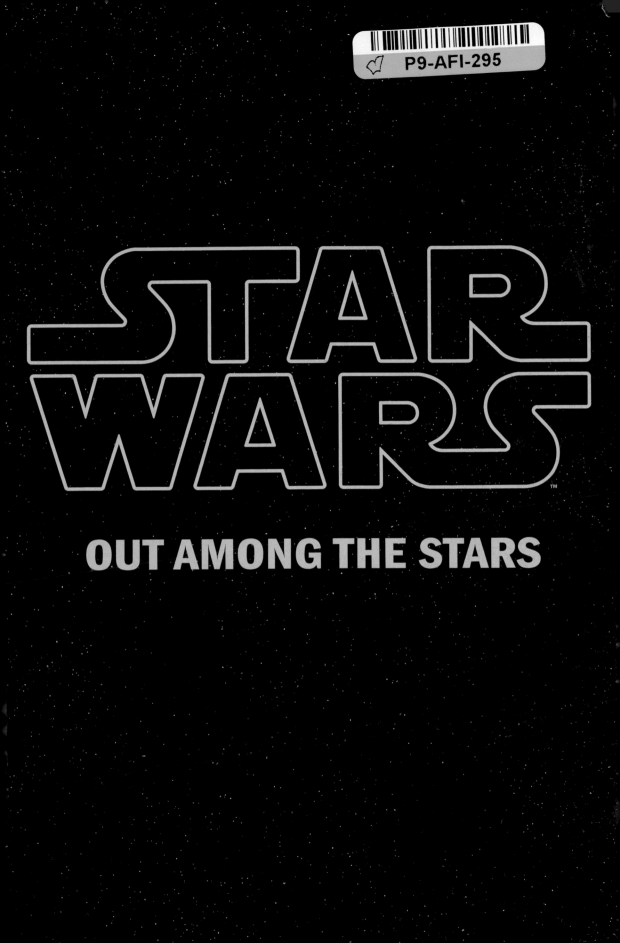

STAR WARS™

OUT AMONG THE STARS

Collection Editor **JENNIFER GRÜNWALD**
Assistant Editor **CAITLIN O'CONNELL**
Associate Managing Editor **KATERI WOODY**
Editor, Special Projects **MARK D. BEAZLEY**

VP Production & Special Projects **JEFF YOUNGQUIST**
SVP Print, Sales & Marketing **DAVID GABRIEL**
Book Designer **ADAM DEL RE**

STAR WARS VOL. 6: OUT AMONG THE STARS. Contains material originally published in magazine form as STAR WARS #33-37 and ANNUAL #3. First printing 2017. ISBN# 978-1-302-90553-8. Published by MARVEL WORLDWIDE, INC., a subsidiary of MARVEL ENTERTAINMENT, LLC. OFFICE OF PUBLICATION: 135 West 50th Street, New York, NY 10020. STAR WARS and related text and illustrations are trademarks and/or copyrights, in the United States and other countries, of Lucasfilm Ltd. and/or its affiliates. © & TM Lucasfilm Ltd. No similarity between any of the names, characters, persons, and/or institutions in this magazine with those of any living or dead person or institution is intended, and any such similarity which may exist is purely coincidental. Marvel and its logos are TM Marvel Characters, Inc. **Printed in the U.S.A.** DAN BUCKLEY, President, Marvel Entertainment; JOE QUESADA, Chief Creative Officer; TOM BREVOORT, SVP of Publishing; DAVID BOGART, SVP of Business Affairs & Operations, Publishing & Partnership; C.B. CEBULSKI, VP of Brand Management & Development, Asia; DAVID GABRIEL, SVP of Sales & Marketing, Publishing; JEFF YOUNGQUIST, VP of Production & Special Projects; DAN CARR, Executive Director of Publishing Technology; ALEX MORALES, Director of Publishing Operations; SUSAN CRESPI, Production Manager; STAN LEE, Chairman Emeritus. For information regarding advertising in Marvel Comics or on Marvel.com, please contact Vit DeBellis, Integrated Sales Manager, at vdebellis@marvel.com. For Marvel subscription inquiries, please call 888-511-5480. Manufactured between 9/29/2017 and 10/30/2017 by QUAD/GRAPHICS WASECA, WASECA, MN, USA.

10 9 8 7 6 5 4 3 2 1

WARS

OUT AMONG THE STARS

ISSUES #33-37
Writer JASON AARON
Artist SALVADOR LARROCA
Colorist EDGAR DELGADO

"THE SAND WILL PROVIDE"
Writers JASON AARON & DASH AARON
Artist ANDREA SORRENTINO
Colorist LEE LOUGHRIDGE

Letterer VC's JOE CARAMAGNA
Cover Art MIKE MAYHEW
Assistant Editor HEATHER ANTOS
Editor JORDAN D. WHITE
Executive Editor C.B. CEBULSKI

ANNUAL #3
Writer JASON LATOUR
Artist/Cover MICHAEL WALSH
Letterer VC'S CLAYTON COWLES
Editor HEATHER ANTOS
Supervising Editor JORDAN D. WHITE
Executive Editor C.B. CEBULSKI

Editor in Chief AXEL ALONSO
Chief Creative Officer JOE QUESADA
President DAN BUCKLEY

For Lucasfilm:
Senior Editor FRANK PARISI
Creative Director MICHAEL SIGLAIN
Lucasfilm Story Group JAMES WAUGH, LELAND CHEE, MATT MARTIN

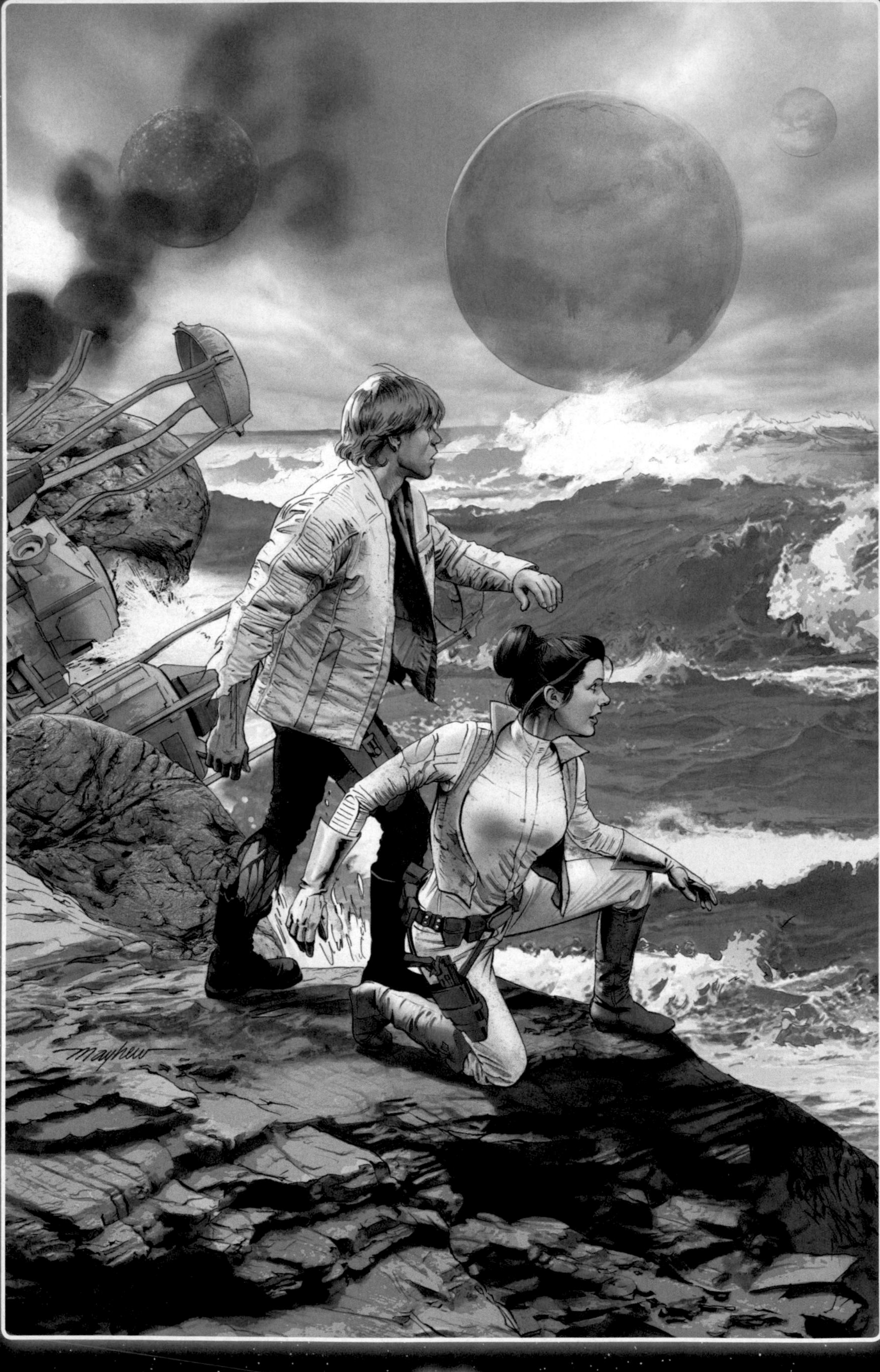
mayhew

REBELS IN THE WILD

It is a time of turmoil for the galaxy. While the evil Galactic Empire remains strong, the Rebel Alliance continues to fight for freedom.

Luke Skywalker struggles with his destiny. He can feel the Force, but lacks the training to become a Jedi Knight. When Doctor Aphra approaches him with an artifact containing the consciousness of an ancient Jedi, Luke accompanies her to the Citadel of Ktath'atn. Overcome with telepathic parasites, Luke is able to overcome their control and free the people of the Citadel along with Rebellion leader Princess Leia.

Despite this, danger still lurks as the surviving parasites aren't the only ones hunting for Luke and Leia....

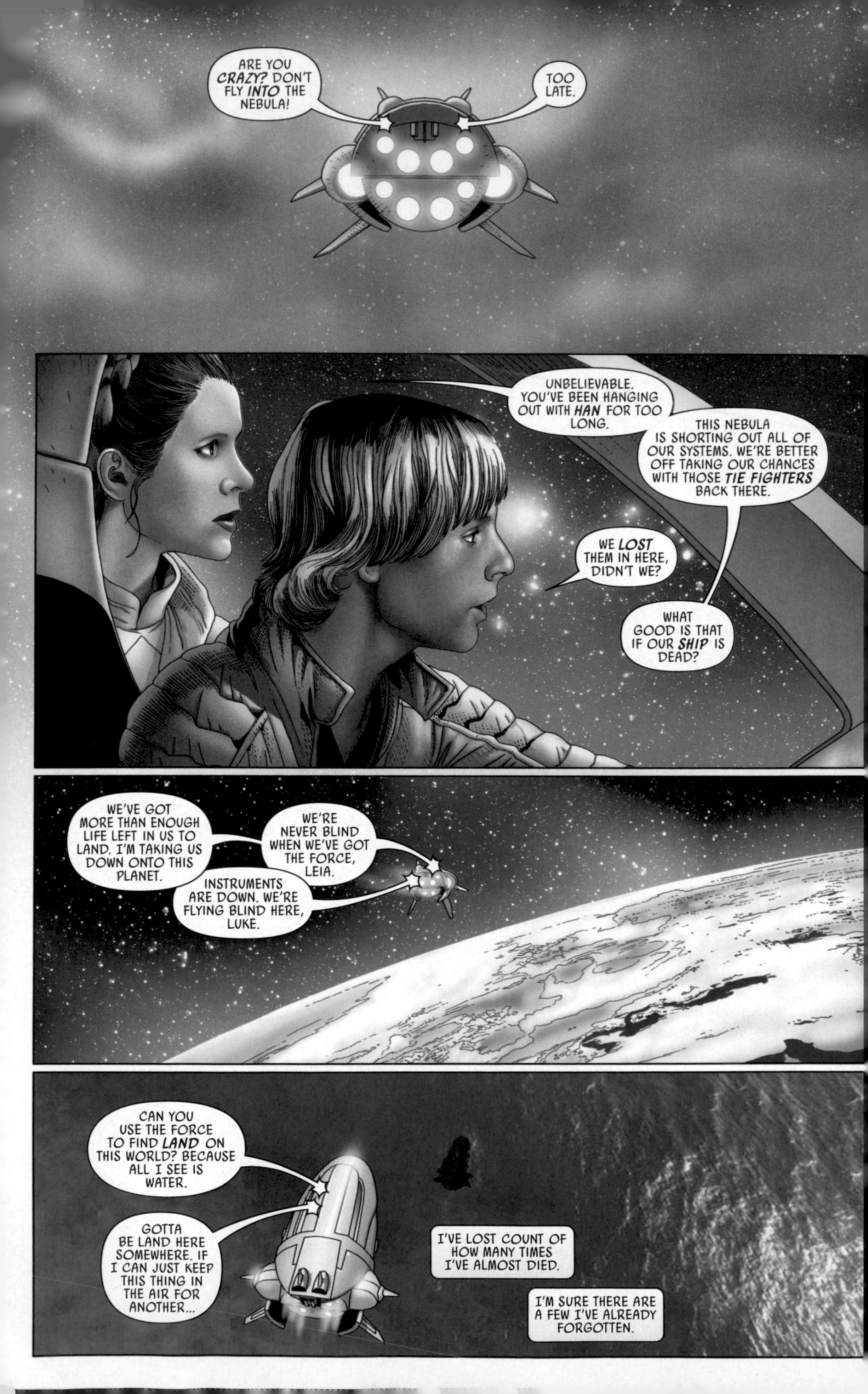
ARE YOU CRAZY? DON'T FLY INTO THE NEBULA!
TOO LATE.
UNBELIEVABLE. YOU'VE BEEN HANGING OUT WITH HAN FOR TOO LONG.
THIS NEBULA IS SHORTING OUT ALL OF OUR SYSTEMS. WE'RE BETTER OFF TAKING OUR CHANCES WITH THOSE TIE FIGHTERS BACK THERE.
WE LOST THEM IN HERE, DIDN'T WE?
WHAT GOOD IS THAT IF OUR SHIP IS DEAD?
WE'VE GOT MORE THAN ENOUGH LIFE LEFT IN US TO LAND. I'M TAKING US DOWN ONTO THIS PLANET.
INSTRUMENTS ARE DOWN. WE'RE FLYING BLIND HERE, LUKE.
WE'RE NEVER BLIND WHEN WE'VE GOT THE FORCE, LEIA.
CAN YOU USE THE FORCE TO FIND LAND ON THIS WORLD? BECAUSE ALL I SEE IS WATER.
GOTTA BE LAND HERE SOMEWHERE. IF I CAN JUST KEEP THIS THING IN THE AIR FOR ANOTHER...
I'VE LOST COUNT OF HOW MANY TIMES I'VE ALMOST DIED.
I'M SURE THERE ARE A FEW I'VE ALREADY FORGOTTEN.

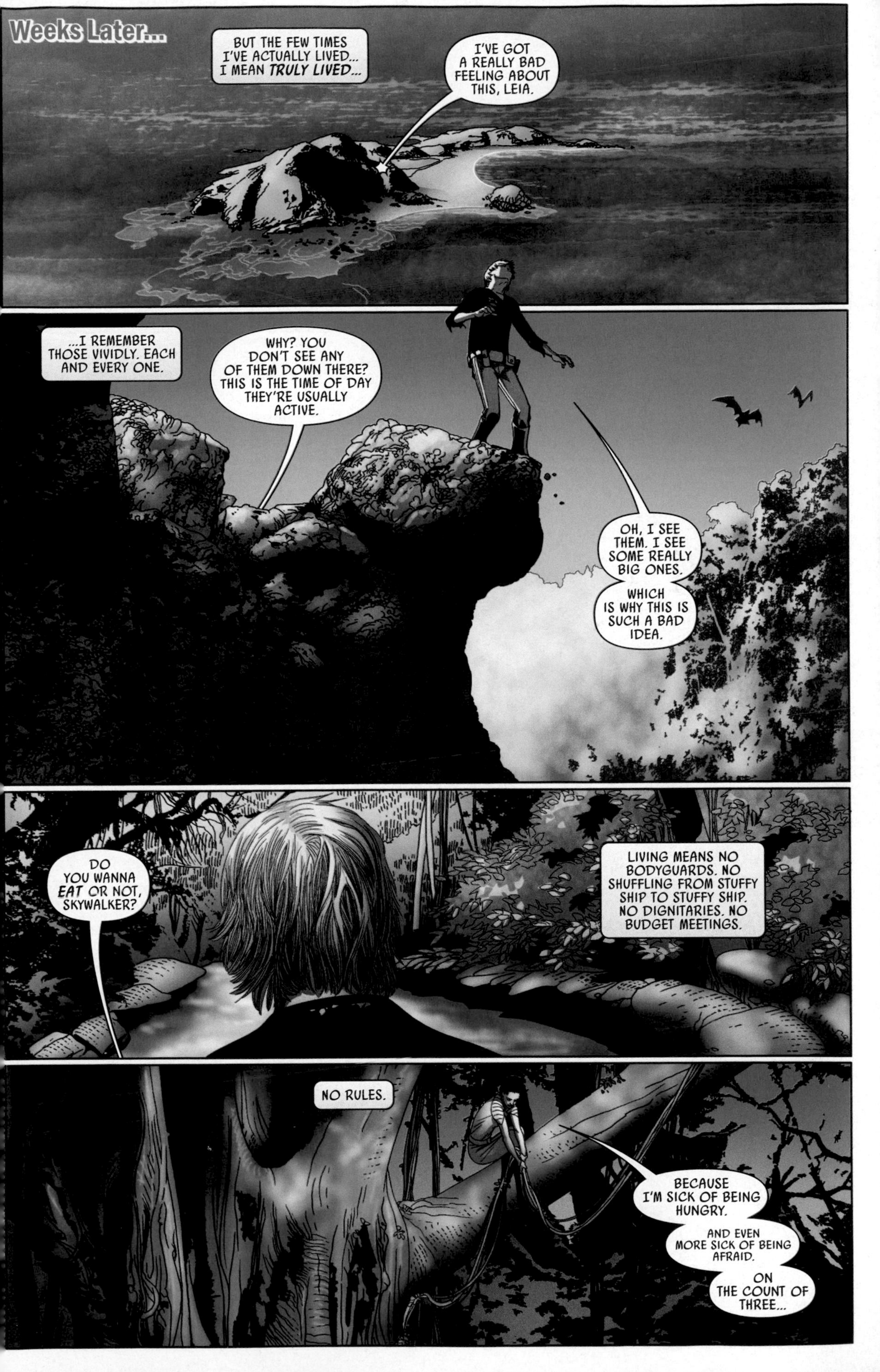
Weeks Later...
BUT THE FEW TIMES I'VE ACTUALLY LIVED... I MEAN *TRULY LIVED*...
I'VE GOT A REALLY BAD FEELING ABOUT THIS, LEIA.
...I REMEMBER THOSE VIVIDLY. EACH AND EVERY ONE.
WHY? YOU DON'T SEE ANY OF THEM DOWN THERE? THIS IS THE TIME OF DAY THEY'RE USUALLY ACTIVE.
OH, I SEE THEM. I SEE SOME REALLY BIG ONES.
WHICH IS WHY THIS IS SUCH A BAD IDEA.
DO YOU WANNA *EAT* OR NOT, SKYWALKER?
LIVING MEANS NO BODYGUARDS. NO SHUFFLING FROM STUFFY SHIP TO STUFFY SHIP. NO DIGNITARIES. NO BUDGET MEETINGS.
NO RULES.
BECAUSE I'M SICK OF BEING HUNGRY.
AND EVEN MORE SICK OF BEING AFRAID.
ON THE COUNT OF THREE...

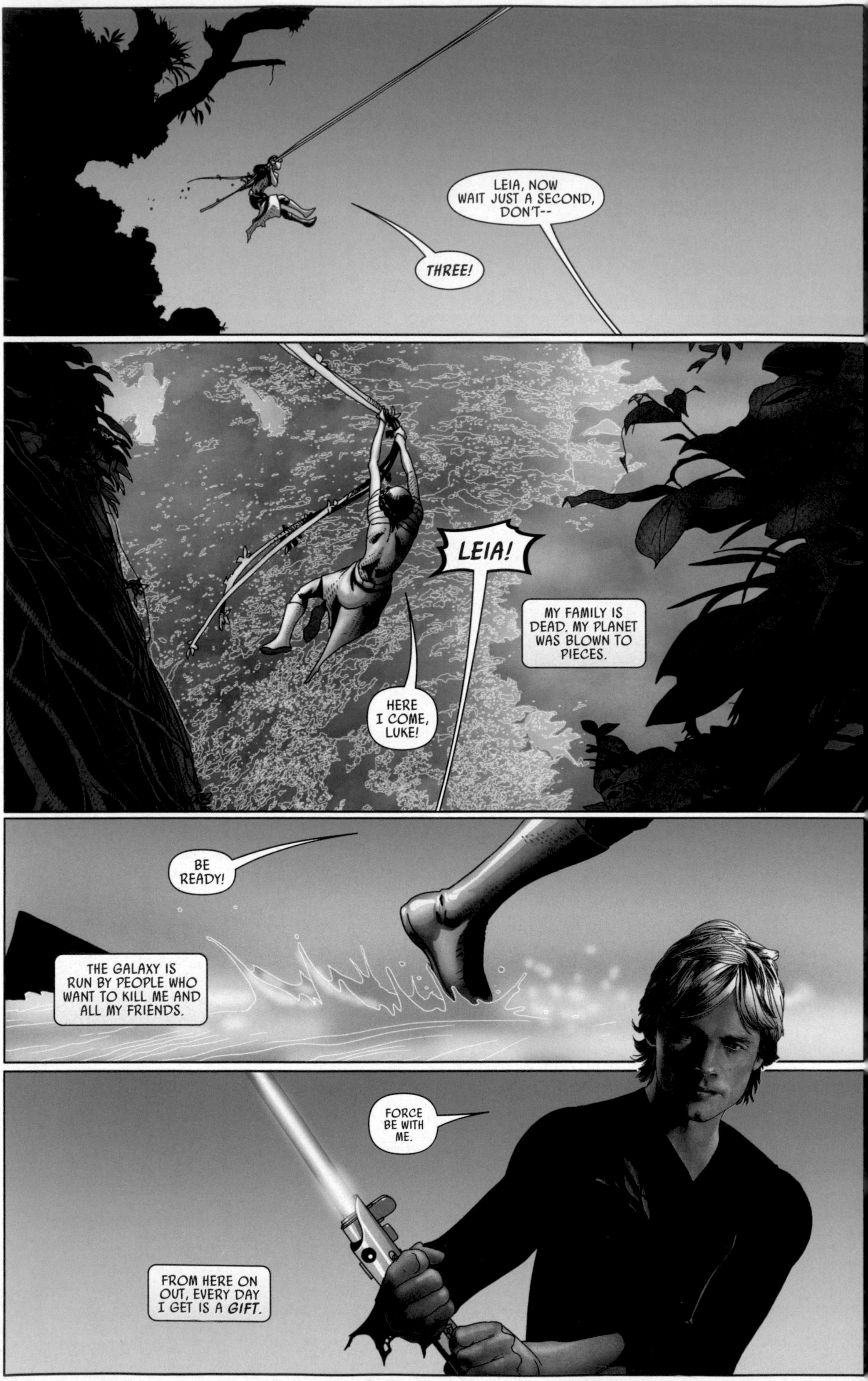
LEIA, NOW WAIT JUST A SECOND, DON'T--
THREE!
LEIA!
HERE I COME, LUKE!
MY FAMILY IS DEAD. MY PLANET WAS BLOWN TO PIECES.
BE READY!
THE GALAXY IS RUN BY PEOPLE WHO WANT TO KILL ME AND ALL MY FRIENDS.
FORCE BE WITH ME.
FROM HERE ON OUT, EVERY DAY I GET IS A *GIFT*.

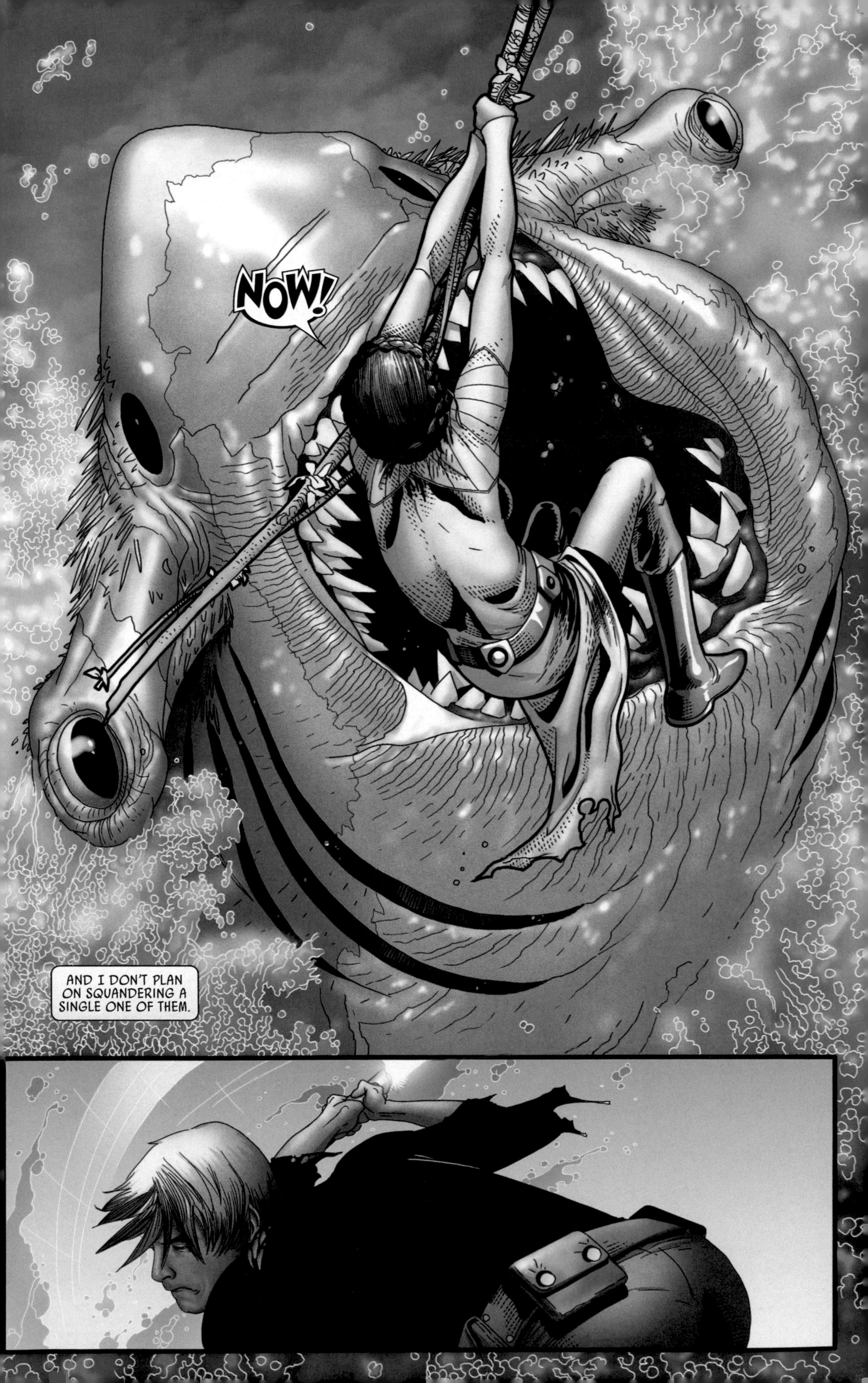
NOW!
AND I DON'T PLAN ON SQUANDERING A SINGLE ONE OF THEM.

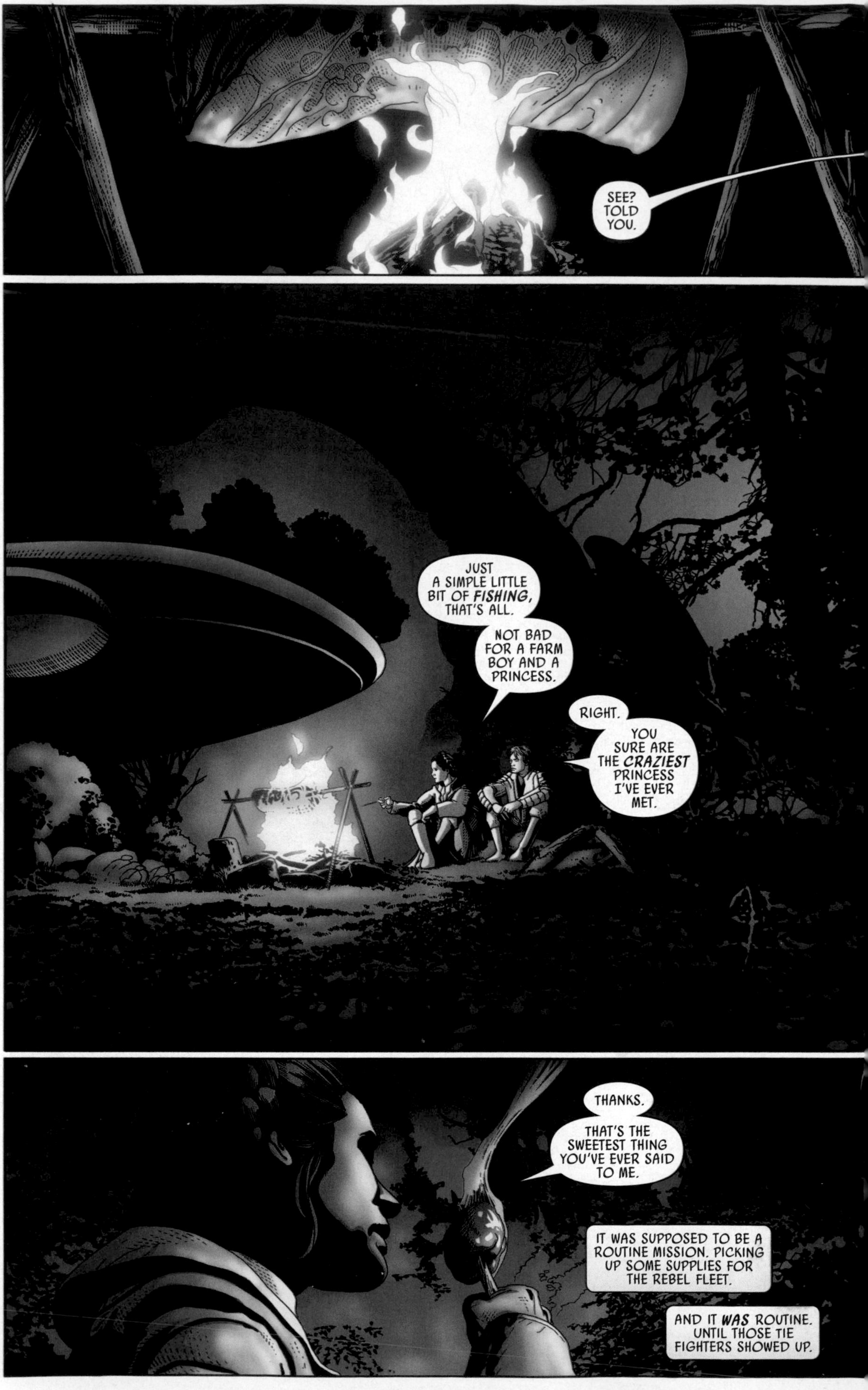

SEE? TOLD YOU.
JUST A SIMPLE LITTLE BIT OF *FISHING*, THAT'S ALL.
NOT BAD FOR A FARM BOY AND A PRINCESS.
RIGHT.
YOU SURE ARE THE *CRAZIEST* PRINCESS I'VE EVER MET.
THANKS.
THAT'S THE SWEETEST THING YOU'VE EVER SAID TO ME.
IT WAS SUPPOSED TO BE A ROUTINE MISSION. PICKING UP SOME SUPPLIES FOR THE REBEL FLEET.
AND IT *WAS* ROUTINE. UNTIL THOSE TIE FIGHTERS SHOWED UP.

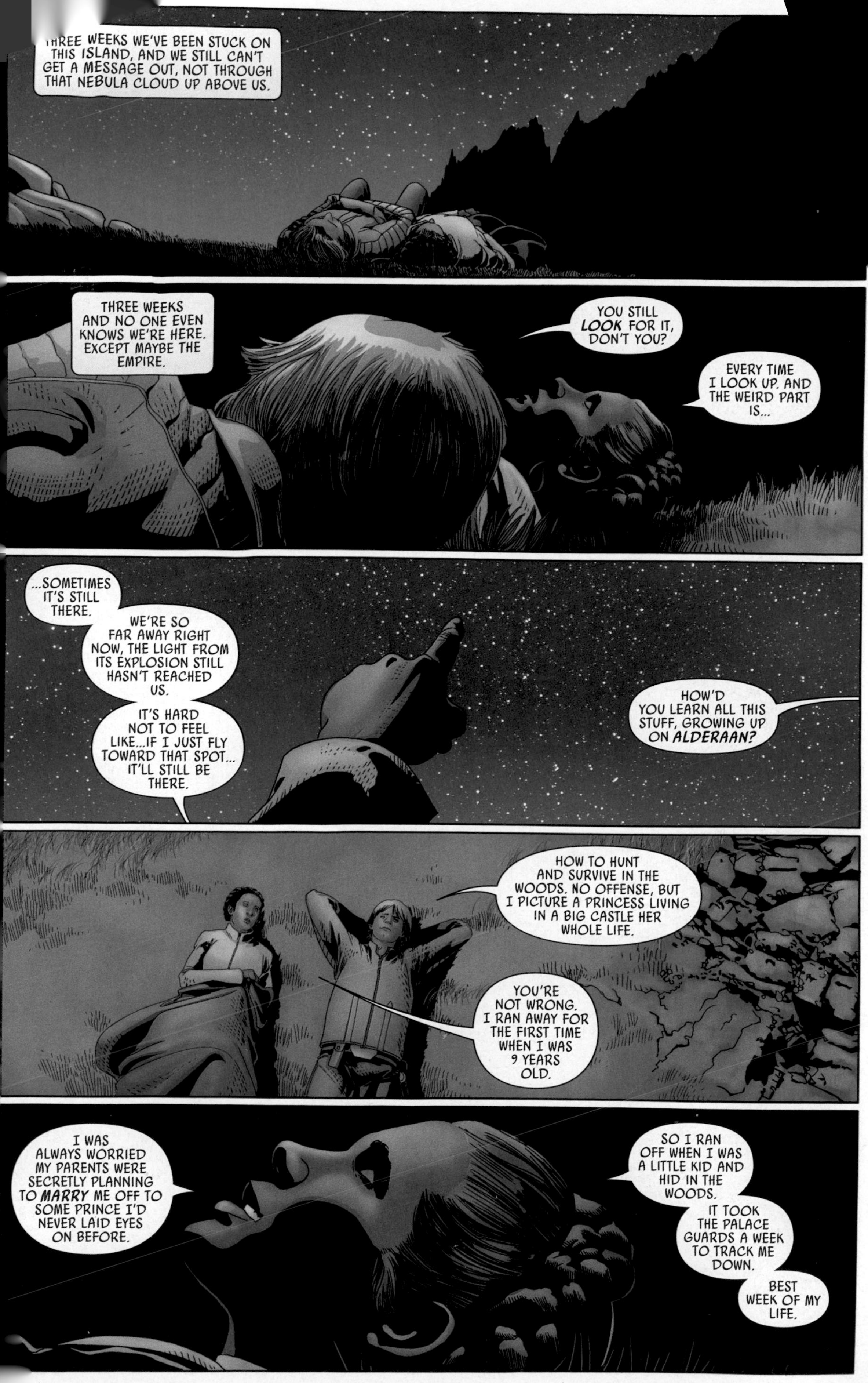
THREE WEEKS WE'VE BEEN STUCK ON THIS ISLAND, AND WE STILL CAN'T GET A MESSAGE OUT, NOT THROUGH THAT NEBULA CLOUD UP ABOVE US.
THREE WEEKS AND NO ONE EVEN KNOWS WE'RE HERE. EXCEPT MAYBE THE EMPIRE.
YOU STILL LOOK FOR IT, DON'T YOU?
EVERY TIME I LOOK UP. AND THE WEIRD PART IS...
...SOMETIMES IT'S STILL THERE.
WE'RE SO FAR AWAY RIGHT NOW, THE LIGHT FROM ITS EXPLOSION STILL HASN'T REACHED US.
IT'S HARD NOT TO FEEL LIKE...IF I JUST FLY TOWARD THAT SPOT... IT'LL STILL BE THERE.
HOW'D YOU LEARN ALL THIS STUFF, GROWING UP ON ALDERAAN?
HOW TO HUNT AND SURVIVE IN THE WOODS. NO OFFENSE, BUT I PICTURE A PRINCESS LIVING IN A BIG CASTLE HER WHOLE LIFE.
YOU'RE NOT WRONG. I RAN AWAY FOR THE FIRST TIME WHEN I WAS 9 YEARS OLD.
I WAS ALWAYS WORRIED MY PARENTS WERE SECRETLY PLANNING TO MARRY ME OFF TO SOME PRINCE I'D NEVER LAID EYES ON BEFORE.
SO I RAN OFF WHEN I WAS A LITTLE KID AND HID IN THE WOODS.
IT TOOK THE PALACE GUARDS A WEEK TO TRACK ME DOWN.
BEST WEEK OF MY LIFE.

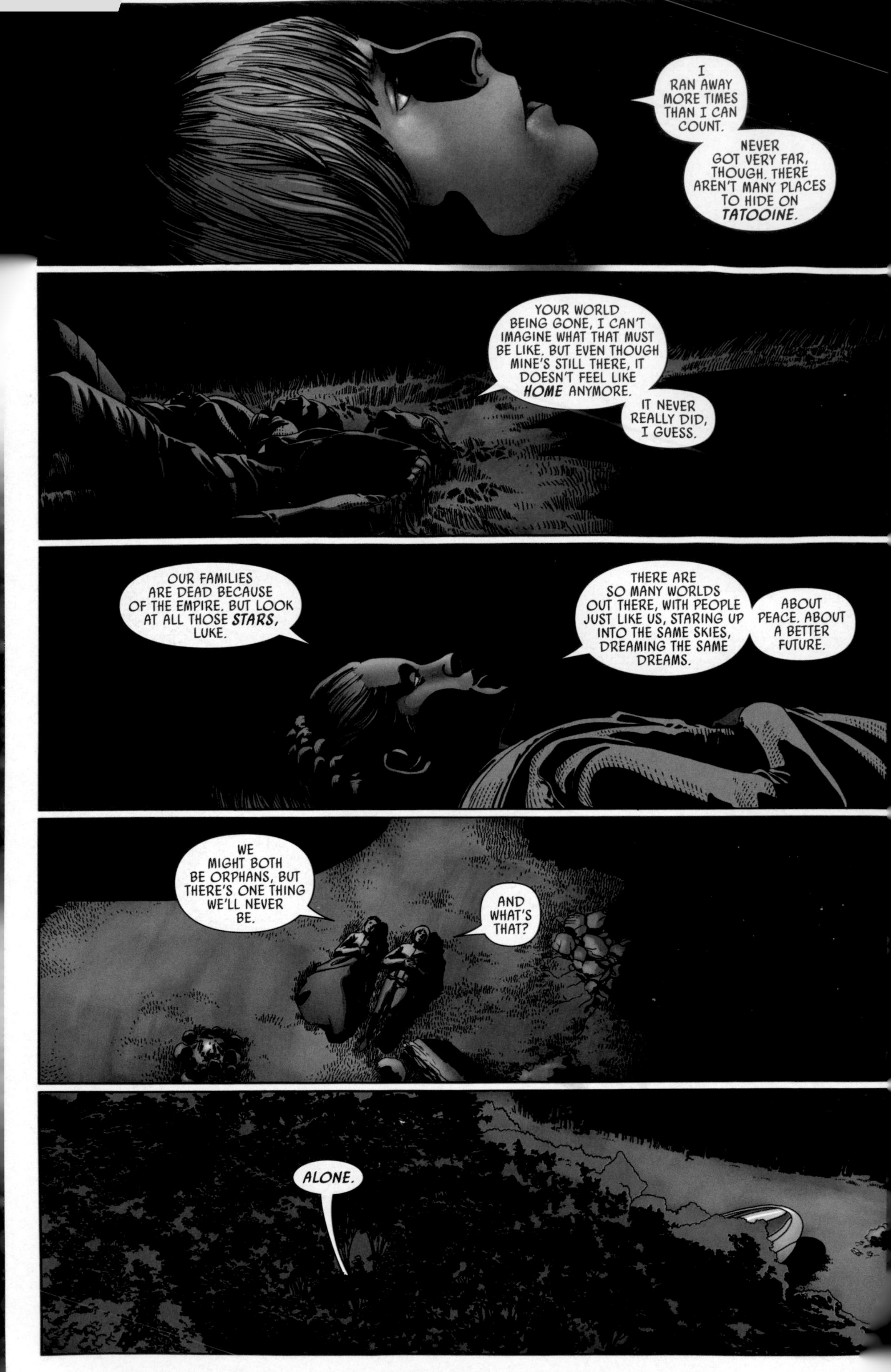
I RAN AWAY MORE TIMES THAN I CAN COUNT.
NEVER GOT VERY FAR, THOUGH. THERE AREN'T MANY PLACES TO HIDE ON TATOOINE.
YOUR WORLD BEING GONE, I CAN'T IMAGINE WHAT THAT MUST BE LIKE. BUT EVEN THOUGH MINE'S STILL THERE, IT DOESN'T FEEL LIKE HOME ANYMORE.
IT NEVER REALLY DID, I GUESS.
OUR FAMILIES ARE DEAD BECAUSE OF THE EMPIRE. BUT LOOK AT ALL THOSE STARS, LUKE.
THERE ARE SO MANY WORLDS OUT THERE, WITH PEOPLE JUST LIKE US, STARING UP INTO THE SAME SKIES, DREAMING THE SAME DREAMS.
ABOUT PEACE. ABOUT A BETTER FUTURE.
WE MIGHT BOTH BE ORPHANS, BUT THERE'S ONE THING WE'LL NEVER BE.
AND WHAT'S THAT?
ALONE.

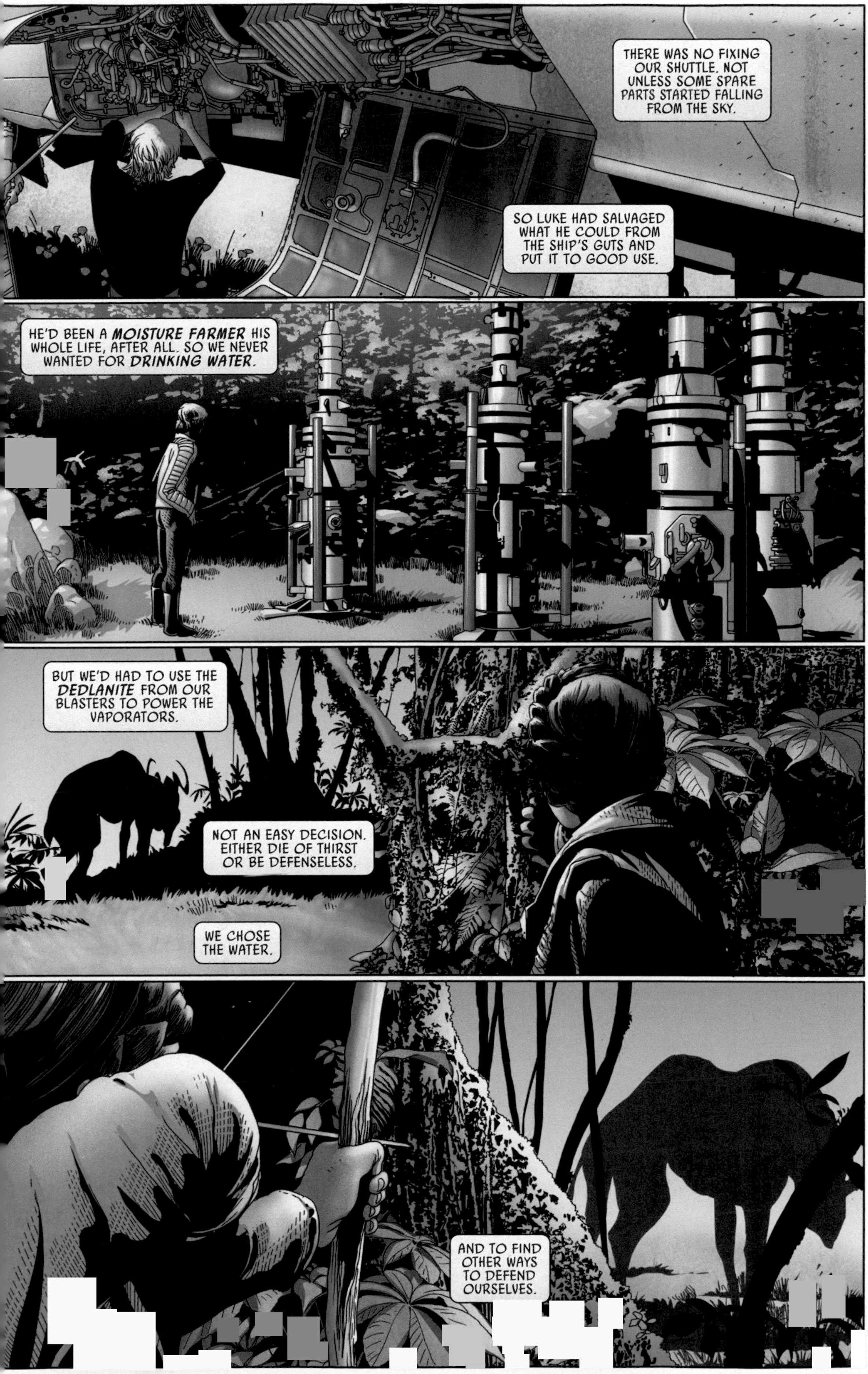
THERE WAS NO FIXING OUR SHUTTLE. NOT UNLESS SOME SPARE PARTS STARTED FALLING FROM THE SKY.
SO LUKE HAD SALVAGED WHAT HE COULD FROM THE SHIP'S GUTS AND PUT IT TO GOOD USE.
HE'D BEEN A MOISTURE FARMER HIS WHOLE LIFE, AFTER ALL. SO WE NEVER WANTED FOR DRINKING WATER.
BUT WE'D HAD TO USE THE DEDLANITE FROM OUR BLASTERS TO POWER THE VAPORATORS.
NOT AN EASY DECISION. EITHER DIE OF THIRST OR BE DEFENSELESS.
WE CHOSE THE WATER.
AND TO FIND OTHER WAYS TO DEFEND OURSELVES.

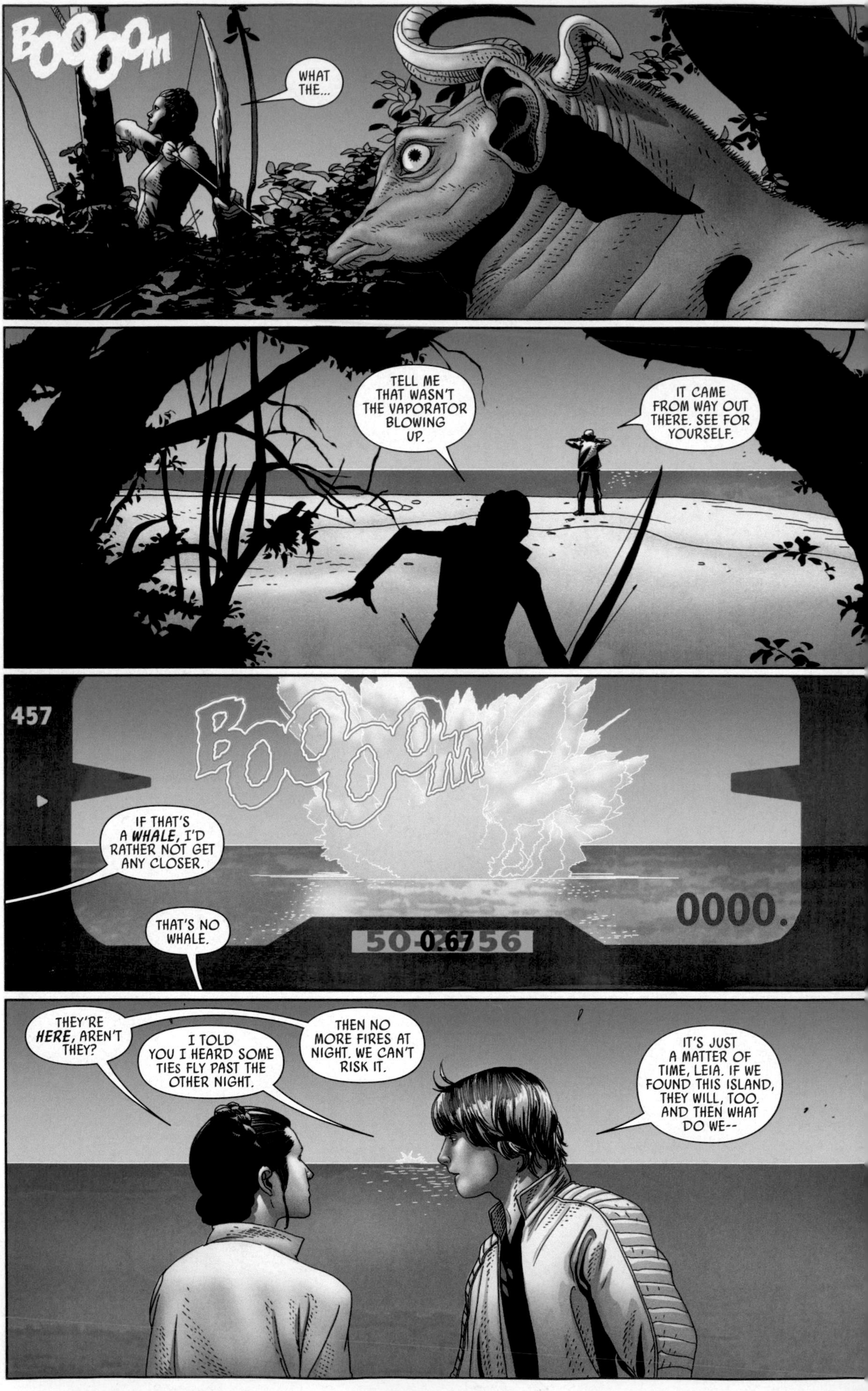
BOOOOOM
WHAT THE...
TELL ME THAT WASN'T THE VAPORATOR BLOWING UP.
IT CAME FROM WAY OUT THERE. SEE FOR YOURSELF.
457
BOOOOOM
IF THAT'S A WHALE, I'D RATHER NOT GET ANY CLOSER.
THAT'S NO WHALE.
0000.
THEY'RE HERE, AREN'T THEY?
I TOLD YOU I HEARD SOME TIEs FLY PAST THE OTHER NIGHT.
THEN NO MORE FIRES AT NIGHT. WE CAN'T RISK IT.
IT'S JUST A MATTER OF TIME, LEIA. IF WE FOUND THIS ISLAND, THEY WILL, TOO. AND THEN WHAT DO WE--

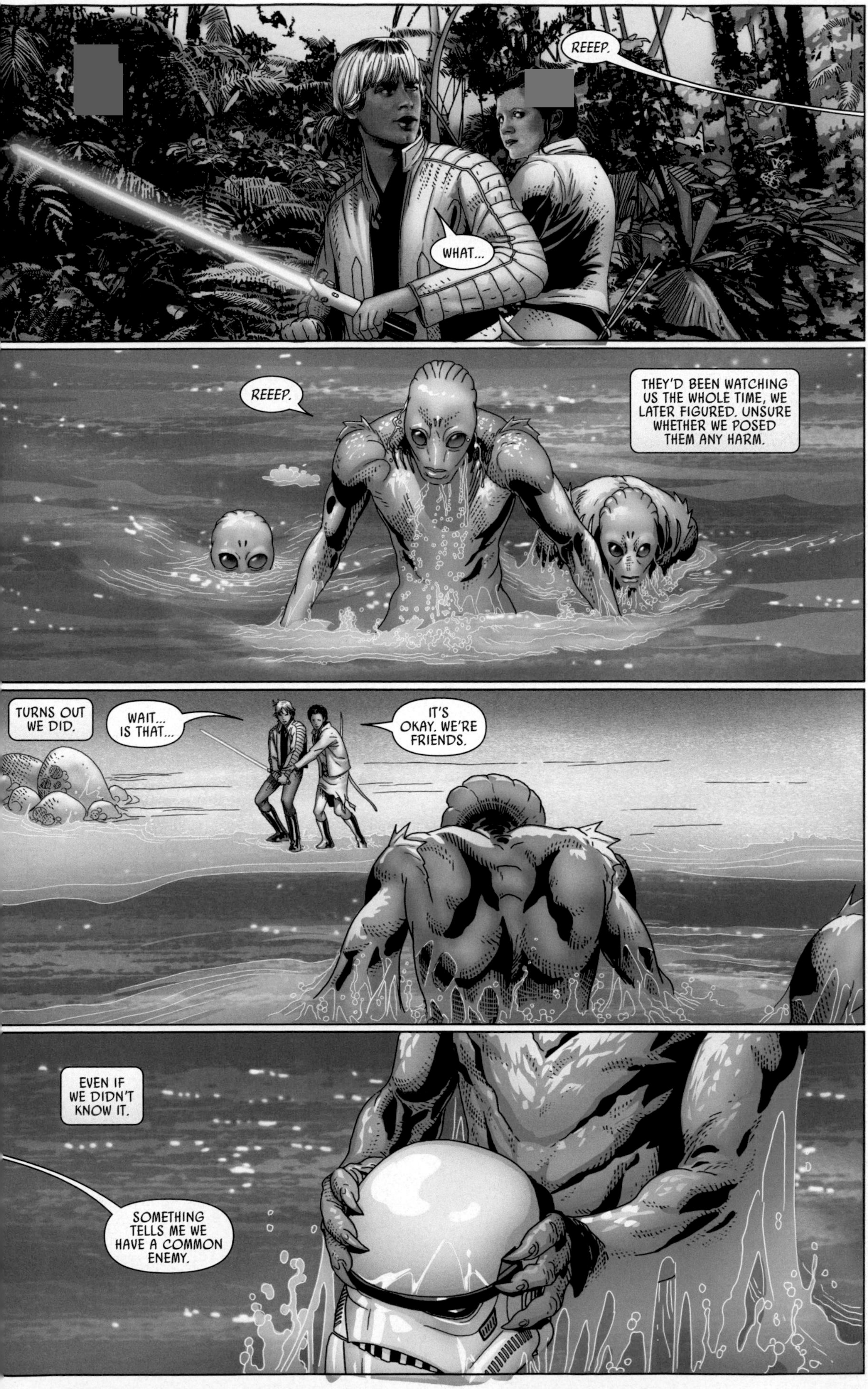
REEEP.
WHAT...
REEEP.
THEY'D BEEN WATCHING US THE WHOLE TIME, WE LATER FIGURED. UNSURE WHETHER WE POSED THEM ANY HARM.
TURNS OUT WE DID.
WAIT... IS THAT...
IT'S OKAY. WE'RE FRIENDS.
EVEN IF WE DIDN'T KNOW IT.
SOMETHING TELLS ME WE HAVE A COMMON ENEMY.

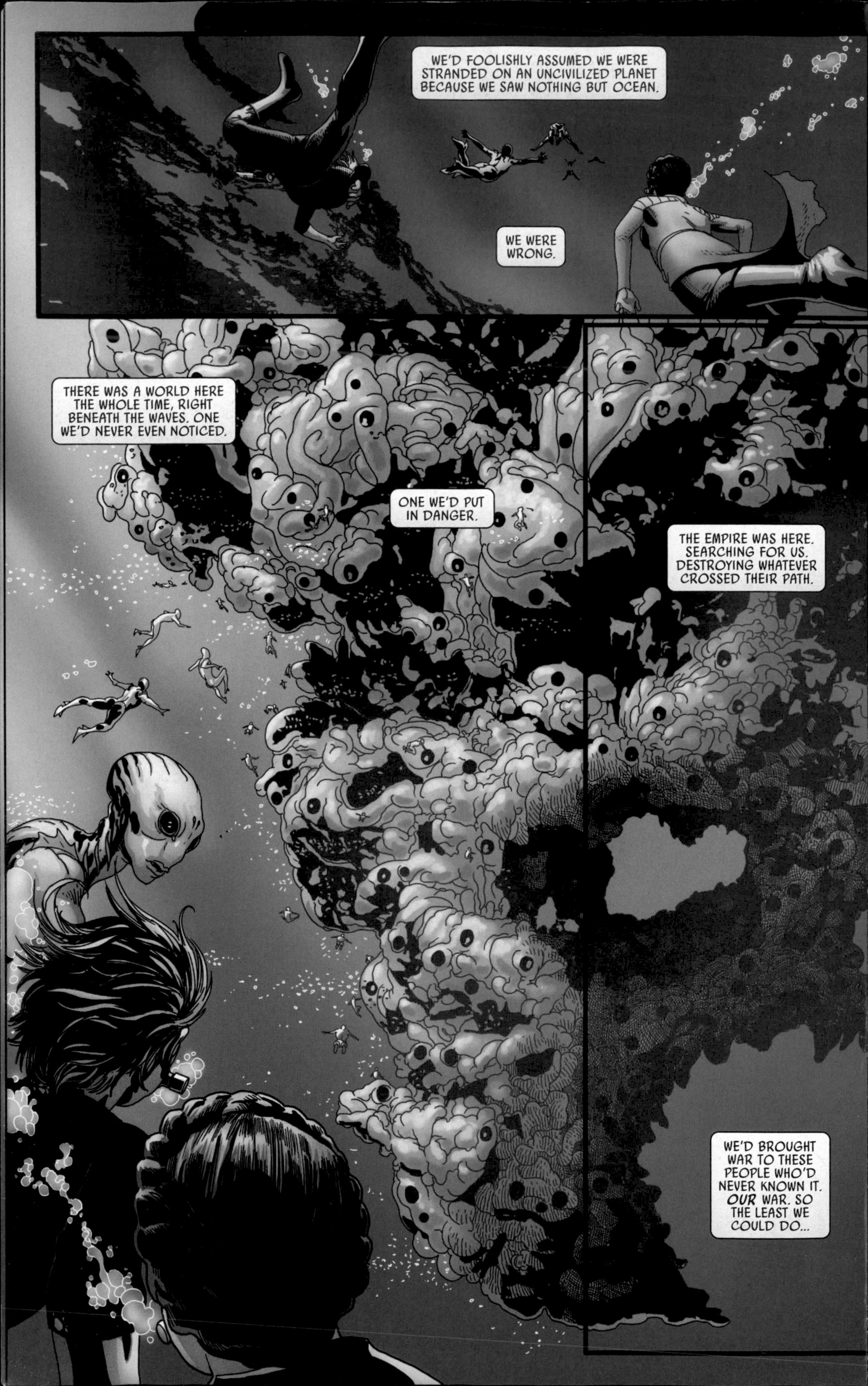
WE'D FOOLISHLY ASSUMED WE WERE STRANDED ON AN UNCIVILIZED PLANET BECAUSE WE SAW NOTHING BUT OCEAN.
WE WERE WRONG.
THERE WAS A WORLD HERE THE WHOLE TIME, RIGHT BENEATH THE WAVES. ONE WE'D NEVER EVEN NOTICED.
ONE WE'D PUT IN DANGER.
THE EMPIRE WAS HERE. SEARCHING FOR US. DESTROYING WHATEVER CROSSED THEIR PATH.
WE'D BROUGHT WAR TO THESE PEOPLE WHO'D NEVER KNOWN IT. ***OUR*** WAR. SO THE LEAST WE COULD DO...

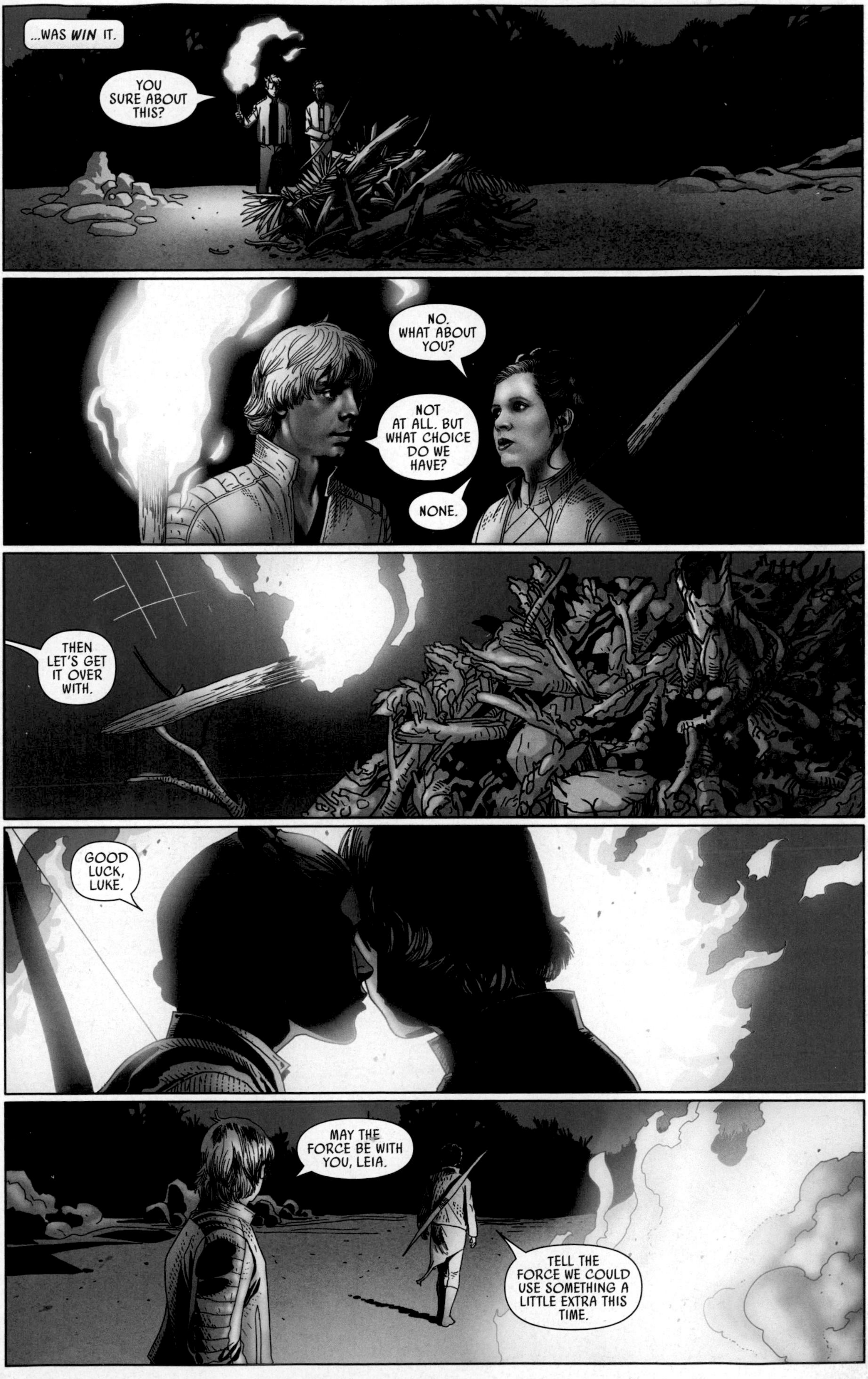
...WAS WIN IT.
YOU SURE ABOUT THIS?
NO. WHAT ABOUT YOU?
NOT AT ALL. BUT WHAT CHOICE DO WE HAVE?
NONE.
THEN LET'S GET IT OVER WITH.
GOOD LUCK, LUKE.
MAY THE FORCE BE WITH YOU, LEIA.
TELL THE FORCE WE COULD USE SOMETHING A LITTLE EXTRA THIS TIME.

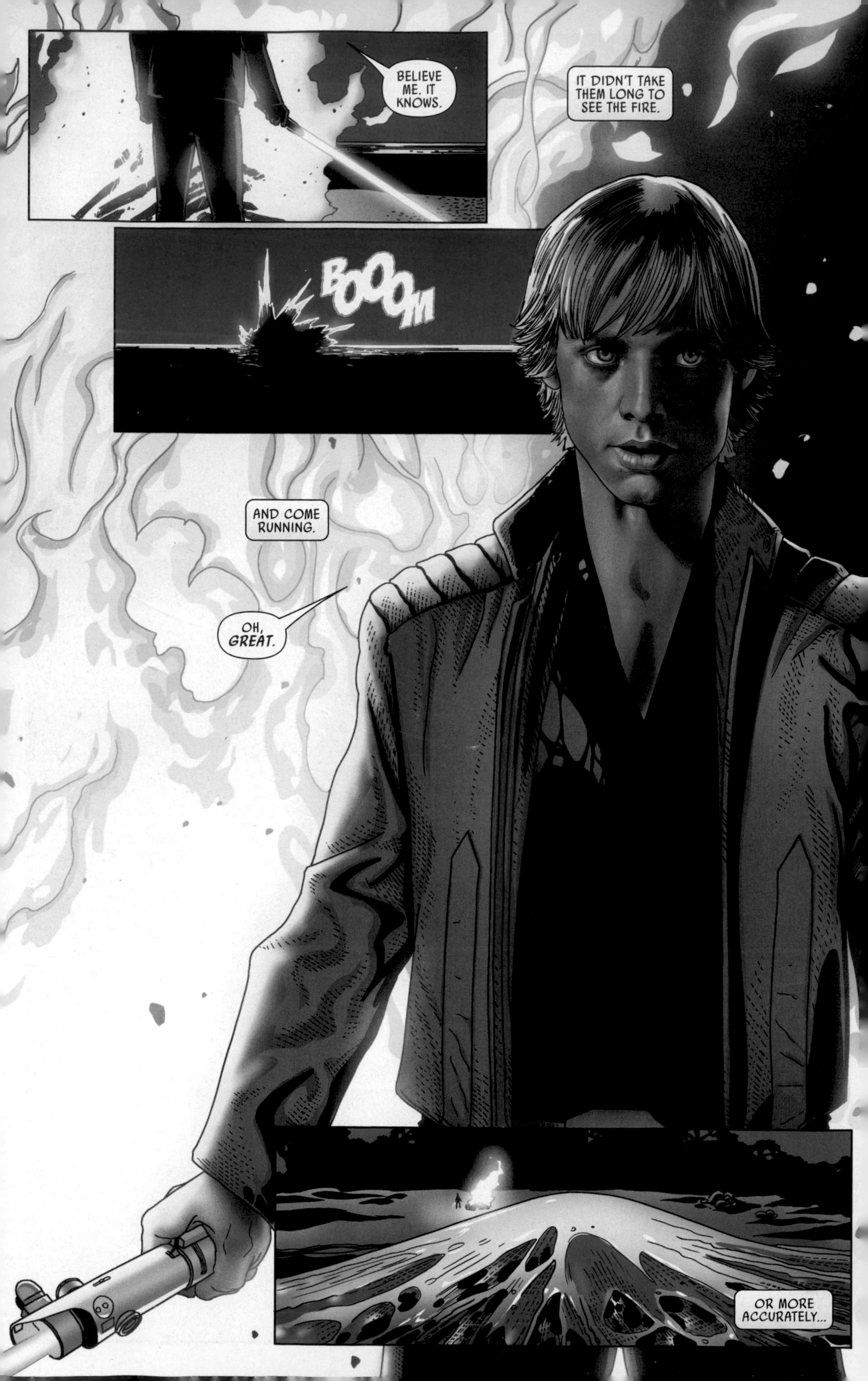
BELIEVE ME. IT KNOWS.
IT DIDN'T TAKE THEM LONG TO SEE THE FIRE.
BOOOM
AND COME RUNNING.
OH, GREAT.
OR MORE ACCURATELY...

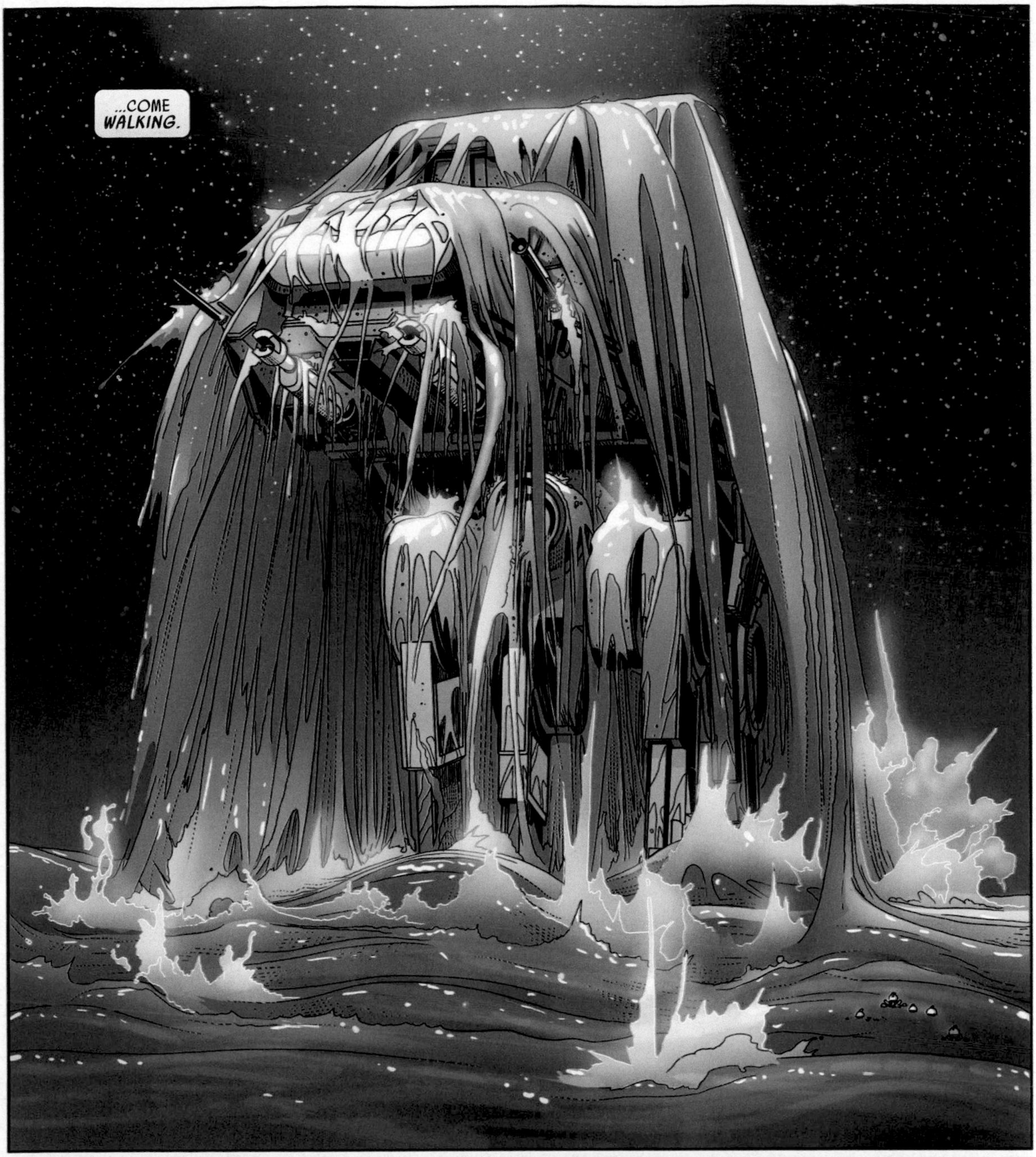
...COME WALKING.
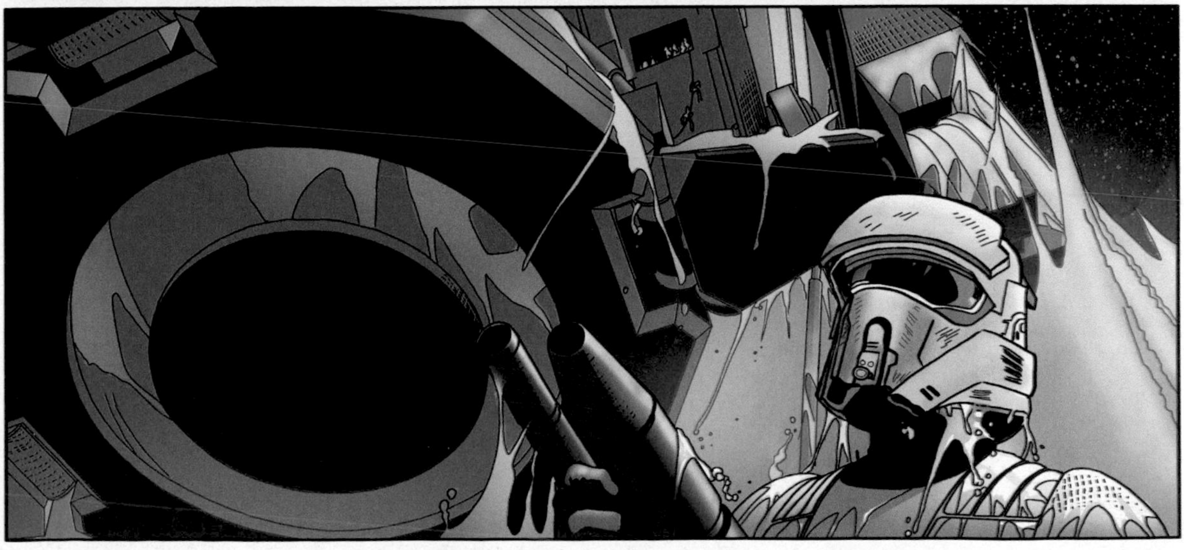

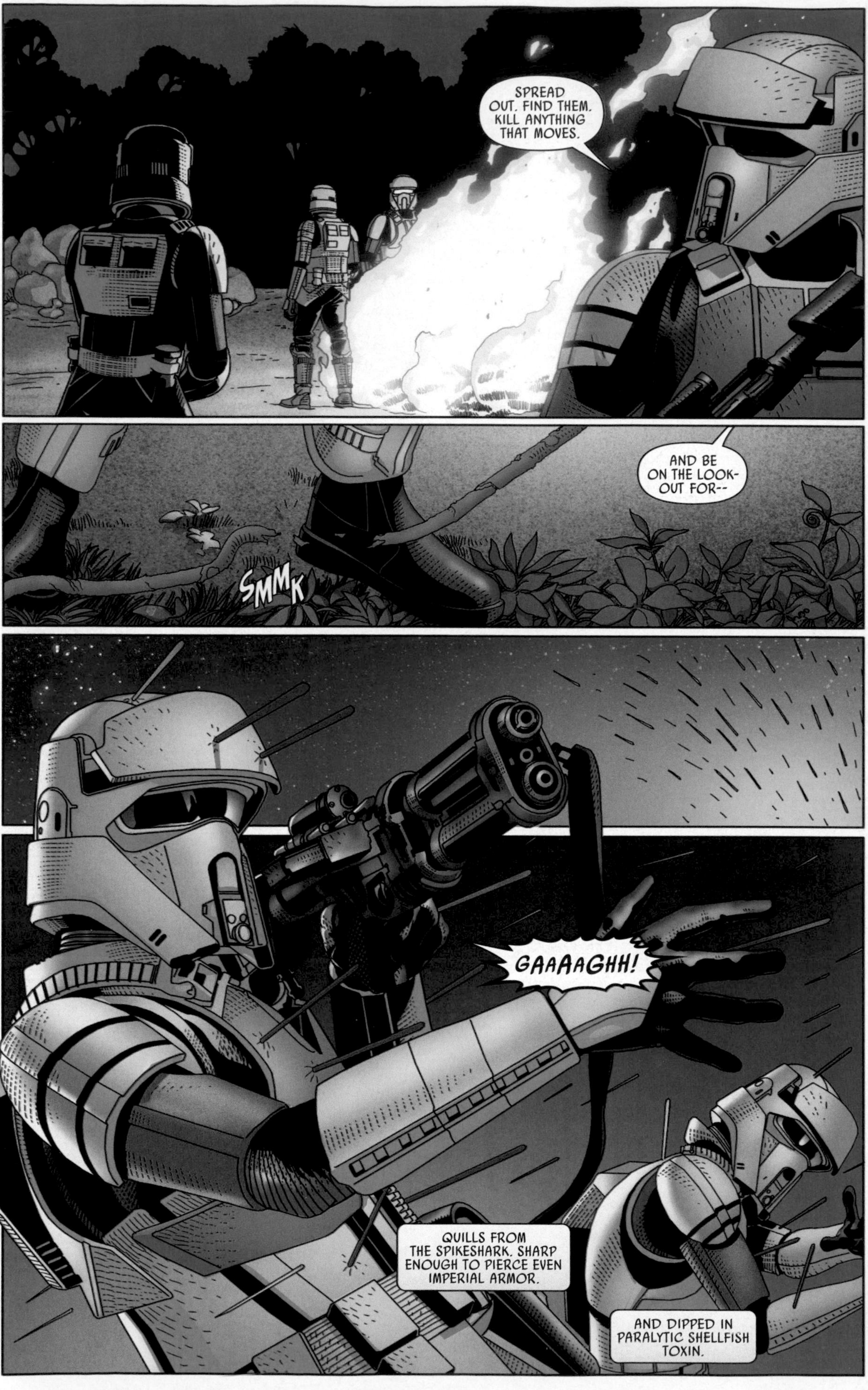
SPREAD OUT. FIND THEM. KILL ANYTHING THAT MOVES.
AND BE ON THE LOOK-OUT FOR--
SMMK
GAAAAGHH!
QUILLS FROM THE SPIKESHARK. SHARP ENOUGH TO PIERCE EVEN IMPERIAL ARMOR.
AND DIPPED IN PARALYTIC SHELLFISH TOXIN.

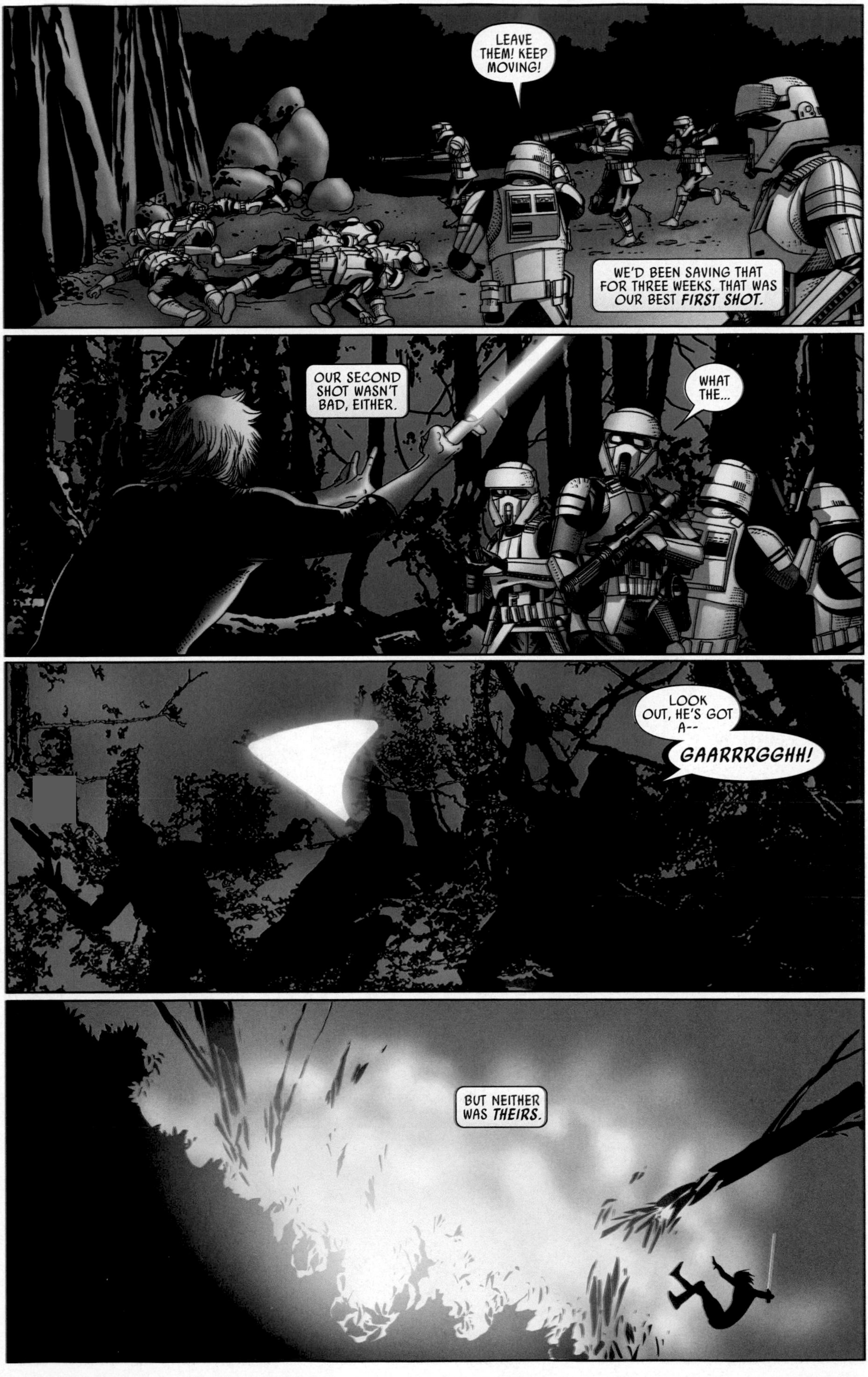
LEAVE THEM! KEEP MOVING!
WE'D BEEN SAVING THAT FOR THREE WEEKS. THAT WAS OUR BEST FIRST SHOT.
OUR SECOND SHOT WASN'T BAD, EITHER.
WHAT THE...
LOOK OUT, HE'S GOT A--
GAARRRGGHH!
BUT NEITHER WAS THEIRS.

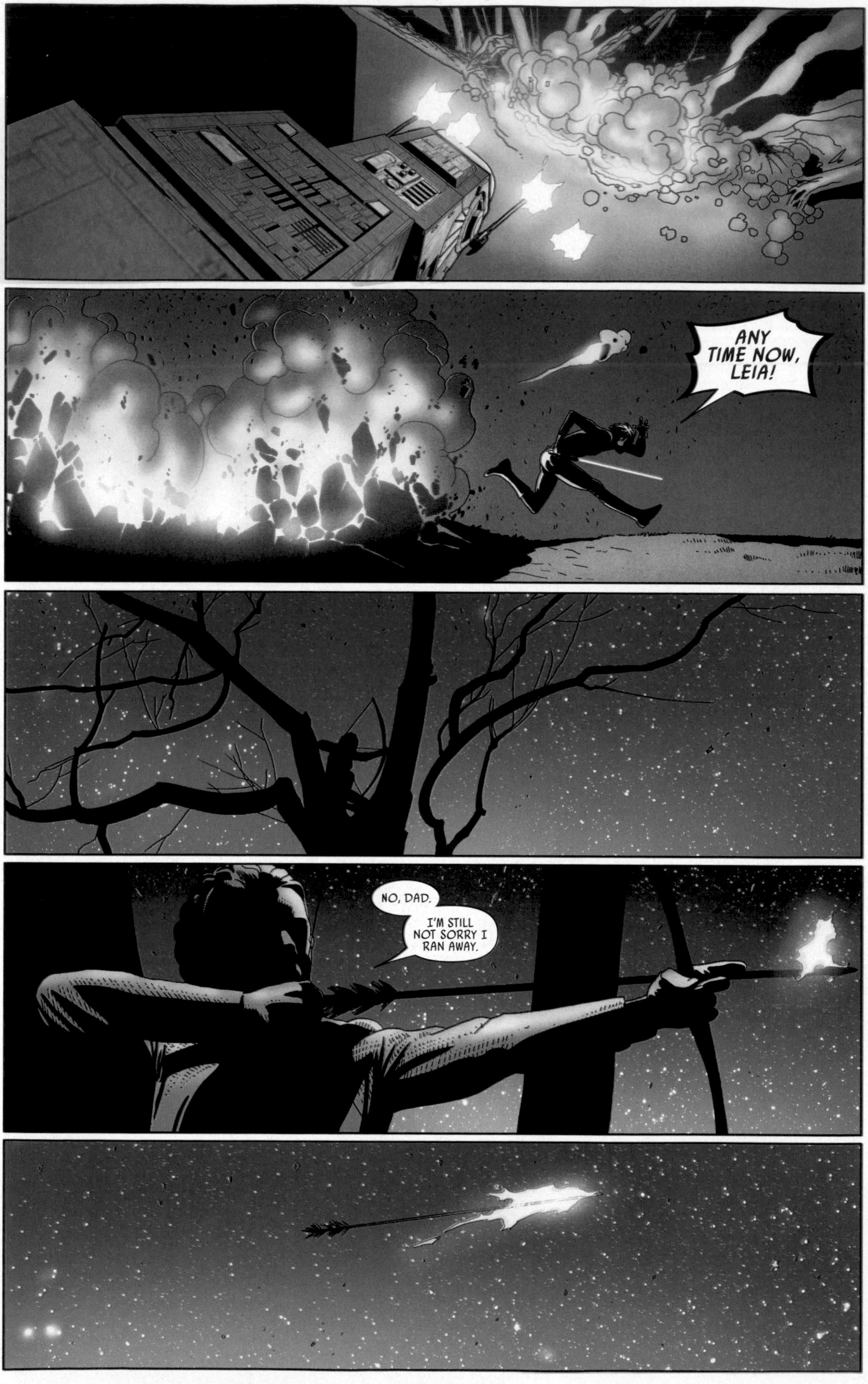
ANY TIME NOW, LEIA!
NO, DAD.
I'M STILL NOT SORRY I RAN AWAY.

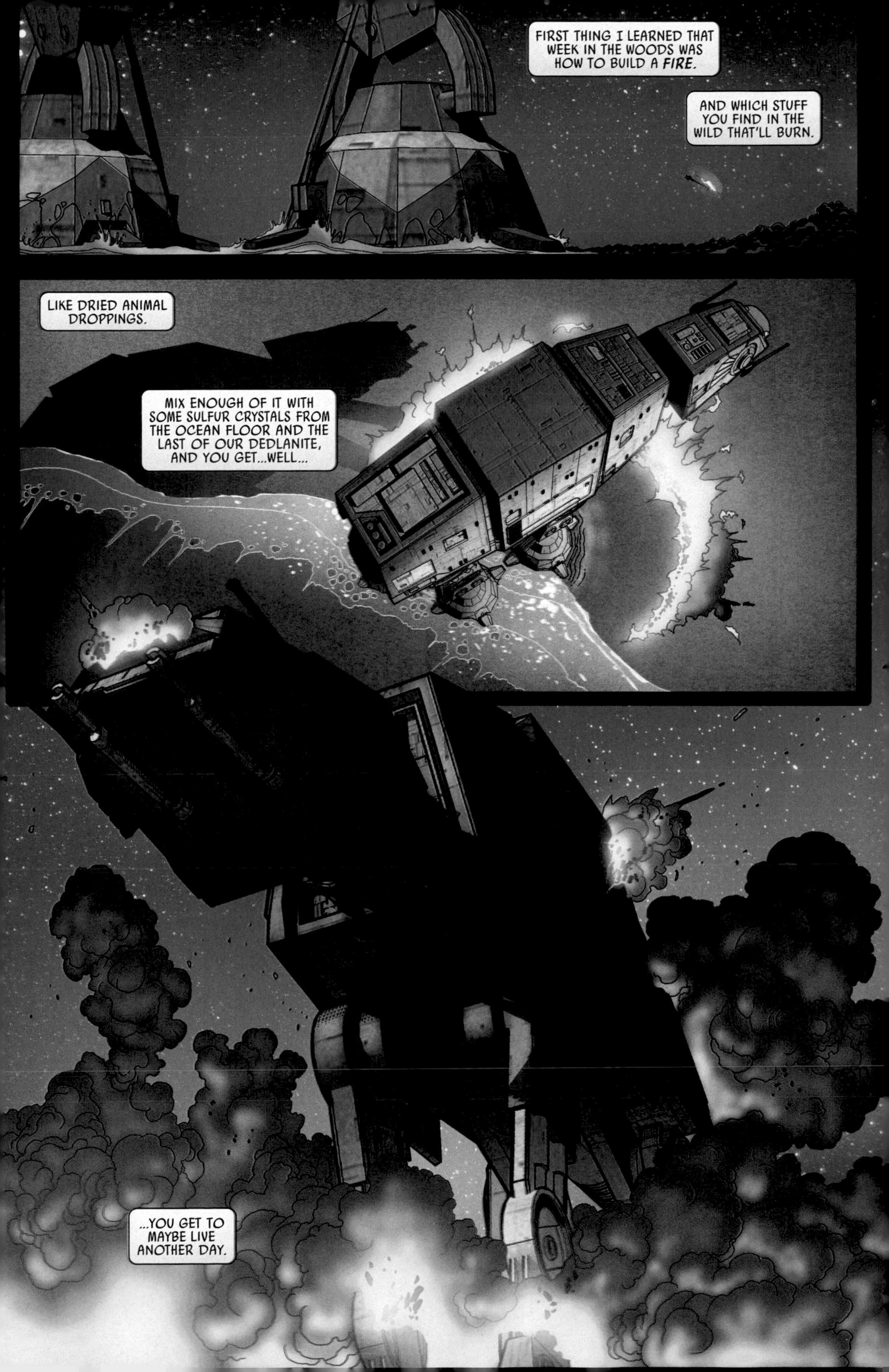
FIRST THING I LEARNED THAT WEEK IN THE WOODS WAS HOW TO BUILD A FIRE.
AND WHICH STUFF YOU FIND IN THE WILD THAT'LL BURN.
LIKE DRIED ANIMAL DROPPINGS.
MIX ENOUGH OF IT WITH SOME SULFUR CRYSTALS FROM THE OCEAN FLOOR AND THE LAST OF OUR DEDLANITE, AND YOU GET...WELL...
...YOU GET TO MAYBE LIVE ANOTHER DAY.

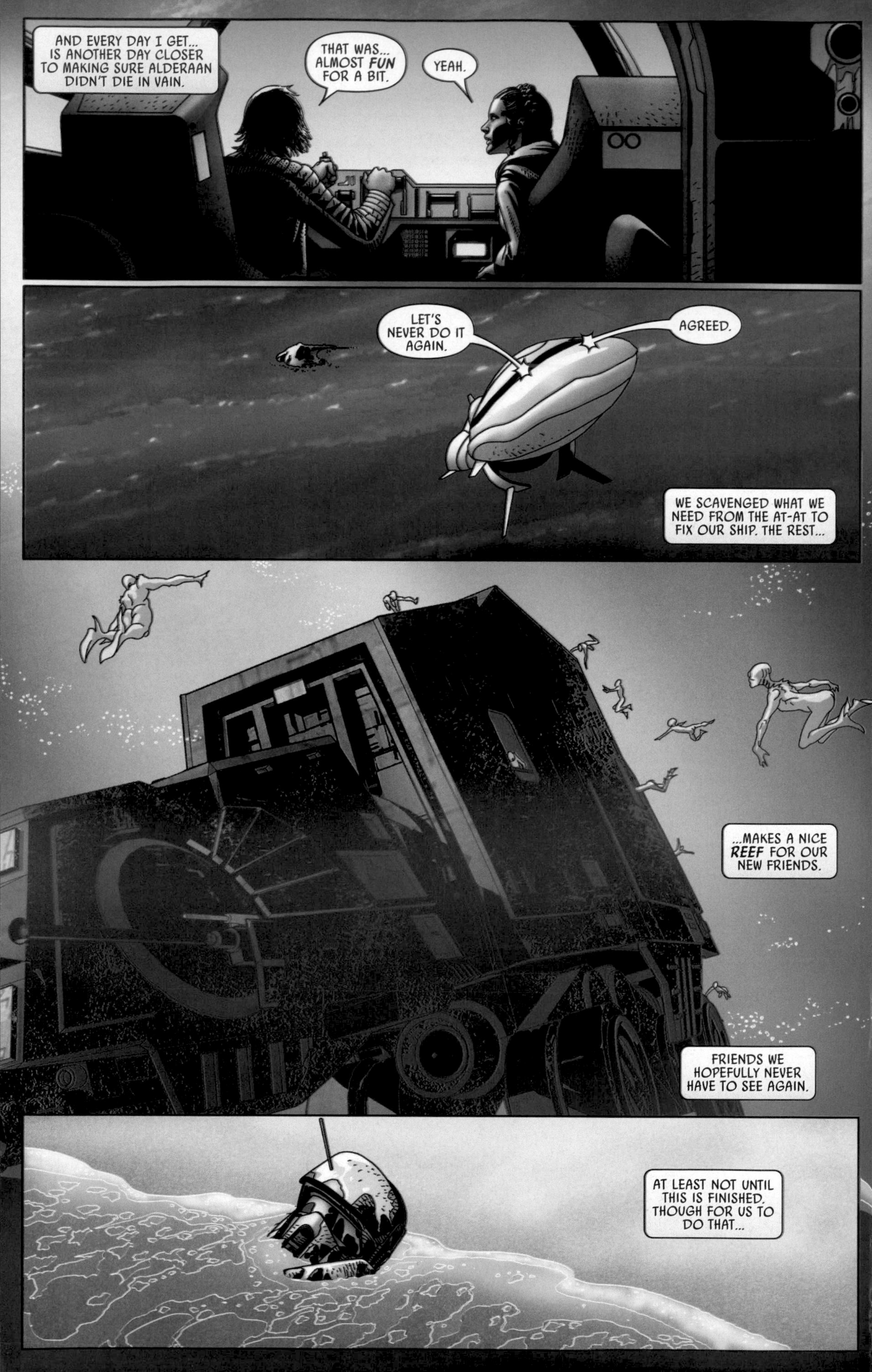
AND EVERY DAY I GET... IS ANOTHER DAY CLOSER TO MAKING SURE ALDERAAN DIDN'T DIE IN VAIN.
THAT WAS... ALMOST **FUN** FOR A BIT.
YEAH.
LET'S NEVER DO IT AGAIN.
AGREED.
WE SCAVENGED WHAT WE NEED FROM THE AT-AT TO FIX OUR SHIP. THE REST...
...MAKES A NICE **REEF** FOR OUR NEW FRIENDS.
FRIENDS WE HOPEFULLY NEVER HAVE TO SEE AGAIN.
AT LEAST NOT UNTIL THIS IS FINISHED. THOUGH FOR US TO DO THAT...

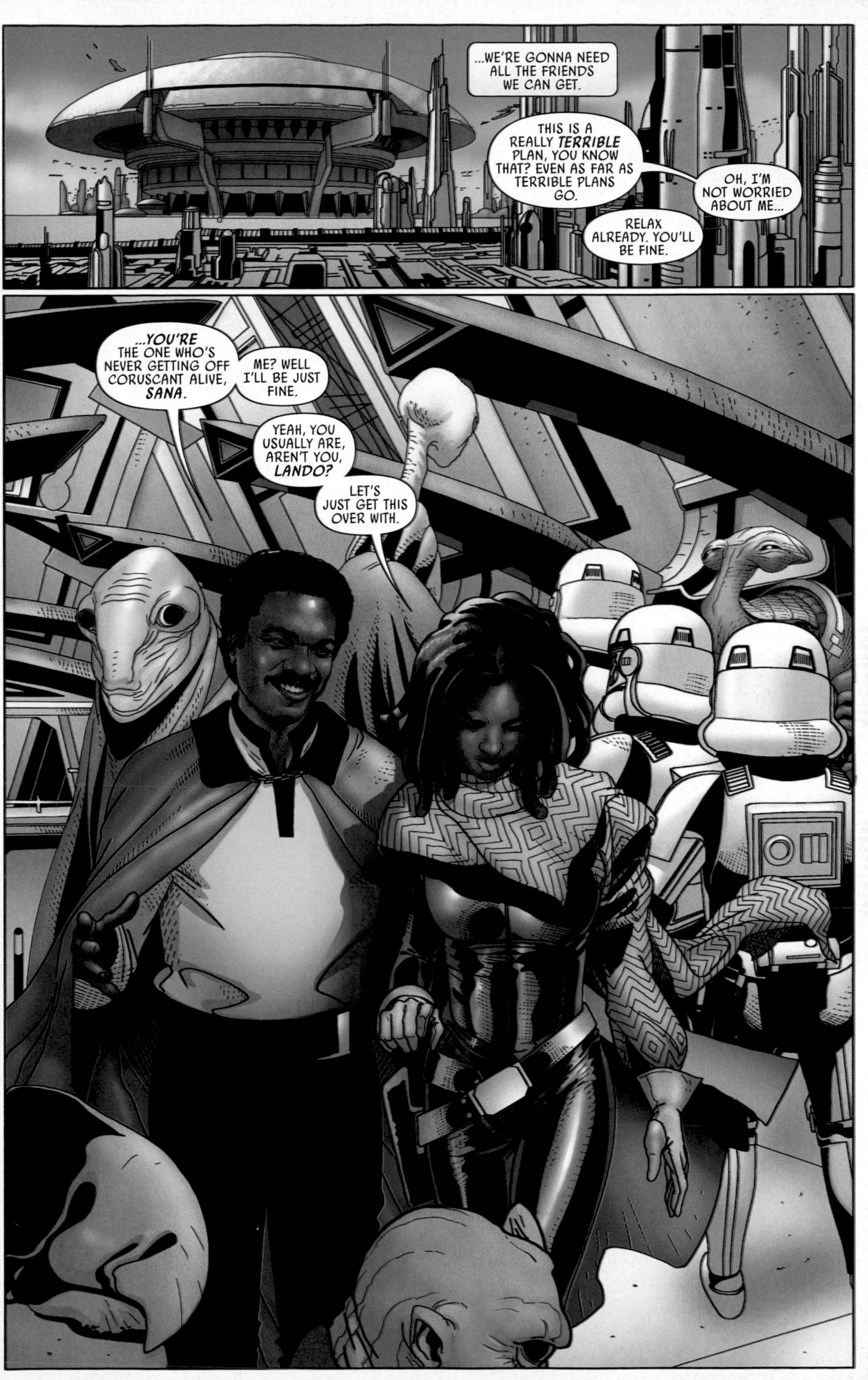
...WE'RE GONNA NEED ALL THE FRIENDS WE CAN GET.
THIS IS A REALLY TERRIBLE PLAN, YOU KNOW THAT? EVEN AS FAR AS TERRIBLE PLANS GO.
OH, I'M NOT WORRIED ABOUT ME...
RELAX ALREADY. YOU'LL BE FINE.
...YOU'RE THE ONE WHO'S NEVER GETTING OFF CORUSCANT ALIVE, SANA.
ME? WELL I'LL BE JUST FINE.
YEAH, YOU USUALLY ARE, AREN'T YOU, LANDO?
LET'S JUST GET THIS OVER WITH.

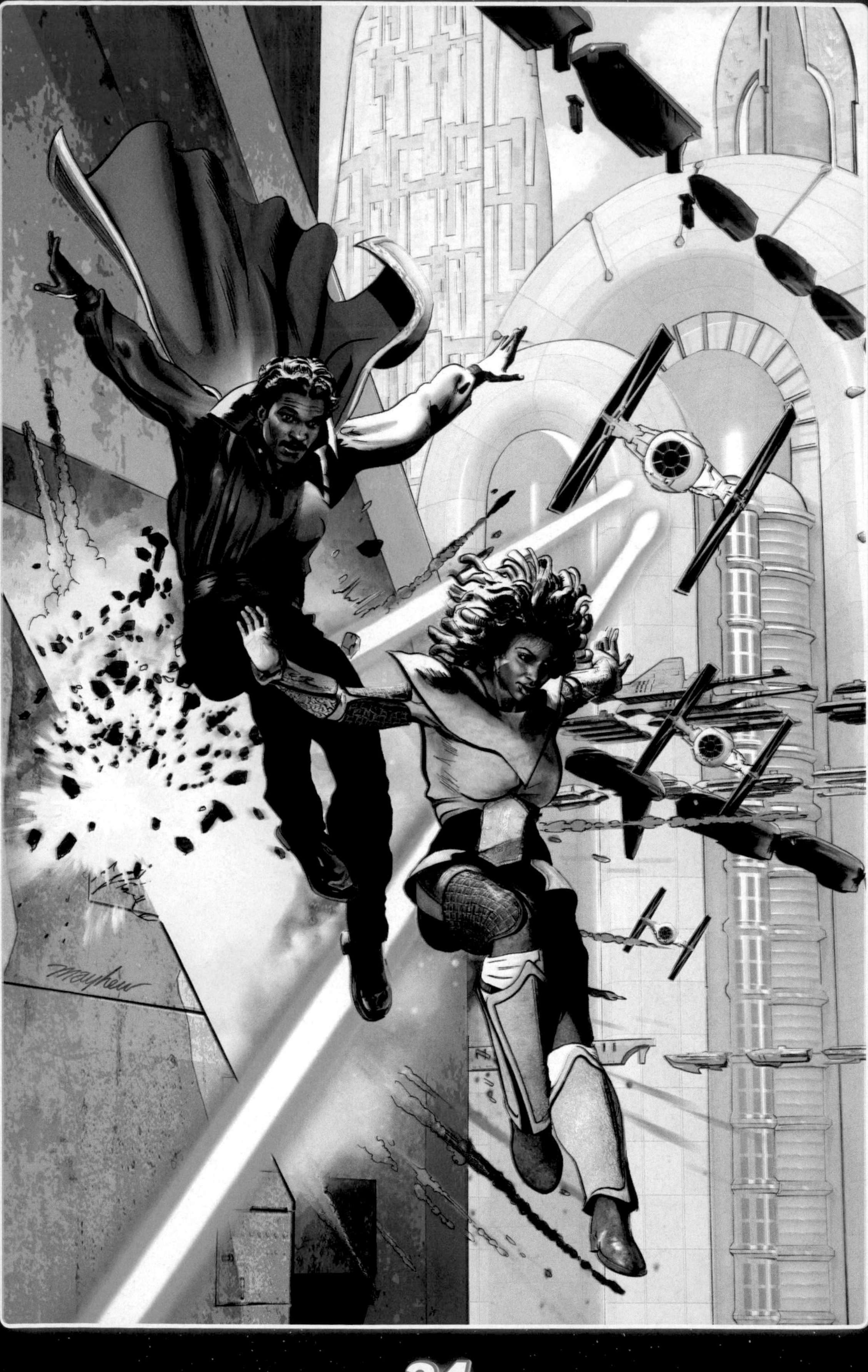
mayhew

THE THIRTEEN CRATES

It is a time of turmoil for the galaxy as the evil galactic Empire rules with an iron fist. However, for those daring and skilled enough to defy and evade Imperial forces, there is potential for profit.

Lando Calrissian, smuggler turned galactic entrepreneur, makes his mark on the universe as a disreputable businessman moving goods and skirting along the edges of Imperial law. When he's approached by skilled bounty hunter and fellow smuggler, Sana Starros, she offers him a deal he can't refuse.

Together Sana and Lando embark on a gamble as they attempt to move one of the biggest scores of their lives—or die trying....

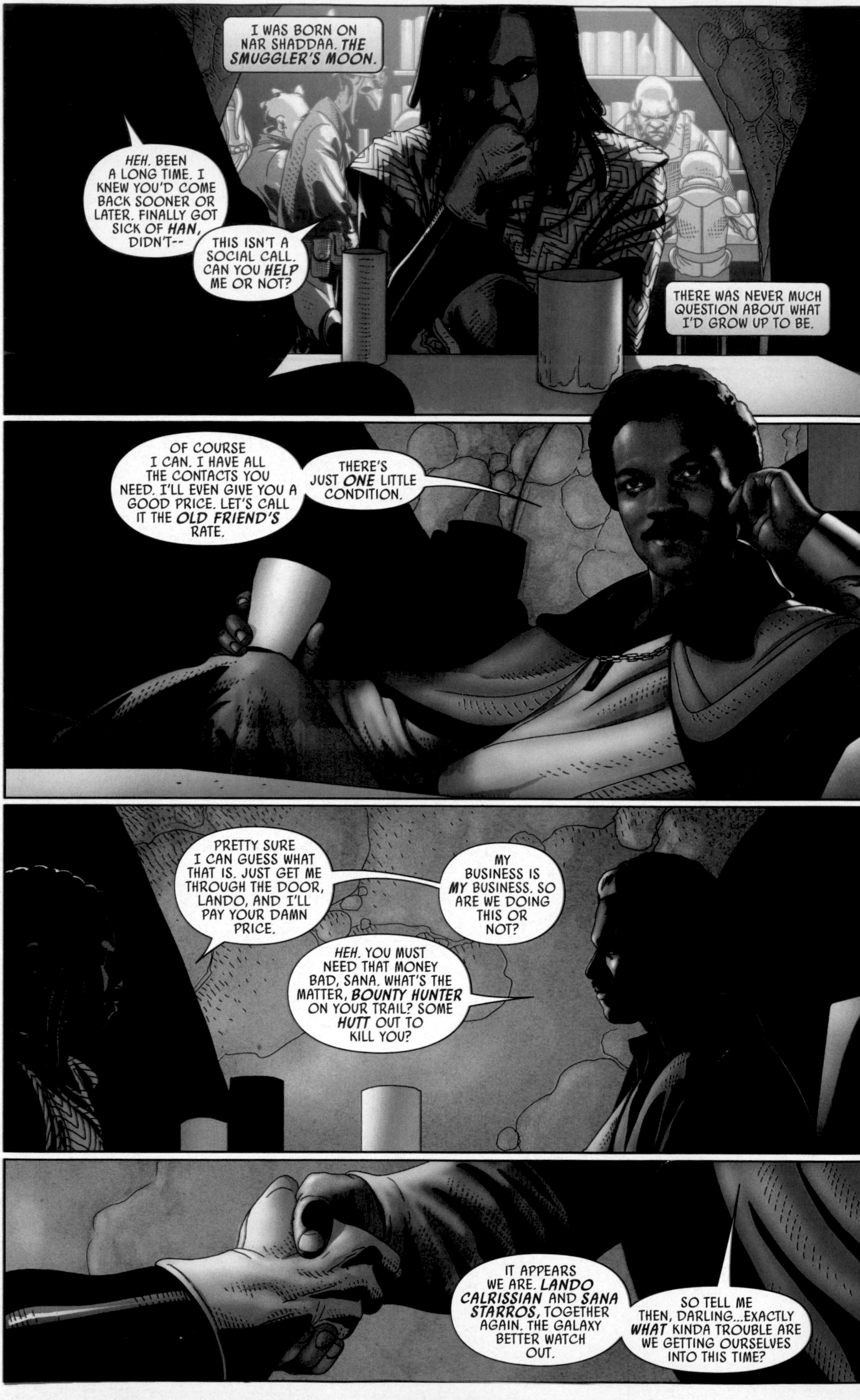
I WAS BORN ON NAR SHADDAA. THE SMUGGLER'S MOON.
HEH. BEEN A LONG TIME. I KNEW YOU'D COME BACK SOONER OR LATER. FINALLY GOT SICK OF HAN, DIDN'T--
THIS ISN'T A SOCIAL CALL. CAN YOU HELP ME OR NOT?
THERE WAS NEVER MUCH QUESTION ABOUT WHAT I'D GROW UP TO BE.
OF COURSE I CAN. I HAVE ALL THE CONTACTS YOU NEED. I'LL EVEN GIVE YOU A GOOD PRICE. LET'S CALL IT THE OLD FRIEND'S RATE.
THERE'S JUST ONE LITTLE CONDITION.
PRETTY SURE I CAN GUESS WHAT THAT IS. JUST GET ME THROUGH THE DOOR, LANDO, AND I'LL PAY YOUR DAMN PRICE.
HEH. YOU MUST NEED THAT MONEY BAD, SANA. WHAT'S THE MATTER, BOUNTY HUNTER ON YOUR TRAIL? SOME HUTT OUT TO KILL YOU?
MY BUSINESS IS MY BUSINESS. SO ARE WE DOING THIS OR NOT?
IT APPEARS WE ARE. LANDO CALRISSIAN AND SANA STARROS, TOGETHER AGAIN. THE GALAXY BETTER WATCH OUT.
SO TELL ME THEN, DARLING...EXACTLY WHAT KINDA TROUBLE ARE WE GETTING OURSELVES INTO THIS TIME?

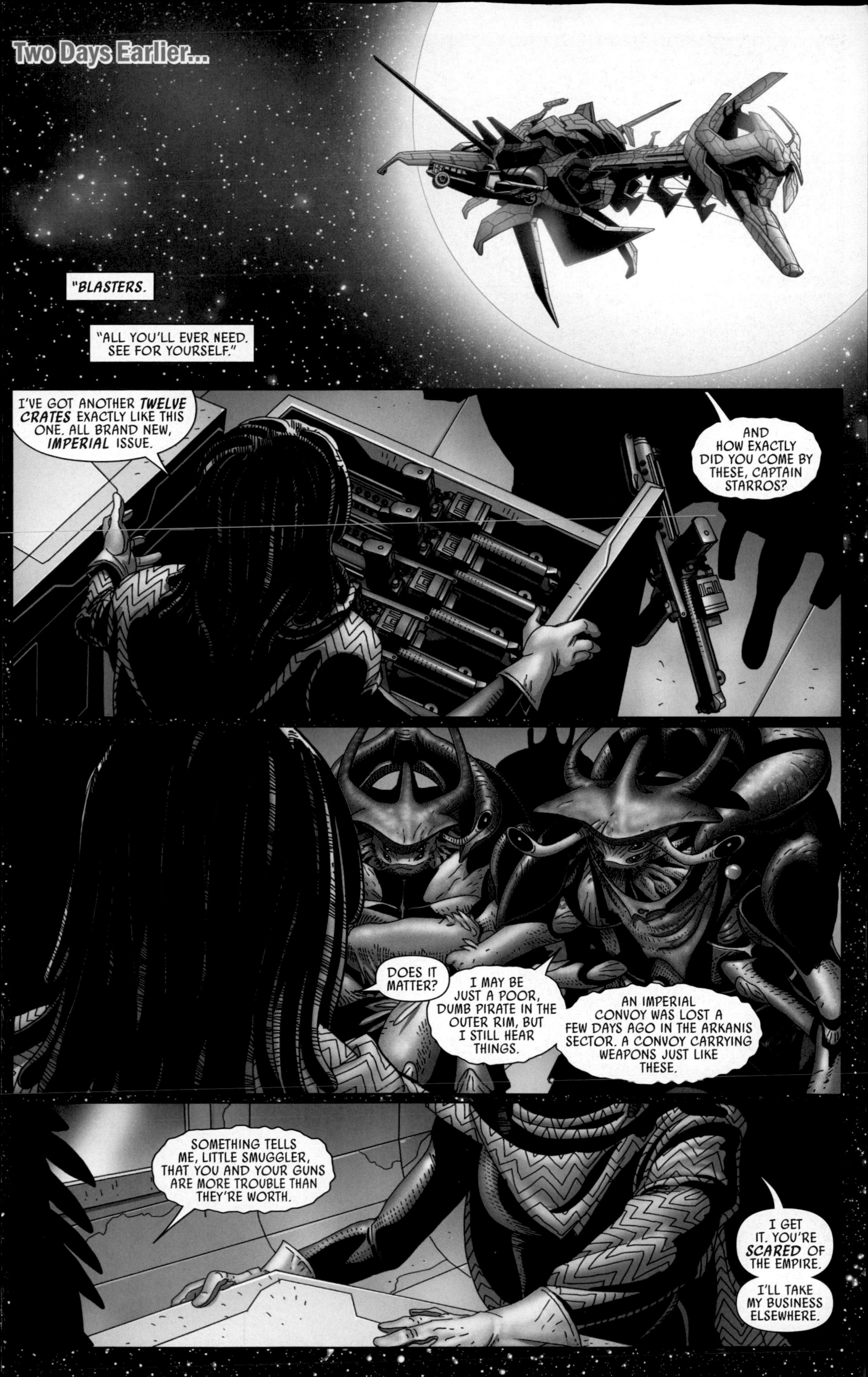
Two Days Earlier...
"BLASTERS.
"ALL YOU'LL EVER NEED. SEE FOR YOURSELF."
I'VE GOT ANOTHER TWELVE CRATES EXACTLY LIKE THIS ONE. ALL BRAND NEW, IMPERIAL ISSUE.
AND HOW EXACTLY DID YOU COME BY THESE, CAPTAIN STARROS?
DOES IT MATTER?
I MAY BE JUST A POOR, DUMB PIRATE IN THE OUTER RIM, BUT I STILL HEAR THINGS.
AN IMPERIAL CONVOY WAS LOST A FEW DAYS AGO IN THE ARKANIS SECTOR. A CONVOY CARRYING WEAPONS JUST LIKE THESE.
SOMETHING TELLS ME, LITTLE SMUGGLER, THAT YOU AND YOUR GUNS ARE MORE TROUBLE THAN THEY'RE WORTH.
I GET IT. YOU'RE SCARED OF THE EMPIRE.
I'LL TAKE MY BUSINESS ELSEWHERE.

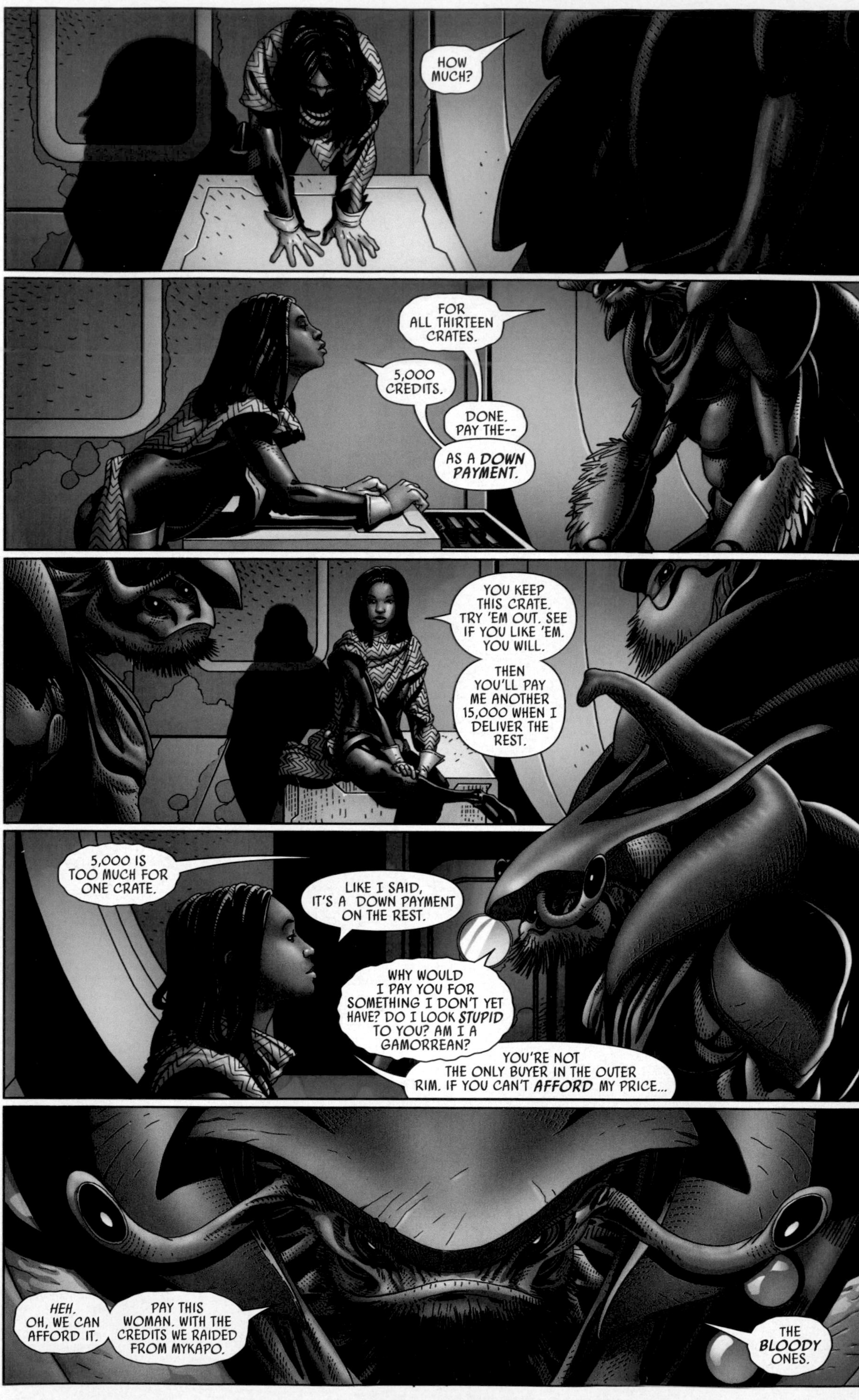
HOW MUCH?
5,000 CREDITS.
FOR ALL THIRTEEN CRATES.
DONE. PAY THE--
AS A *DOWN PAYMENT.*
YOU KEEP THIS CRATE. TRY 'EM OUT. SEE IF YOU LIKE 'EM. YOU WILL.
THEN YOU'LL PAY ME ANOTHER 15,000 WHEN I DELIVER THE REST.
5,000 IS TOO MUCH FOR ONE CRATE.
LIKE I SAID, IT'S A DOWN PAYMENT ON THE REST.
WHY WOULD I PAY YOU FOR SOMETHING I DON'T YET HAVE? DO I LOOK *STUPID* TO YOU? AM I A GAMORREAN?
YOU'RE NOT THE ONLY BUYER IN THE OUTER RIM. IF YOU CAN'T *AFFORD* MY PRICE...
HEH. OH, WE CAN AFFORD IT.
PAY THIS WOMAN. WITH THE CREDITS WE RAIDED FROM MYKAPO.
THE *BLOODY* ONES.

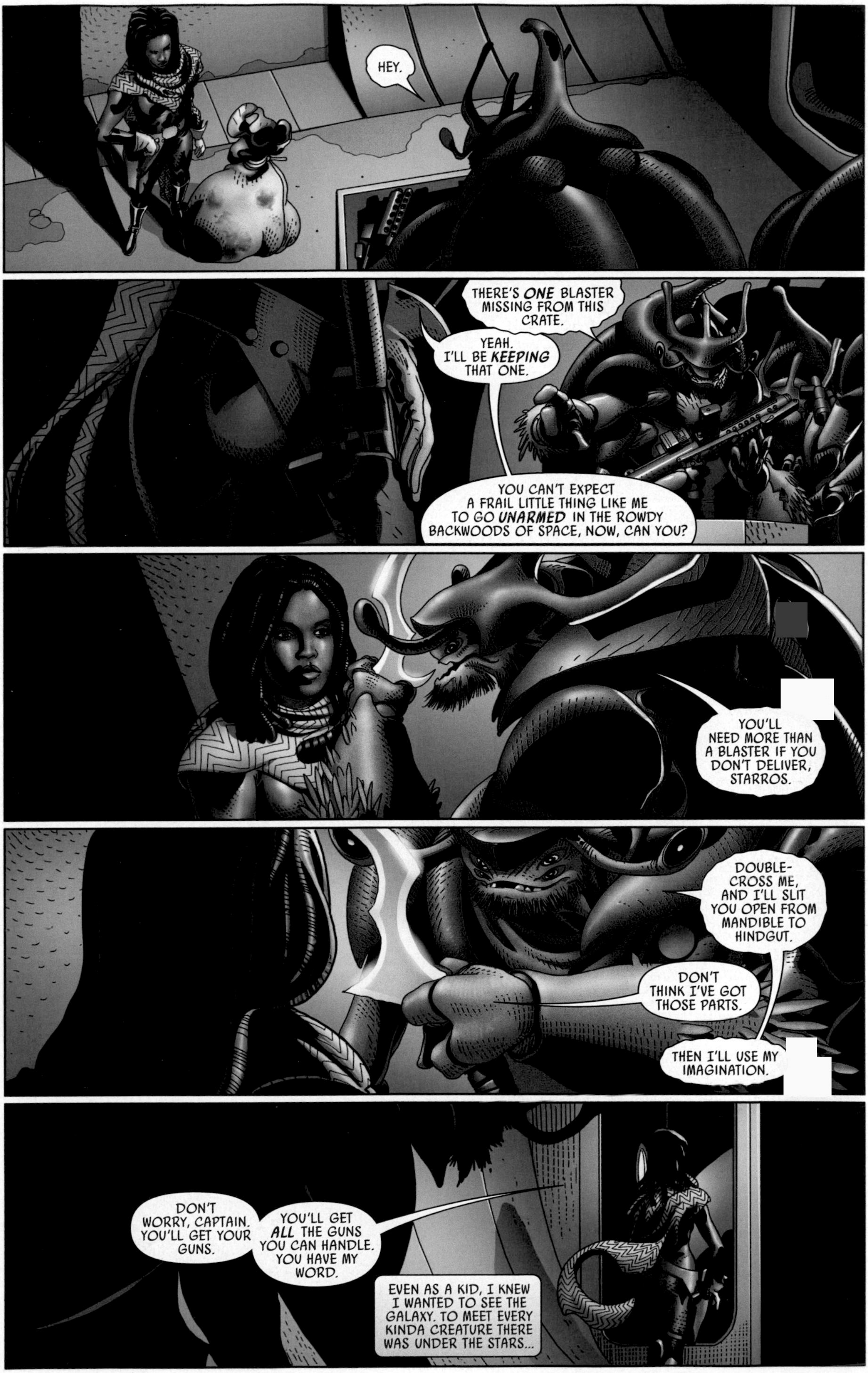
HEY.
THERE'S ONE BLASTER MISSING FROM THIS CRATE.
YEAH. I'LL BE KEEPING THAT ONE.
YOU CAN'T EXPECT A FRAIL LITTLE THING LIKE ME TO GO UNARMED IN THE ROWDY BACKWOODS OF SPACE, NOW, CAN YOU?
YOU'LL NEED MORE THAN A BLASTER IF YOU DON'T DELIVER, STARROS.
DOUBLE-CROSS ME, AND I'LL SLIT YOU OPEN FROM MANDIBLE TO HINDGUT.
DON'T THINK I'VE GOT THOSE PARTS.
THEN I'LL USE MY IMAGINATION.
DON'T WORRY, CAPTAIN. YOU'LL GET YOUR GUNS.
YOU'LL GET ALL THE GUNS YOU CAN HANDLE. YOU HAVE MY WORD.
EVEN AS A KID, I KNEW I WANTED TO SEE THE GALAXY. TO MEET EVERY KINDA CREATURE THERE WAS UNDER THE STARS...

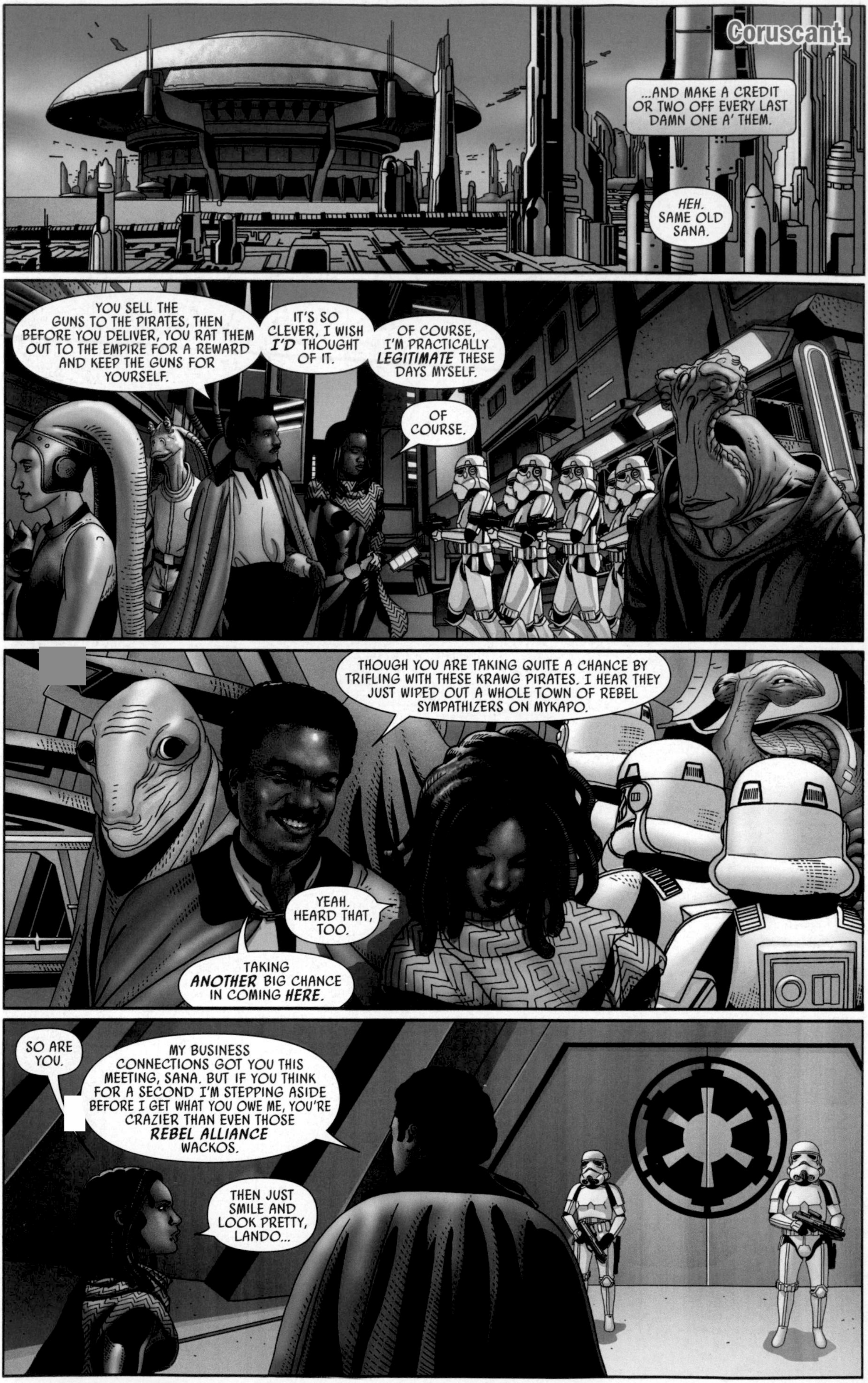
Coruscant.
...AND MAKE A CREDIT OR TWO OFF EVERY LAST DAMN ONE A' THEM.
HEH. SAME OLD SANA.
YOU SELL THE GUNS TO THE PIRATES, THEN BEFORE YOU DELIVER, YOU RAT THEM OUT TO THE EMPIRE FOR A REWARD AND KEEP THE GUNS FOR YOURSELF.
IT'S SO CLEVER, I WISH *I'D* THOUGHT OF IT.
OF COURSE, I'M PRACTICALLY *LEGITIMATE* THESE DAYS MYSELF.
OF COURSE.
THOUGH YOU ARE TAKING QUITE A CHANCE BY TRIFLING WITH THESE KRAWG PIRATES. I HEAR THEY JUST WIPED OUT A WHOLE TOWN OF REBEL SYMPATHIZERS ON MYKAPO.
YEAH. HEARD THAT, TOO.
TAKING *ANOTHER* BIG CHANCE IN COMING *HERE.*
SO ARE YOU.
MY BUSINESS CONNECTIONS GOT YOU THIS MEETING, SANA. BUT IF YOU THINK FOR A SECOND I'M STEPPING ASIDE BEFORE I GET WHAT YOU OWE ME, YOU'RE CRAZIER THAN EVEN THOSE *REBEL ALLIANCE* WACKOS.
THEN JUST SMILE AND LOOK PRETTY, LANDO...

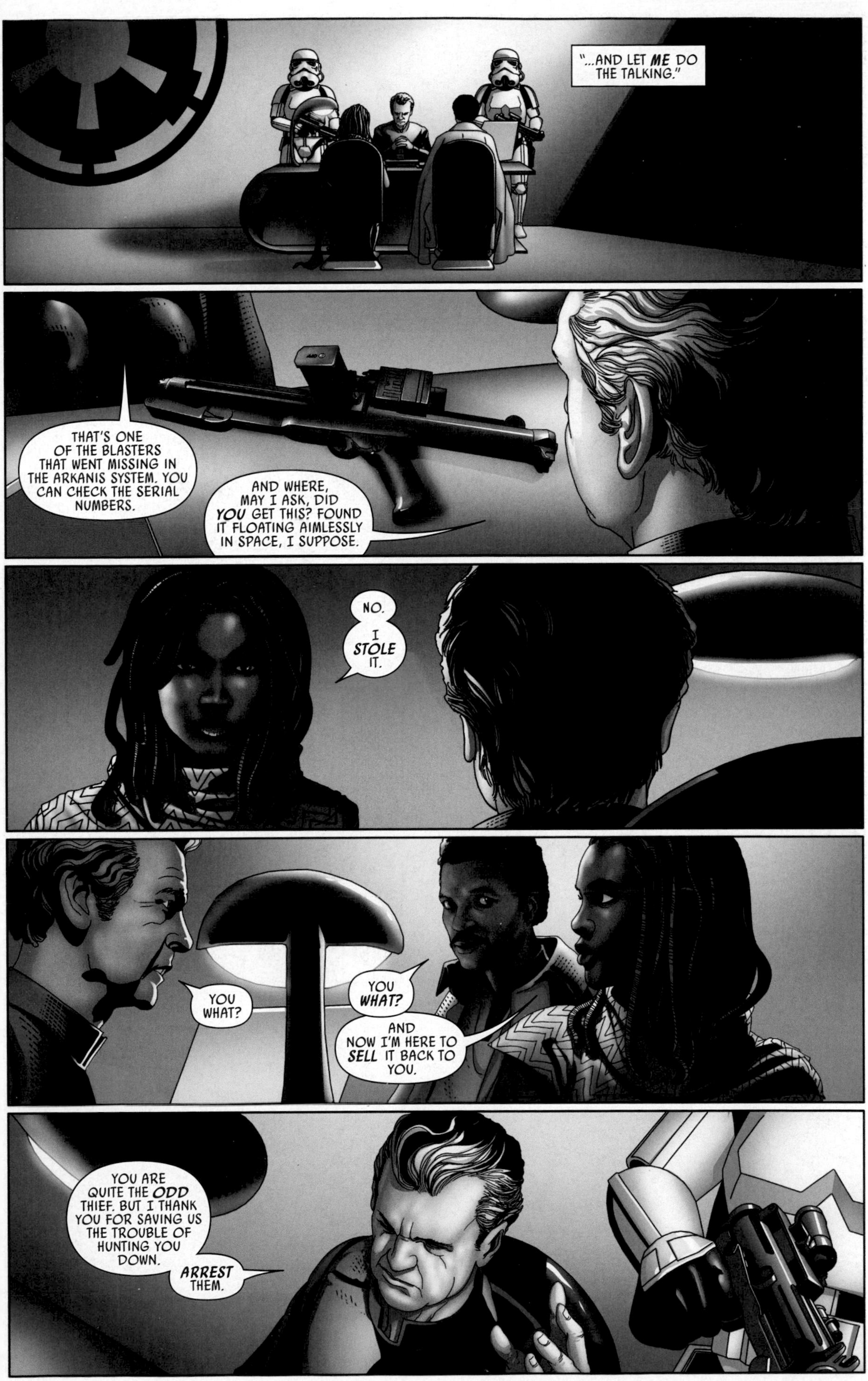
"...AND LET ME DO THE TALKING."
THAT'S ONE OF THE BLASTERS THAT WENT MISSING IN THE ARKANIS SYSTEM. YOU CAN CHECK THE SERIAL NUMBERS.
AND WHERE, MAY I ASK, DID YOU GET THIS? FOUND IT FLOATING AIMLESSLY IN SPACE, I SUPPOSE.
NO.
I STOLE IT.
YOU WHAT?
YOU WHAT?
AND NOW I'M HERE TO SELL IT BACK TO YOU.
YOU ARE QUITE THE ODD THIEF. BUT I THANK YOU FOR SAVING US THE TROUBLE OF HUNTING YOU DOWN.
ARREST THEM.

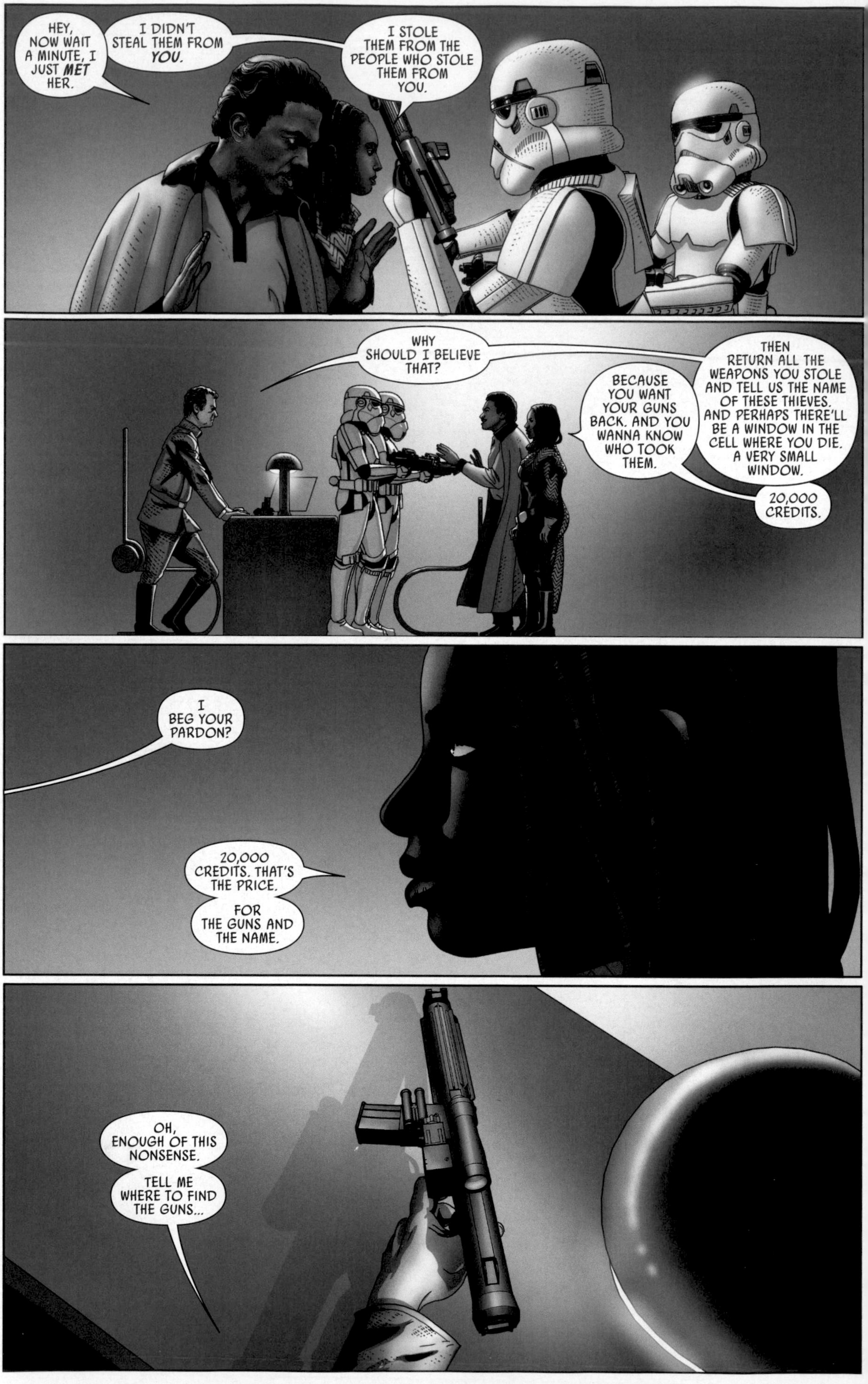
HEY, NOW WAIT A MINUTE, I JUST *MET* HER.
I DIDN'T STEAL THEM FROM *YOU.*
I STOLE THEM FROM THE PEOPLE WHO STOLE THEM FROM YOU.
WHY SHOULD I BELIEVE THAT?
BECAUSE YOU WANT YOUR GUNS BACK. AND YOU WANNA KNOW WHO TOOK THEM.
THEN RETURN ALL THE WEAPONS YOU STOLE AND TELL US THE NAME OF THESE THIEVES. AND PERHAPS THERE'LL BE A WINDOW IN THE CELL WHERE YOU DIE. A VERY SMALL WINDOW.
20,000 CREDITS.
I BEG YOUR PARDON?
20,000 CREDITS. THAT'S THE PRICE.
FOR THE GUNS AND THE NAME.
OH, ENOUGH OF THIS NONSENSE.
TELL ME WHERE TO FIND THE GUNS...

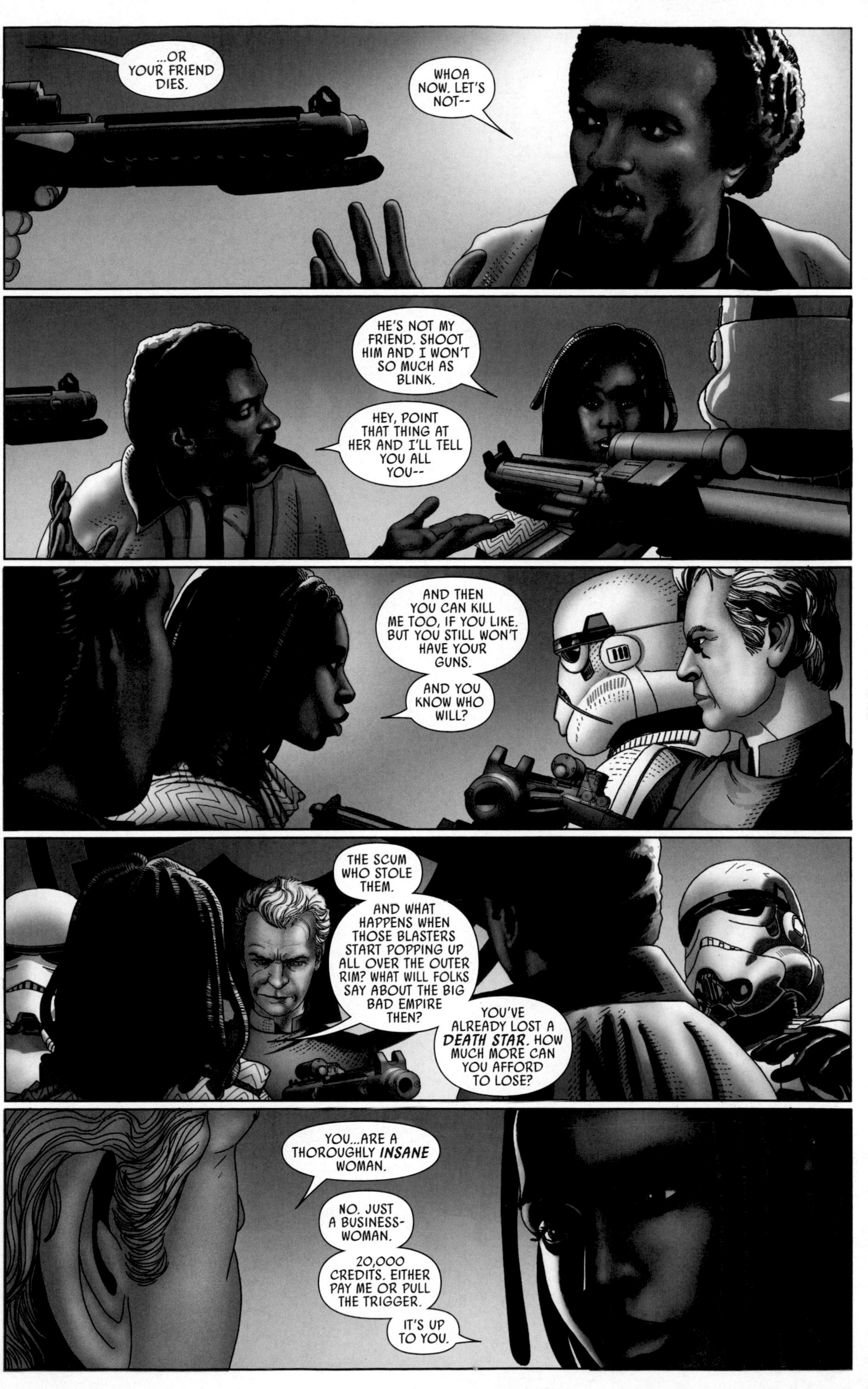
...OR YOUR FRIEND DIES.
WHOA NOW. LET'S NOT--
HE'S NOT MY FRIEND. SHOOT HIM AND I WON'T SO MUCH AS BLINK.
HEY, POINT THAT THING AT HER AND I'LL TELL YOU ALL YOU--
AND THEN YOU CAN KILL ME TOO, IF YOU LIKE. BUT YOU STILL WON'T HAVE YOUR GUNS.
AND YOU KNOW WHO WILL?
THE SCUM WHO STOLE THEM.
AND WHAT HAPPENS WHEN THOSE BLASTERS START POPPING UP ALL OVER THE OUTER RIM? WHAT WILL FOLKS SAY ABOUT THE BIG BAD EMPIRE THEN?
YOU'VE ALREADY LOST A DEATH STAR. HOW MUCH MORE CAN YOU AFFORD TO LOSE?
YOU...ARE A THOROUGHLY INSANE WOMAN.
NO. JUST A BUSINESS-WOMAN.
20,000 CREDITS. EITHER PAY ME OR PULL THE TRIGGER.
IT'S UP TO YOU.

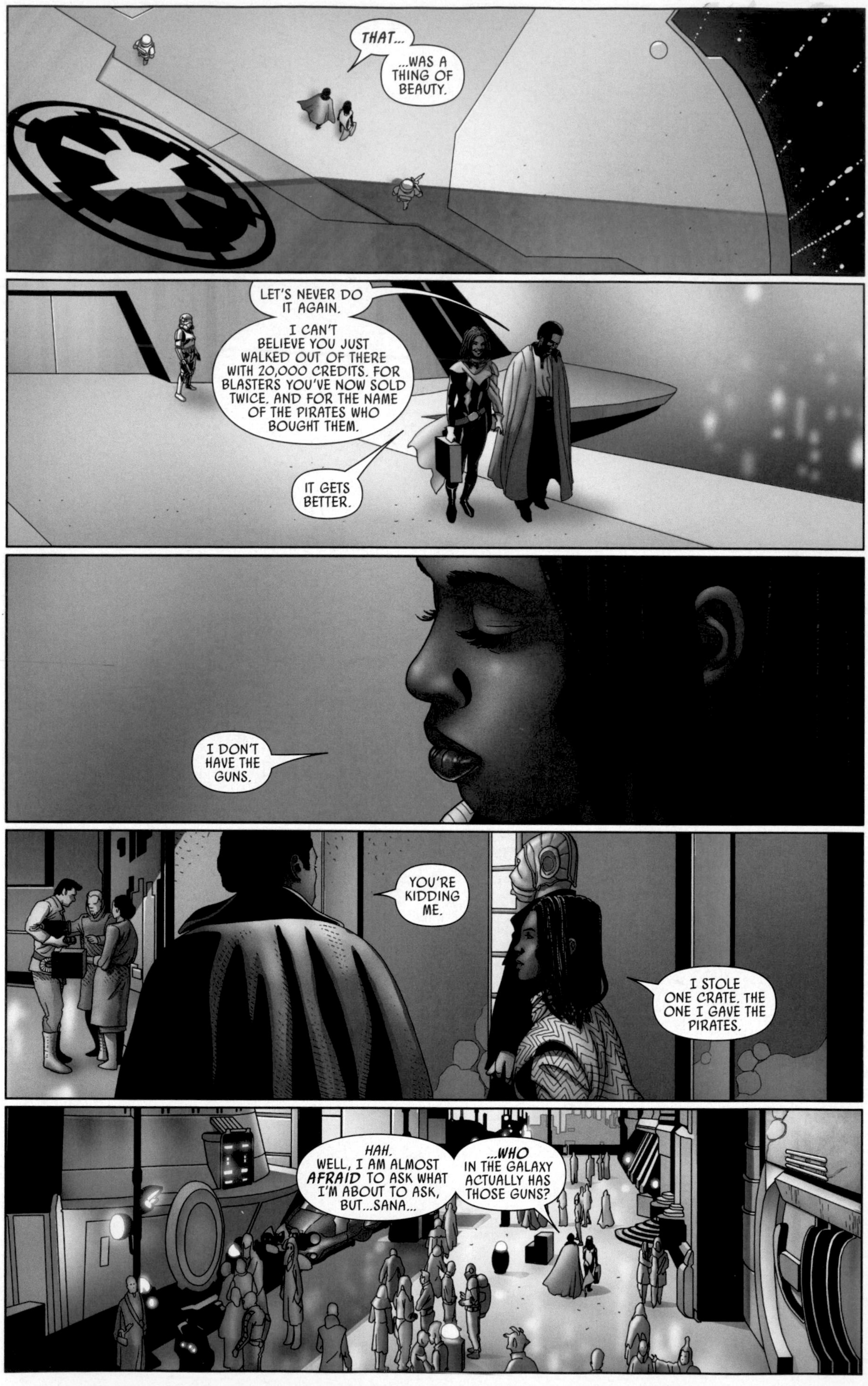
THAT...
...WAS A THING OF BEAUTY.
LET'S NEVER DO IT AGAIN.
I CAN'T BELIEVE YOU JUST WALKED OUT OF THERE WITH 20,000 CREDITS. FOR BLASTERS YOU'VE NOW SOLD TWICE. AND FOR THE NAME OF THE PIRATES WHO BOUGHT THEM.
IT GETS BETTER.
I DON'T HAVE THE GUNS.
YOU'RE KIDDING ME.
I STOLE ONE CRATE. THE ONE I GAVE THE PIRATES.
HAH. WELL, I AM ALMOST AFRAID TO ASK WHAT I'M ABOUT TO ASK, BUT...SANA...
...WHO IN THE GALAXY ACTUALLY HAS THOSE GUNS?

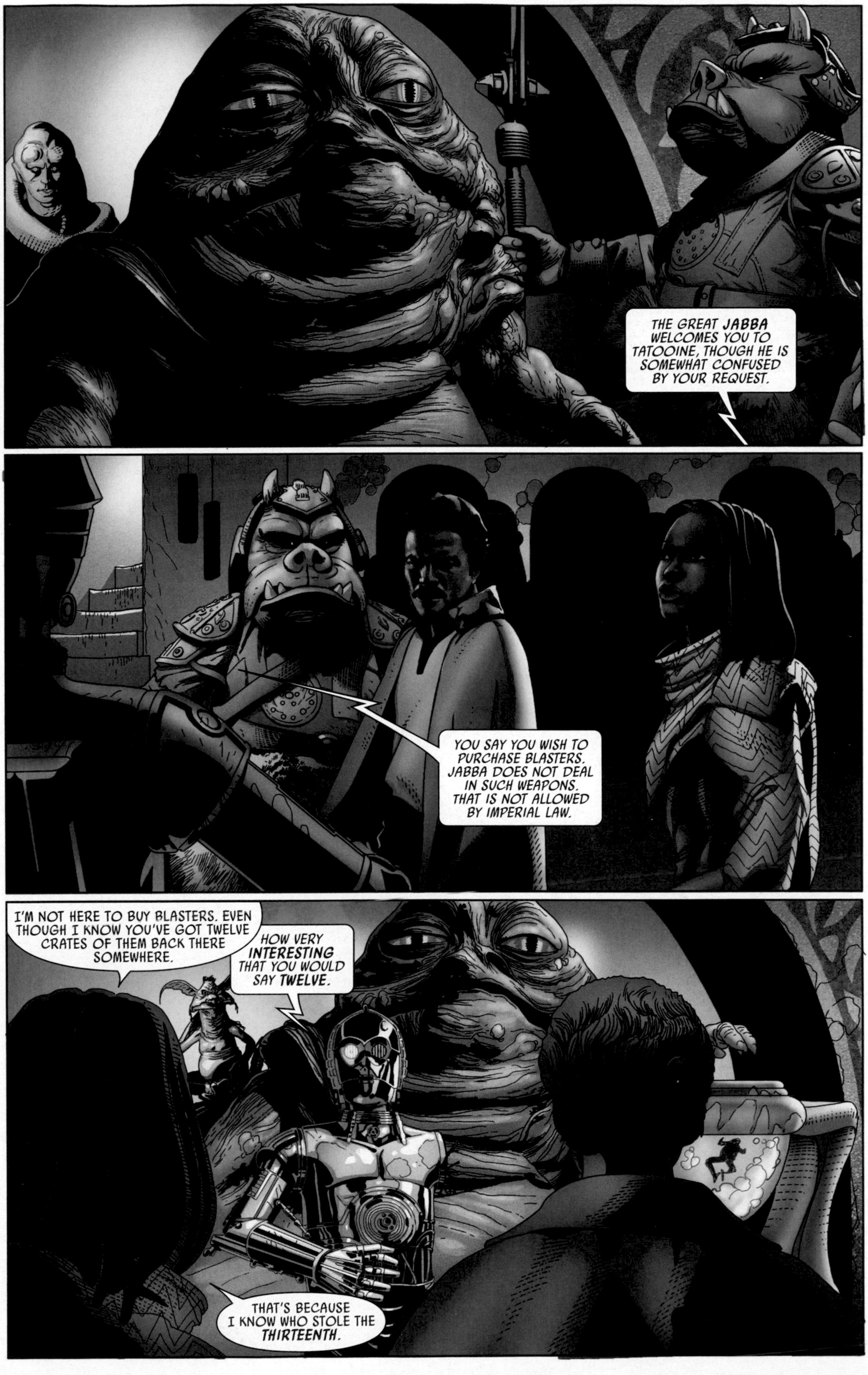
THE GREAT JABBA WELCOMES YOU TO TATOOINE, THOUGH HE IS SOMEWHAT CONFUSED BY YOUR REQUEST.
YOU SAY YOU WISH TO PURCHASE BLASTERS. JABBA DOES NOT DEAL IN SUCH WEAPONS. THAT IS NOT ALLOWED BY IMPERIAL LAW.
I'M NOT HERE TO BUY BLASTERS. EVEN THOUGH I KNOW YOU'VE GOT TWELVE CRATES OF THEM BACK THERE SOMEWHERE.
HOW VERY INTERESTING THAT YOU WOULD SAY TWELVE.
THAT'S BECAUSE I KNOW WHO STOLE THE THIRTEENTH.

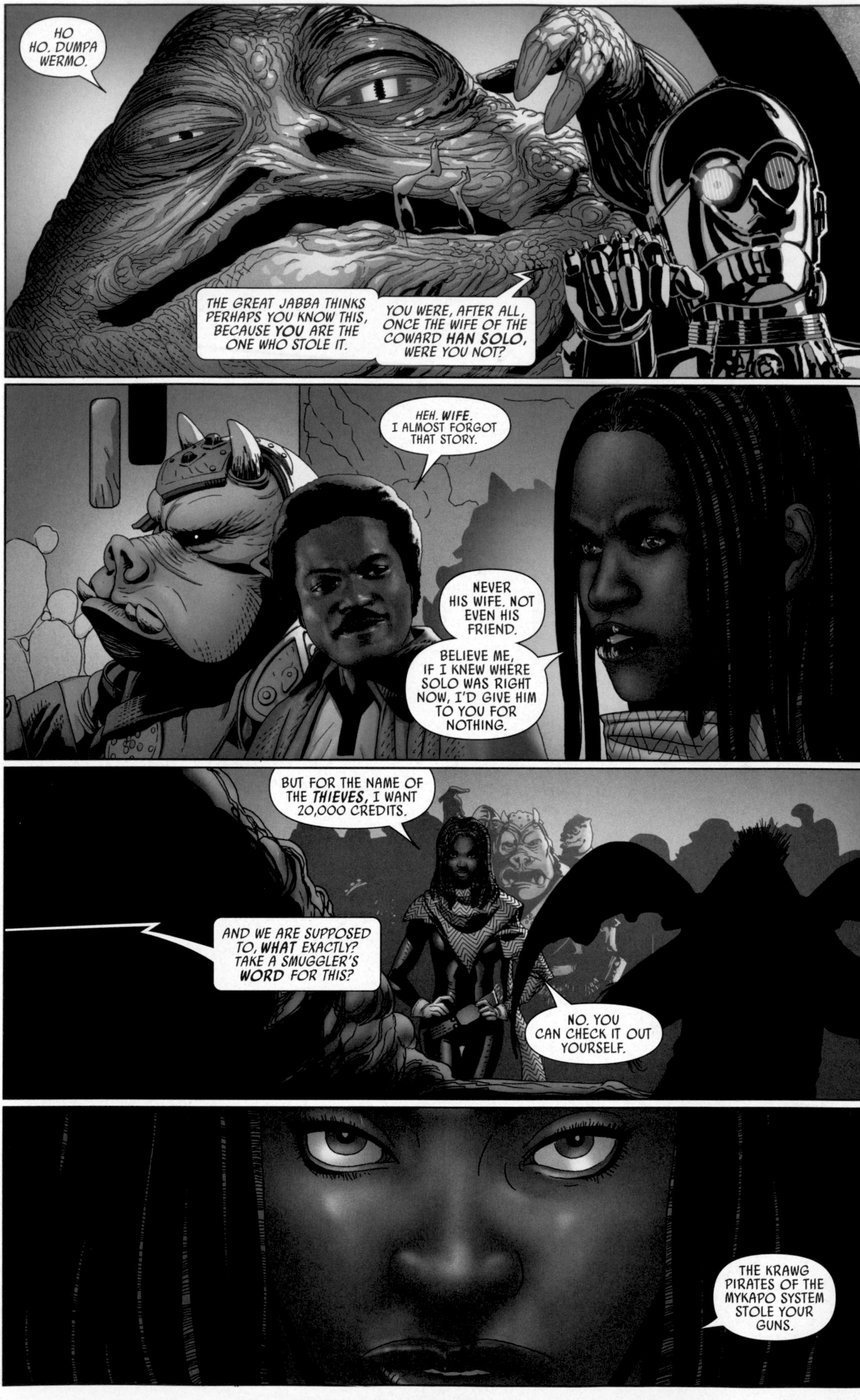
HO HO. DUMPA WERMO.
THE GREAT JABBA THINKS PERHAPS YOU KNOW THIS, BECAUSE YOU ARE THE ONE WHO STOLE IT.
YOU WERE, AFTER ALL, ONCE THE WIFE OF THE COWARD HAN SOLO, WERE YOU NOT?
HEH. WIFE. I ALMOST FORGOT THAT STORY.
NEVER HIS WIFE. NOT EVEN HIS FRIEND.
BELIEVE ME, IF I KNEW WHERE SOLO WAS RIGHT NOW, I'D GIVE HIM TO YOU FOR NOTHING.
BUT FOR THE NAME OF THE THIEVES, I WANT 20,000 CREDITS.
AND WE ARE SUPPOSED TO, WHAT EXACTLY? TAKE A SMUGGLER'S WORD FOR THIS?
NO. YOU CAN CHECK IT OUT YOURSELF.
THE KRAWG PIRATES OF THE MYKAPO SYSTEM STOLE YOUR GUNS.

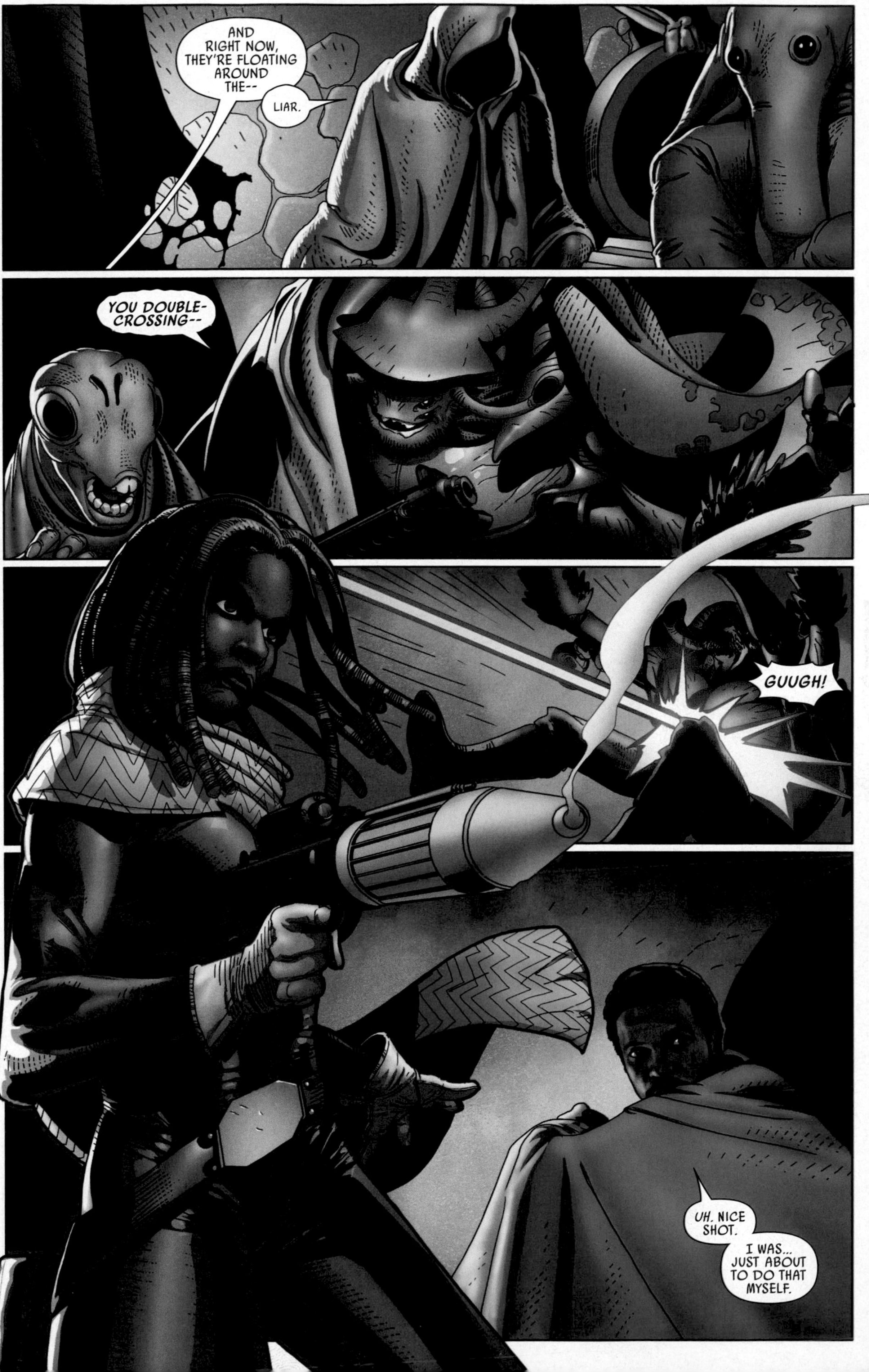
AND RIGHT NOW, THEY'RE FLOATING AROUND THE--
LIAR.
YOU DOUBLE-CROSSING--
GUUGH!
UH. NICE SHOT.
I WAS... JUST ABOUT TO DO THAT MYSELF.

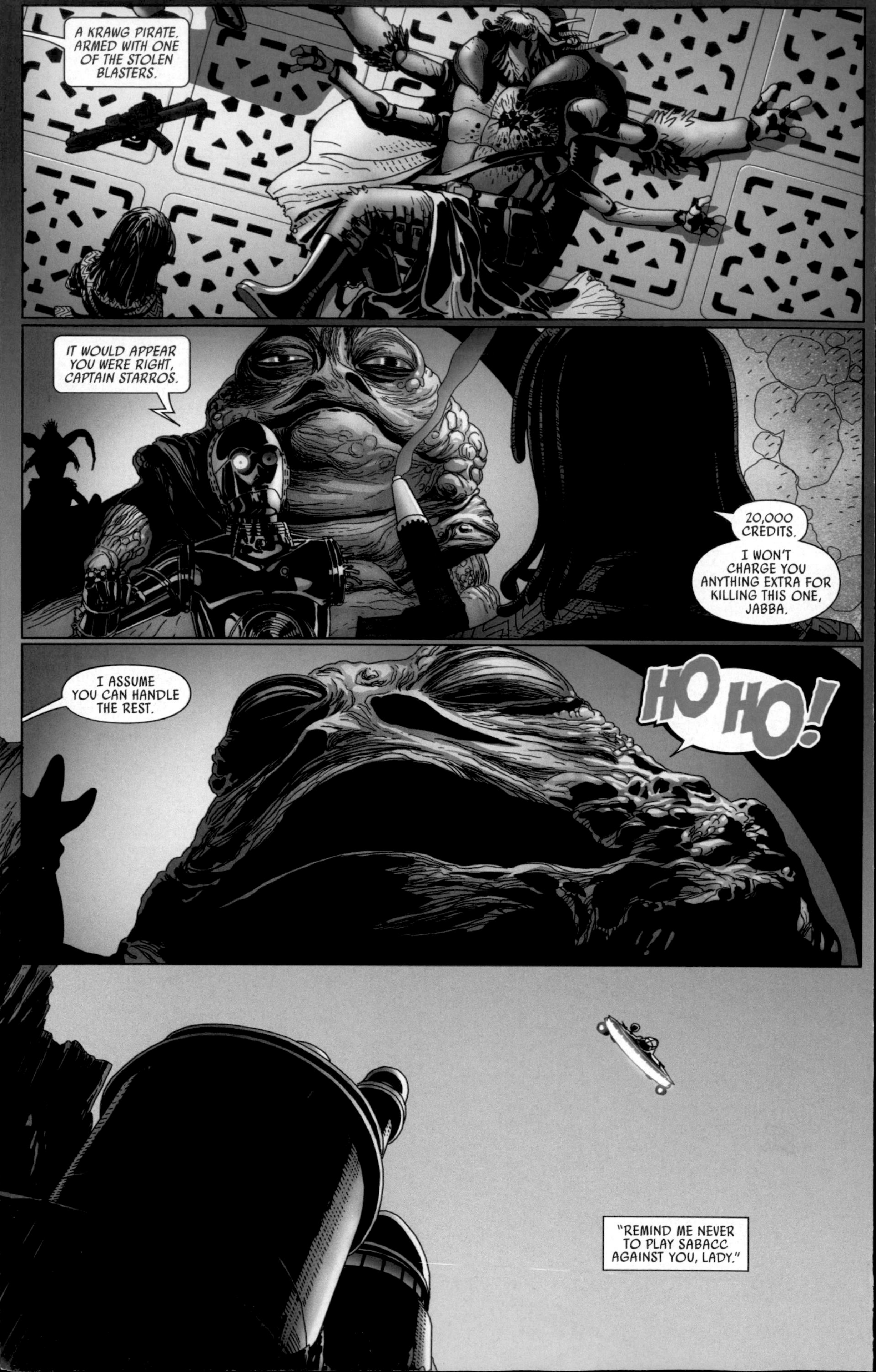

A KRAWG PIRATE. ARMED WITH ONE OF THE STOLEN BLASTERS.
IT WOULD APPEAR YOU WERE RIGHT, CAPTAIN STARROS.
20,000 CREDITS.
I WON'T CHARGE YOU ANYTHING EXTRA FOR KILLING THIS ONE, JABBA.
I ASSUME YOU CAN HANDLE THE REST.
HO HO!
"REMIND ME NEVER TO PLAY SABACC AGAINST YOU, LADY."

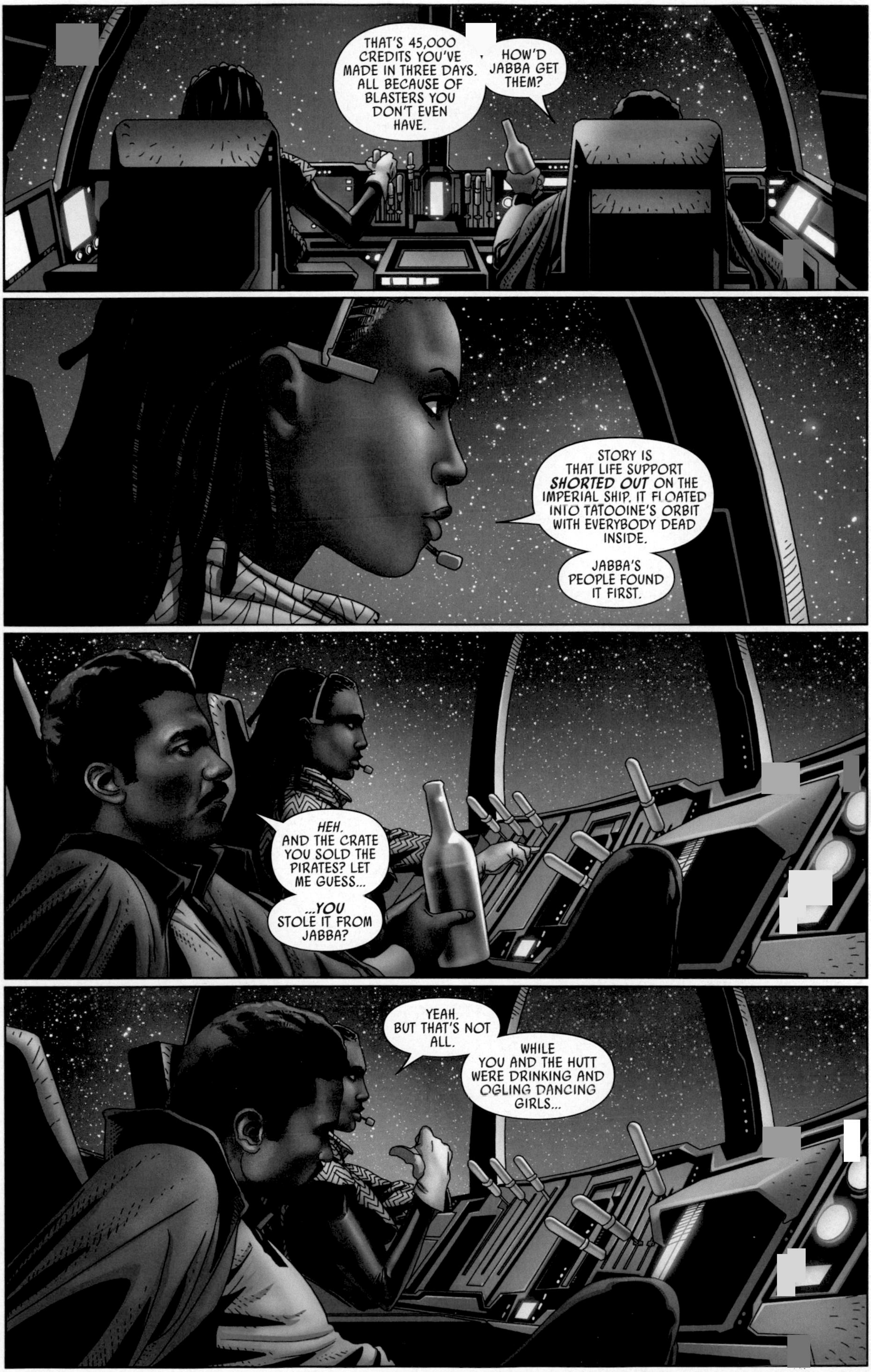
THAT'S 45,000 CREDITS YOU'VE MADE IN THREE DAYS. ALL BECAUSE OF BLASTERS YOU DON'T EVEN HAVE.
HOW'D JABBA GET THEM?
STORY IS THAT LIFE SUPPORT **SHORTED OUT** ON THE IMPERIAL SHIP. IT FLOATED INTO TATOOINE'S ORBIT WITH EVERYBODY DEAD INSIDE.
JABBA'S PEOPLE FOUND IT FIRST.
HEH. AND THE CRATE YOU SOLD THE PIRATES? LET ME GUESS...
...YOU STOLE IT FROM JABBA?
YEAH. BUT THAT'S NOT ALL.
WHILE YOU AND THE HUTT WERE DRINKING AND OGLING DANCING GIRLS...

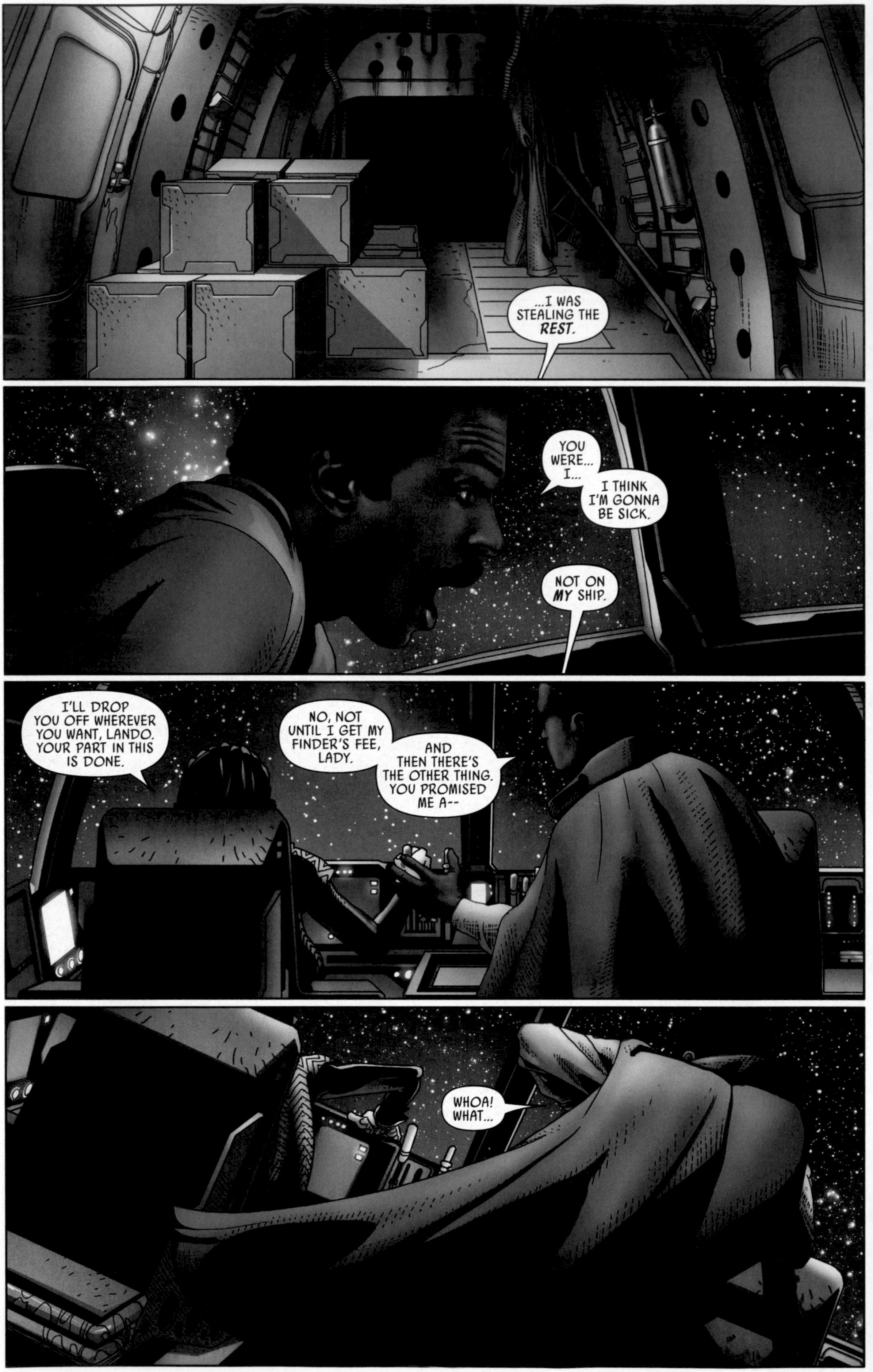

...I WAS STEALING THE REST.
YOU WERE... I...
I THINK I'M GONNA BE SICK.
NOT ON MY SHIP.
I'LL DROP YOU OFF WHEREVER YOU WANT, LANDO. YOUR PART IN THIS IS DONE.
NO, NOT UNTIL I GET MY FINDER'S FEE, LADY.
AND THEN THERE'S THE OTHER THING. YOU PROMISED ME A--
WHOA! WHAT...

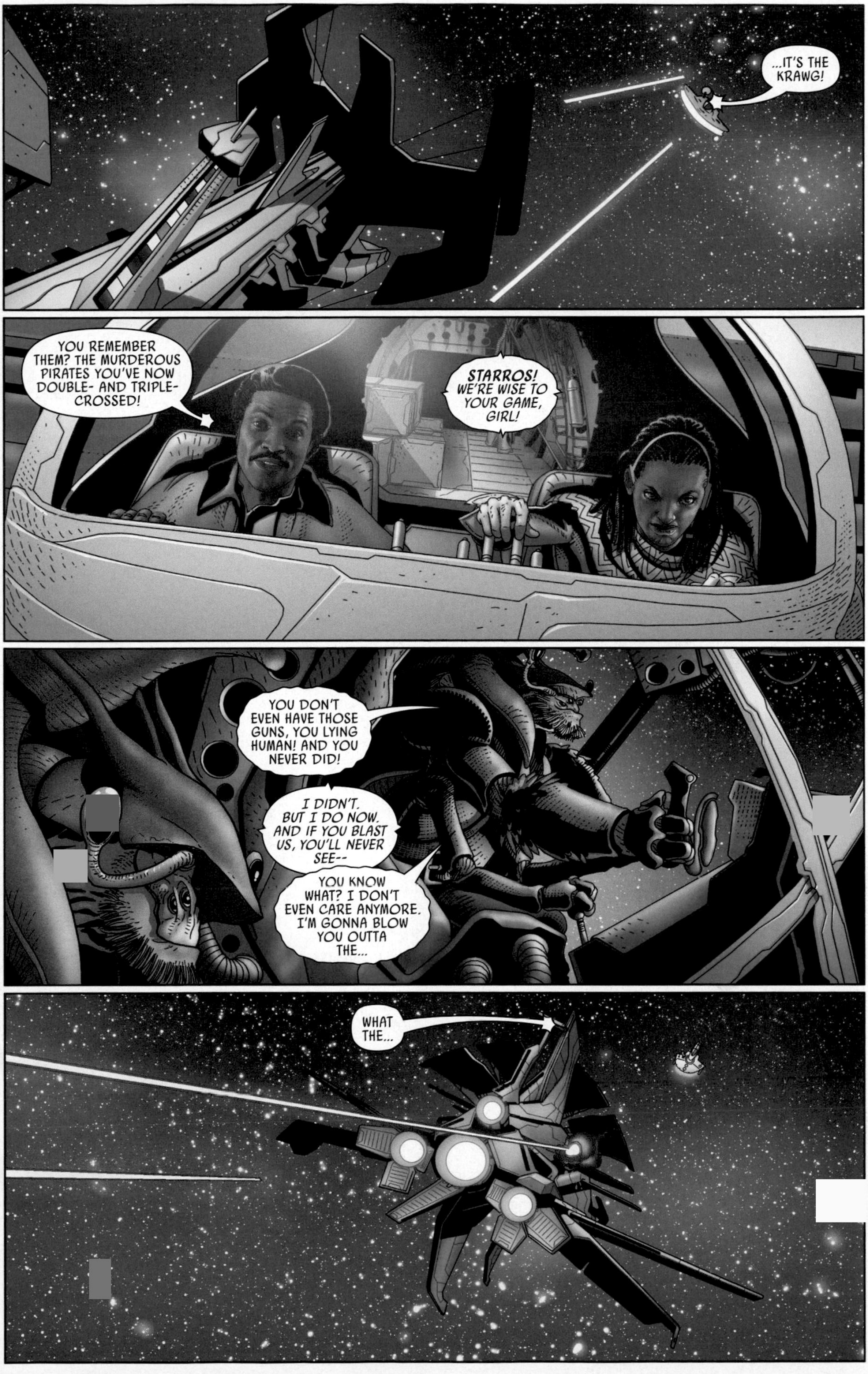
...IT'S THE KRAWG!
YOU REMEMBER THEM? THE MURDEROUS PIRATES YOU'VE NOW DOUBLE- AND TRIPLE-CROSSED!
STARROS! WE'RE WISE TO YOUR GAME, GIRL!
YOU DON'T EVEN HAVE THOSE GUNS, YOU LYING HUMAN! AND YOU NEVER DID!
I DIDN'T. BUT I DO NOW. AND IF YOU BLAST US, YOU'LL NEVER SEE--
YOU KNOW WHAT? I DON'T EVEN CARE ANYMORE. I'M GONNA BLOW YOU OUTTA THE...
WHAT THE...

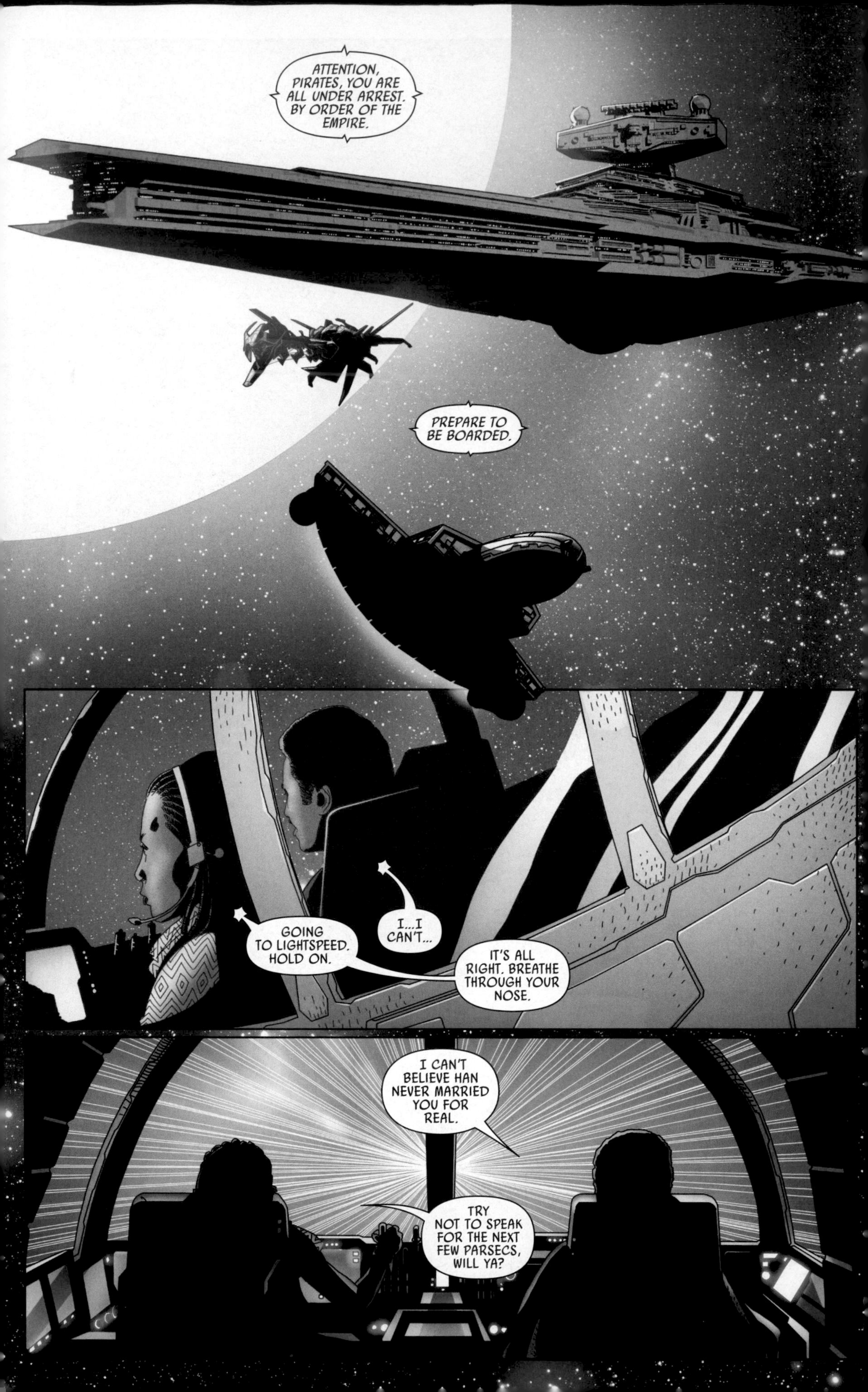
ATTENTION, PIRATES, YOU ARE ALL UNDER ARREST. BY ORDER OF THE EMPIRE.
PREPARE TO BE BOARDED.
GOING TO LIGHTSPEED. HOLD ON.
I...I CAN'T...
IT'S ALL RIGHT. BREATHE THROUGH YOUR NOSE.
I CAN'T BELIEVE HAN NEVER MARRIED YOU FOR REAL.
TRY NOT TO SPEAK FOR THE NEXT FEW PARSECS, WILL YA?

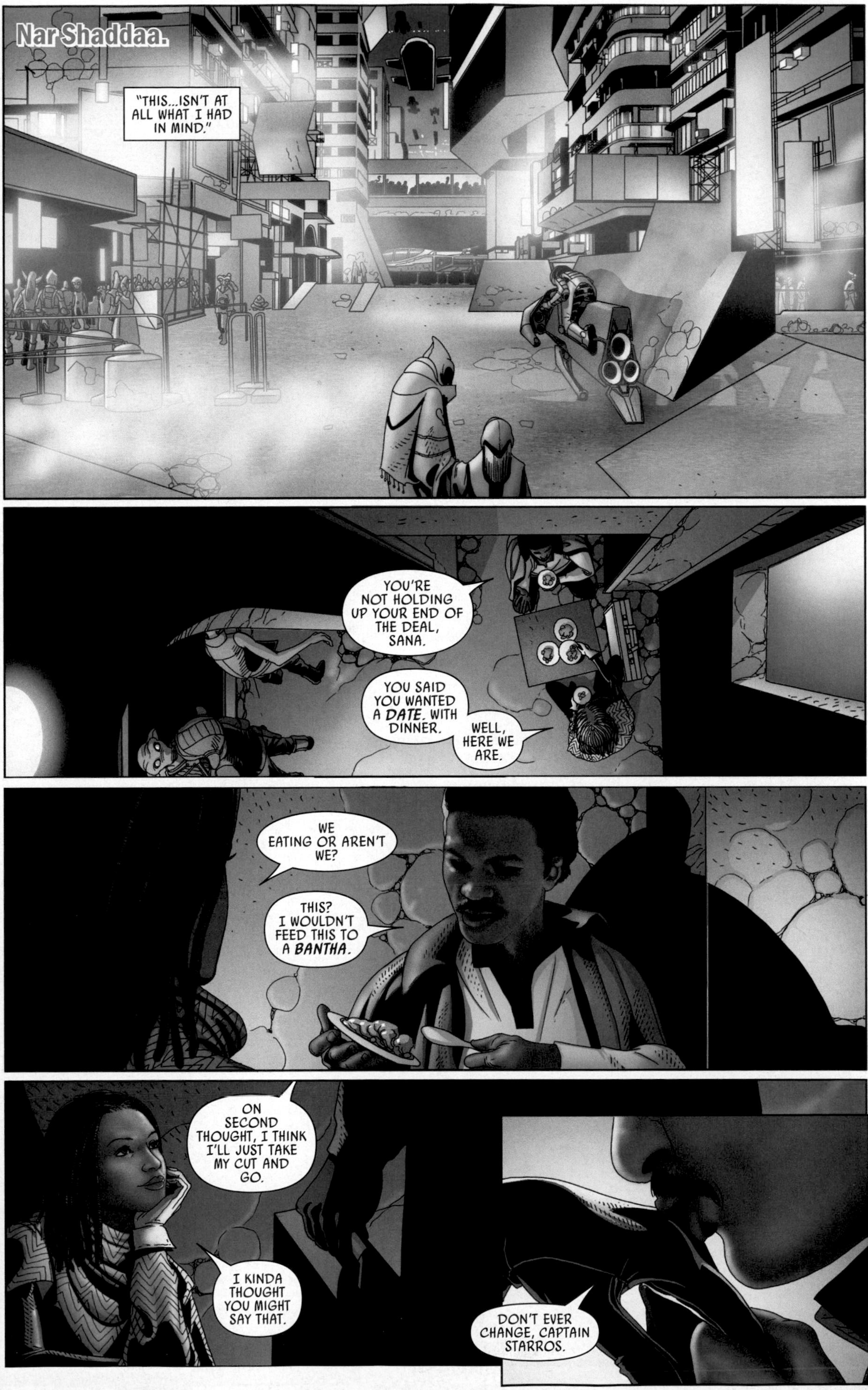
Nar Shaddaa.
"THIS...ISN'T AT ALL WHAT I HAD IN MIND."
YOU'RE NOT HOLDING UP YOUR END OF THE DEAL, SANA.
YOU SAID YOU WANTED A DATE. WITH DINNER.
WELL, HERE WE ARE.
WE EATING OR AREN'T WE?
THIS? I WOULDN'T FEED THIS TO A BANTHA.
ON SECOND THOUGHT, I THINK I'LL JUST TAKE MY CUT AND GO.
I KINDA THOUGHT YOU MIGHT SAY THAT.
DON'T EVER CHANGE, CAPTAIN STARROS.

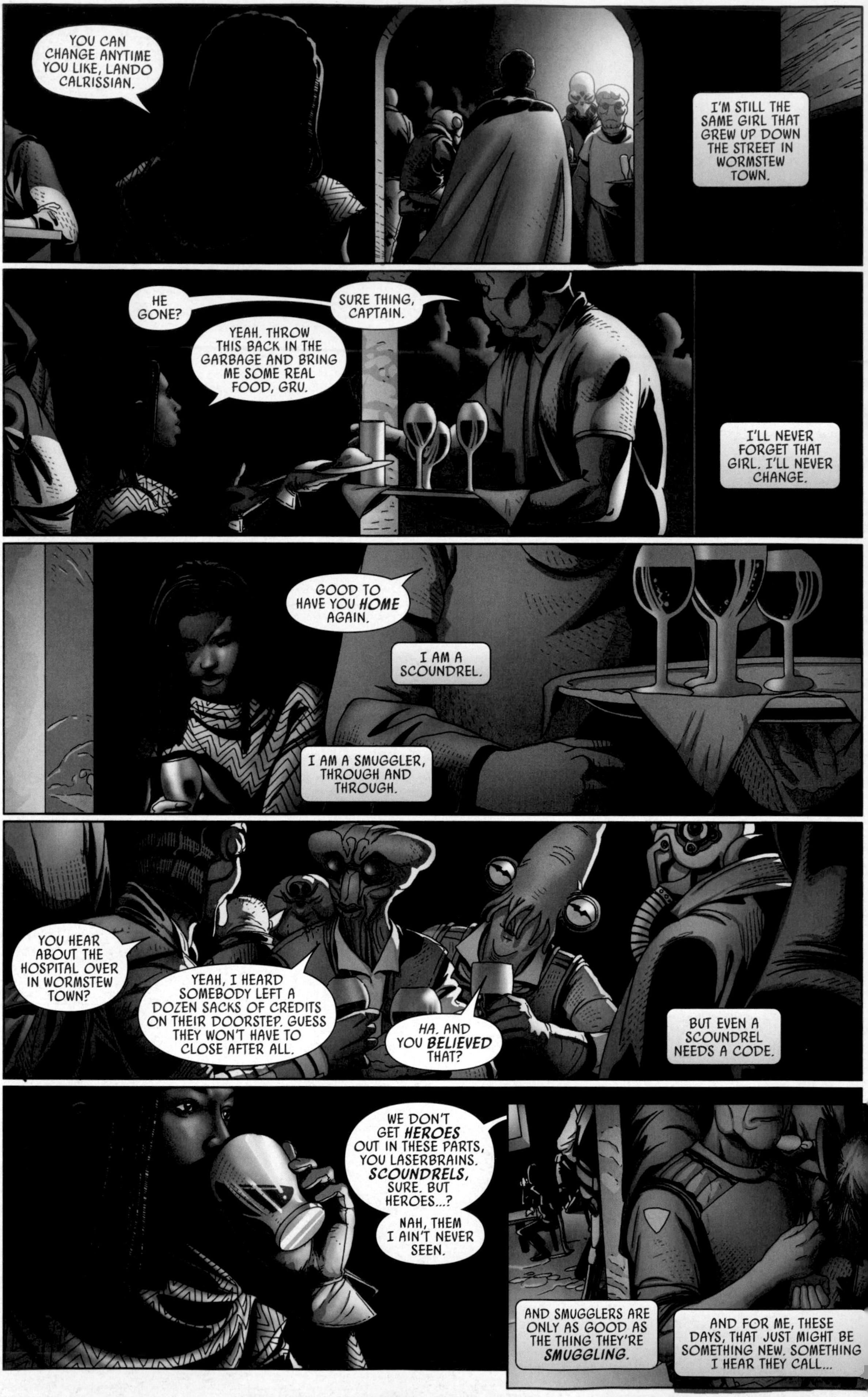
YOU CAN CHANGE ANYTIME YOU LIKE, LANDO CALRISSIAN.
I'M STILL THE SAME GIRL THAT GREW UP DOWN THE STREET IN WORMSTEW TOWN.
HE GONE?
SURE THING, CAPTAIN.
YEAH. THROW THIS BACK IN THE GARBAGE AND BRING ME SOME REAL FOOD, GRU.
I'LL NEVER FORGET THAT GIRL. I'LL NEVER CHANGE.
GOOD TO HAVE YOU HOME AGAIN.
I AM A SCOUNDREL.
I AM A SMUGGLER, THROUGH AND THROUGH.
YOU HEAR ABOUT THE HOSPITAL OVER IN WORMSTEW TOWN?
YEAH, I HEARD SOMEBODY LEFT A DOZEN SACKS OF CREDITS ON THEIR DOORSTEP. GUESS THEY WON'T HAVE TO CLOSE AFTER ALL.
HA. AND YOU BELIEVED THAT?
BUT EVEN A SCOUNDREL NEEDS A CODE.
WE DON'T GET HEROES OUT IN THESE PARTS, YOU LASERBRAINS. SCOUNDRELS, SURE. BUT HEROES...?
NAH, THEM I AIN'T NEVER SEEN.
AND SMUGGLERS ARE ONLY AS GOOD AS THE THING THEY'RE SMUGGLING.
AND FOR ME, THESE DAYS, THAT JUST MIGHT BE SOMETHING NEW. SOMETHING I HEAR THEY CALL...

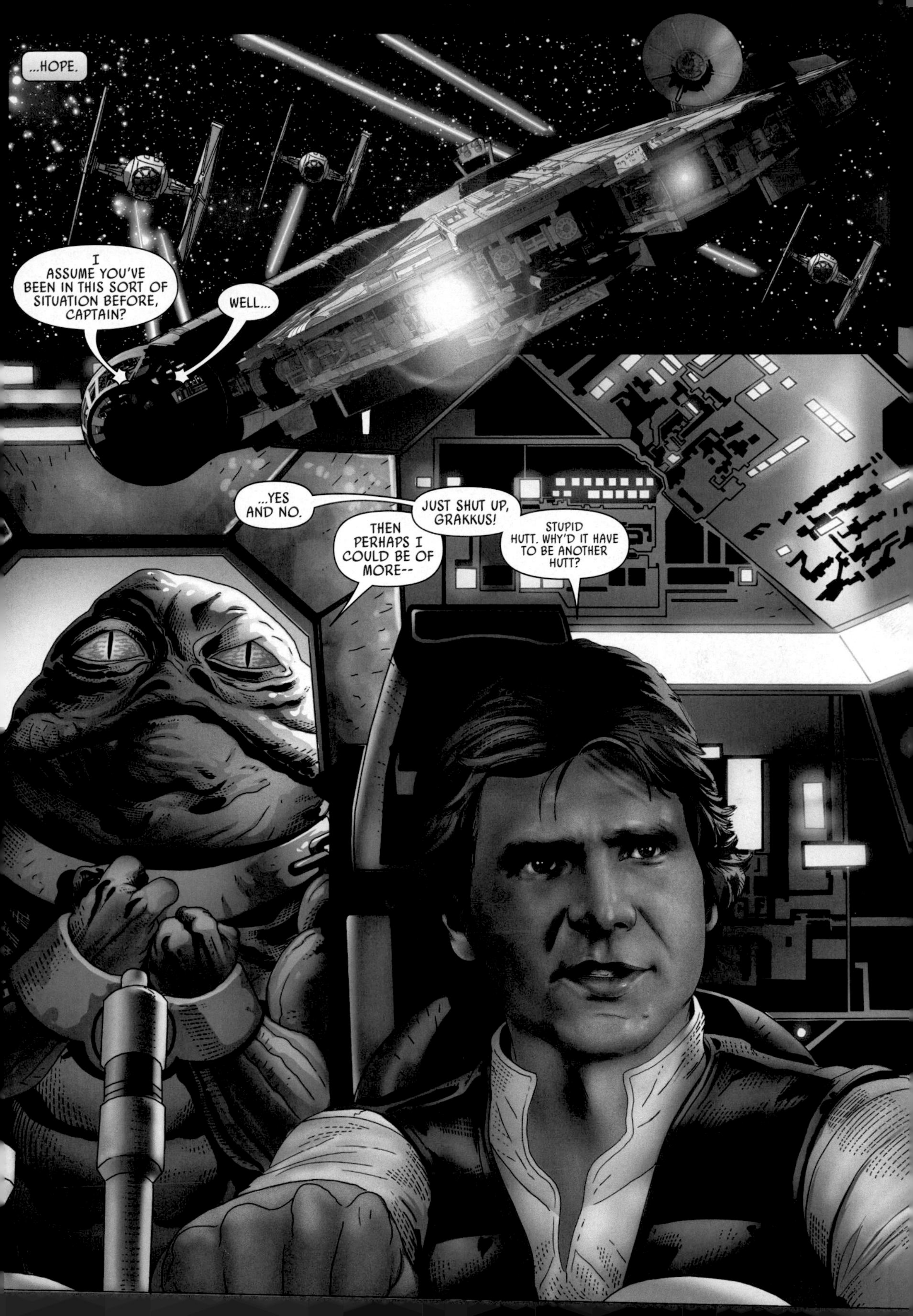
...HOPE.
I ASSUME YOU'VE BEEN IN THIS SORT OF SITUATION BEFORE, CAPTAIN?
WELL...
...YES AND NO.
THEN PERHAPS I COULD BE OF MORE--
JUST SHUT UP, GRAKKUS!
STUPID HUTT. WHY'D IT HAVE TO BE ANOTHER HUTT?

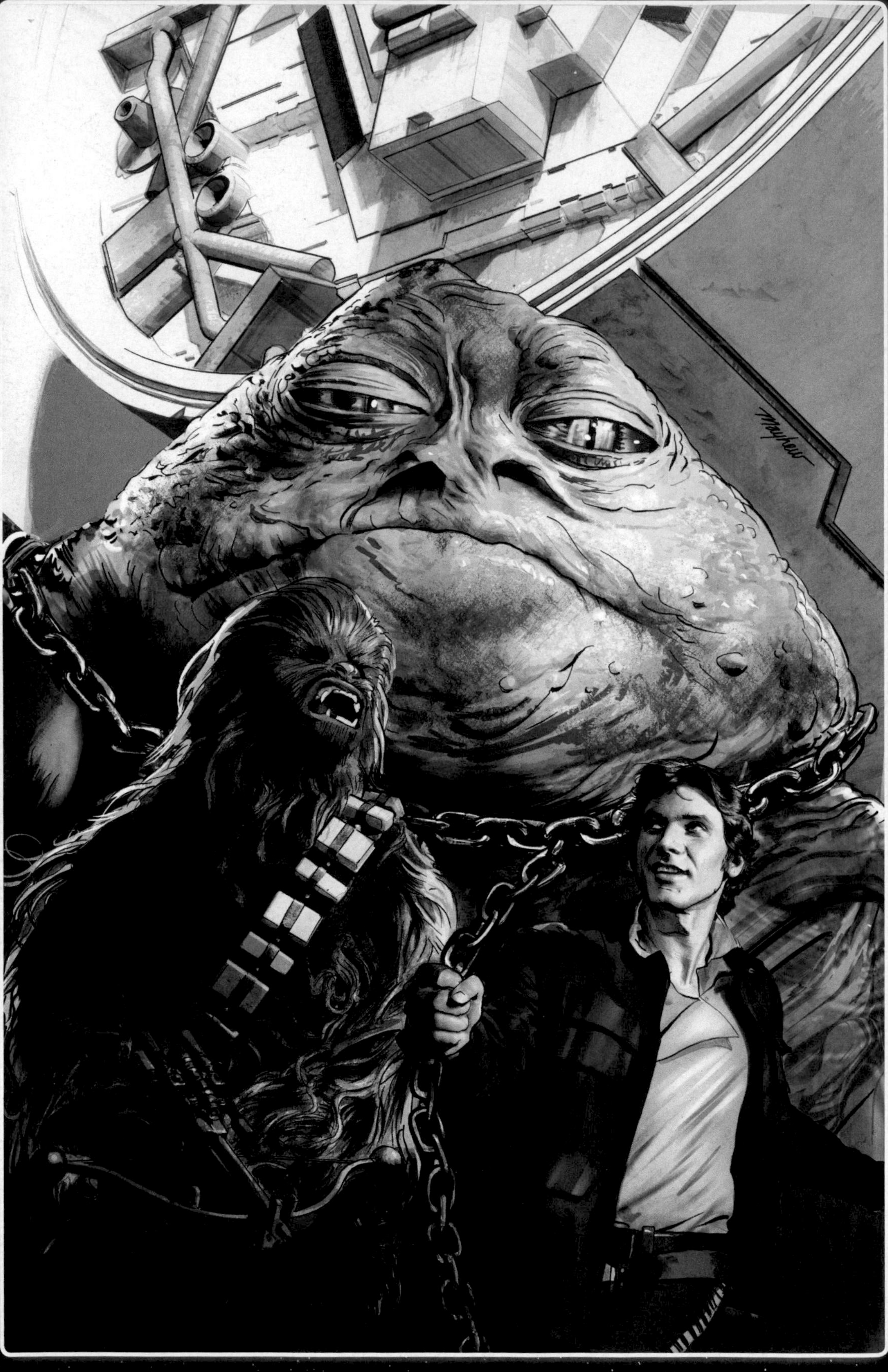

THE HUTT RUN

It is a time of turmoil for the galaxy. While the evil Galactic Empire remains strong, the Rebel Alliance continues to fight for freedom.

Legendary smuggler and all-around scoundrel Han Solo was roped into the Rebellion after a simple charter trip taken to pay off his debt to notorious crime lord, Jabba the Hutt, turned into rescuing the Rebellion leader, Princess Leia, from the Death Star.

Since then, Han Solo and his Wookiee co-pilot, Chewbacca, have performed odd jobs and miraculous feats alike in order to keep their friends alive and the Rebellion running– usually to the chagrin of everyone involved....

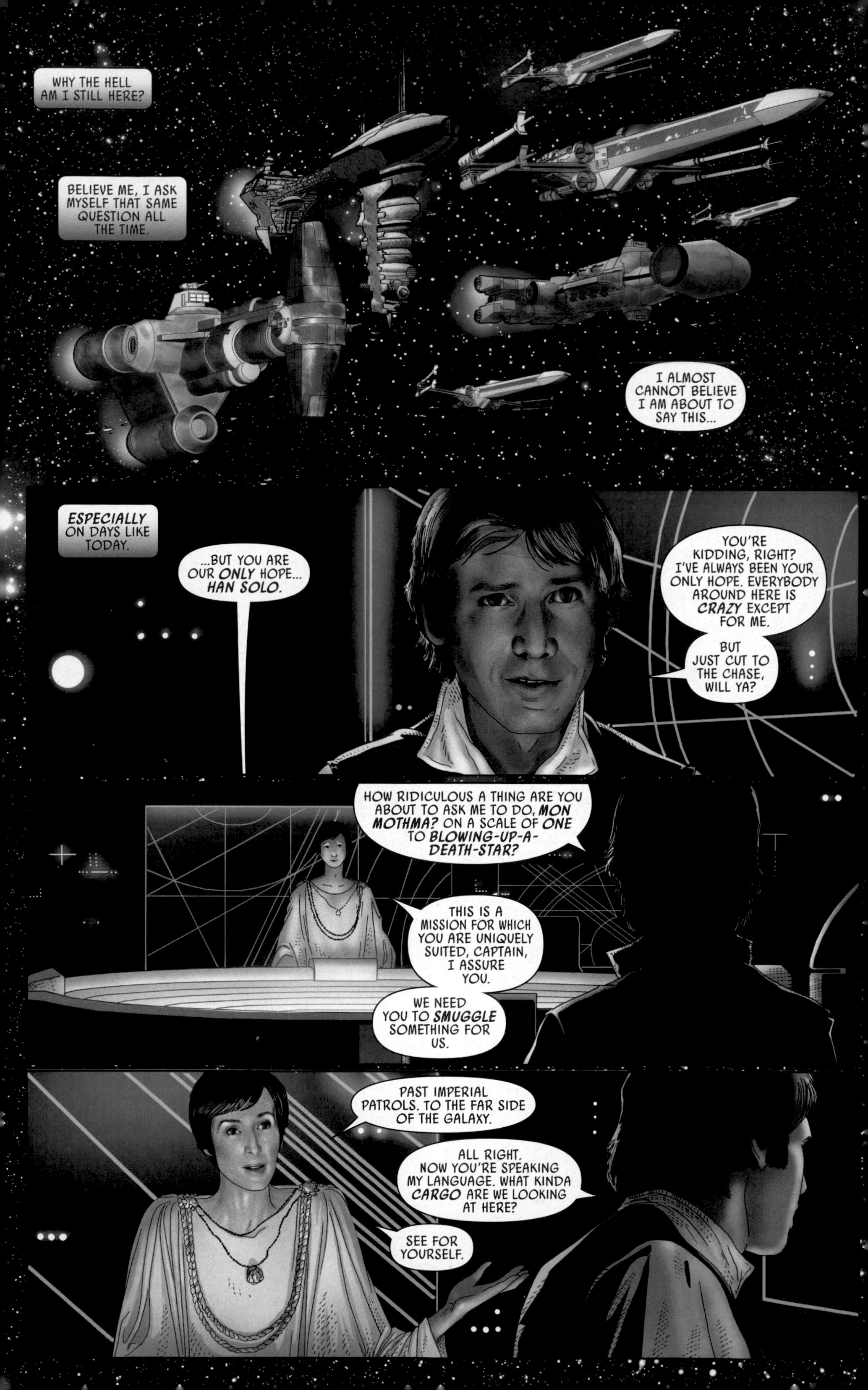
WHY THE HELL AM I STILL HERE?
BELIEVE ME, I ASK MYSELF THAT SAME QUESTION ALL THE TIME.
I ALMOST CANNOT BELIEVE I AM ABOUT TO SAY THIS...
ESPECIALLY ON DAYS LIKE TODAY.
...BUT YOU ARE OUR ONLY HOPE... HAN SOLO.
YOU'RE KIDDING, RIGHT? I'VE ALWAYS BEEN YOUR ONLY HOPE. EVERYBODY AROUND HERE IS CRAZY EXCEPT FOR ME.
BUT JUST CUT TO THE CHASE, WILL YA?
HOW RIDICULOUS A THING ARE YOU ABOUT TO ASK ME TO DO, MON MOTHMA? ON A SCALE OF ONE TO BLOWING-UP-A-DEATH-STAR?
THIS IS A MISSION FOR WHICH YOU ARE UNIQUELY SUITED, CAPTAIN, I ASSURE YOU.
WE NEED YOU TO SMUGGLE SOMETHING FOR US.
PAST IMPERIAL PATROLS. TO THE FAR SIDE OF THE GALAXY.
ALL RIGHT. NOW YOU'RE SPEAKING MY LANGUAGE. WHAT KINDA CARGO ARE WE LOOKING AT HERE?
SEE FOR YOURSELF.

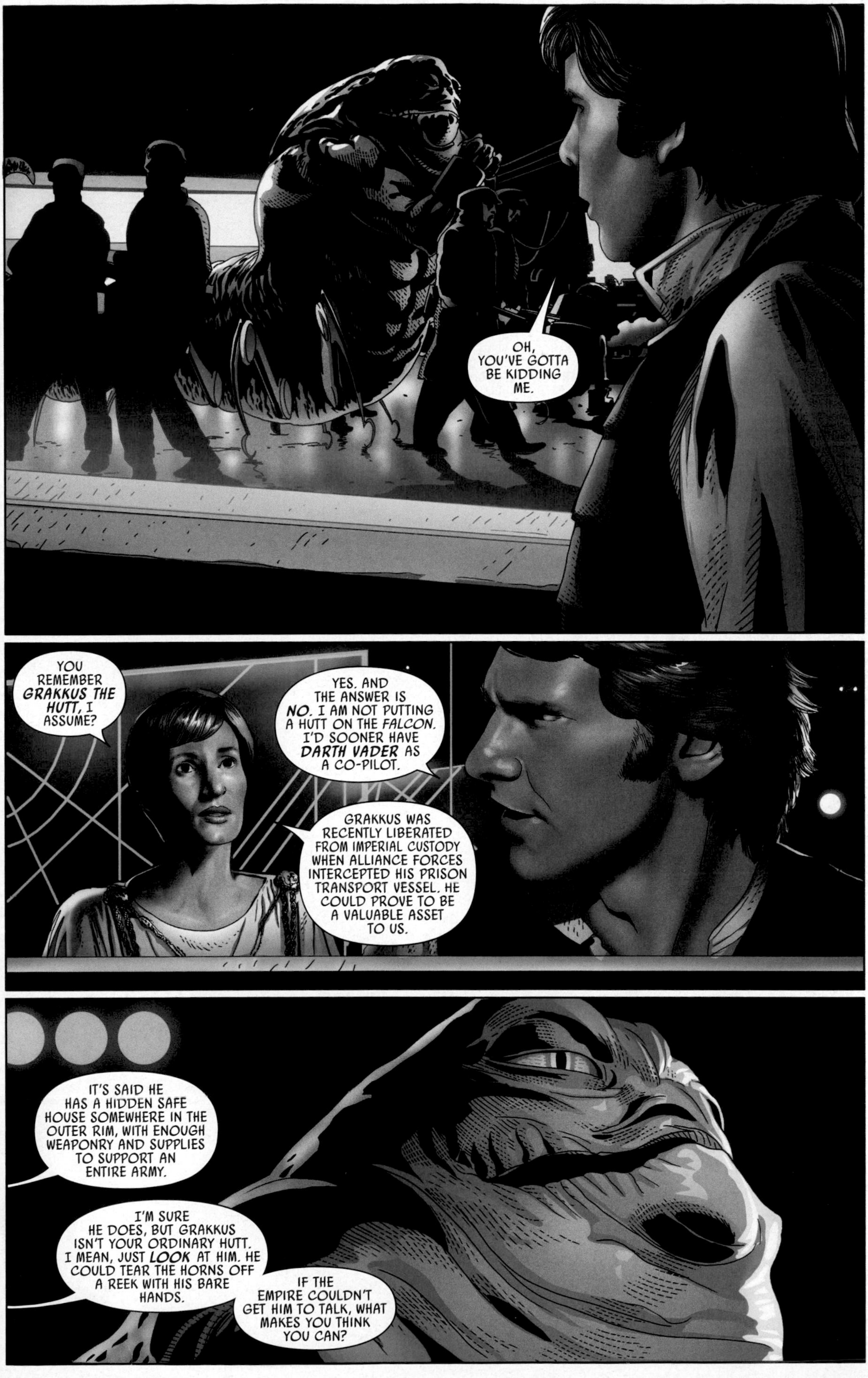
OH, YOU'VE GOTTA BE KIDDING ME.
YOU REMEMBER GRAKKUS THE HUTT, I ASSUME?
YES. AND THE ANSWER IS NO. I AM NOT PUTTING A HUTT ON THE FALCON. I'D SOONER HAVE DARTH VADER AS A CO-PILOT.
GRAKKUS WAS RECENTLY LIBERATED FROM IMPERIAL CUSTODY WHEN ALLIANCE FORCES INTERCEPTED HIS PRISON TRANSPORT VESSEL. HE COULD PROVE TO BE A VALUABLE ASSET TO US.
IT'S SAID HE HAS A HIDDEN SAFE HOUSE SOMEWHERE IN THE OUTER RIM, WITH ENOUGH WEAPONRY AND SUPPLIES TO SUPPORT AN ENTIRE ARMY.
I'M SURE HE DOES, BUT GRAKKUS ISN'T YOUR ORDINARY HUTT. I MEAN, JUST LOOK AT HIM. HE COULD TEAR THE HORNS OFF A REEK WITH HIS BARE HANDS.
IF THE EMPIRE COULDN'T GET HIM TO TALK, WHAT MAKES YOU THINK YOU CAN?

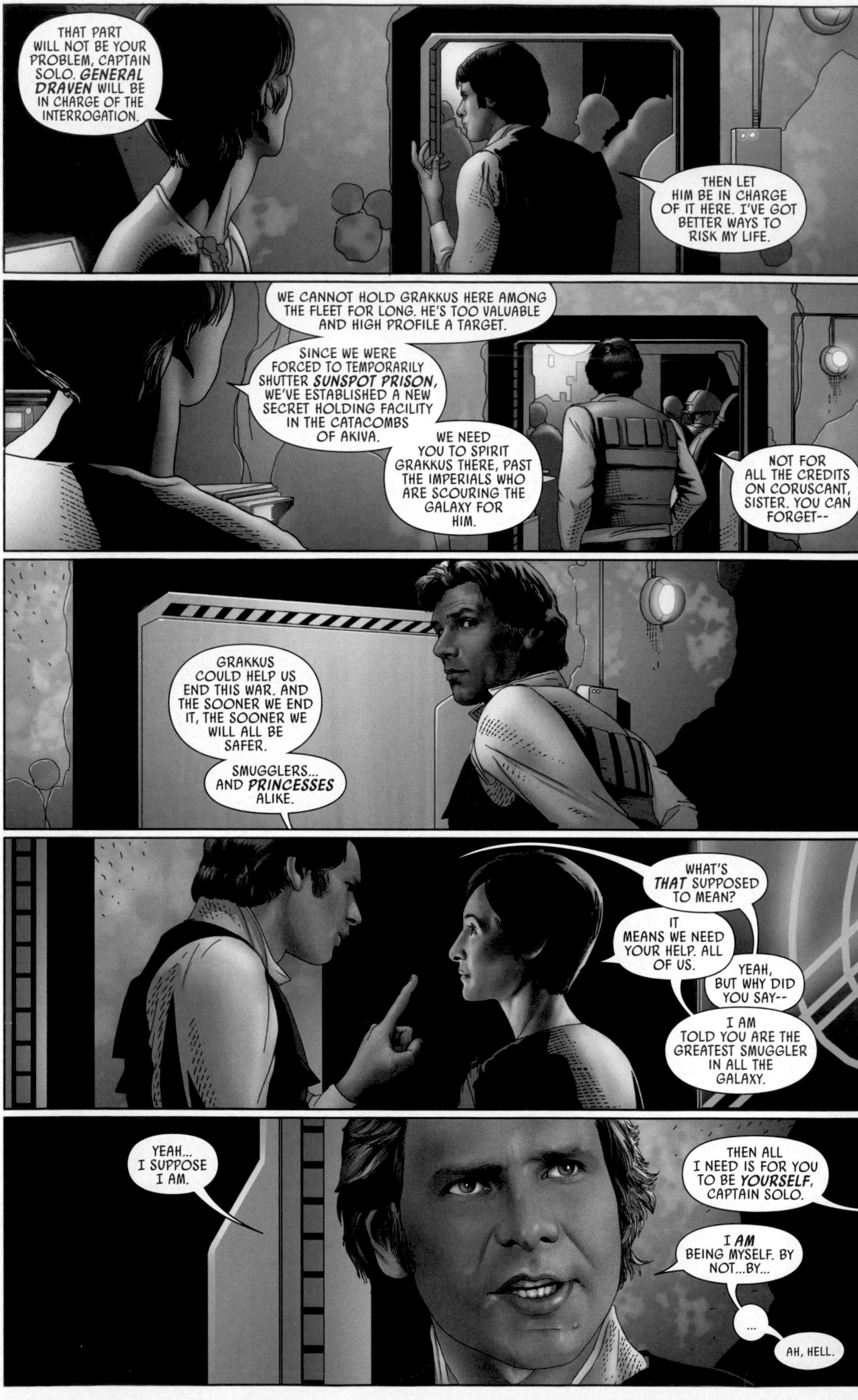
THAT PART WILL NOT BE YOUR PROBLEM, CAPTAIN SOLO. GENERAL DRAVEN WILL BE IN CHARGE OF THE INTERROGATION.
THEN LET HIM BE IN CHARGE OF IT HERE. I'VE GOT BETTER WAYS TO RISK MY LIFE.
WE CANNOT HOLD GRAKKUS HERE AMONG THE FLEET FOR LONG. HE'S TOO VALUABLE AND HIGH PROFILE A TARGET.
SINCE WE WERE FORCED TO TEMPORARILY SHUTTER SUNSPOT PRISON, WE'VE ESTABLISHED A NEW SECRET HOLDING FACILITY IN THE CATACOMBS OF AKIVA.
WE NEED YOU TO SPIRIT GRAKKUS THERE, PAST THE IMPERIALS WHO ARE SCOURING THE GALAXY FOR HIM.
NOT FOR ALL THE CREDITS ON CORUSCANT, SISTER. YOU CAN FORGET--
GRAKKUS COULD HELP US END THIS WAR. AND THE SOONER WE END IT, THE SOONER WE WILL ALL BE SAFER.
SMUGGLERS... AND PRINCESSES ALIKE.
WHAT'S THAT SUPPOSED TO MEAN?
IT MEANS WE NEED YOUR HELP. ALL OF US.
YEAH, BUT WHY DID YOU SAY--
I AM TOLD YOU ARE THE GREATEST SMUGGLER IN ALL THE GALAXY.
YEAH... I SUPPOSE I AM.
THEN ALL I NEED IS FOR YOU TO BE YOURSELF, CAPTAIN SOLO.
I AM BEING MYSELF. BY NOT...BY...
...
AH, HELL.

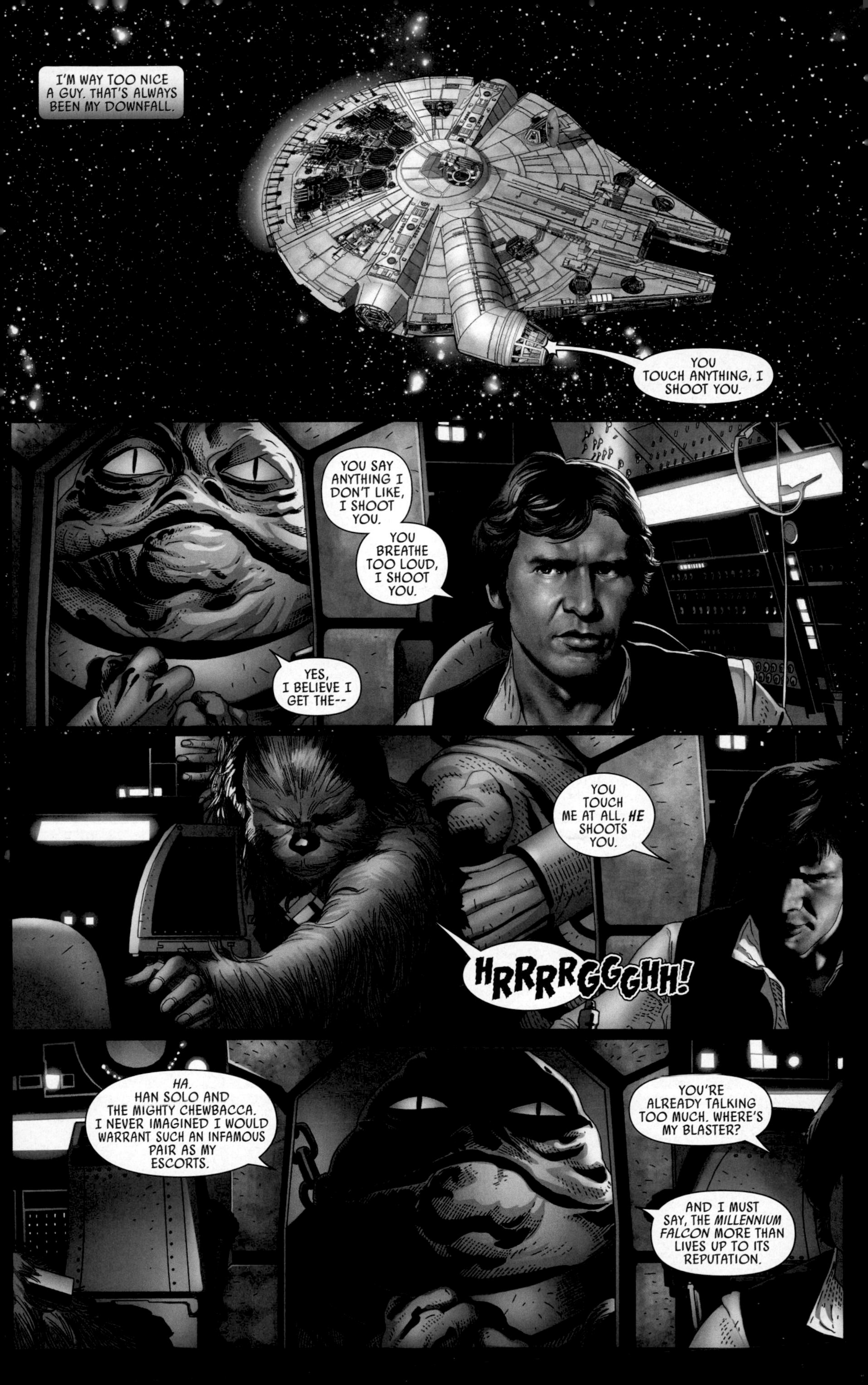
I'M WAY TOO NICE A GUY. THAT'S ALWAYS BEEN MY DOWNFALL.
YOU TOUCH ANYTHING, I SHOOT YOU.
YOU SAY ANYTHING I DON'T LIKE, I SHOOT YOU.
YOU BREATHE TOO LOUD, I SHOOT YOU.
YES, I BELIEVE I GET THE--
YOU TOUCH ME AT ALL, *HE* SHOOTS YOU.
HRRRRGGGHH!
HA. HAN SOLO AND THE MIGHTY CHEWBACCA. I NEVER IMAGINED I WOULD WARRANT SUCH AN INFAMOUS PAIR AS MY ESCORTS.
YOU'RE ALREADY TALKING TOO MUCH. WHERE'S MY BLASTER?
AND I MUST SAY, THE *MILLENNIUM FALCON* MORE THAN LIVES UP TO ITS REPUTATION.

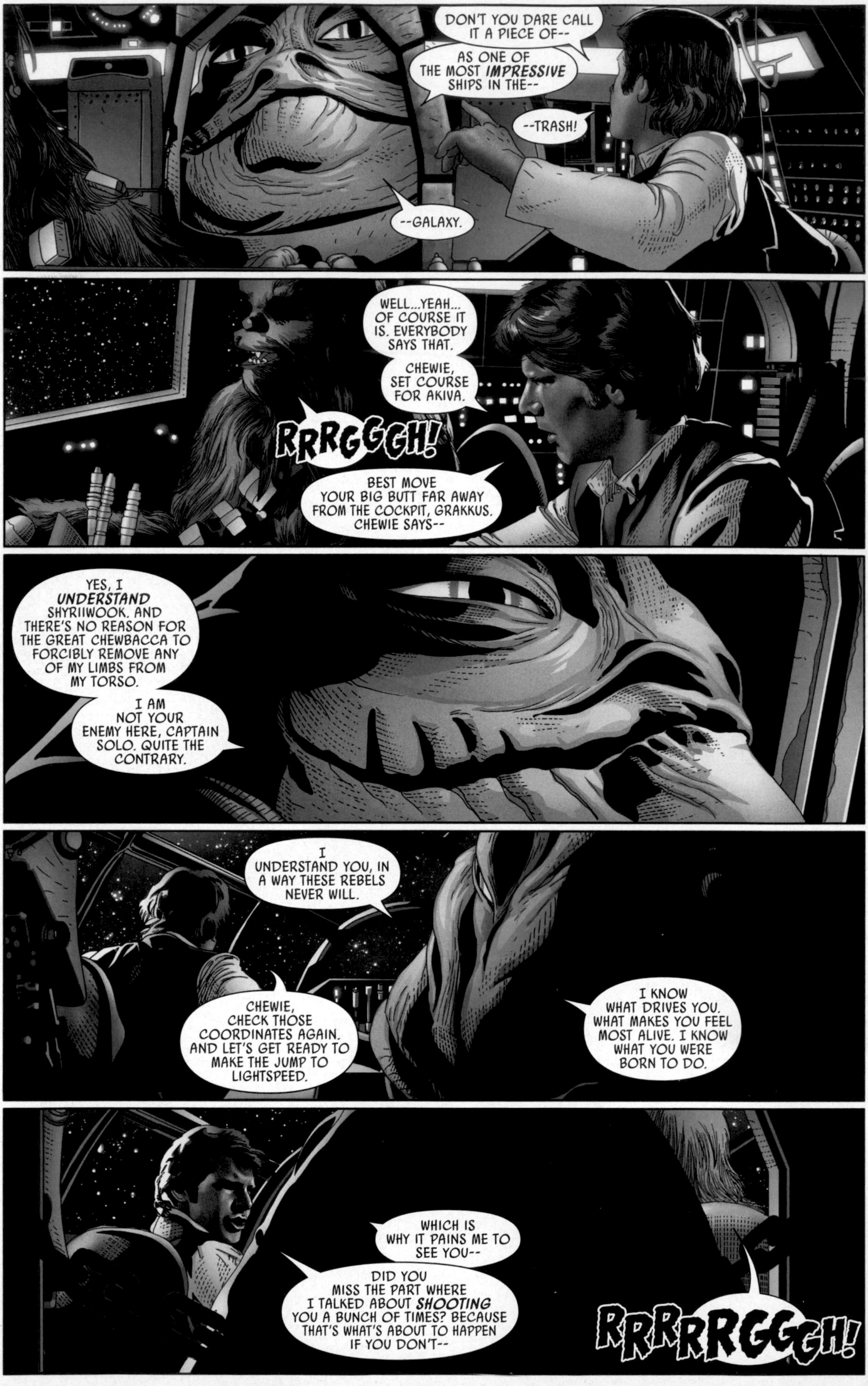
DON'T YOU DARE CALL IT A PIECE OF--
AS ONE OF THE MOST IMPRESSIVE SHIPS IN THE--
--TRASH!
--GALAXY.
WELL...YEAH... OF COURSE IT IS. EVERYBODY SAYS THAT.
CHEWIE, SET COURSE FOR AKIVA.
RRRGGGH!
BEST MOVE YOUR BIG BUTT FAR AWAY FROM THE COCKPIT, GRAKKUS. CHEWIE SAYS--
YES, I UNDERSTAND SHYRIIWOOK. AND THERE'S NO REASON FOR THE GREAT CHEWBACCA TO FORCIBLY REMOVE ANY OF MY LIMBS FROM MY TORSO.
I AM NOT YOUR ENEMY HERE, CAPTAIN SOLO. QUITE THE CONTRARY.
I UNDERSTAND YOU, IN A WAY THESE REBELS NEVER WILL.
CHEWIE, CHECK THOSE COORDINATES AGAIN. AND LET'S GET READY TO MAKE THE JUMP TO LIGHTSPEED.
I KNOW WHAT DRIVES YOU. WHAT MAKES YOU FEEL MOST ALIVE. I KNOW WHAT YOU WERE BORN TO DO.
WHICH IS WHY IT PAINS ME TO SEE YOU--
DID YOU MISS THE PART WHERE I TALKED ABOUT SHOOTING YOU A BUNCH OF TIMES? BECAUSE THAT'S WHAT'S ABOUT TO HAPPEN IF YOU DON'T--
RRRRRGGGH!

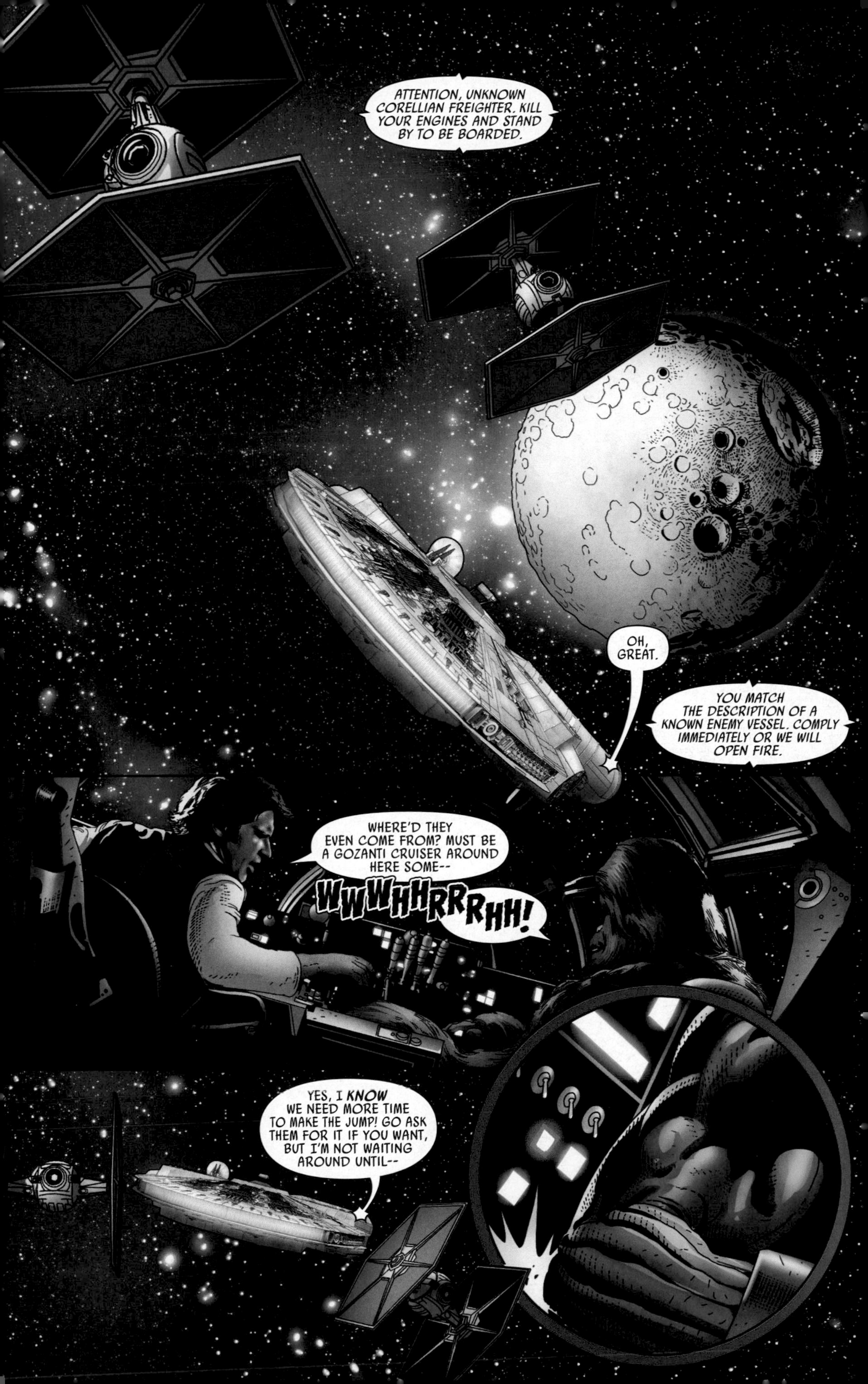
ATTENTION, UNKNOWN CORELLIAN FREIGHTER. KILL YOUR ENGINES AND STAND BY TO BE BOARDED.
OH, GREAT.
YOU MATCH THE DESCRIPTION OF A KNOWN ENEMY VESSEL. COMPLY IMMEDIATELY OR WE WILL OPEN FIRE.
WHERE'D THEY EVEN COME FROM? MUST BE A GOZANTI CRUISER AROUND HERE SOME--
WWWHHRRRRHH!
YES, I KNOW WE NEED MORE TIME TO MAKE THE JUMP! GO ASK THEM FOR IT IF YOU WANT, BUT I'M NOT WAITING AROUND UNTIL--

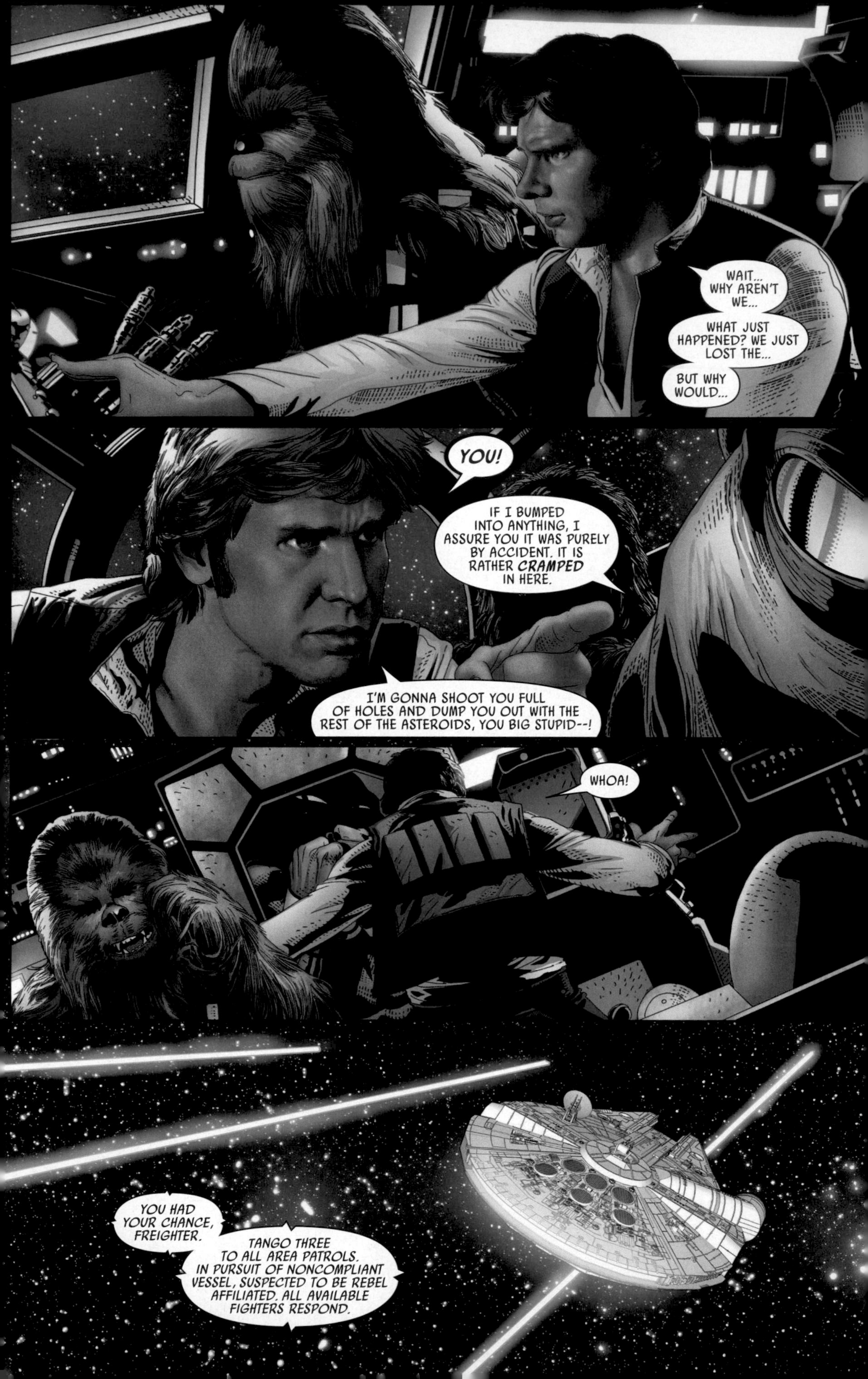
WAIT... WHY AREN'T WE...
WHAT JUST HAPPENED? WE JUST LOST THE...
BUT WHY WOULD...
YOU!
IF I BUMPED INTO ANYTHING, I ASSURE YOU IT WAS PURELY BY ACCIDENT. IT IS RATHER CRAMPED IN HERE.
I'M GONNA SHOOT YOU FULL OF HOLES AND DUMP YOU OUT WITH THE REST OF THE ASTEROIDS, YOU BIG STUPID--!
WHOA!
YOU HAD YOUR CHANCE, FREIGHTER.
TANGO THREE TO ALL AREA PATROLS. IN PURSUIT OF NONCOMPLIANT VESSEL, SUSPECTED TO BE REBEL AFFILIATED. ALL AVAILABLE FIGHTERS RESPOND.

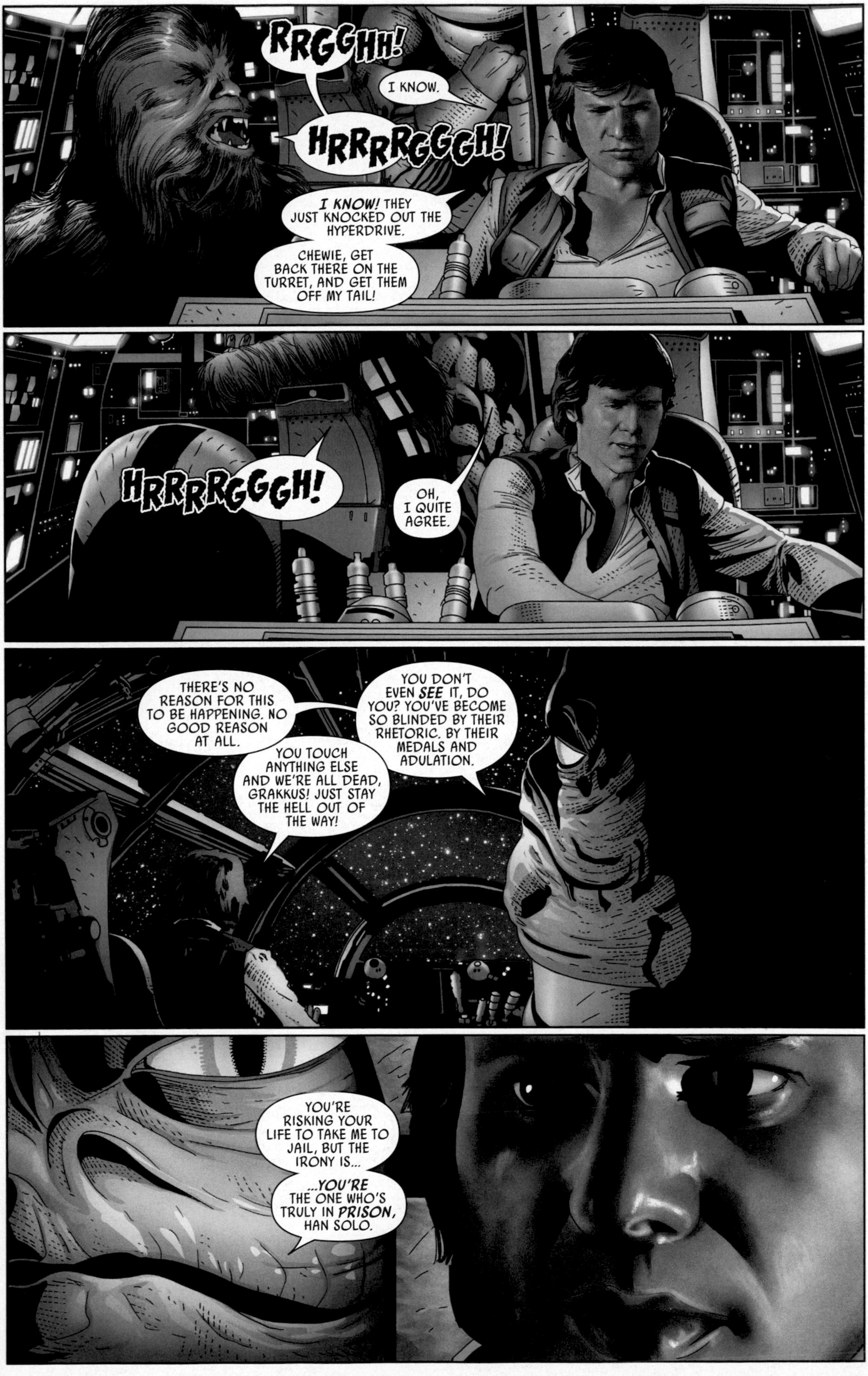
RRGGHH!
I KNOW.
HRRRRGGGH!
I KNOW! THEY JUST KNOCKED OUT THE HYPERDRIVE.
CHEWIE, GET BACK THERE ON THE TURRET, AND GET THEM OFF MY TAIL!
HRRRRGGGH!
OH, I QUITE AGREE.
THERE'S NO REASON FOR THIS TO BE HAPPENING. NO GOOD REASON AT ALL.
YOU DON'T EVEN SEE IT, DO YOU? YOU'VE BECOME SO BLINDED BY THEIR RHETORIC. BY THEIR MEDALS AND ADULATION.
YOU TOUCH ANYTHING ELSE AND WE'RE ALL DEAD, GRAKKUS! JUST STAY THE HELL OUT OF THE WAY!
YOU'RE RISKING YOUR LIFE TO TAKE ME TO JAIL, BUT THE IRONY IS...
...YOU'RE THE ONE WHO'S TRULY IN PRISON, HAN SOLO.

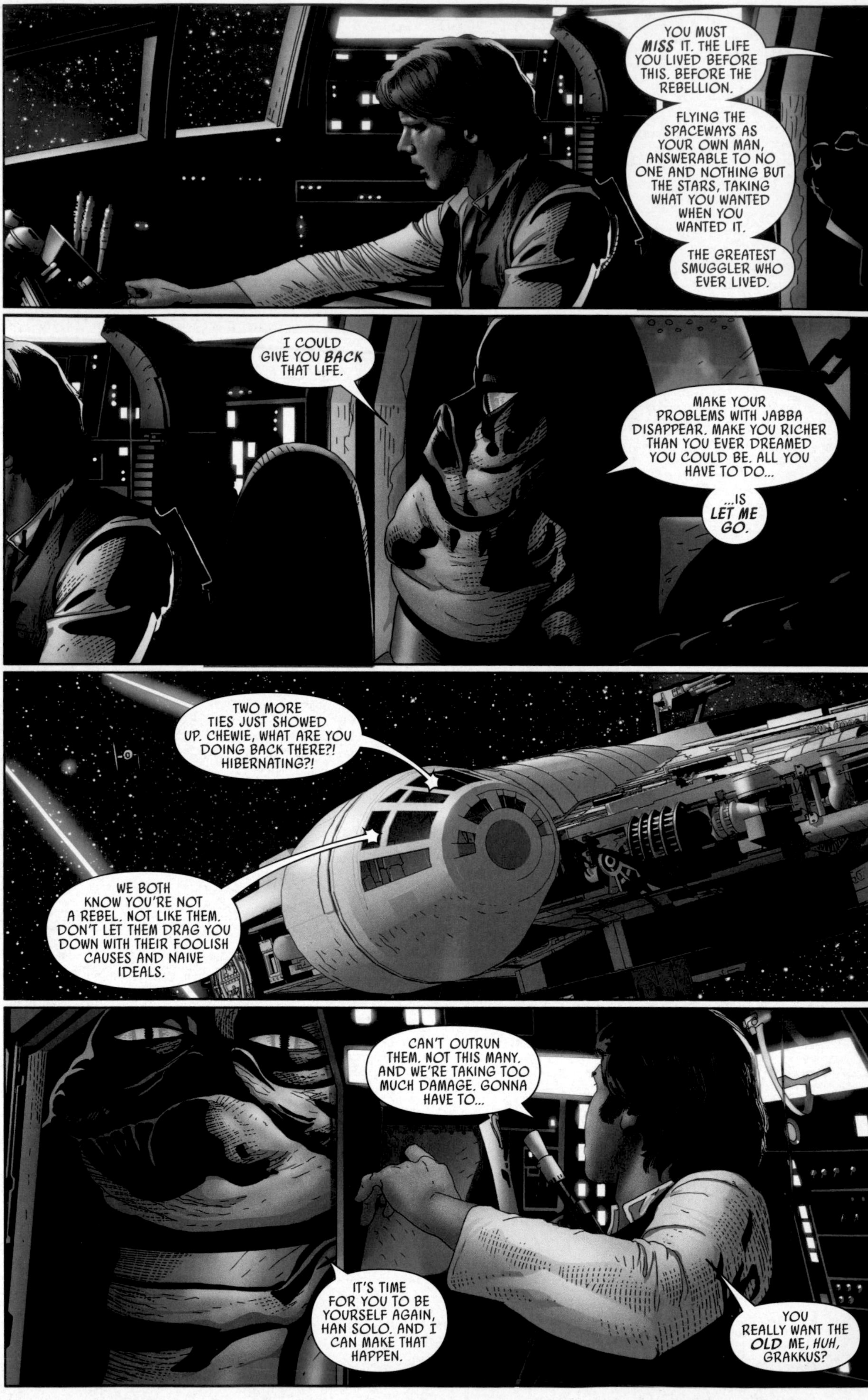
YOU MUST MISS IT. THE LIFE YOU LIVED BEFORE THIS. BEFORE THE REBELLION.
FLYING THE SPACEWAYS AS YOUR OWN MAN, ANSWERABLE TO NO ONE AND NOTHING BUT THE STARS, TAKING WHAT YOU WANTED WHEN YOU WANTED IT.
THE GREATEST SMUGGLER WHO EVER LIVED.
I COULD GIVE YOU BACK THAT LIFE.
MAKE YOUR PROBLEMS WITH JABBA DISAPPEAR. MAKE YOU RICHER THAN YOU EVER DREAMED YOU COULD BE. ALL YOU HAVE TO DO...
...IS LET ME GO.
TWO MORE TIES JUST SHOWED UP. CHEWIE, WHAT ARE YOU DOING BACK THERE?! HIBERNATING?!
WE BOTH KNOW YOU'RE NOT A REBEL. NOT LIKE THEM. DON'T LET THEM DRAG YOU DOWN WITH THEIR FOOLISH CAUSES AND NAIVE IDEALS.
CAN'T OUTRUN THEM. NOT THIS MANY. AND WE'RE TAKING TOO MUCH DAMAGE. GONNA HAVE TO...
IT'S TIME FOR YOU TO BE YOURSELF AGAIN, HAN SOLO. AND I CAN MAKE THAT HAPPEN.
YOU REALLY WANT THE OLD ME, HUH, GRAKKUS?

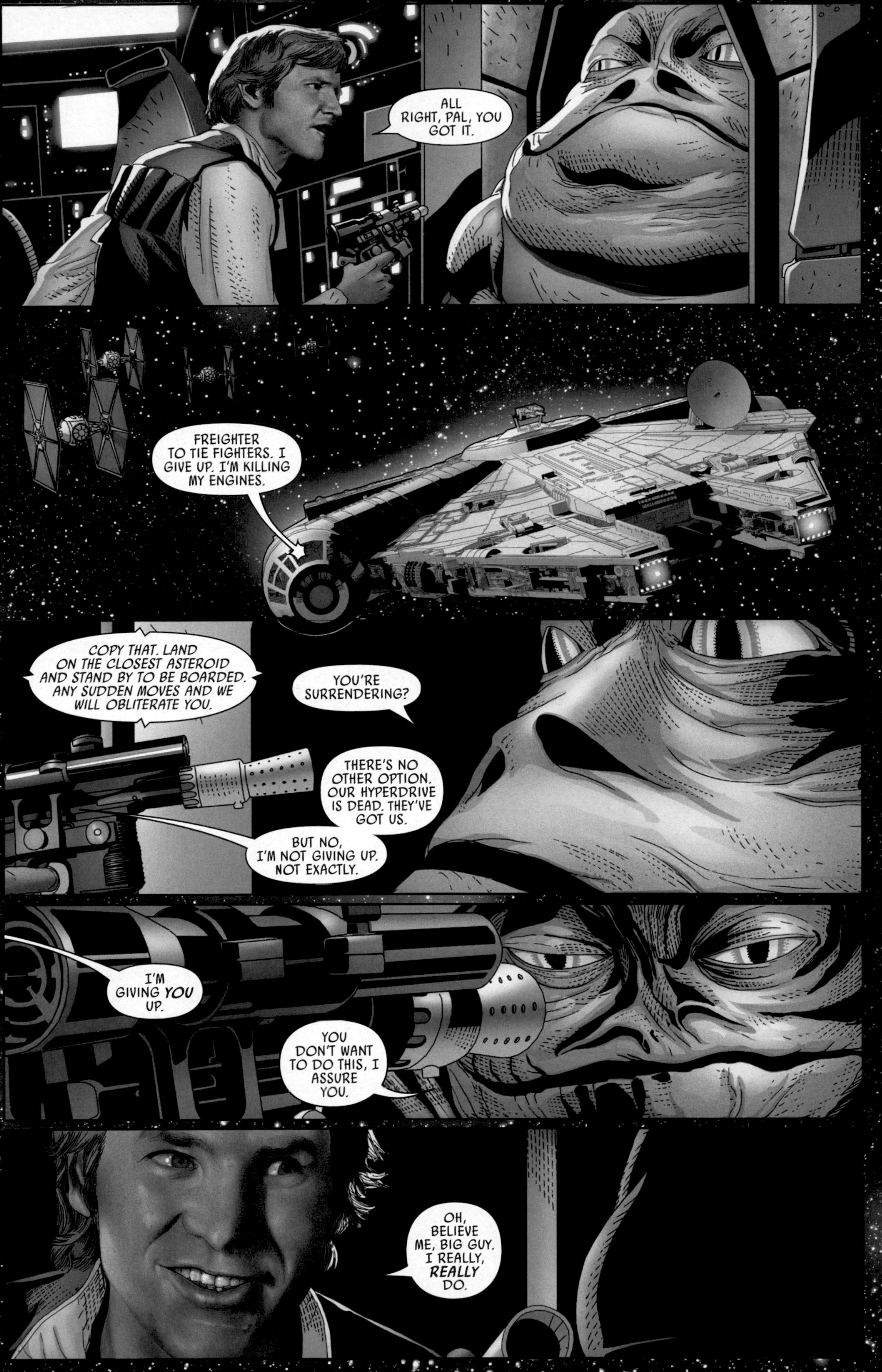
ALL RIGHT, PAL, YOU GOT IT.
FREIGHTER TO TIE FIGHTERS. I GIVE UP. I'M KILLING MY ENGINES.
COPY THAT. LAND ON THE CLOSEST ASTEROID AND STAND BY TO BE BOARDED. ANY SUDDEN MOVES AND WE WILL OBLITERATE YOU.
YOU'RE SURRENDERING?
THERE'S NO OTHER OPTION. OUR HYPERDRIVE IS DEAD. THEY'VE GOT US.
BUT NO, I'M NOT GIVING UP. NOT EXACTLY.
I'M GIVING *YOU* UP.
YOU DON'T WANT TO DO THIS, I ASSURE YOU.
OH, BELIEVE ME, BIG GUY. I REALLY, *REALLY* DO.

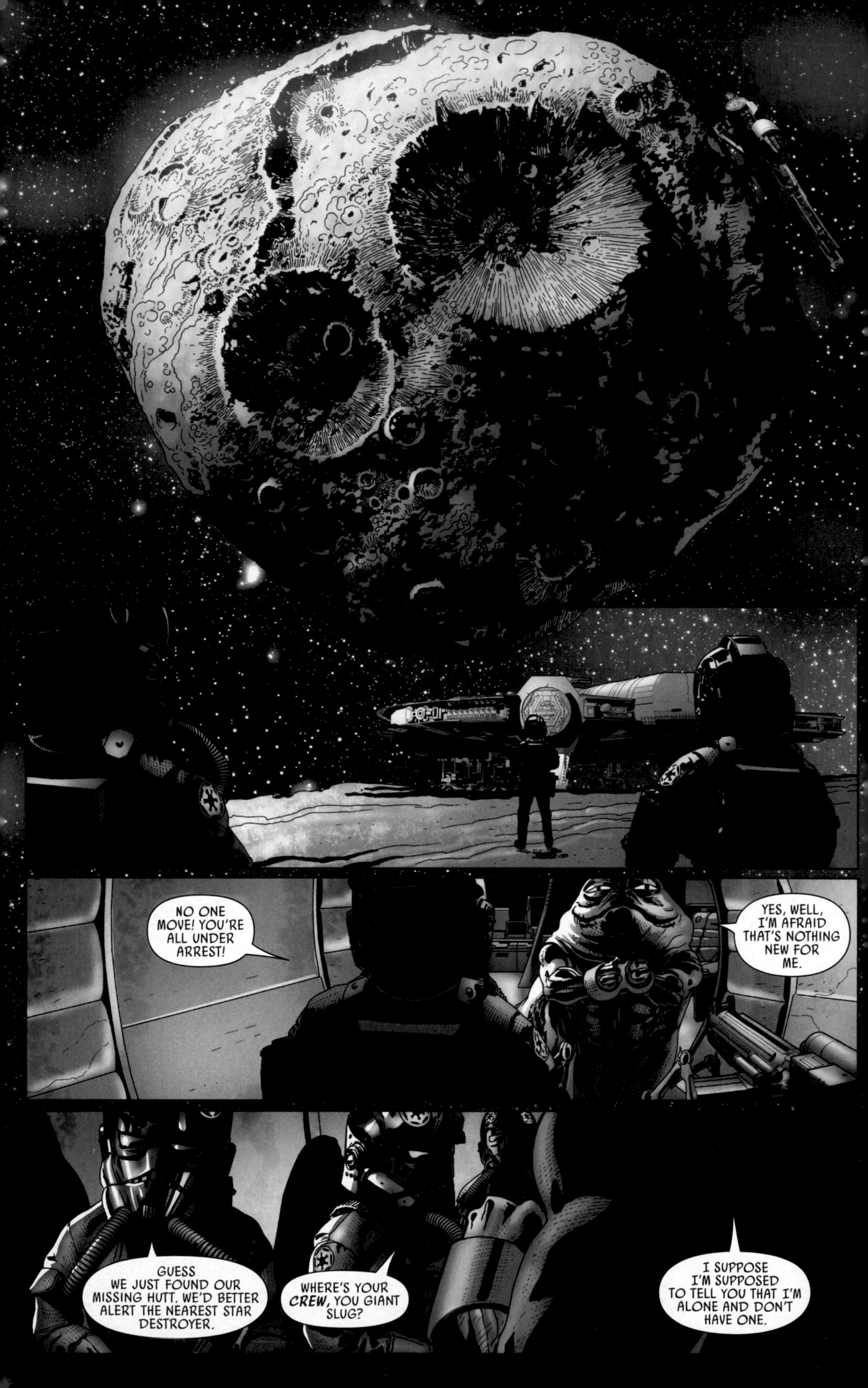
NO ONE MOVE! YOU'RE ALL UNDER ARREST!
YES, WELL, I'M AFRAID THAT'S NOTHING NEW FOR ME.
GUESS WE JUST FOUND OUR MISSING HUTT. WE'D BETTER ALERT THE NEAREST STAR DESTROYER.
WHERE'S YOUR CREW, YOU GIANT SLUG?
I SUPPOSE I'M SUPPOSED TO TELL YOU THAT I'M ALONE AND DON'T HAVE ONE.

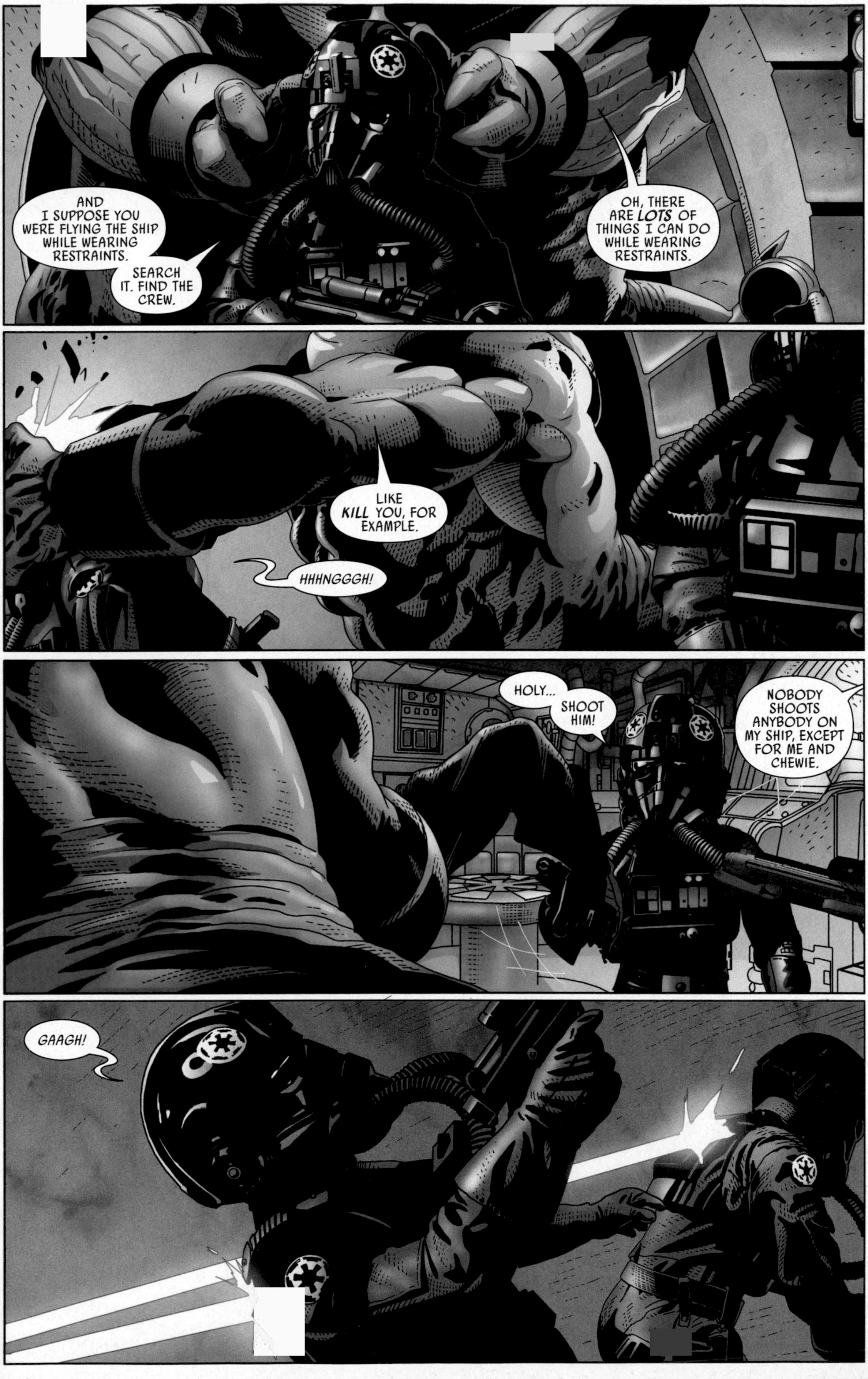
AND I SUPPOSE YOU WERE FLYING THE SHIP WHILE WEARING RESTRAINTS.
SEARCH IT. FIND THE CREW.
OH, THERE ARE LOTS OF THINGS I CAN DO WHILE WEARING RESTRAINTS.
LIKE KILL YOU, FOR EXAMPLE.
HHHNGGGH!
HOLY...
SHOOT HIM!
NOBODY SHOOTS ANYBODY ON MY SHIP, EXCEPT FOR ME AND CHEWIE.
GAAGH!

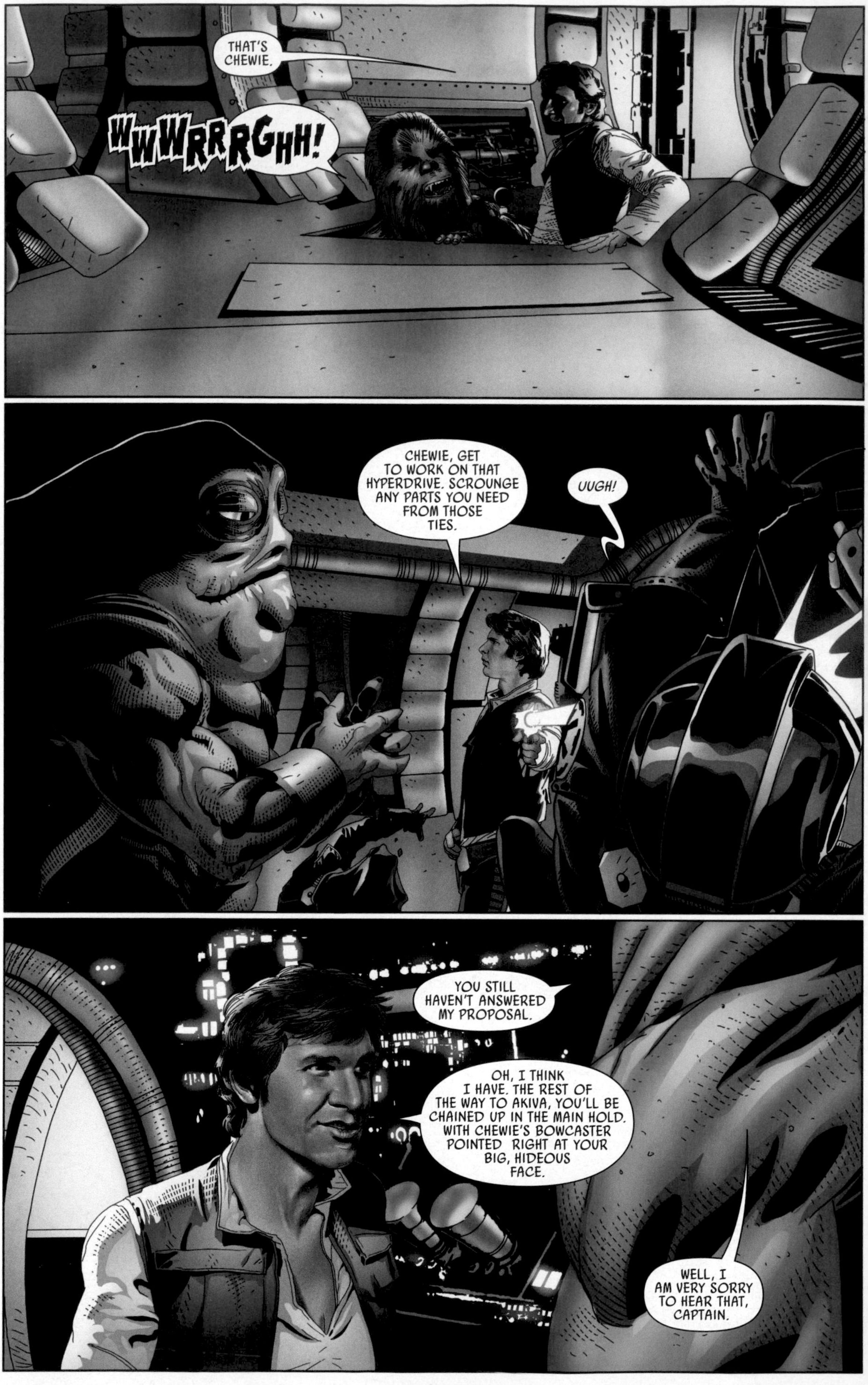
THAT'S CHEWIE.
WWWRRRGHH!
CHEWIE, GET TO WORK ON THAT HYPERDRIVE. SCROUNGE ANY PARTS YOU NEED FROM THOSE TIES.
UUGH!
YOU STILL HAVEN'T ANSWERED MY PROPOSAL.
OH, I THINK I HAVE. THE REST OF THE WAY TO AKIVA, YOU'LL BE CHAINED UP IN THE MAIN HOLD. WITH CHEWIE'S BOWCASTER POINTED RIGHT AT YOUR BIG, HIDEOUS FACE.
WELL, I AM VERY SORRY TO HEAR THAT, CAPTAIN.

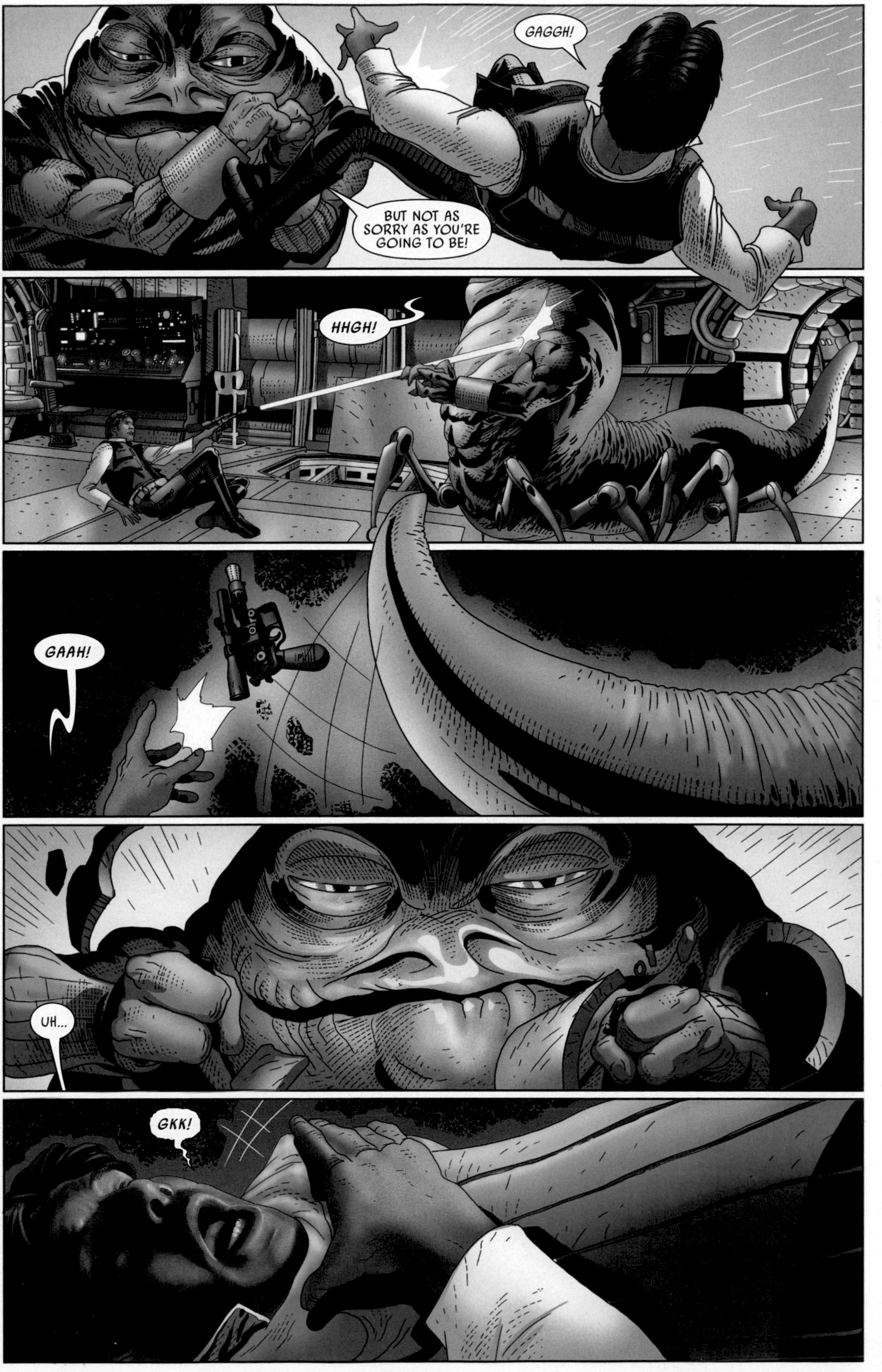
GAGGH!
BUT NOT AS SORRY AS YOU'RE GOING TO BE!
HHGH!
GAAH!
UH...
GKK!

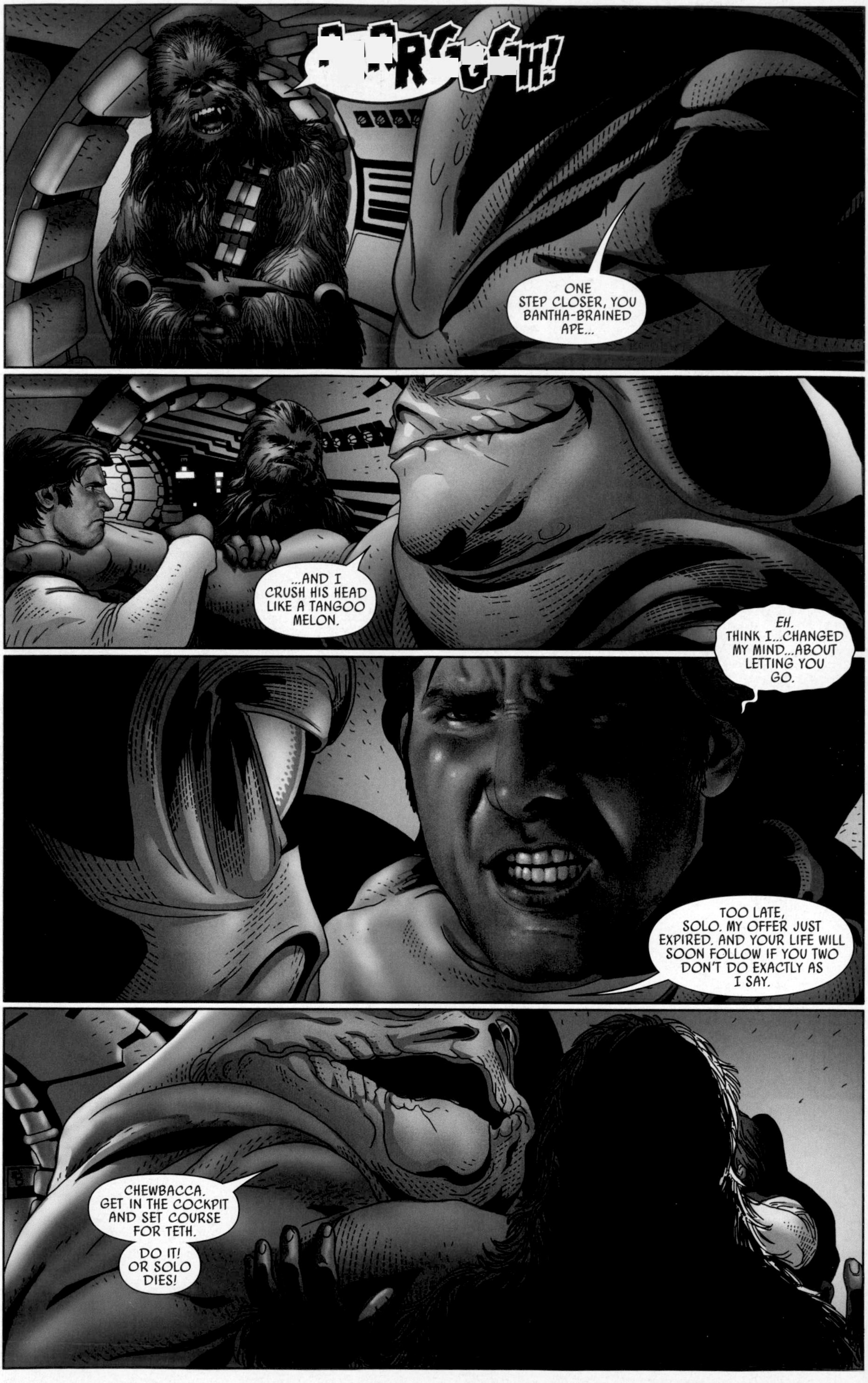
ONE STEP CLOSER, YOU BANTHA-BRAINED APE...
...AND I CRUSH HIS HEAD LIKE A TANGOO MELON.
EH. THINK I...CHANGED MY MIND...ABOUT LETTING YOU GO.
TOO LATE, SOLO. MY OFFER JUST EXPIRED. AND YOUR LIFE WILL SOON FOLLOW IF YOU TWO DON'T DO EXACTLY AS I SAY.
CHEWBACCA. GET IN THE COCKPIT AND SET COURSE FOR TETH.
DO IT! OR SOLO DIES!

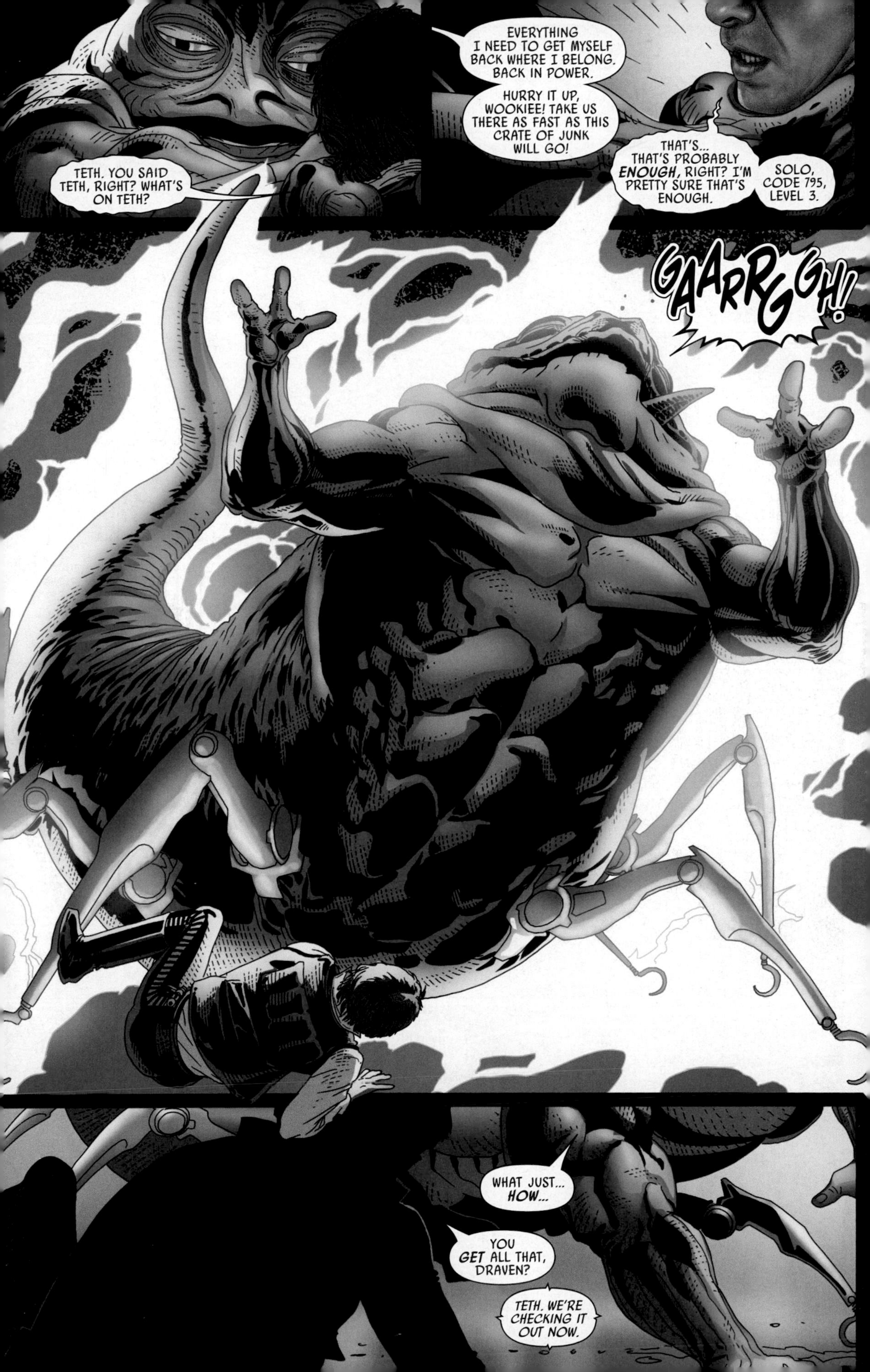
TETH. YOU SAID TETH, RIGHT? WHAT'S ON TETH?
EVERYTHING I NEED TO GET MYSELF BACK WHERE I BELONG. BACK IN POWER.
HURRY IT UP, WOOKIEE! TAKE US THERE AS FAST AS THIS CRATE OF JUNK WILL GO!
THAT'S... THAT'S PROBABLY ENOUGH, RIGHT? I'M PRETTY SURE THAT'S ENOUGH.
SOLO, CODE 795, LEVEL 3.
GAARRGGH!
WHAT JUST... HOW...
YOU GET ALL THAT, DRAVEN?
TETH. WE'RE CHECKING IT OUT NOW.

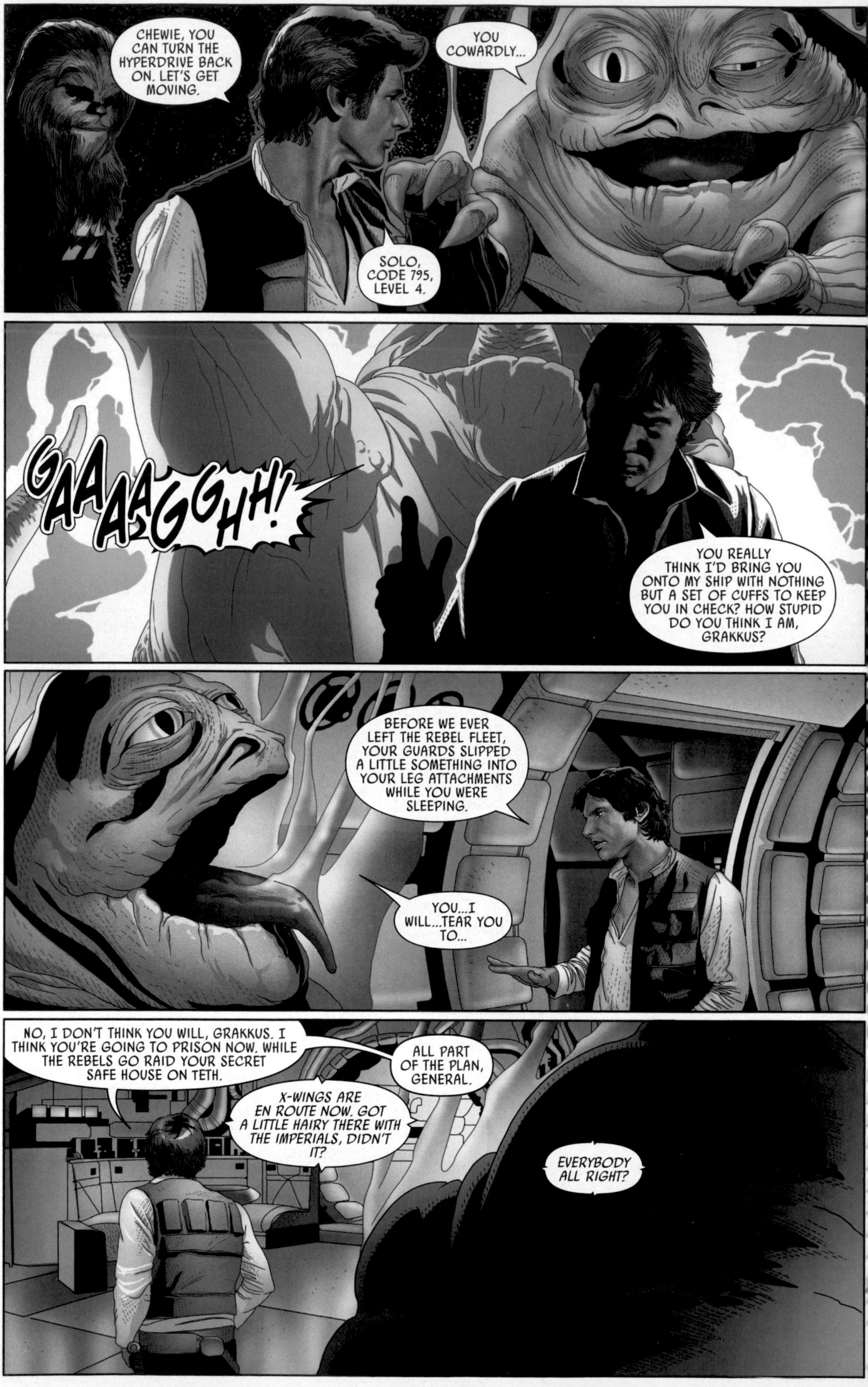
CHEWIE, YOU CAN TURN THE HYPERDRIVE BACK ON. LET'S GET MOVING.
YOU COWARDLY...
SOLO, CODE 795, LEVEL 4.
GAAAAAGGHH!
YOU REALLY THINK I'D BRING YOU ONTO MY SHIP WITH NOTHING BUT A SET OF CUFFS TO KEEP YOU IN CHECK? HOW STUPID DO YOU THINK I AM, GRAKKUS?
BEFORE WE EVER LEFT THE REBEL FLEET, YOUR GUARDS SLIPPED A LITTLE SOMETHING INTO YOUR LEG ATTACHMENTS WHILE YOU WERE SLEEPING.
YOU...I WILL...TEAR YOU TO...
NO, I DON'T THINK YOU WILL, GRAKKUS. I THINK YOU'RE GOING TO PRISON NOW. WHILE THE REBELS GO RAID YOUR SECRET SAFE HOUSE ON TETH.
ALL PART OF THE PLAN, GENERAL.
X-WINGS ARE EN ROUTE NOW. GOT A LITTLE HAIRY THERE WITH THE IMPERIALS, DIDN'T IT?
EVERYBODY ALL RIGHT?

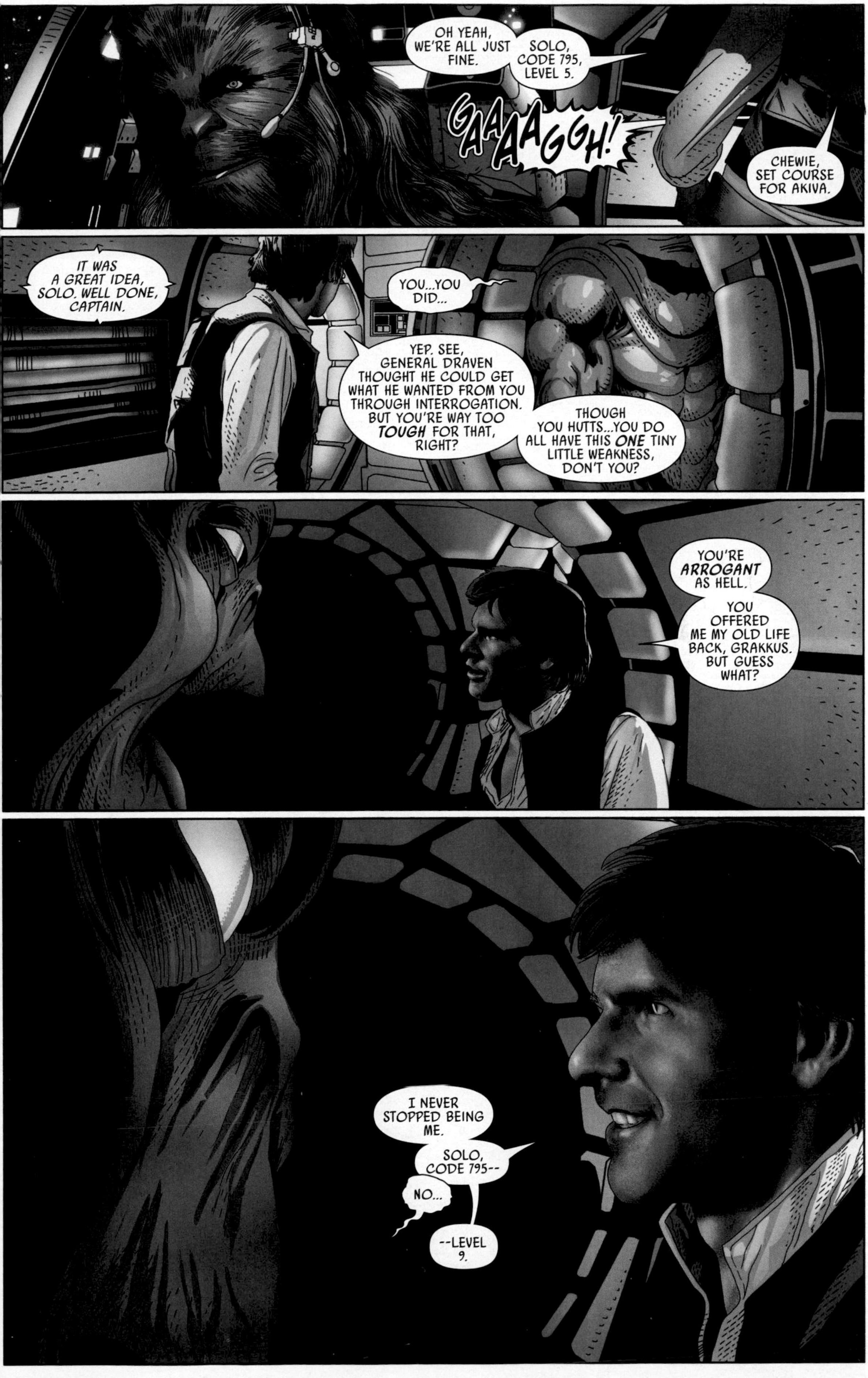
OH YEAH, WE'RE ALL JUST FINE.
SOLO, CODE 795, LEVEL 5.
GAAAAGGH!
CHEWIE, SET COURSE FOR AKIVA.
IT WAS A GREAT IDEA, SOLO. WELL DONE, CAPTAIN.
YOU...YOU DID...
YEP. SEE, GENERAL DRAVEN THOUGHT HE COULD GET WHAT HE WANTED FROM YOU THROUGH INTERROGATION. BUT YOU'RE WAY TOO TOUGH FOR THAT, RIGHT?
THOUGH YOU HUTTS...YOU DO ALL HAVE THIS ONE TINY LITTLE WEAKNESS, DON'T YOU?
YOU'RE ARROGANT AS HELL.
YOU OFFERED ME MY OLD LIFE BACK, GRAKKUS. BUT GUESS WHAT?
I NEVER STOPPED BEING ME.
SOLO, CODE 795--
NO...
--LEVEL 9.

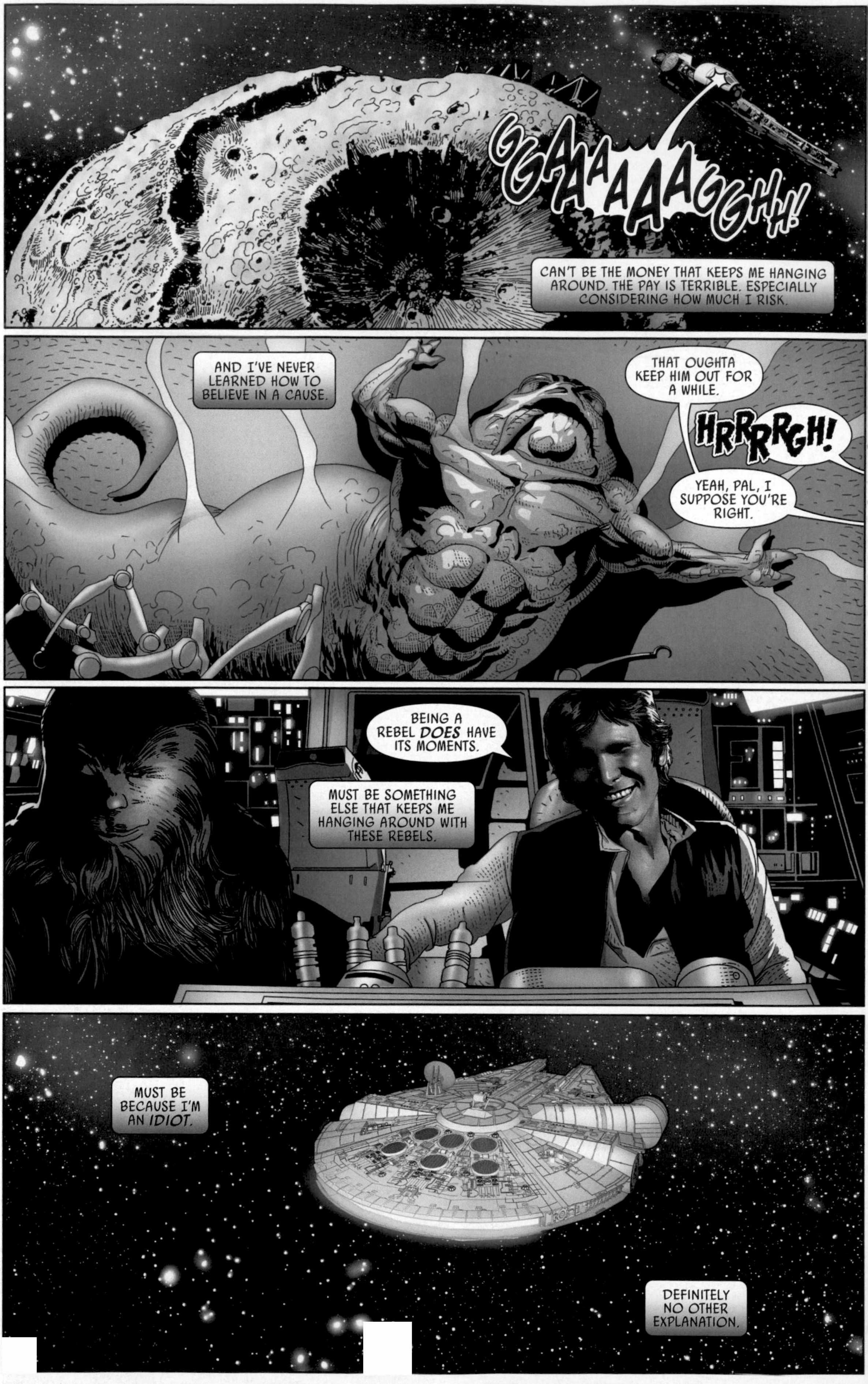
GGAAAAAAAGGHH!
CAN'T BE THE MONEY THAT KEEPS ME HANGING AROUND. THE PAY IS TERRIBLE. ESPECIALLY CONSIDERING HOW MUCH I RISK.
AND I'VE NEVER LEARNED HOW TO BELIEVE IN A CAUSE.
THAT OUGHTA KEEP HIM OUT FOR A WHILE.
HRRRRGH!
YEAH, PAL, I SUPPOSE YOU'RE RIGHT.
BEING A REBEL DOES HAVE ITS MOMENTS.
MUST BE SOMETHING ELSE THAT KEEPS ME HANGING AROUND WITH THESE REBELS.
MUST BE BECAUSE I'M AN IDIOT.
DEFINITELY NO OTHER EXPLANATION.

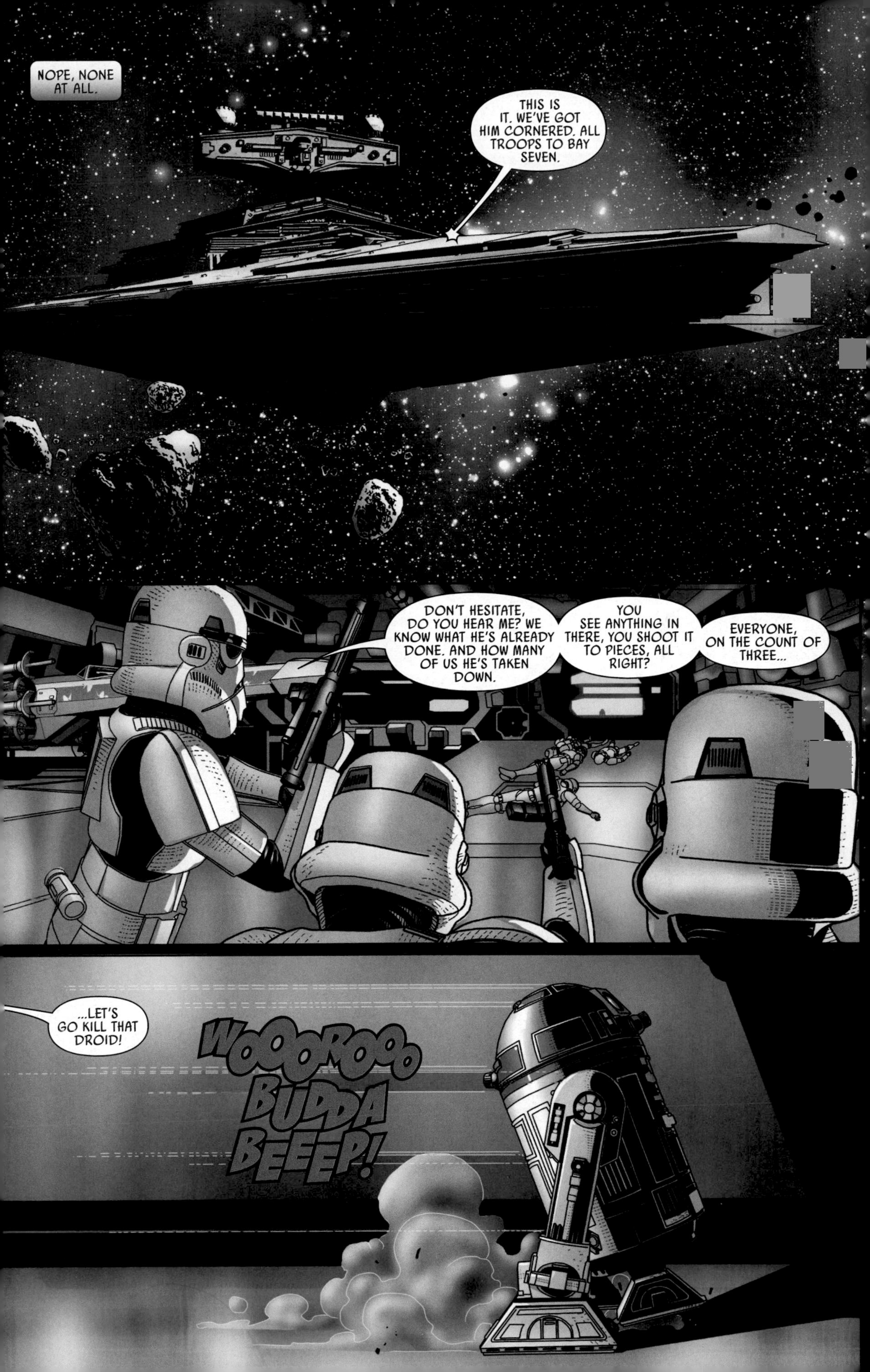
NOPE, NONE AT ALL.
THIS IS IT. WE'VE GOT HIM CORNERED. ALL TROOPS TO BAY SEVEN.
DON'T HESITATE, DO YOU HEAR ME? WE KNOW WHAT HE'S ALREADY DONE. AND HOW MANY OF US HE'S TAKEN DOWN.
YOU SEE ANYTHING IN THERE, YOU SHOOT IT TO PIECES, ALL RIGHT?
EVERYONE, ON THE COUNT OF THREE...
...LET'S GO KILL THAT DROID!
WOOOROOO BUDDA BEEEP!

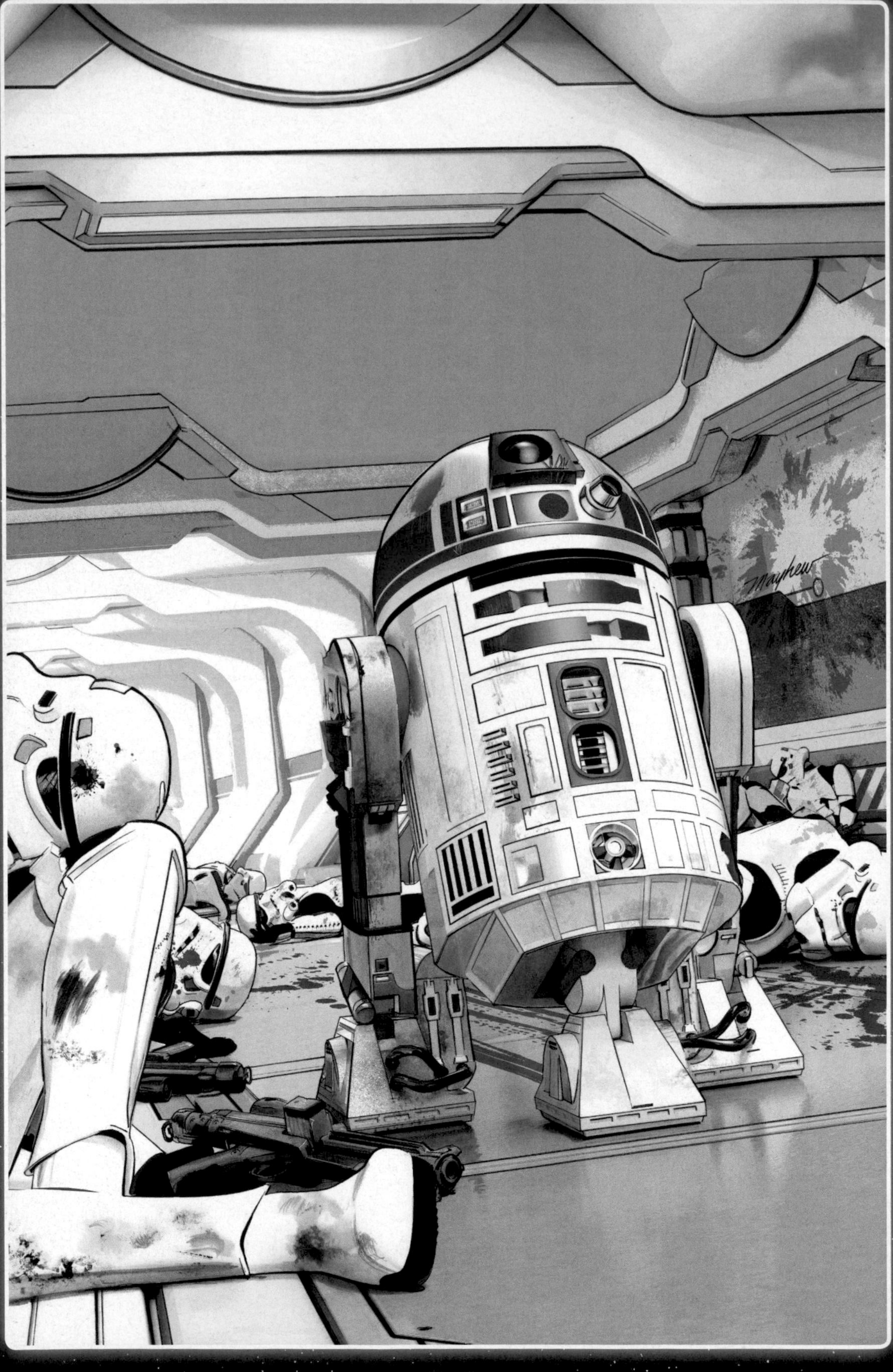
Mayhew

REVENGE OF THE ASTROMECH

It is a time of turmoil in the galaxy. While the evil Galactic Empire remains strong, the Rebel Alliance continues to undermine Imperial forces throughout the galaxy in their fight for freedom.

An Imperial siege on Tureen VII compelled Alliance heroes Luke Skywalker, Princess Leia, and Han Solo, to intervene. Darth Vader dispatched Scar Squadron, an elite group of stormtroopers, to stop them. Although humiliated and disgraced when the rebel forces were able to break the siege, Scar Squadron did not emerge empty handed–they captured C-3PO.

Scar Squadron has turned their focus to extracting as many rebel secrets as possible from the protocol droid. Meanwhile, R2-D2, concerned for his fellow droid and friend, has abandoned the rest of the rebel force in order to launch a solo rescue mission....

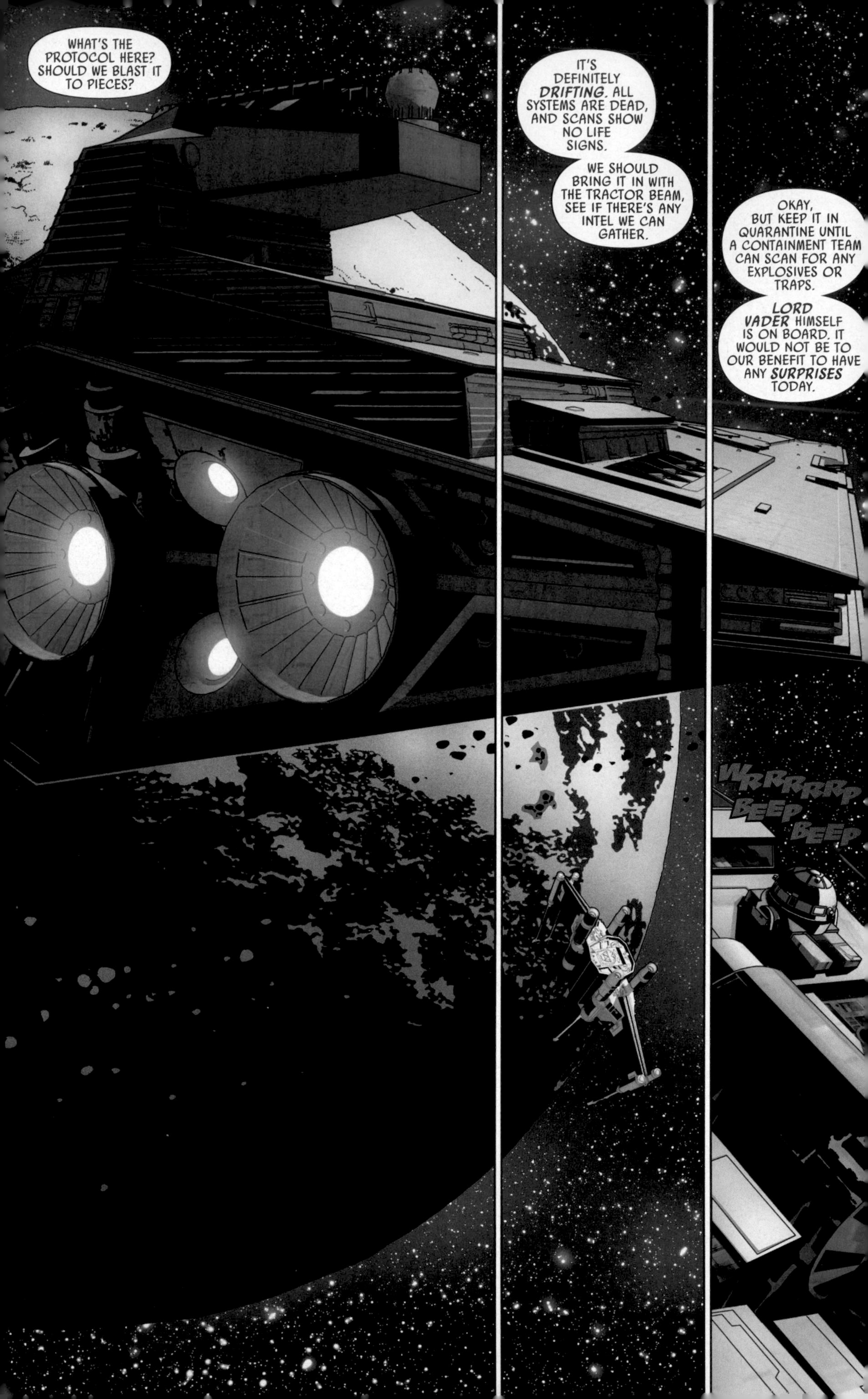
WHAT'S THE PROTOCOL HERE? SHOULD WE BLAST IT TO PIECES?
IT'S DEFINITELY DRIFTING. ALL SYSTEMS ARE DEAD, AND SCANS SHOW NO LIFE SIGNS.
WE SHOULD BRING IT IN WITH THE TRACTOR BEAM, SEE IF THERE'S ANY INTEL WE CAN GATHER.
OKAY, BUT KEEP IT IN QUARANTINE UNTIL A CONTAINMENT TEAM CAN SCAN FOR ANY EXPLOSIVES OR TRAPS.
LORD VADER HIMSELF IS ON BOARD. IT WOULD NOT BE TO OUR BENEFIT TO HAVE ANY SURPRISES TODAY.
WRRRRRP
BEEP
BEEP

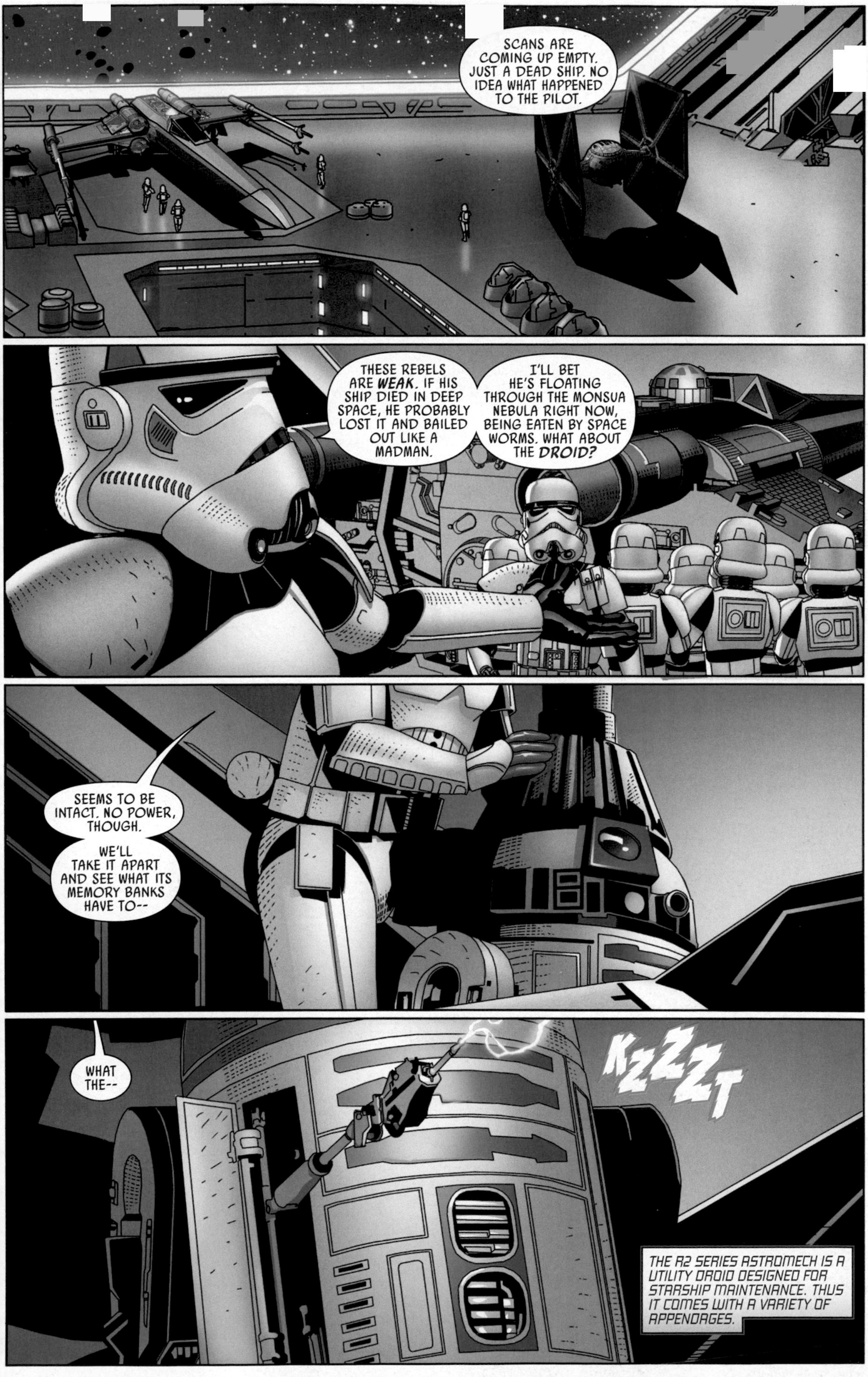
SCANS ARE COMING UP EMPTY. JUST A DEAD SHIP. NO IDEA WHAT HAPPENED TO THE PILOT.
THESE REBELS ARE WEAK. IF HIS SHIP DIED IN DEEP SPACE, HE PROBABLY LOST IT AND BAILED OUT LIKE A MADMAN.
I'LL BET HE'S FLOATING THROUGH THE MONSUA NEBULA RIGHT NOW, BEING EATEN BY SPACE WORMS. WHAT ABOUT THE DROID?
SEEMS TO BE INTACT. NO POWER, THOUGH.
WE'LL TAKE IT APART AND SEE WHAT ITS MEMORY BANKS HAVE TO--
WHAT THE--
KZZZZT
THE R2 SERIES ASTROMECH IS A UTILITY DROID DESIGNED FOR STARSHIP MAINTENANCE. THUS IT COMES WITH A VARIETY OF APPENDAGES.

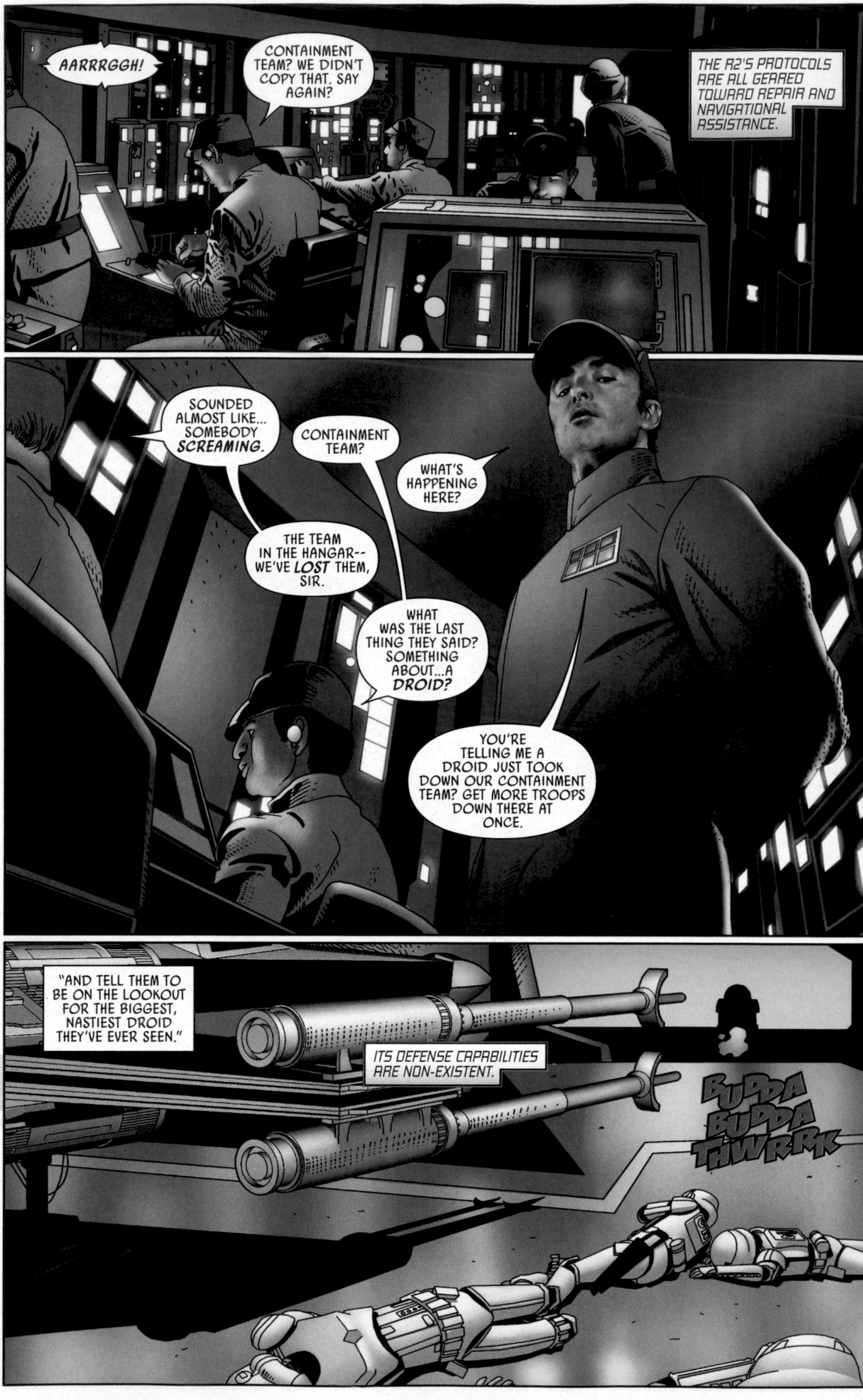
AARRRGGH!
CONTAINMENT TEAM? WE DIDN'T COPY THAT. SAY AGAIN?
THE R2'S PROTOCOLS ARE ALL GEARED TOWARD REPAIR AND NAVIGATIONAL ASSISTANCE.
SOUNDED ALMOST LIKE... SOMEBODY SCREAMING.
CONTAINMENT TEAM?
WHAT'S HAPPENING HERE?
THE TEAM IN THE HANGAR-- WE'VE LOST THEM, SIR.
WHAT WAS THE LAST THING THEY SAID? SOMETHING ABOUT...A DROID?
YOU'RE TELLING ME A DROID JUST TOOK DOWN OUR CONTAINMENT TEAM? GET MORE TROOPS DOWN THERE AT ONCE.
"AND TELL THEM TO BE ON THE LOOKOUT FOR THE BIGGEST, NASTIEST DROID THEY'VE EVER SEEN."
ITS DEFENSE CAPABILITIES ARE NON-EXISTENT.
BUDDA BUDDA THWRRK

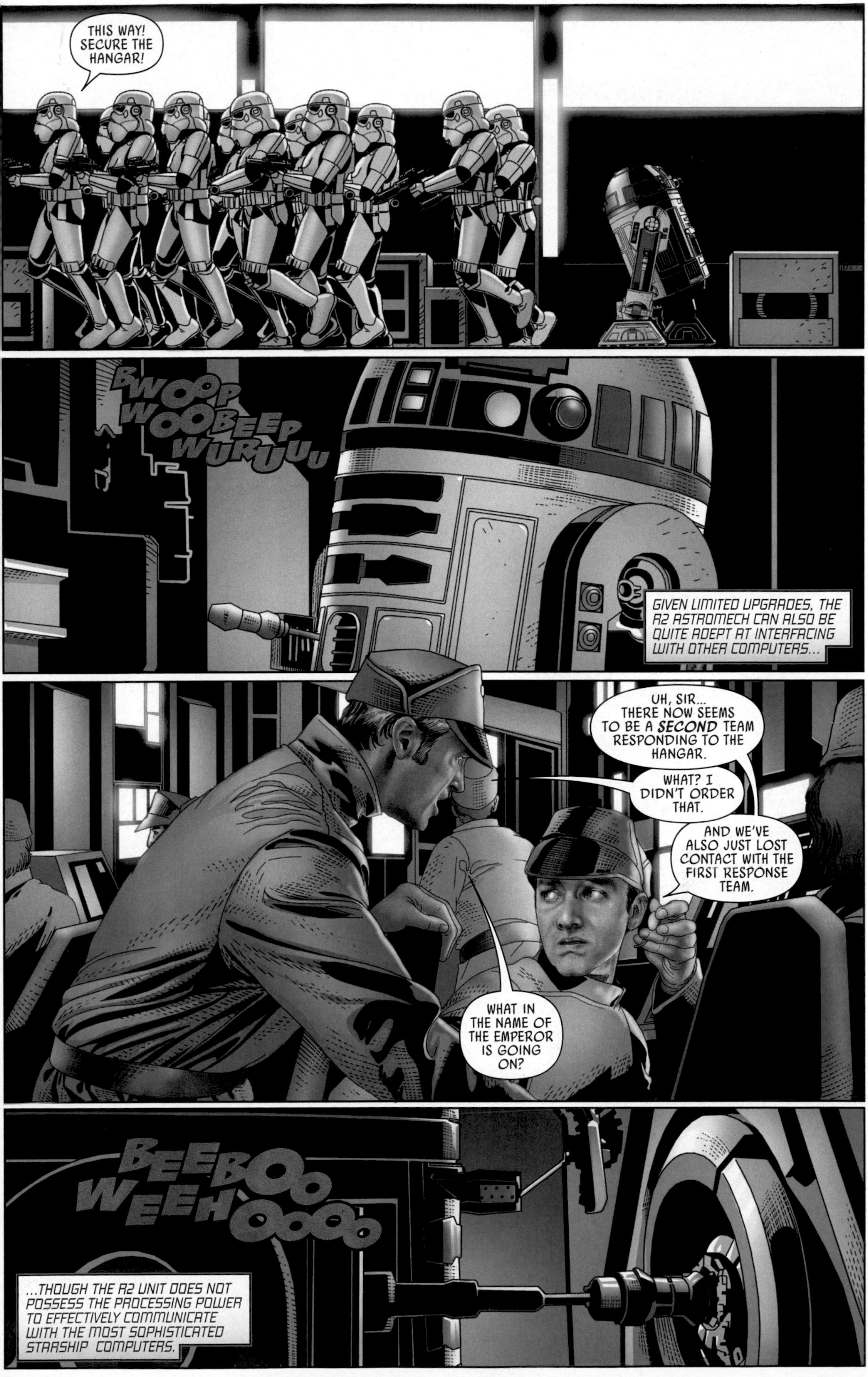
THIS WAY! SECURE THE HANGAR!
BWOOP WOOBEEP WURUUU
GIVEN LIMITED UPGRADES, THE R2 ASTROMECH CAN ALSO BE QUITE ADEPT AT INTERFACING WITH OTHER COMPUTERS...
UH, SIR... THERE NOW SEEMS TO BE A SECOND TEAM RESPONDING TO THE HANGAR.
WHAT? I DIDN'T ORDER THAT.
AND WE'VE ALSO JUST LOST CONTACT WITH THE FIRST RESPONSE TEAM.
WHAT IN THE NAME OF THE EMPEROR IS GOING ON?
BEEBOO WEEHOOOO
...THOUGH THE R2 UNIT DOES NOT POSSESS THE PROCESSING POWER TO EFFECTIVELY COMMUNICATE WITH THE MOST SOPHISTICATED STARSHIP COMPUTERS.

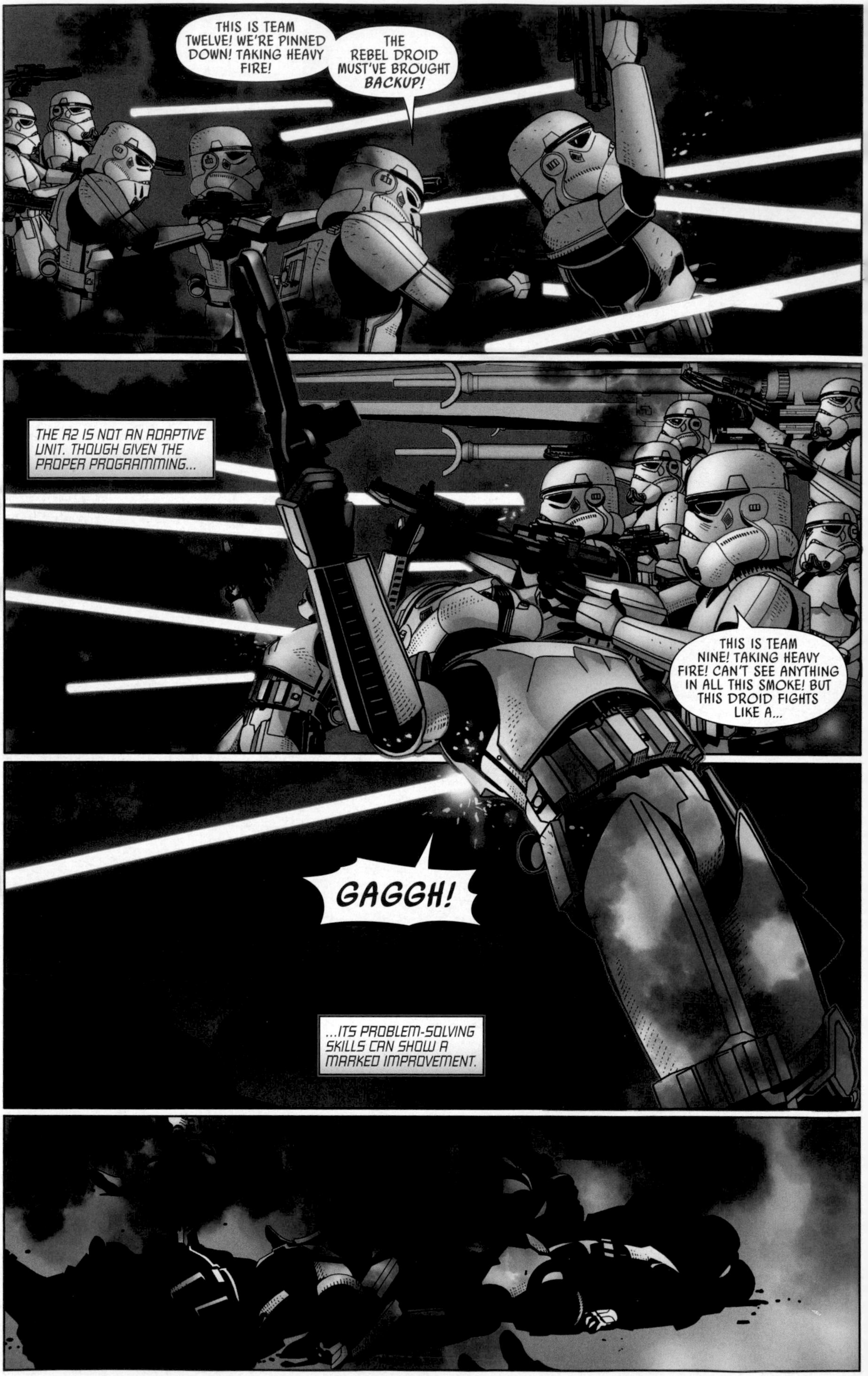

THIS IS TEAM TWELVE! WE'RE PINNED DOWN! TAKING HEAVY FIRE!
THE REBEL DROID MUST'VE BROUGHT BACKUP!
THE R2 IS NOT AN ADAPTIVE UNIT. THOUGH GIVEN THE PROPER PROGRAMMING...
THIS IS TEAM NINE! TAKING HEAVY FIRE! CAN'T SEE ANYTHING IN ALL THIS SMOKE! BUT THIS DROID FIGHTS LIKE A...
GAGGH!
...ITS PROBLEM-SOLVING SKILLS CAN SHOW A MARKED IMPROVEMENT.

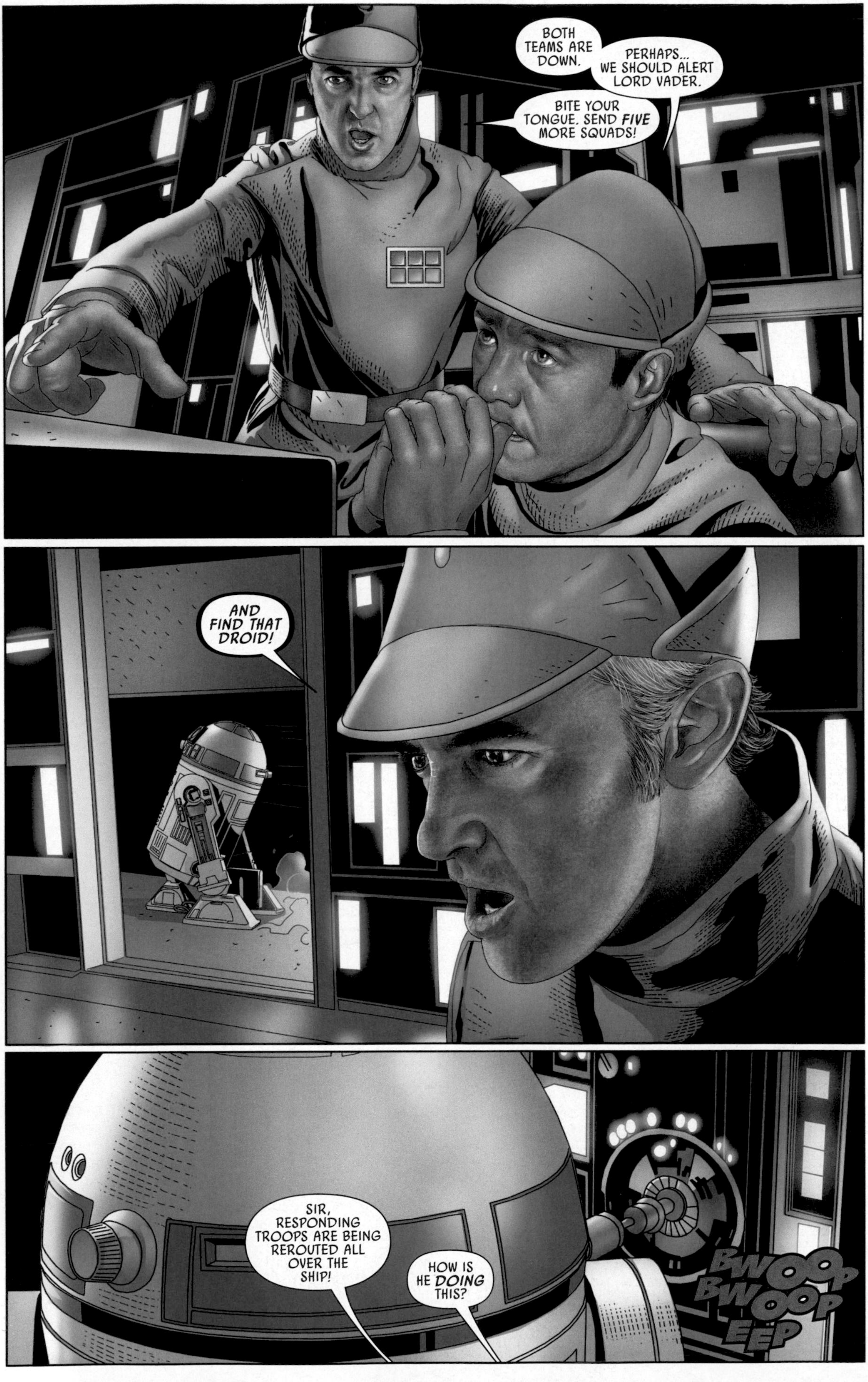
BOTH TEAMS ARE DOWN.
PERHAPS... WE SHOULD ALERT LORD VADER.
BITE YOUR TONGUE. SEND FIVE MORE SQUADS!
AND FIND THAT DROID!
SIR, RESPONDING TROOPS ARE BEING REROUTED ALL OVER THE SHIP!
HOW IS HE DOING THIS?
BWOOP BWOOP EEP

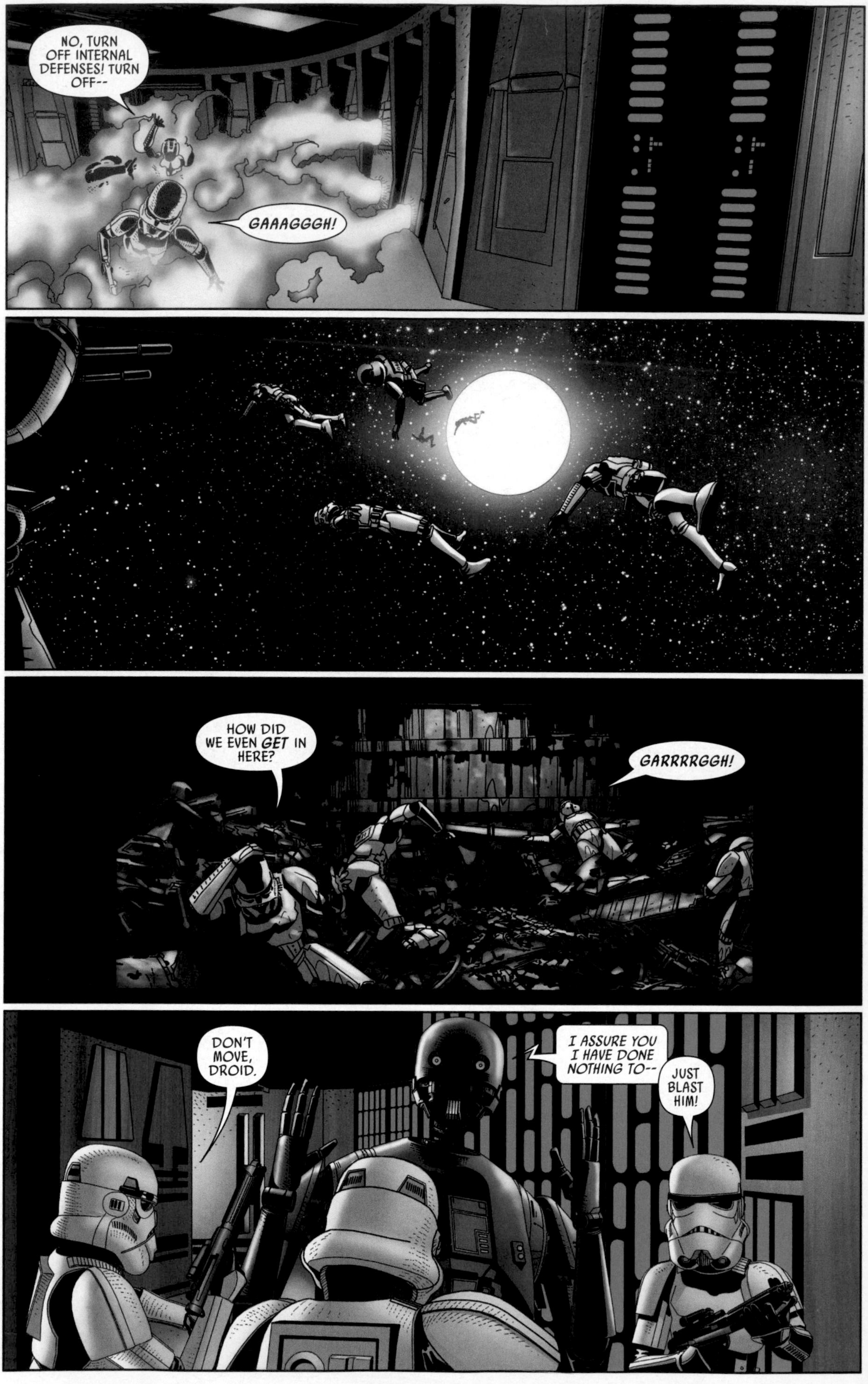
NO, TURN OFF INTERNAL DEFENSES! TURN OFF--
GAAAGGGH!
HOW DID WE EVEN GET IN HERE?
GARRRRGGH!
DON'T MOVE, DROID.
I ASSURE YOU I HAVE DONE NOTHING TO--
JUST BLAST HIM!

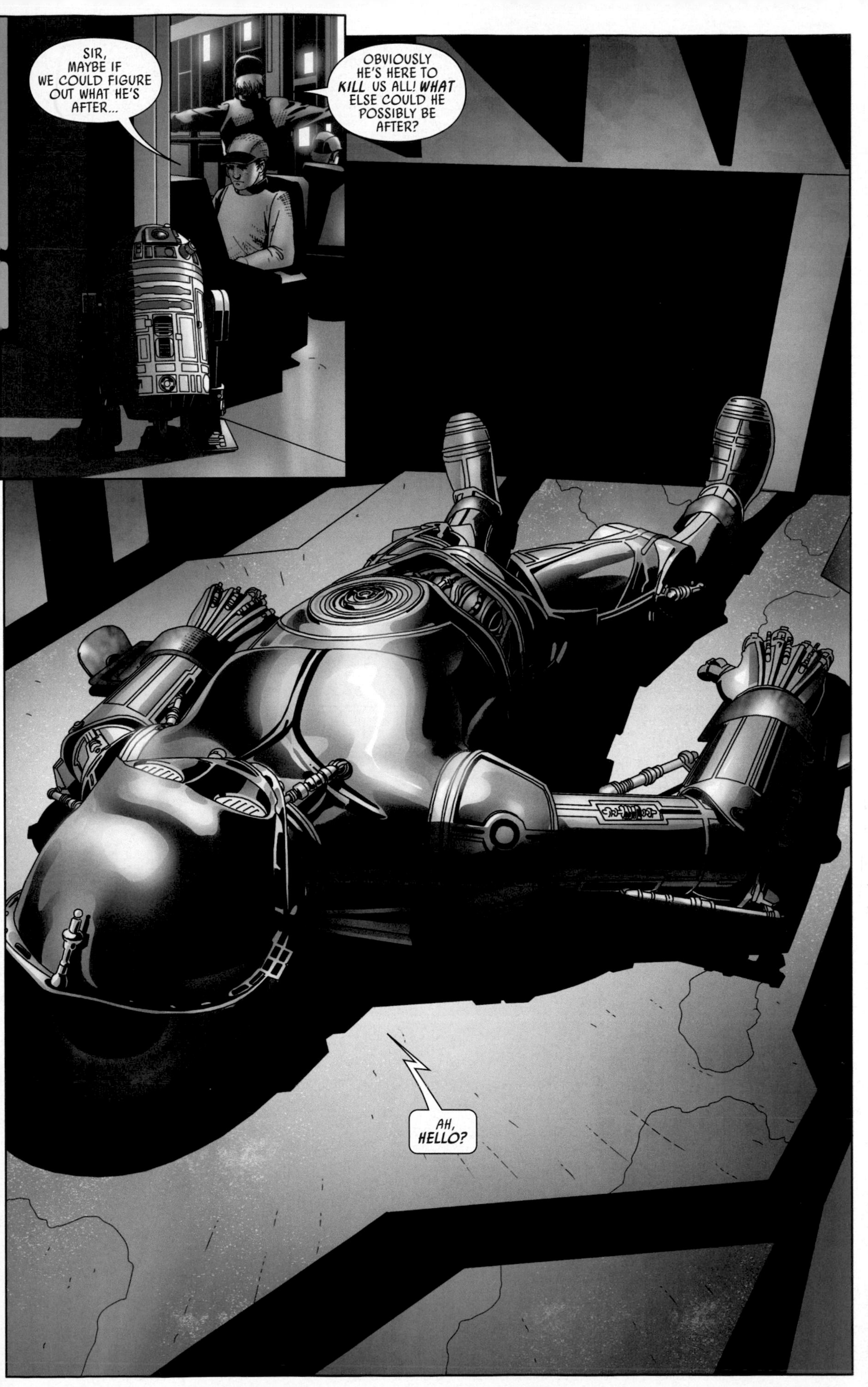
SIR, MAYBE IF WE COULD FIGURE OUT WHAT HE'S AFTER...
OBVIOUSLY HE'S HERE TO KILL US ALL! WHAT ELSE COULD HE POSSIBLY BE AFTER?
AH, HELLO?

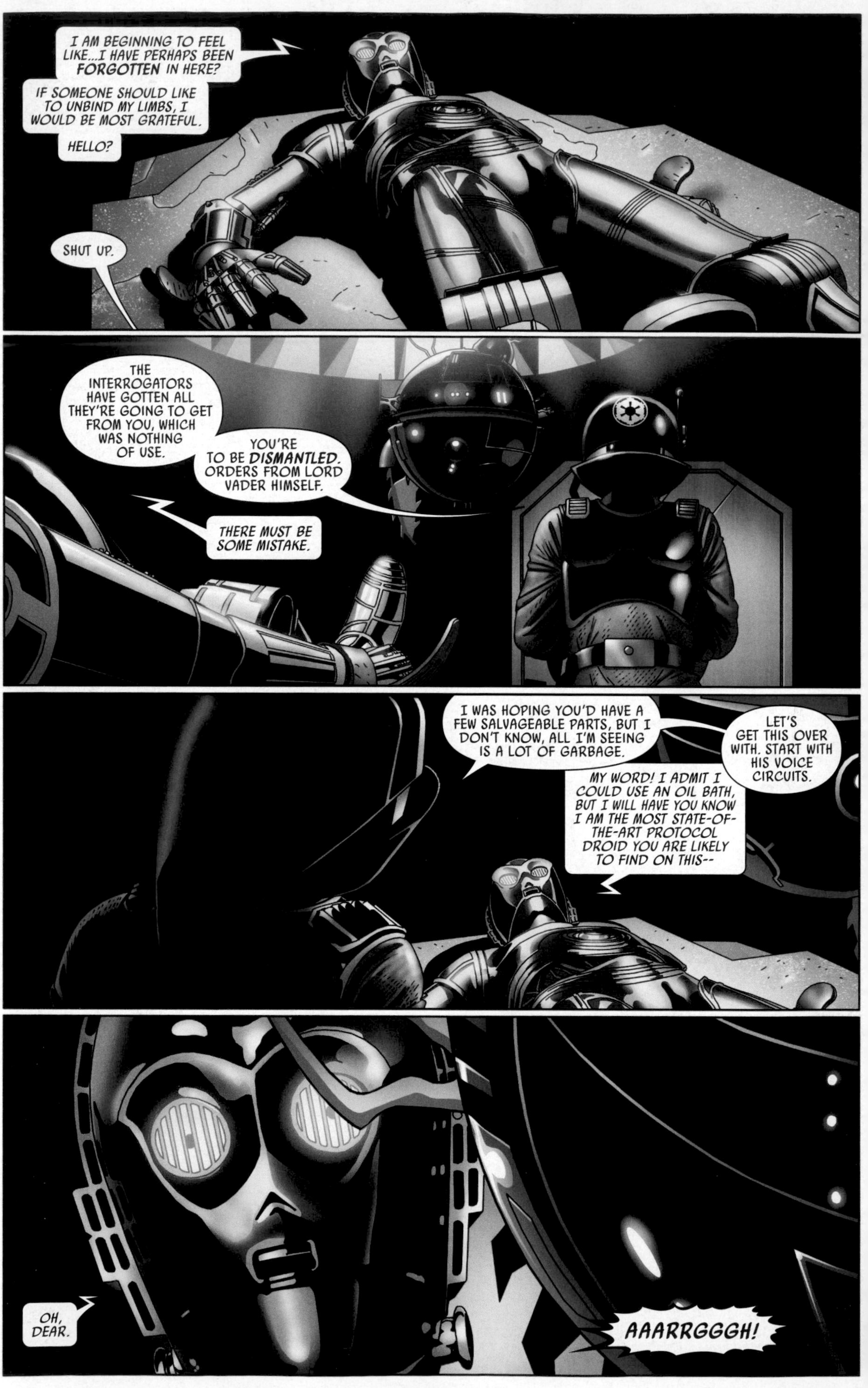
I AM BEGINNING TO FEEL LIKE...I HAVE PERHAPS BEEN FORGOTTEN IN HERE?
IF SOMEONE SHOULD LIKE TO UNBIND MY LIMBS, I WOULD BE MOST GRATEFUL.
HELLO?
SHUT UP.
THE INTERROGATORS HAVE GOTTEN ALL THEY'RE GOING TO GET FROM YOU, WHICH WAS NOTHING OF USE.
YOU'RE TO BE DISMANTLED. ORDERS FROM LORD VADER HIMSELF.
THERE MUST BE SOME MISTAKE.
I WAS HOPING YOU'D HAVE A FEW SALVAGEABLE PARTS, BUT I DON'T KNOW, ALL I'M SEEING IS A LOT OF GARBAGE.
LET'S GET THIS OVER WITH. START WITH HIS VOICE CIRCUITS.
MY WORD! I ADMIT I COULD USE AN OIL BATH, BUT I WILL HAVE YOU KNOW I AM THE MOST STATE-OF-THE-ART PROTOCOL DROID YOU ARE LIKELY TO FIND ON THIS--
OH, DEAR.
AAARRGGGH!

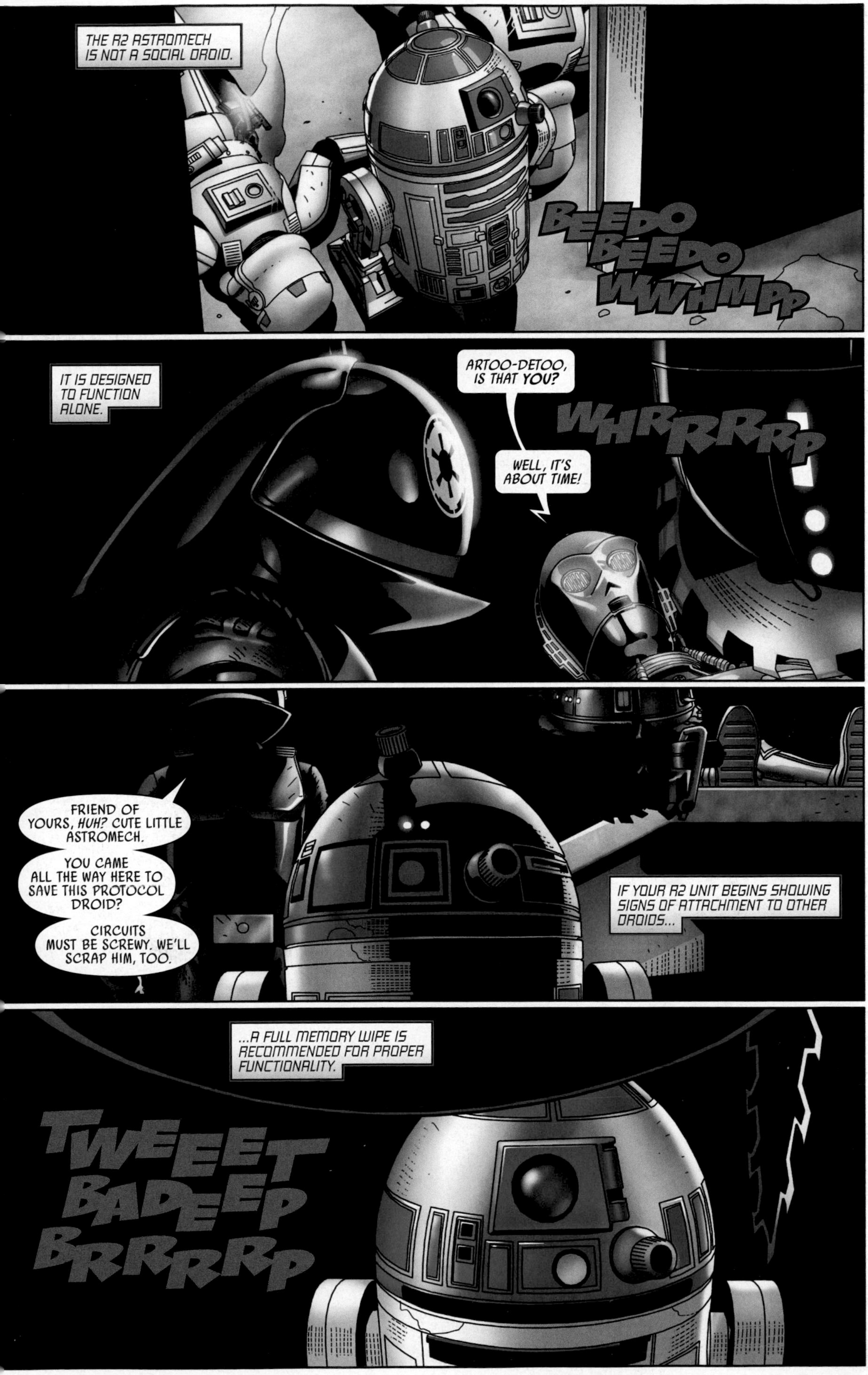
THE R2 ASTROMECH IS NOT A SOCIAL DROID.
BEEDO BEEDO WWHMPP
IT IS DESIGNED TO FUNCTION ALONE.
ARTOO-DETOO, IS THAT YOU?
WELL, IT'S ABOUT TIME!
WHRRRRRP
FRIEND OF YOURS, HUH? CUTE LITTLE ASTROMECH.
YOU CAME ALL THE WAY HERE TO SAVE THIS PROTOCOL DROID?
CIRCUITS MUST BE SCREWY. WE'LL SCRAP HIM, TOO.
IF YOUR R2 UNIT BEGINS SHOWING SIGNS OF ATTACHMENT TO OTHER DROIDS...
...A FULL MEMORY WIPE IS RECOMMENDED FOR PROPER FUNCTIONALITY.
TWEEET BADEEP BRRRRRP

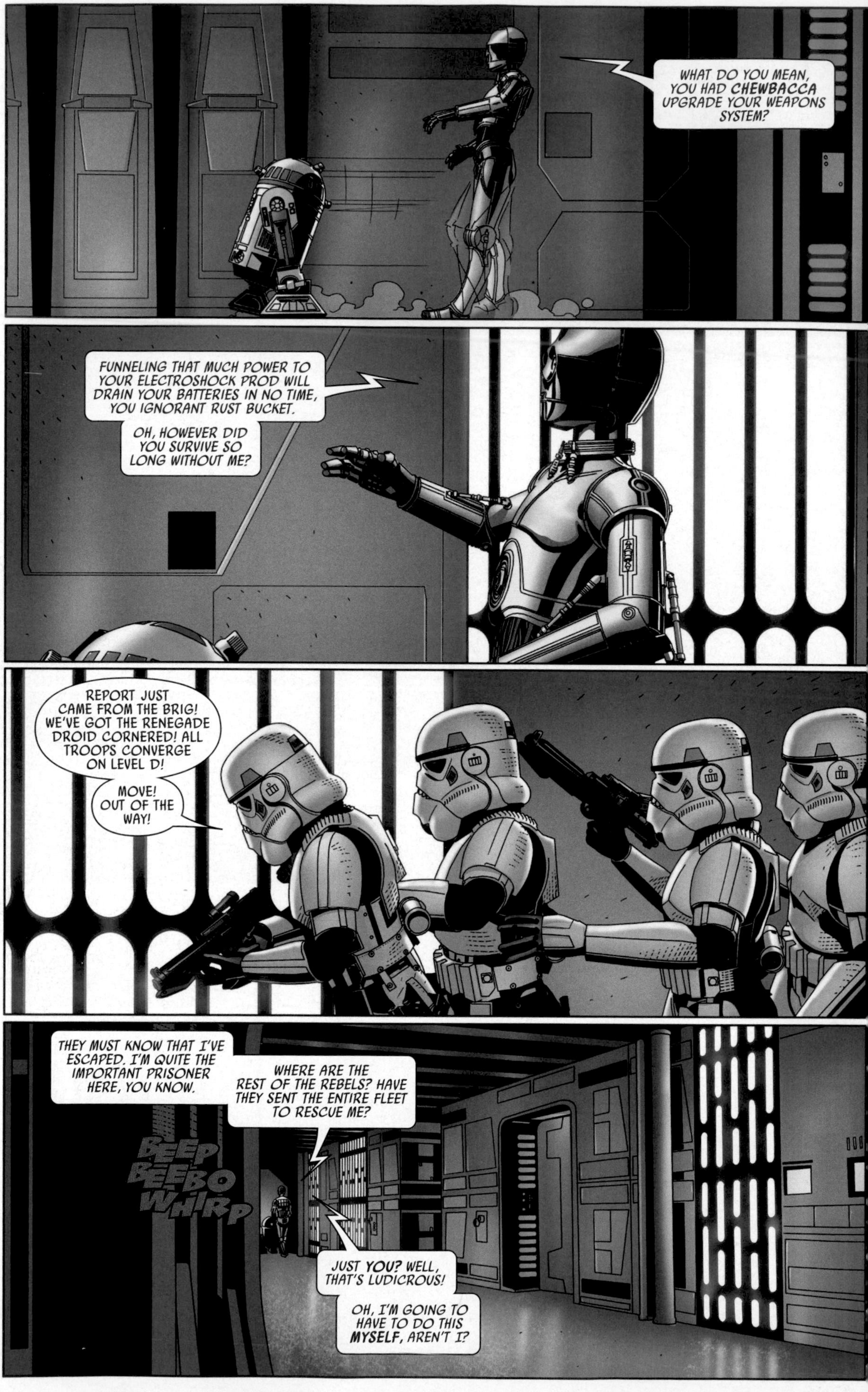
WHAT DO YOU MEAN, YOU HAD CHEWBACCA UPGRADE YOUR WEAPONS SYSTEM?
FUNNELING THAT MUCH POWER TO YOUR ELECTROSHOCK PROD WILL DRAIN YOUR BATTERIES IN NO TIME, YOU IGNORANT RUST BUCKET.
OH, HOWEVER DID YOU SURVIVE SO LONG WITHOUT ME?
REPORT JUST CAME FROM THE BRIG! WE'VE GOT THE RENEGADE DROID CORNERED! ALL TROOPS CONVERGE ON LEVEL D!
MOVE! OUT OF THE WAY!
THEY MUST KNOW THAT I'VE ESCAPED. I'M QUITE THE IMPORTANT PRISONER HERE, YOU KNOW.
WHERE ARE THE REST OF THE REBELS? HAVE THEY SENT THE ENTIRE FLEET TO RESCUE ME?
BEEP BEEBO WHIRP
JUST YOU? WELL, THAT'S LUDICROUS!
OH, I'M GOING TO HAVE TO DO THIS MYSELF, AREN'T I?

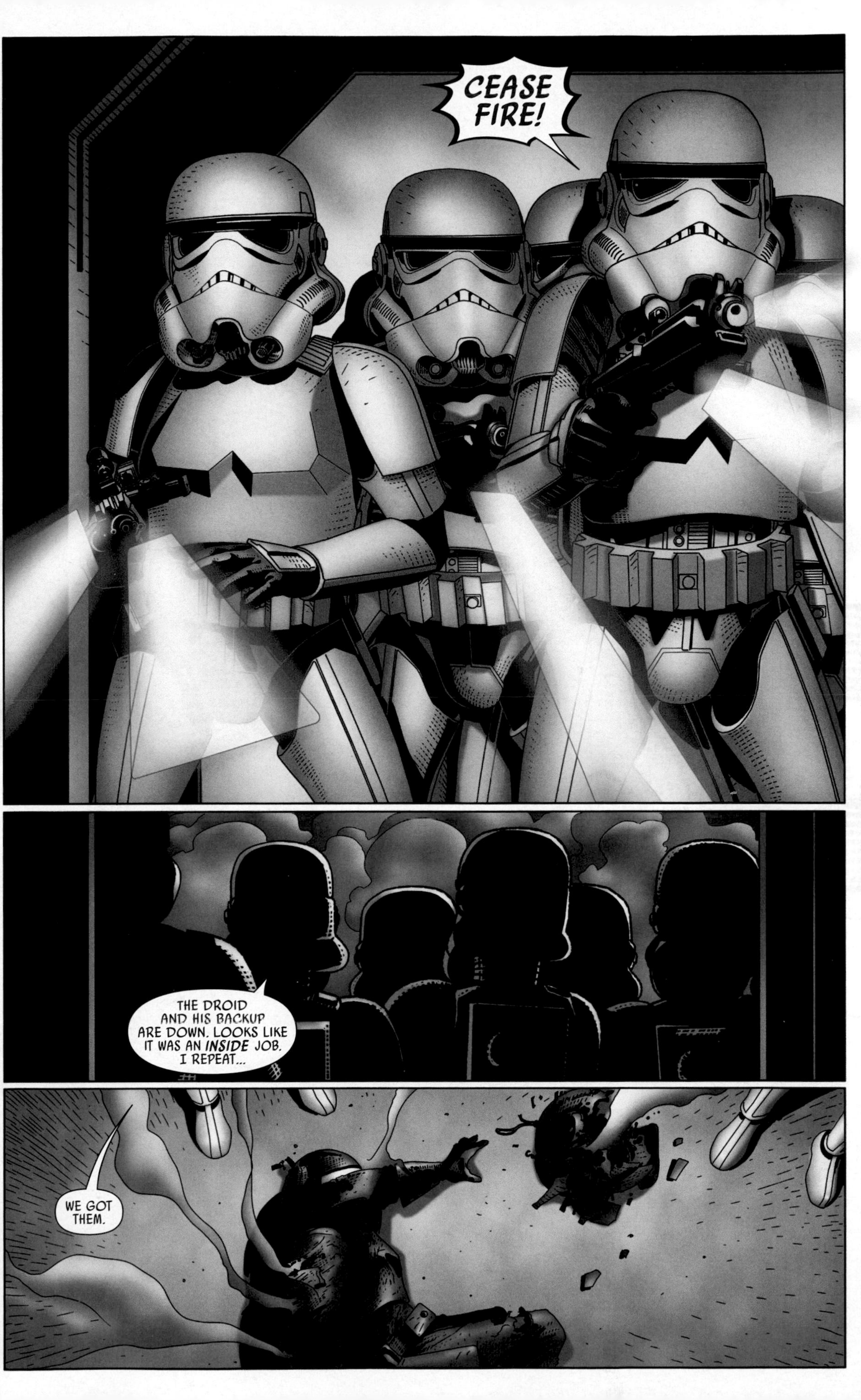
CEASE FIRE!
THE DROID AND HIS BACKUP ARE DOWN. LOOKS LIKE IT WAS AN *INSIDE* JOB. I REPEAT...
WE GOT THEM.

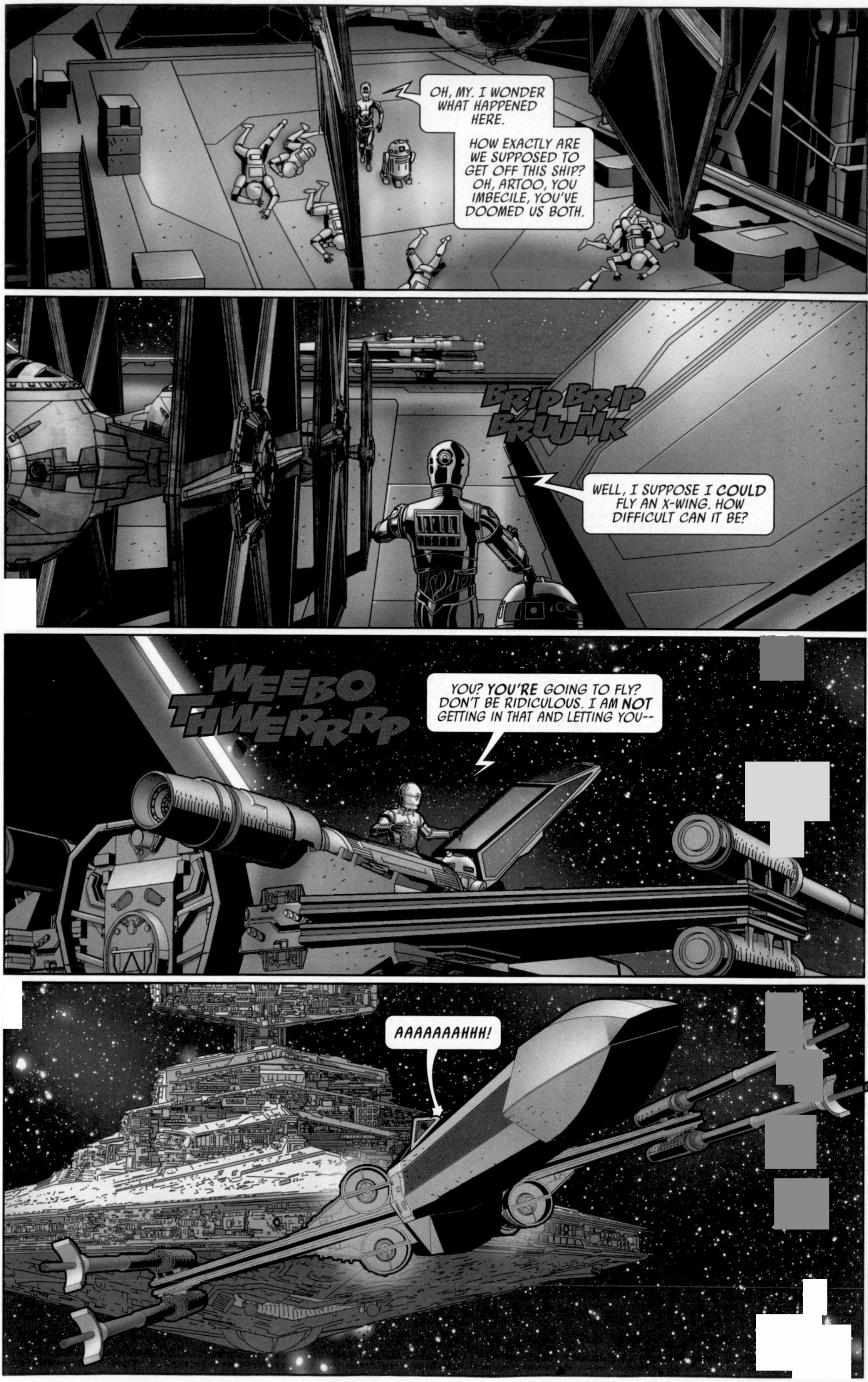
OH, MY. I WONDER WHAT HAPPENED HERE.
HOW EXACTLY ARE WE SUPPOSED TO GET OFF THIS SHIP? OH, ARTOO, YOU IMBECILE, YOU'VE DOOMED US BOTH.
BRIP BRIP BRUUNK
WELL, I SUPPOSE I **COULD** FLY AN X-WING. HOW DIFFICULT CAN IT BE?
WEEBO THWERRRP
YOU? **YOU'RE** GOING TO FLY? DON'T BE RIDICULOUS. I AM **NOT** GETTING IN THAT AND LETTING YOU--
AAAAAAAHHH!

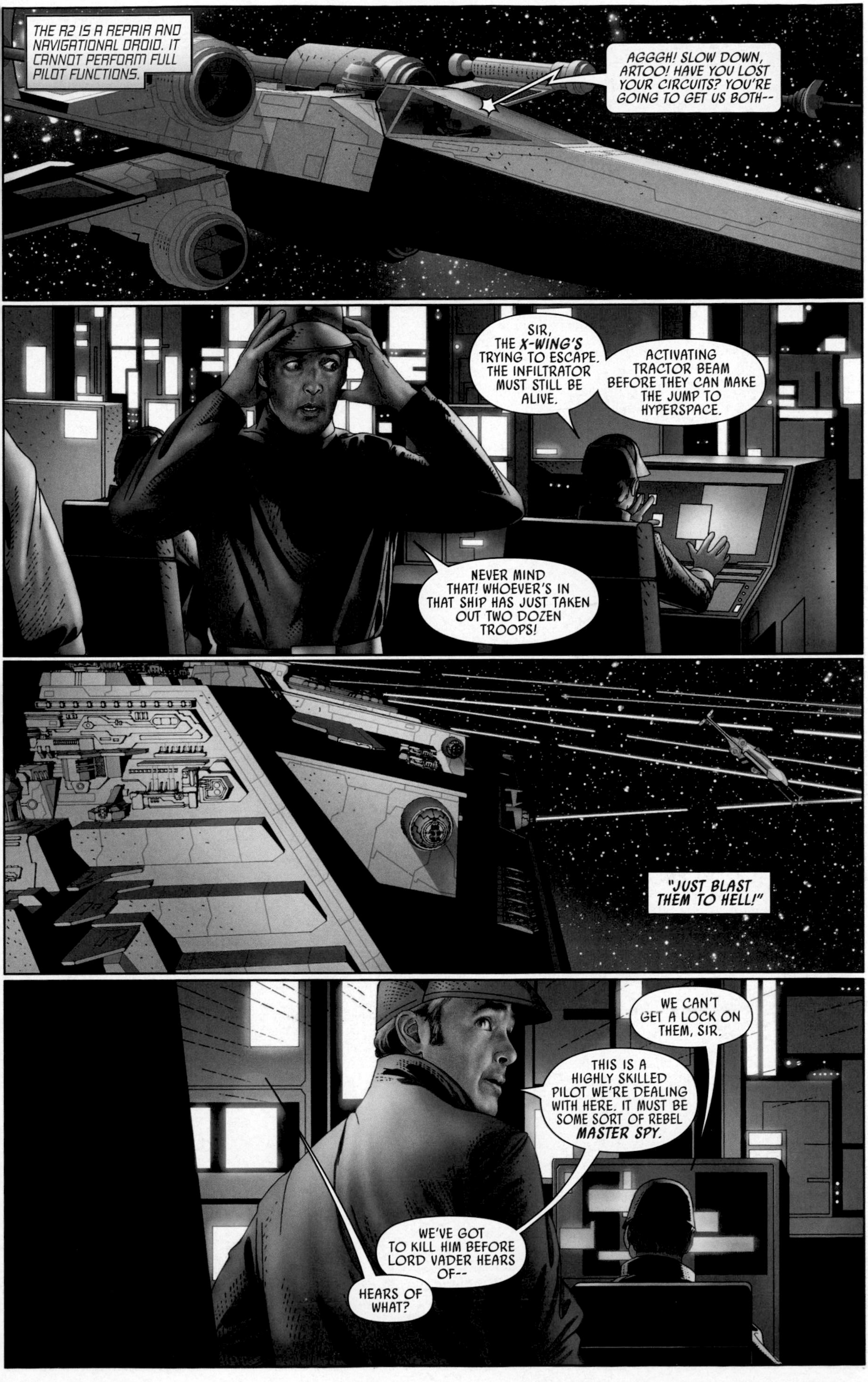
THE R2 IS A REPAIR AND NAVIGATIONAL DROID. IT CANNOT PERFORM FULL PILOT FUNCTIONS.
AGGGH! SLOW DOWN, ARTOO! HAVE YOU LOST YOUR CIRCUITS? YOU'RE GOING TO GET US BOTH--
SIR, THE X-WING'S TRYING TO ESCAPE. THE INFILTRATOR MUST STILL BE ALIVE.
ACTIVATING TRACTOR BEAM BEFORE THEY CAN MAKE THE JUMP TO HYPERSPACE.
NEVER MIND THAT! WHOEVER'S IN THAT SHIP HAS JUST TAKEN OUT TWO DOZEN TROOPS!
"JUST BLAST THEM TO HELL!"
WE CAN'T GET A LOCK ON THEM, SIR.
THIS IS A HIGHLY SKILLED PILOT WE'RE DEALING WITH HERE. IT MUST BE SOME SORT OF REBEL MASTER SPY.
WE'VE GOT TO KILL HIM BEFORE LORD VADER HEARS OF--
HEARS OF WHAT?

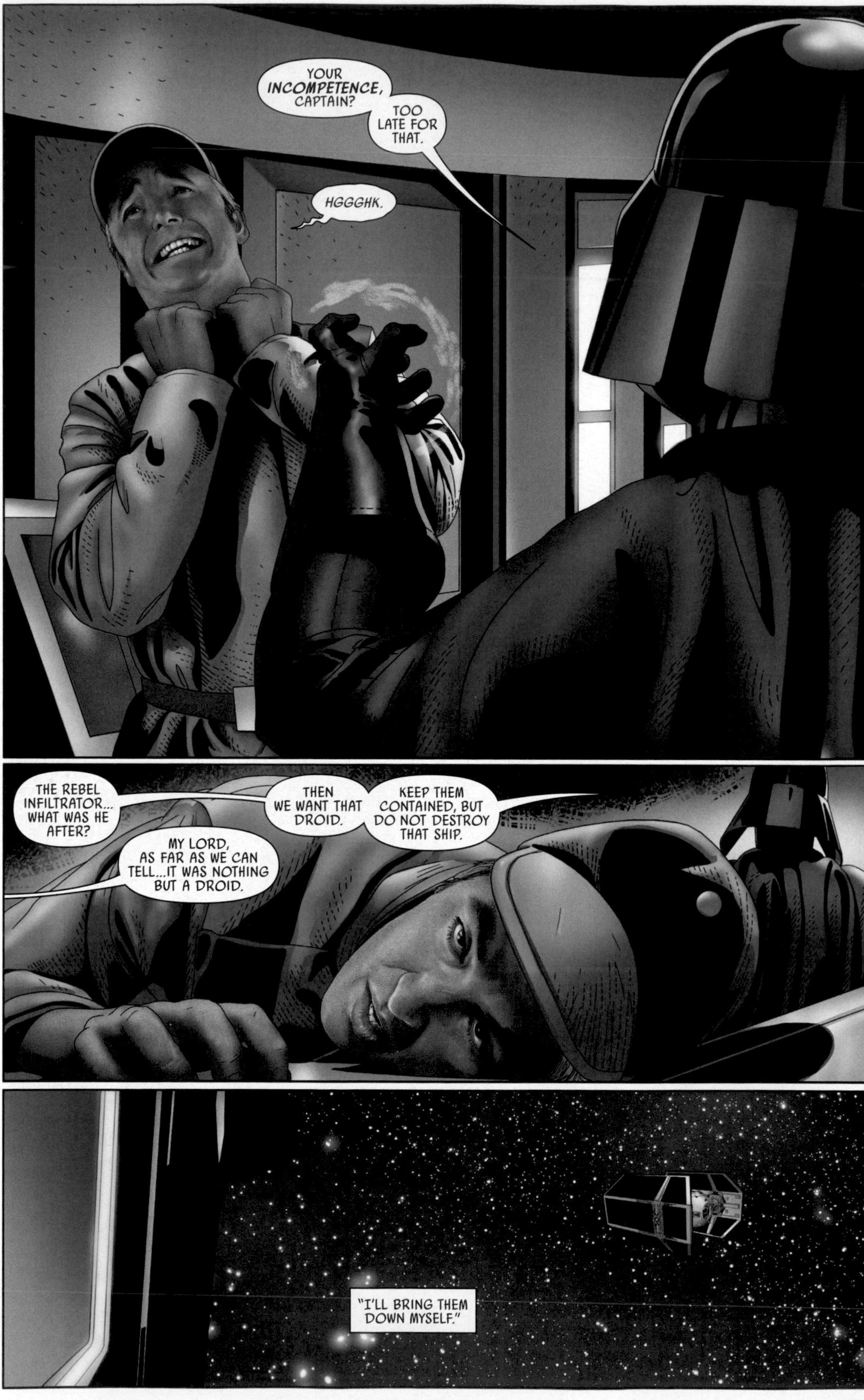
YOUR INCOMPETENCE, CAPTAIN?
TOO LATE FOR THAT.
HGGGHK.
THE REBEL INFILTRATOR... WHAT WAS HE AFTER?
MY LORD, AS FAR AS WE CAN TELL...IT WAS NOTHING BUT A DROID.
THEN WE WANT THAT DROID.
KEEP THEM CONTAINED, BUT DO NOT DESTROY THAT SHIP.
"I'LL BRING THEM DOWN MYSELF."

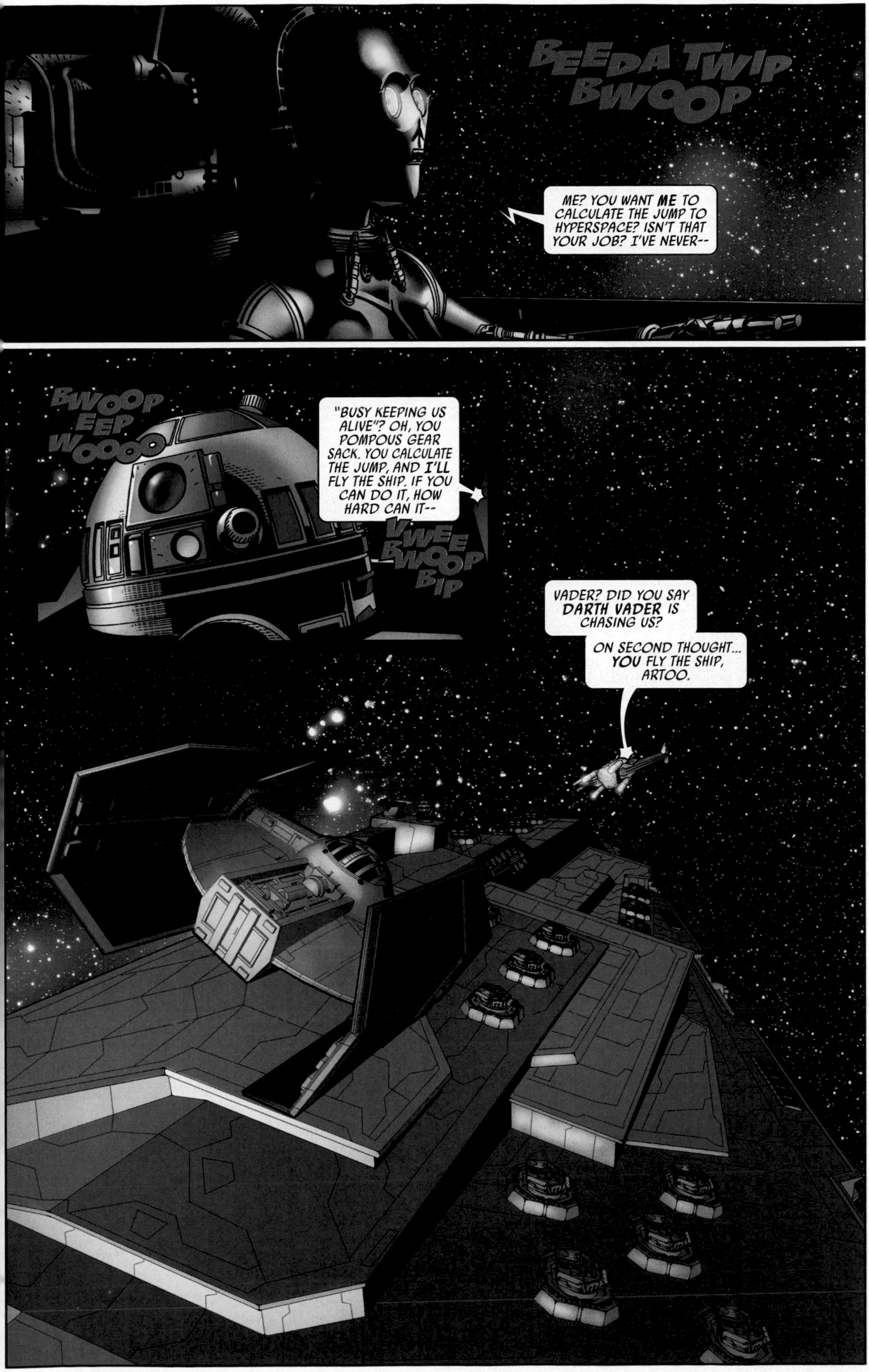
BEEDA TWIP BWOOP
ME? YOU WANT ME TO CALCULATE THE JUMP TO HYPERSPACE? ISN'T THAT YOUR JOB? I'VE NEVER--
BWOOP EEP WOOOOO
"BUSY KEEPING US ALIVE"? OH, YOU POMPOUS GEAR SACK. YOU CALCULATE THE JUMP, AND I'LL FLY THE SHIP. IF YOU CAN DO IT, HOW HARD CAN IT--
VWEE BWOOP BIP
VADER? DID YOU SAY DARTH VADER IS CHASING US?
ON SECOND THOUGHT... YOU FLY THE SHIP, ARTOO.

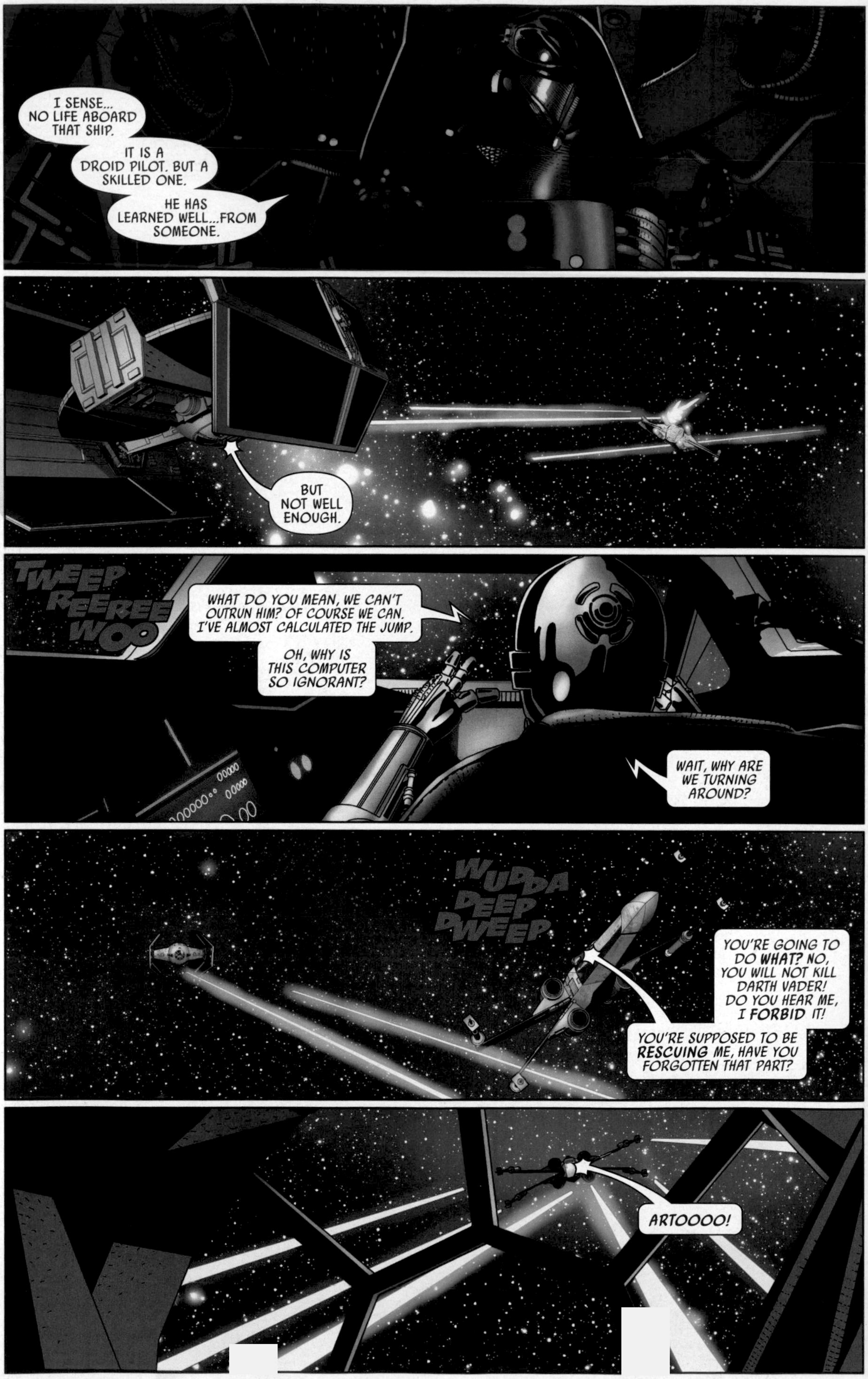
I SENSE... NO LIFE ABOARD THAT SHIP.
IT IS A DROID PILOT. BUT A SKILLED ONE.
HE HAS LEARNED WELL...FROM SOMEONE.
BUT NOT WELL ENOUGH.
TWEEP REEREE WOO
WHAT DO YOU MEAN, WE CAN'T OUTRUN HIM? OF COURSE WE CAN. I'VE ALMOST CALCULATED THE JUMP.
OH, WHY IS THIS COMPUTER SO IGNORANT?
WAIT, WHY ARE WE TURNING AROUND?
WUDDA DEEP DWEEP
YOU'RE GOING TO DO **WHAT?** NO, YOU WILL NOT KILL DARTH VADER! DO YOU HEAR ME, I **FORBID** IT!
YOU'RE SUPPOSED TO BE **RESCUING** ME, HAVE YOU FORGOTTEN THAT PART?
ARTOOOO!

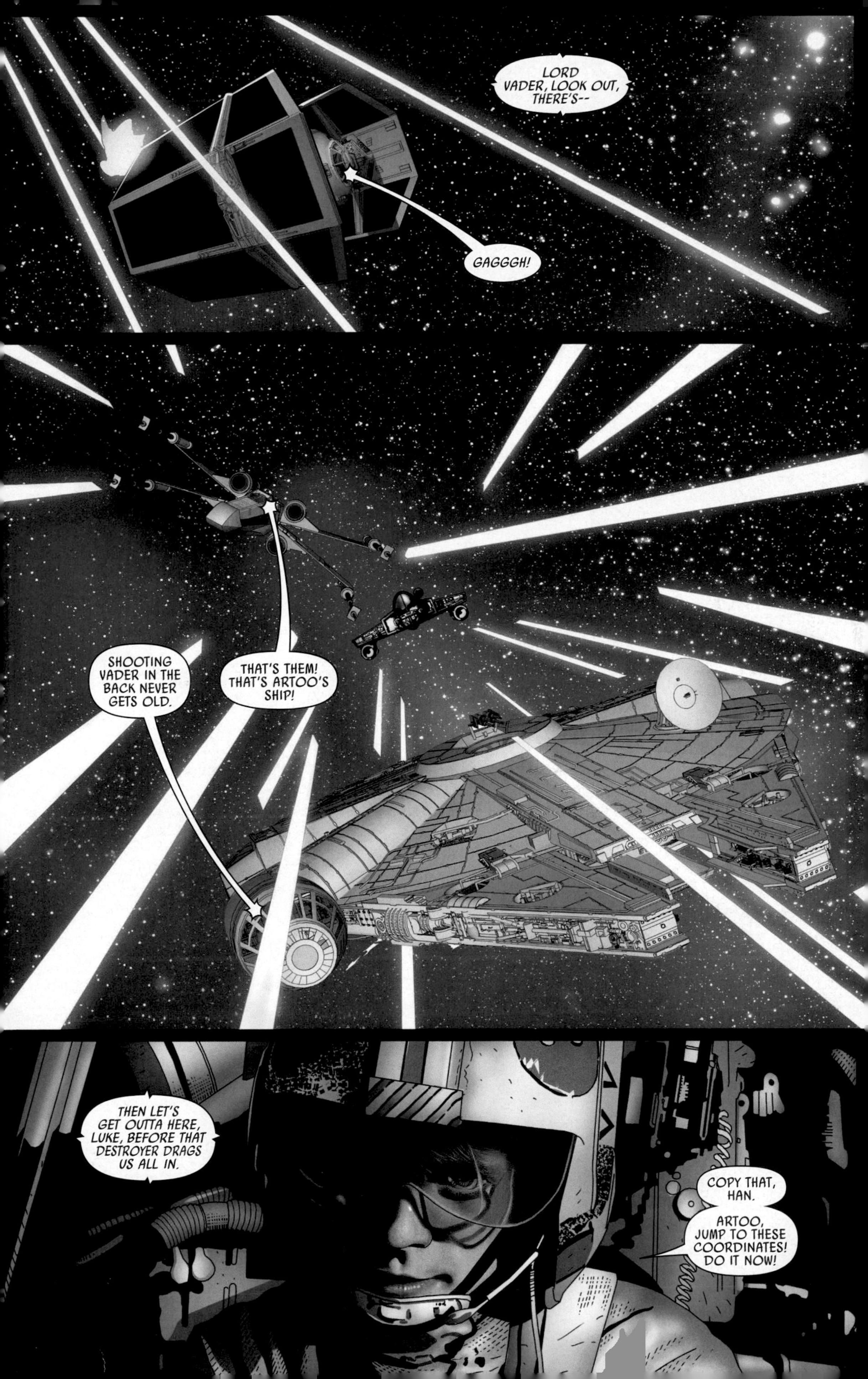
LORD VADER, LOOK OUT, THERE'S--
GAGGGH!
SHOOTING VADER IN THE BACK NEVER GETS OLD.
THAT'S THEM! THAT'S ARTOO'S SHIP!
THEN LET'S GET OUTTA HERE, LUKE, BEFORE THAT DESTROYER DRAGS US ALL IN.
COPY THAT, HAN.
ARTOO, JUMP TO THESE COORDINATES! DO IT NOW!

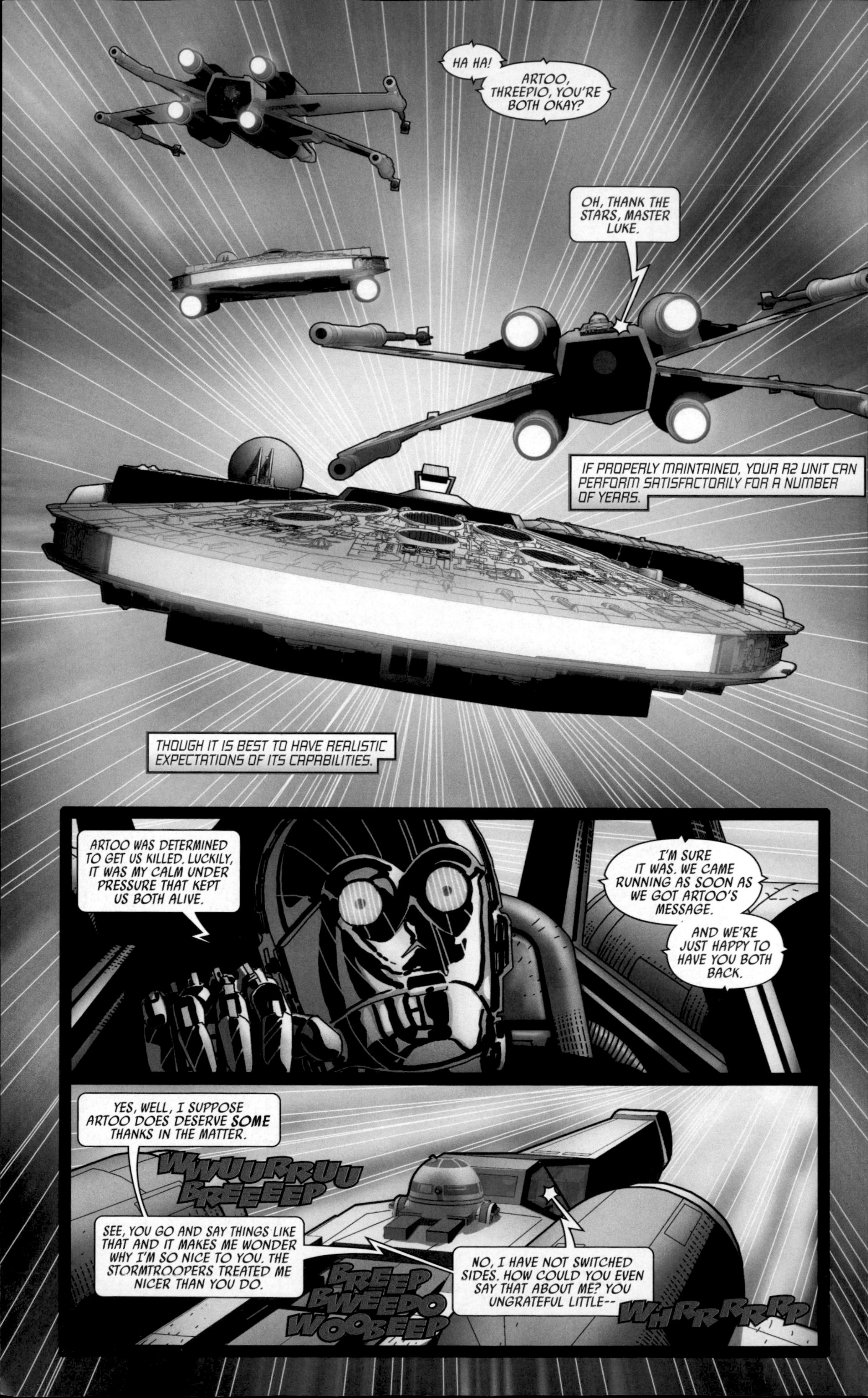
HA HA!
ARTOO, THREEPIO, YOU'RE BOTH OKAY?
OH, THANK THE STARS, MASTER LUKE.
IF PROPERLY MAINTAINED, YOUR R2 UNIT CAN PERFORM SATISFACTORILY FOR A NUMBER OF YEARS.
THOUGH IT IS BEST TO HAVE REALISTIC EXPECTATIONS OF ITS CAPABILITIES.
ARTOO WAS DETERMINED TO GET US KILLED. LUCKILY, IT WAS MY CALM UNDER PRESSURE THAT KEPT US BOTH ALIVE.
I'M SURE IT WAS. WE CAME RUNNING AS SOON AS WE GOT ARTOO'S MESSAGE.
AND WE'RE JUST HAPPY TO HAVE YOU BOTH BACK.
YES, WELL, I SUPPOSE ARTOO DOES DESERVE **SOME** THANKS IN THE MATTER.
WWUURRUU BREEEEP
SEE, YOU GO AND SAY THINGS LIKE THAT AND IT MAKES ME WONDER WHY I'M SO NICE TO YOU. THE STORMTROOPERS TREATED ME NICER THAN YOU DO.
BREEP BWEEDO WOOBEEP
NO, I HAVE NOT SWITCHED SIDES. HOW COULD YOU EVEN SAY THAT ABOUT ME? YOU UNGRATEFUL LITTLE--
WHRRRRRP

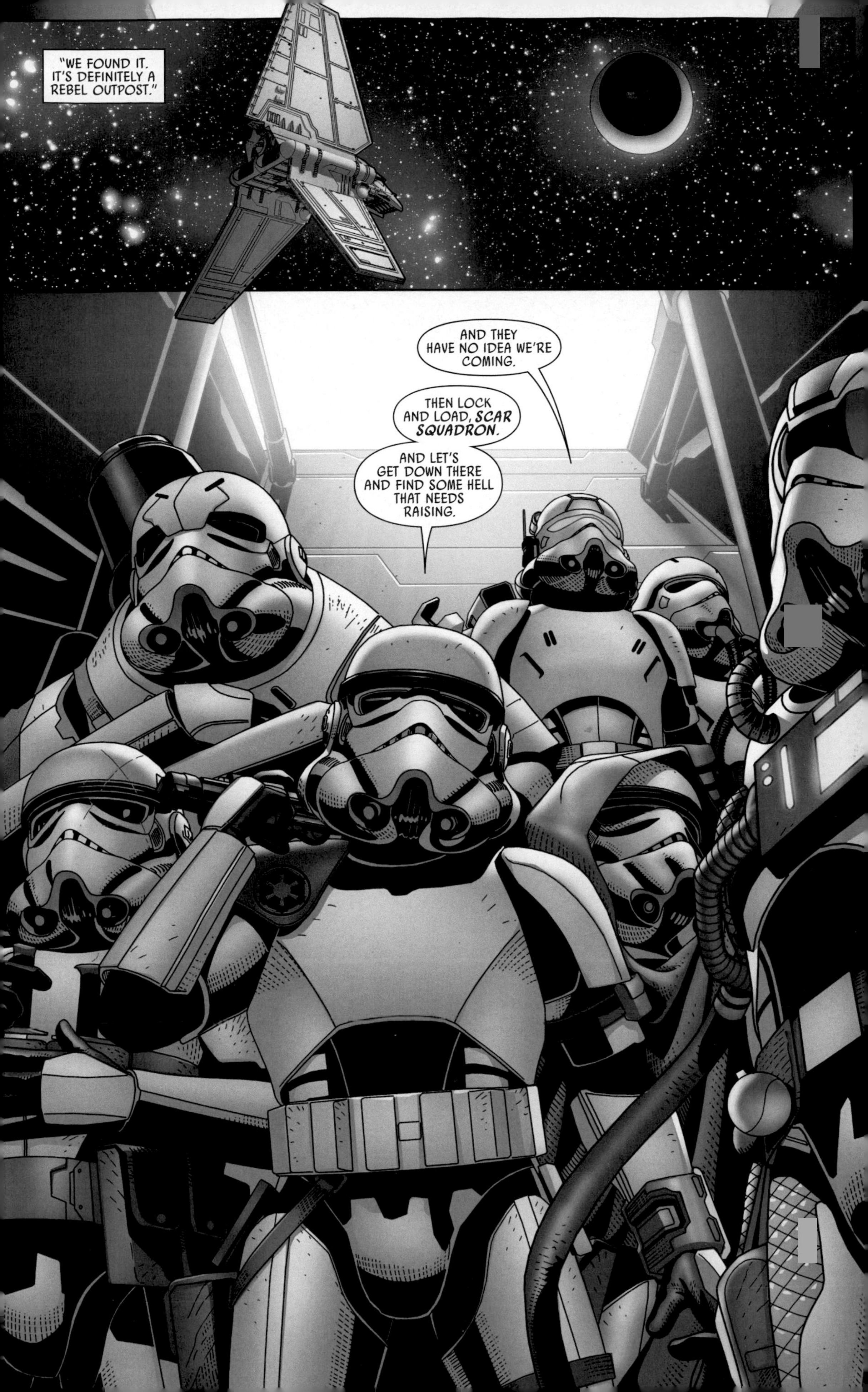
"WE FOUND IT. IT'S DEFINITELY A REBEL OUTPOST."
AND THEY HAVE NO IDEA WE'RE COMING.
THEN LOCK AND LOAD, SCAR SQUADRON.
AND LET'S GET DOWN THERE AND FIND SOME HELL THAT NEEDS RAISING.

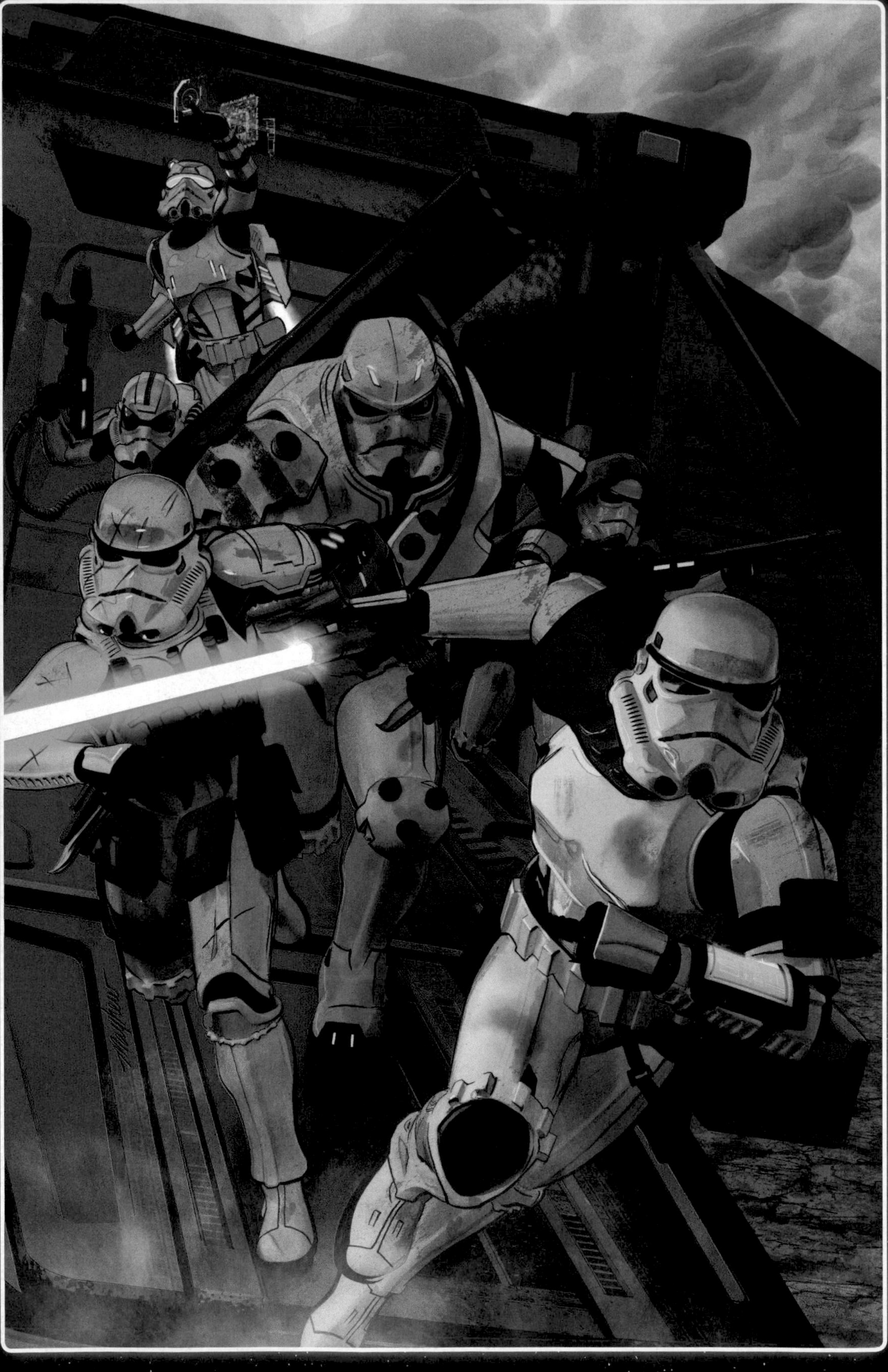

IMPERIAL PRIDE

It is a crucial time for the Empire. Rebel forces are proliferating across the galaxy, and their elimination is imperative for Imperial reign.

For a mission this vital, the right team is essential – an elite group of stormtroopers, handpicked for their skills, loyalty to the Empire, and complete dedication to destroying the Rebellion.

Leading this team is the ruthless Sergeant Kreel – a man who answers directly to Darth Vader. Rebel heroes Luke Skywalker, Princess Leia, and Han Solo have evaded SCAR Squadron before, but they have not seen the last of the Empire's wrath....

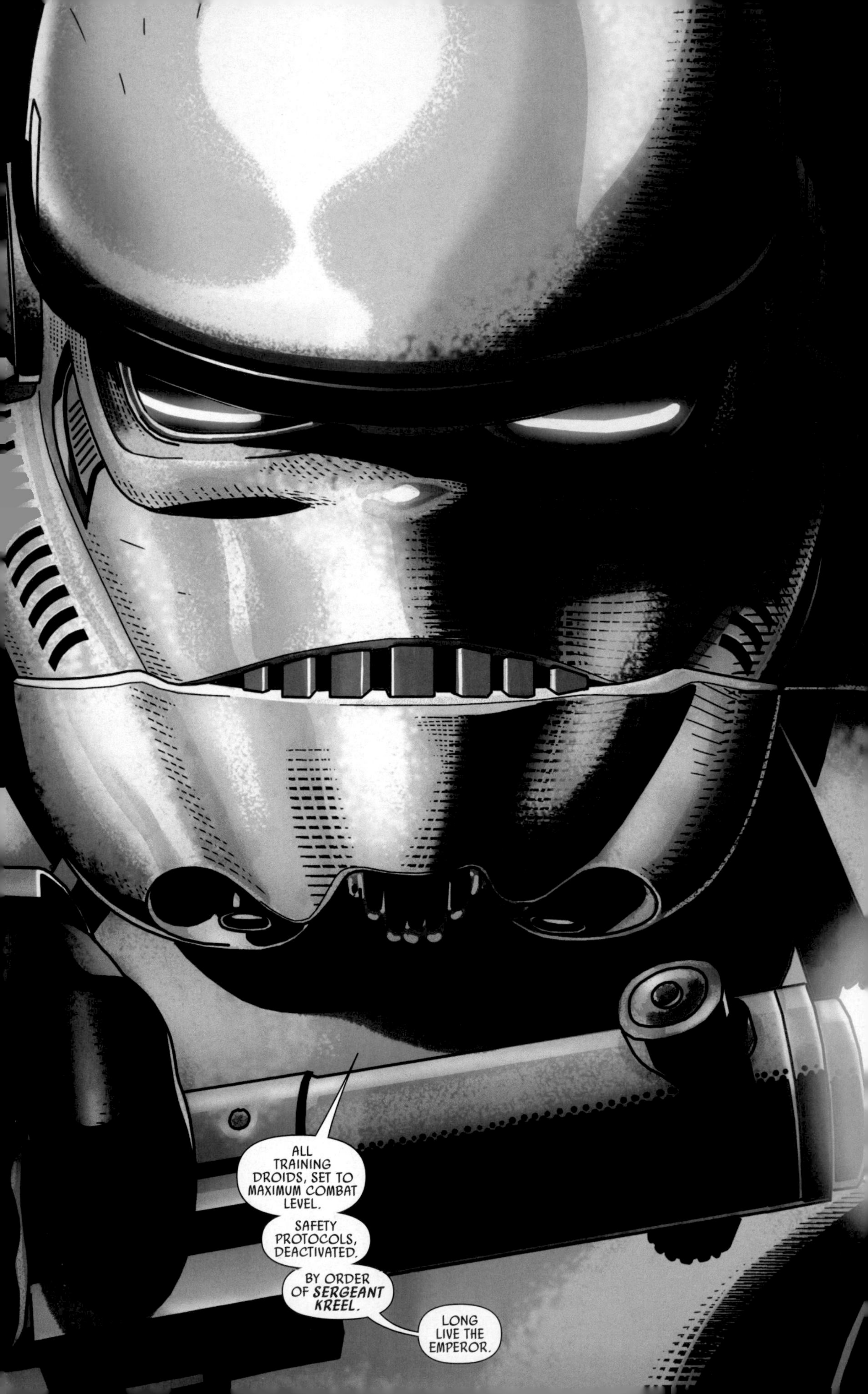
ALL TRAINING DROIDS, SET TO MAXIMUM COMBAT LEVEL.
SAFETY PROTOCOLS, DEACTIVATED.
BY ORDER OF SERGEANT KREEL.
LONG LIVE THE EMPEROR.

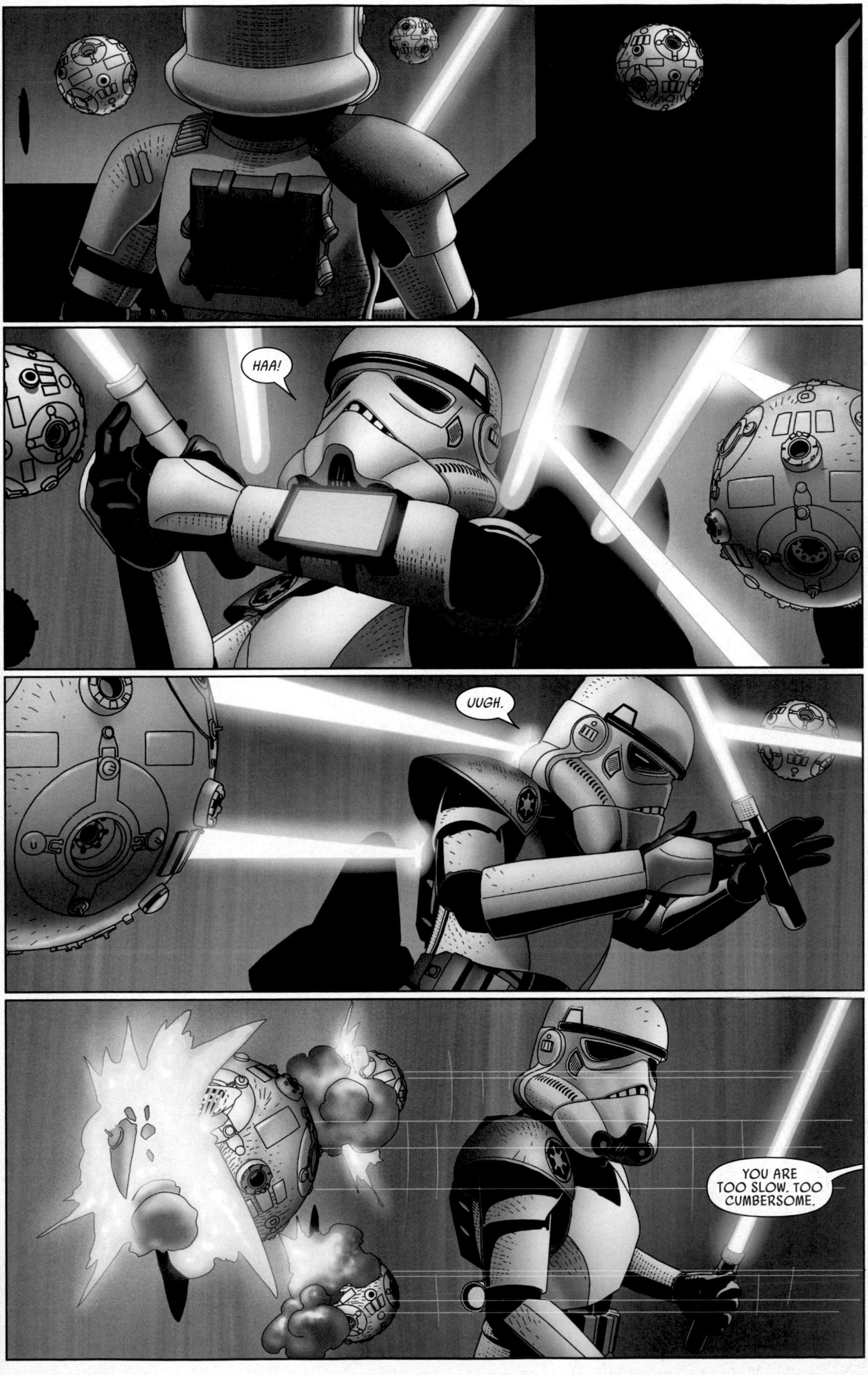
HAA!
UUGH.
YOU ARE TOO SLOW. TOO CUMBERSOME.

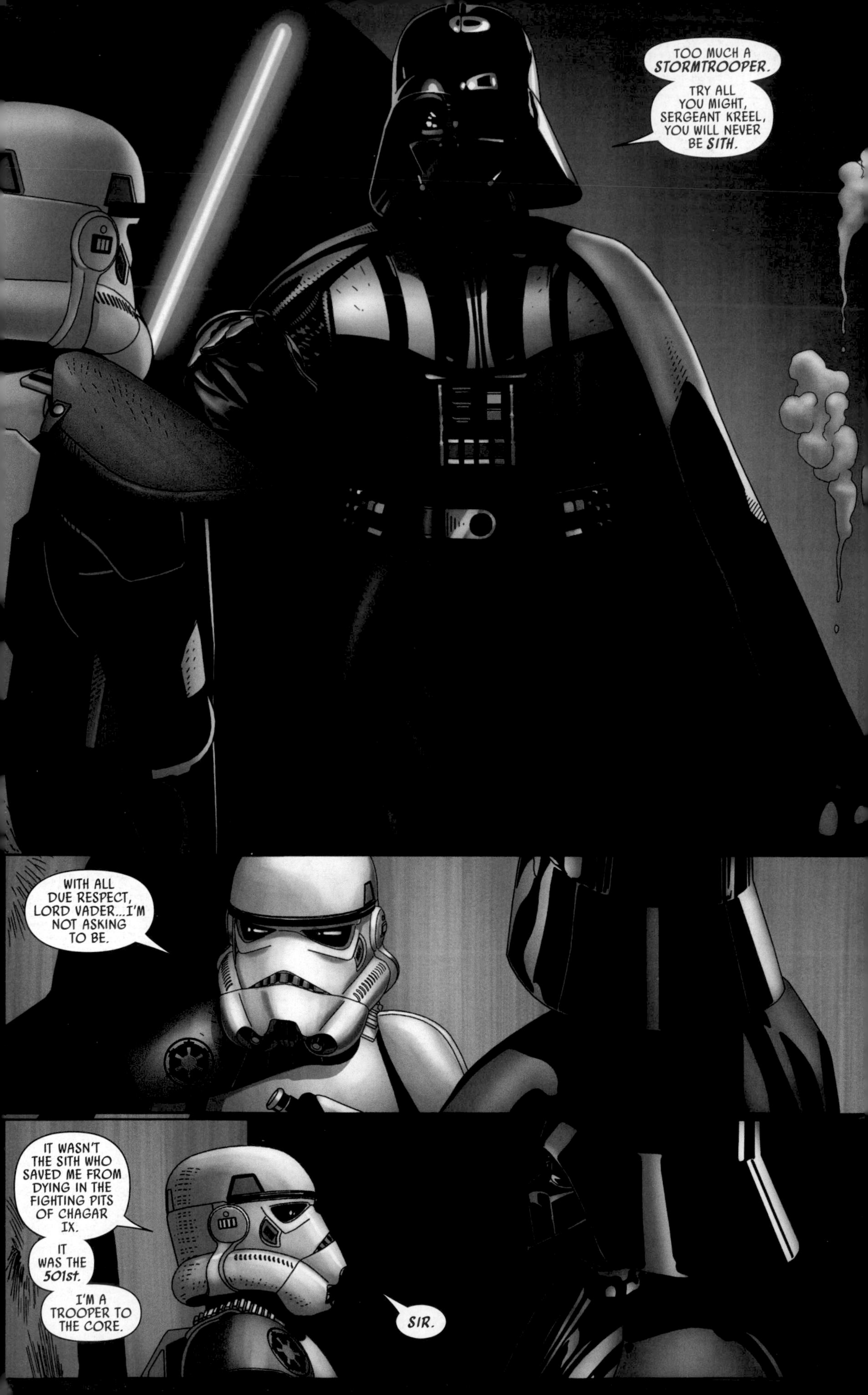
TOO MUCH A STORMTROOPER.
TRY ALL YOU MIGHT, SERGEANT KREEL, YOU WILL NEVER BE SITH.
WITH ALL DUE RESPECT, LORD VADER...I'M NOT ASKING TO BE.
IT WASN'T THE SITH WHO SAVED ME FROM DYING IN THE FIGHTING PITS OF CHAGAR IX.
IT WAS THE 501st.
I'M A TROOPER TO THE CORE.
SIR.

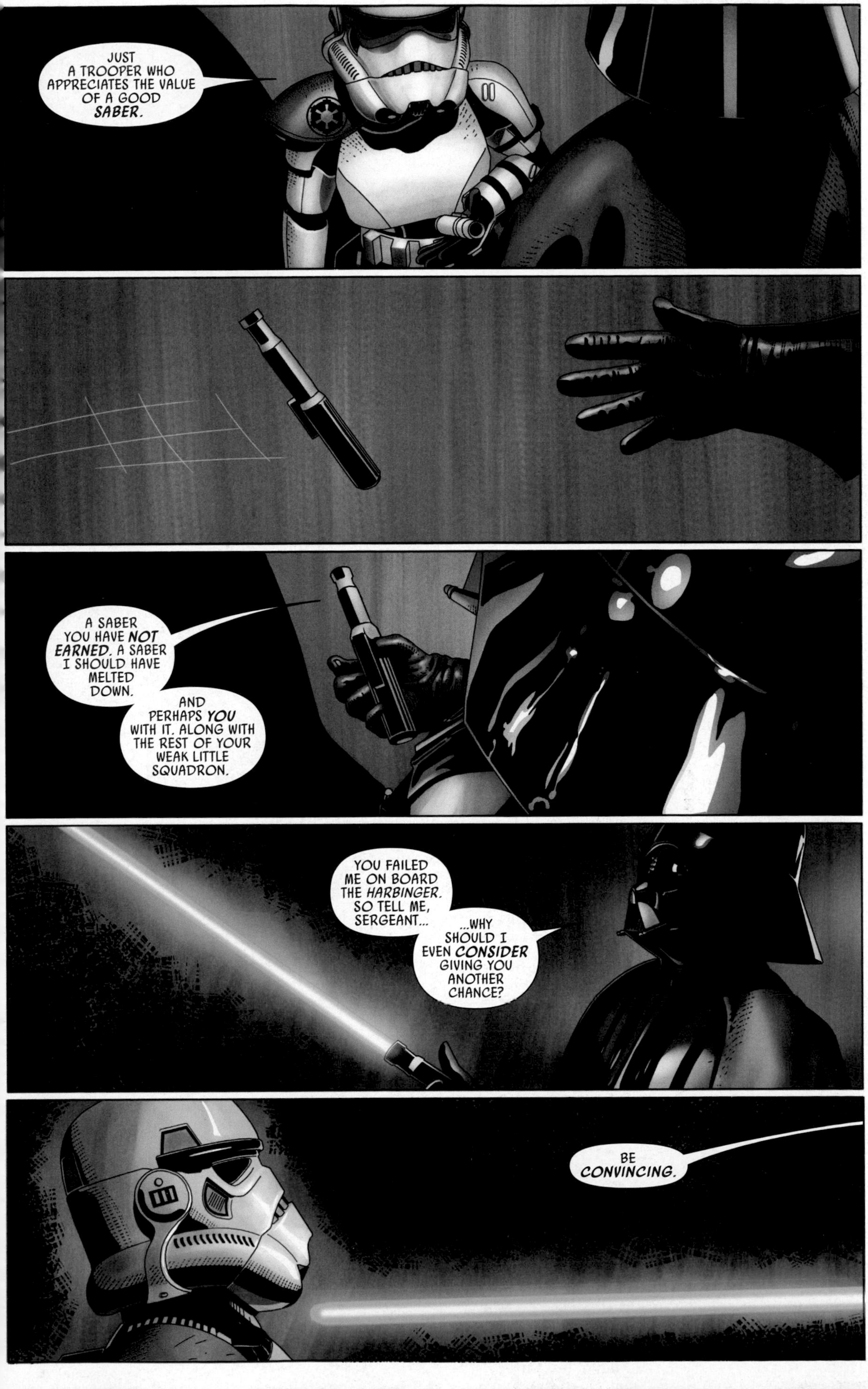
JUST A TROOPER WHO APPRECIATES THE VALUE OF A GOOD SABER.
A SABER YOU HAVE NOT EARNED. A SABER I SHOULD HAVE MELTED DOWN.
AND PERHAPS YOU WITH IT. ALONG WITH THE REST OF YOUR WEAK LITTLE SQUADRON.
YOU FAILED ME ON BOARD THE HARBINGER. SO TELL ME, SERGEANT...
...WHY SHOULD I EVEN CONSIDER GIVING YOU ANOTHER CHANCE?
BE CONVINCING.

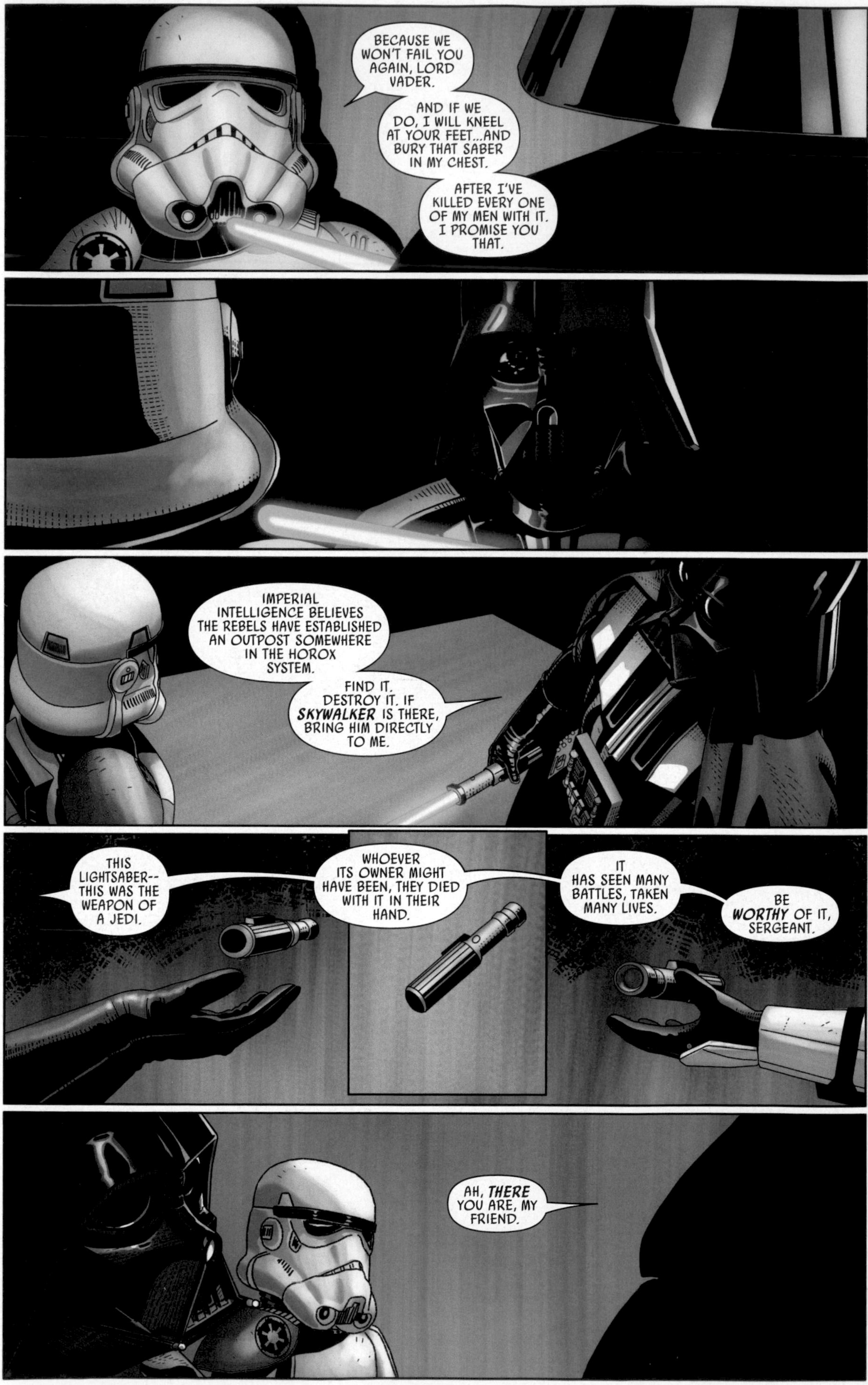

BECAUSE WE WON'T FAIL YOU AGAIN, LORD VADER.
AND IF WE DO, I WILL KNEEL AT YOUR FEET...AND BURY THAT SABER IN MY CHEST.
AFTER I'VE KILLED EVERY ONE OF MY MEN WITH IT. I PROMISE YOU THAT.
IMPERIAL INTELLIGENCE BELIEVES THE REBELS HAVE ESTABLISHED AN OUTPOST SOMEWHERE IN THE HOROX SYSTEM.
FIND IT. DESTROY IT. IF *SKYWALKER* IS THERE, BRING HIM DIRECTLY TO ME.
THIS LIGHTSABER--THIS WAS THE WEAPON OF A JEDI.
WHOEVER ITS OWNER MIGHT HAVE BEEN, THEY DIED WITH IT IN THEIR HAND.
IT HAS SEEN MANY BATTLES, TAKEN MANY LIVES.
BE *WORTHY* OF IT, SERGEANT.
AH, *THERE* YOU ARE, MY FRIEND.

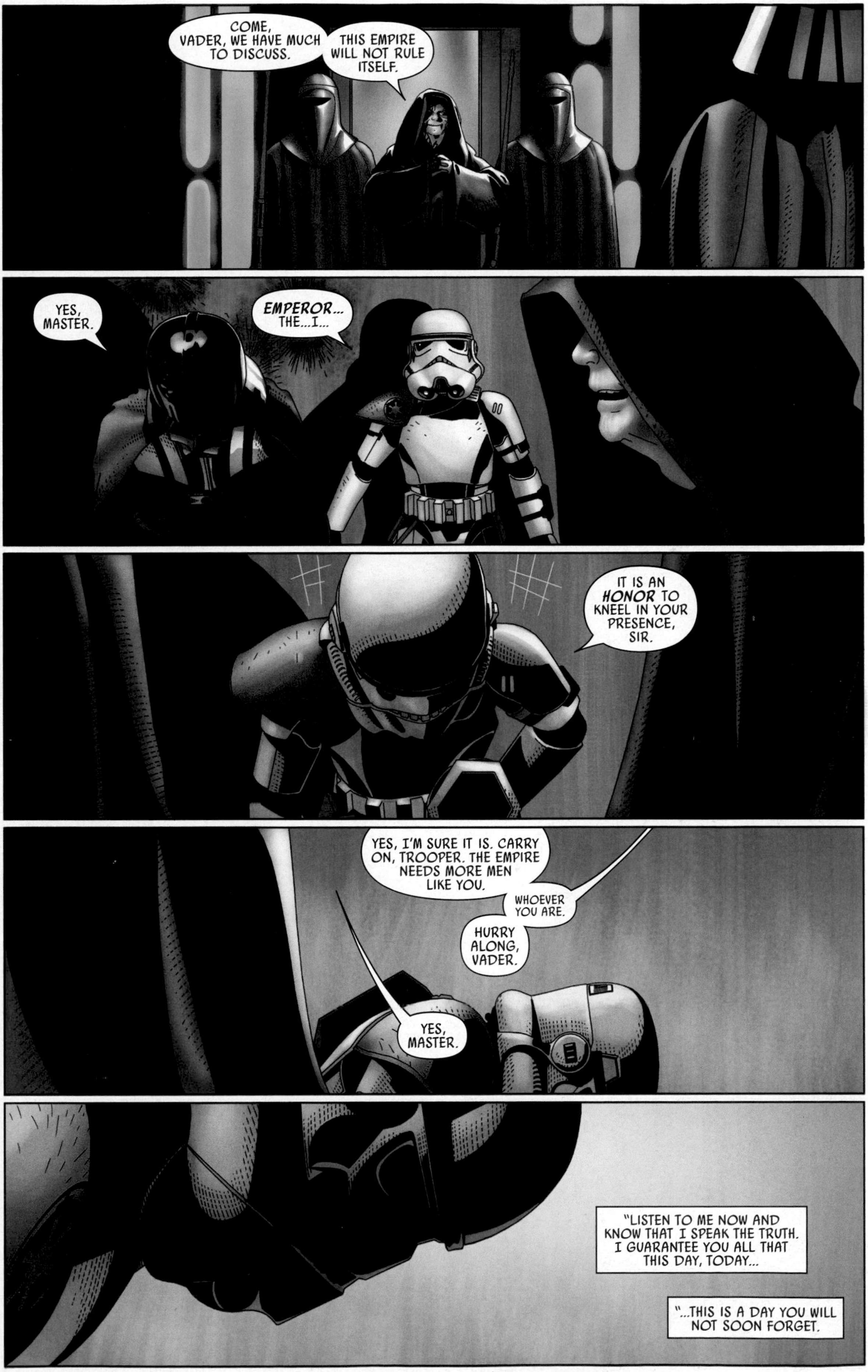
COME, VADER, WE HAVE MUCH TO DISCUSS.
THIS EMPIRE WILL NOT RULE ITSELF.
YES, MASTER.
EMPEROR... THE...I...
IT IS AN HONOR TO KNEEL IN YOUR PRESENCE, SIR.
YES, I'M SURE IT IS. CARRY ON, TROOPER. THE EMPIRE NEEDS MORE MEN LIKE YOU.
WHOEVER YOU ARE.
HURRY ALONG, VADER.
YES, MASTER.
"LISTEN TO ME NOW AND KNOW THAT I SPEAK THE TRUTH. I GUARANTEE YOU ALL THAT THIS DAY, TODAY...
"...THIS IS A DAY YOU WILL NOT SOON FORGET.

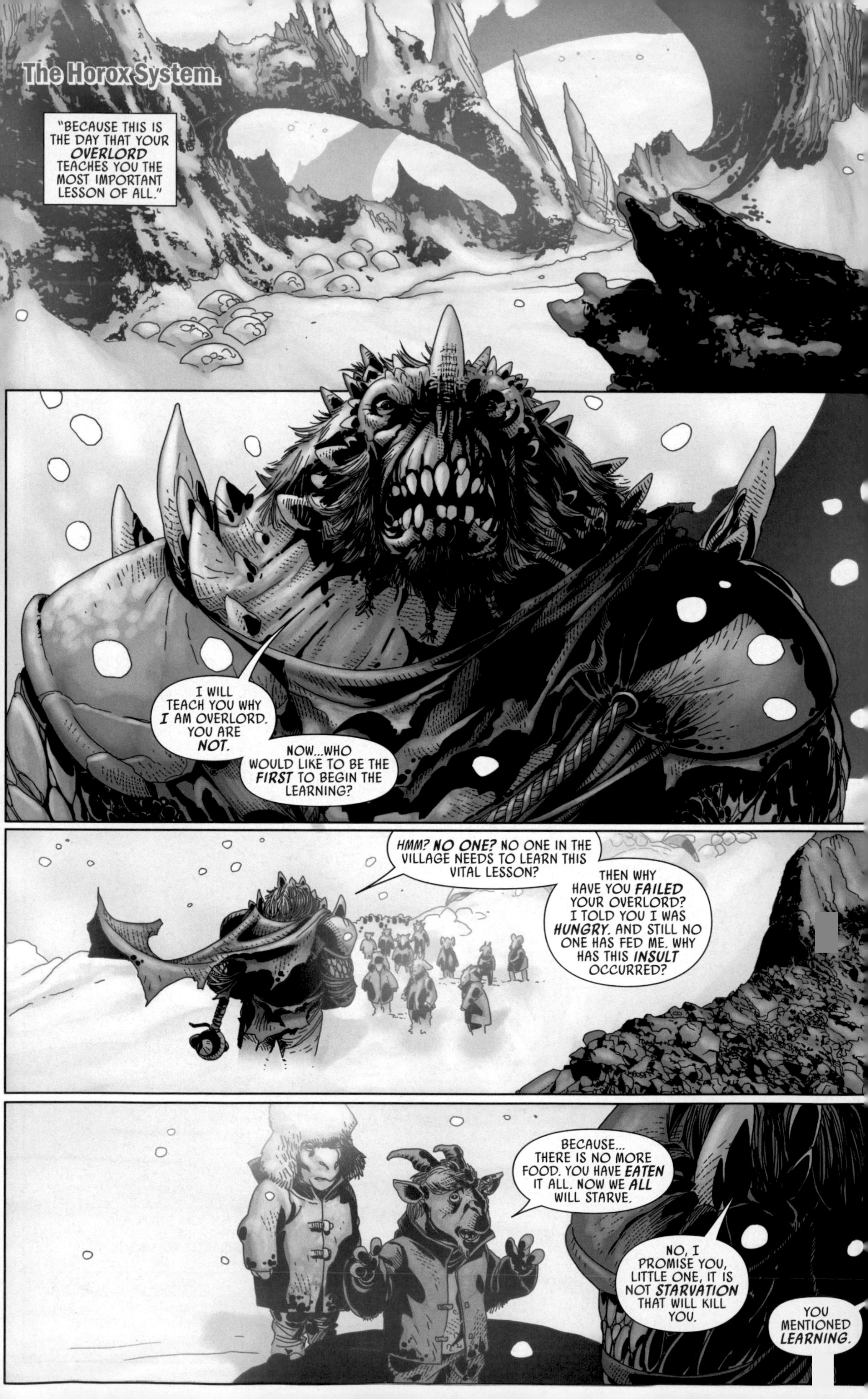
The Horox System.
"BECAUSE THIS IS THE DAY THAT YOUR OVERLORD TEACHES YOU THE MOST IMPORTANT LESSON OF ALL."
I WILL TEACH YOU WHY I AM OVERLORD. YOU ARE NOT.
NOW...WHO WOULD LIKE TO BE THE FIRST TO BEGIN THE LEARNING?
HMM? NO ONE? NO ONE IN THE VILLAGE NEEDS TO LEARN THIS VITAL LESSON?
THEN WHY HAVE YOU FAILED YOUR OVERLORD? I TOLD YOU I WAS HUNGRY. AND STILL NO ONE HAS FED ME. WHY HAS THIS INSULT OCCURRED?
BECAUSE... THERE IS NO MORE FOOD. YOU HAVE EATEN IT ALL. NOW WE ALL WILL STARVE.
NO, I PROMISE YOU, LITTLE ONE, IT IS NOT STARVATION THAT WILL KILL YOU.
YOU MENTIONED LEARNING.

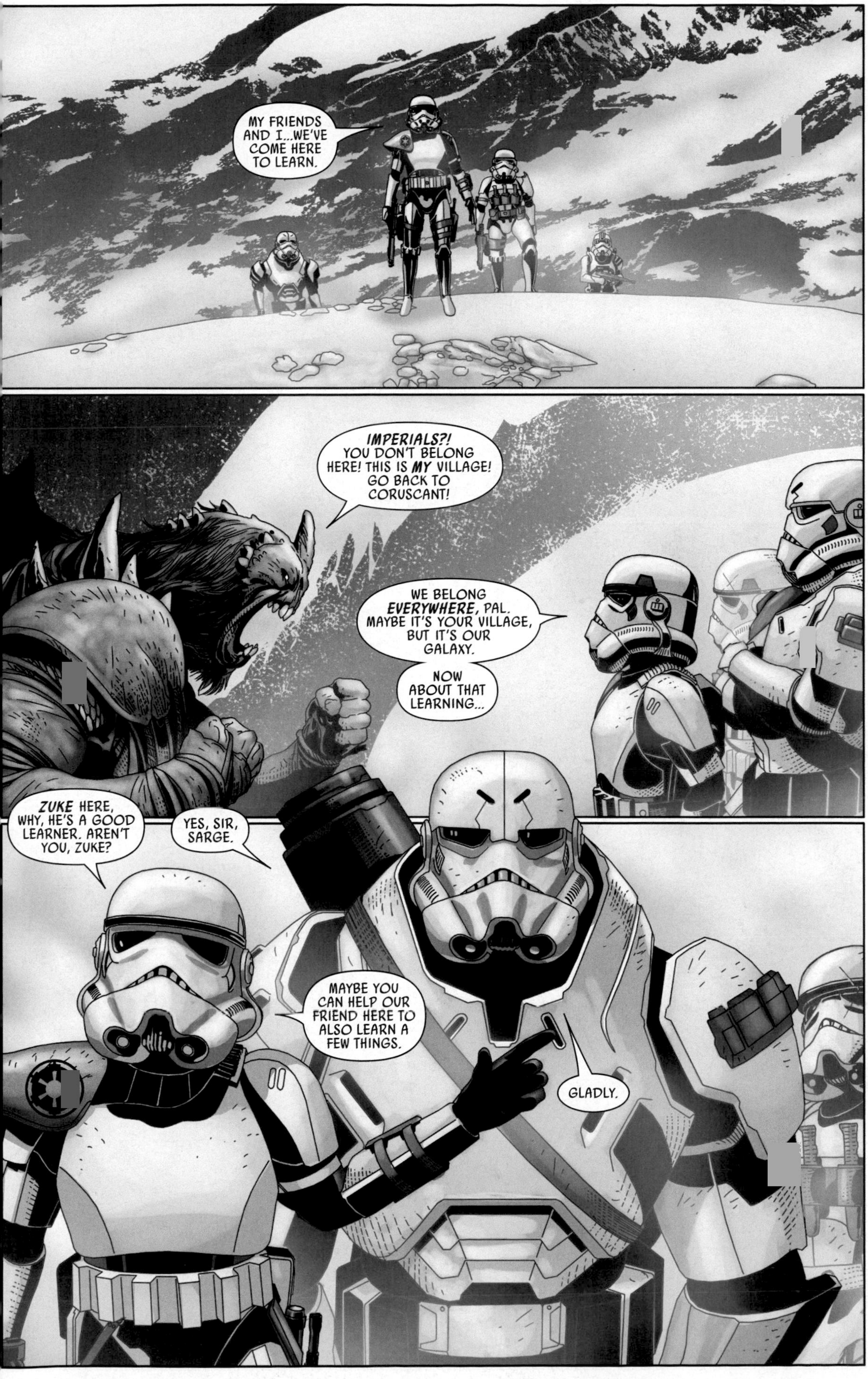
MY FRIENDS AND I...WE'VE COME HERE TO LEARN.
IMPERIALS?! YOU DON'T BELONG HERE! THIS IS MY VILLAGE! GO BACK TO CORUSCANT!
WE BELONG EVERYWHERE, PAL. MAYBE IT'S YOUR VILLAGE, BUT IT'S OUR GALAXY.
NOW ABOUT THAT LEARNING...
ZUKE HERE, WHY, HE'S A GOOD LEARNER. AREN'T YOU, ZUKE?
YES, SIR, SARGE.
MAYBE YOU CAN HELP OUR FRIEND HERE TO ALSO LEARN A FEW THINGS.
GLADLY.

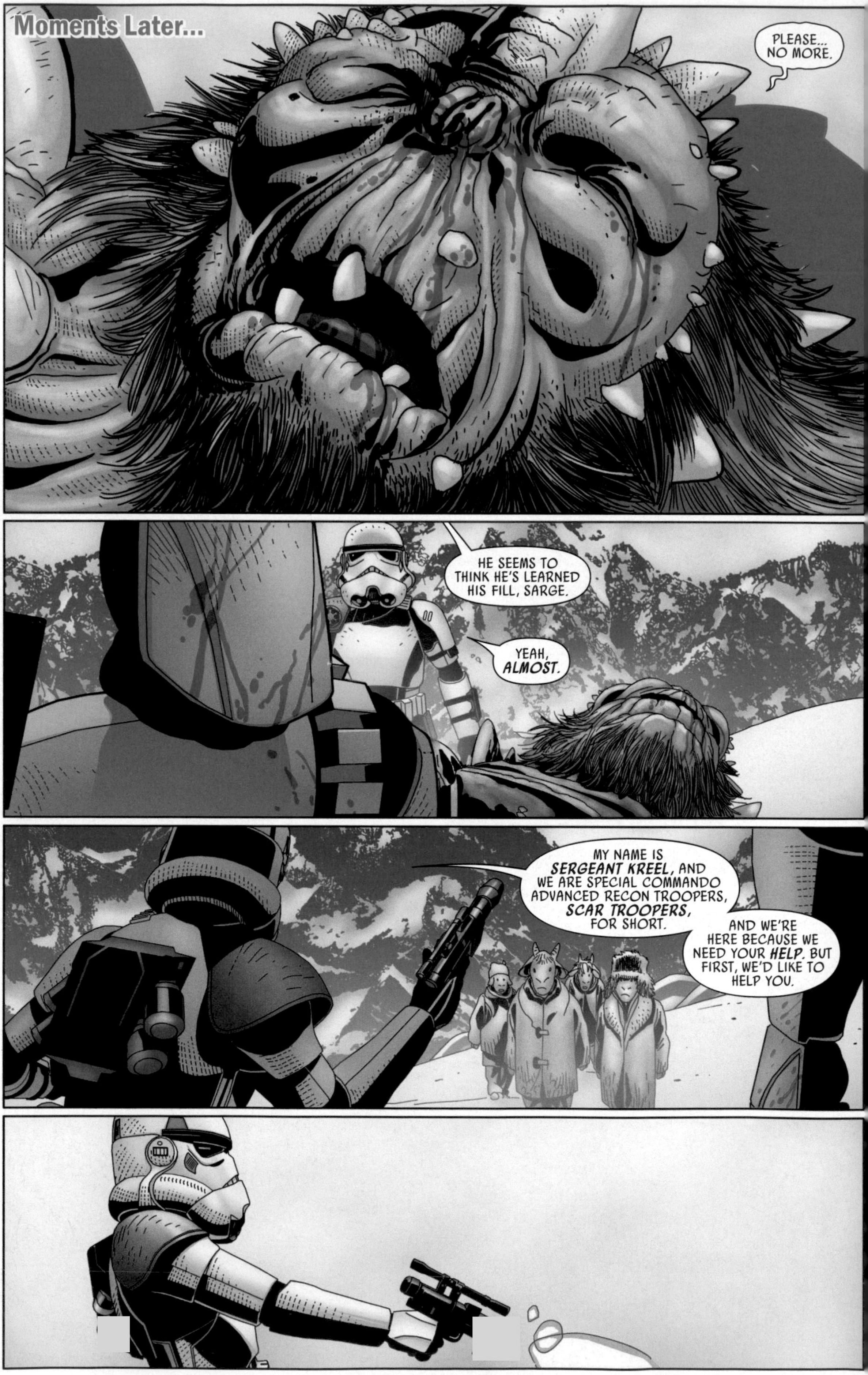

Moments Later...
PLEASE... NO MORE.
HE SEEMS TO THINK HE'S LEARNED HIS FILL, SARGE.
YEAH, ALMOST.
MY NAME IS SERGEANT KREEL, AND WE ARE SPECIAL COMMANDO ADVANCED RECON TROOPERS, SCAR TROOPERS, FOR SHORT.
AND WE'RE HERE BECAUSE WE NEED YOUR HELP. BUT FIRST, WE'D LIKE TO HELP YOU.

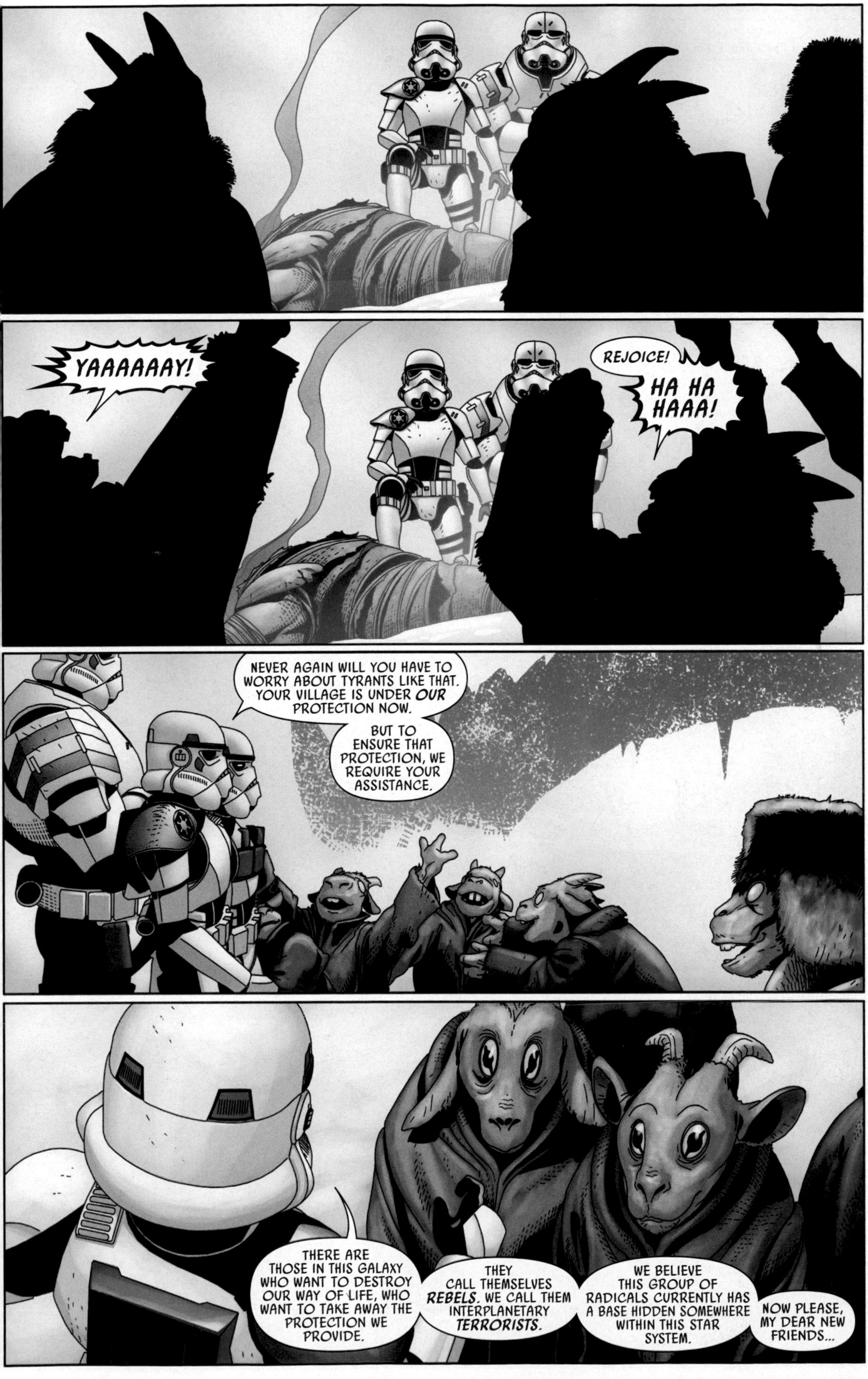
YAAAAAAY!
REJOICE!
HA HA HAAA!
NEVER AGAIN WILL YOU HAVE TO WORRY ABOUT TYRANTS LIKE THAT. YOUR VILLAGE IS UNDER *OUR* PROTECTION NOW.
BUT TO ENSURE THAT PROTECTION, WE REQUIRE YOUR ASSISTANCE.
THERE ARE THOSE IN THIS GALAXY WHO WANT TO DESTROY OUR WAY OF LIFE, WHO WANT TO TAKE AWAY THE PROTECTION WE PROVIDE.
THEY CALL THEMSELVES *REBELS*. WE CALL THEM INTERPLANETARY *TERRORISTS*.
WE BELIEVE THIS GROUP OF RADICALS CURRENTLY HAS A BASE HIDDEN SOMEWHERE WITHIN THIS STAR SYSTEM.
NOW PLEASE, MY DEAR NEW FRIENDS...

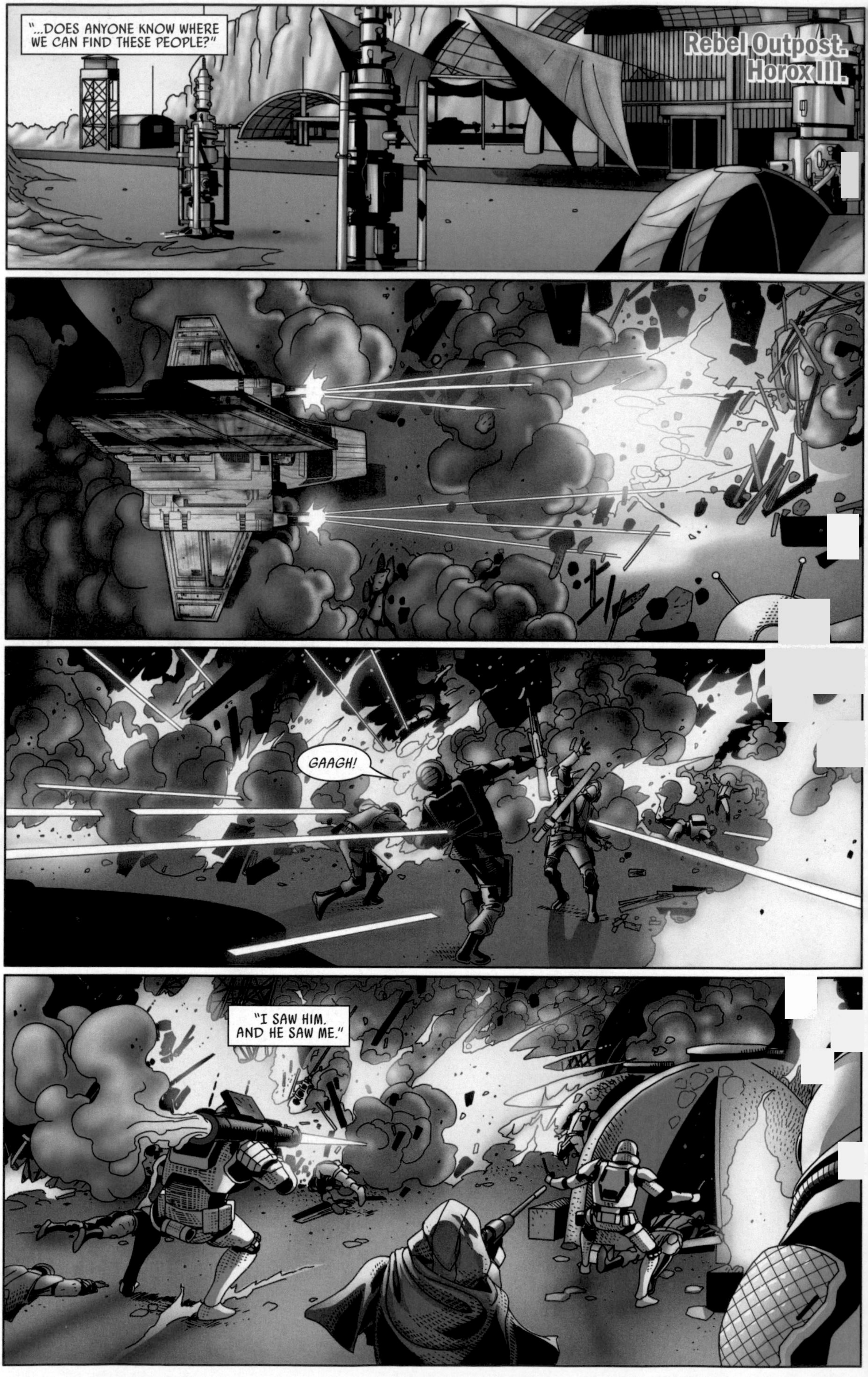
"...DOES ANYONE KNOW WHERE WE CAN FIND THESE PEOPLE?"
Rebel Outpost. Horox III.
GAAGH!
"I SAW HIM. AND HE SAW ME."

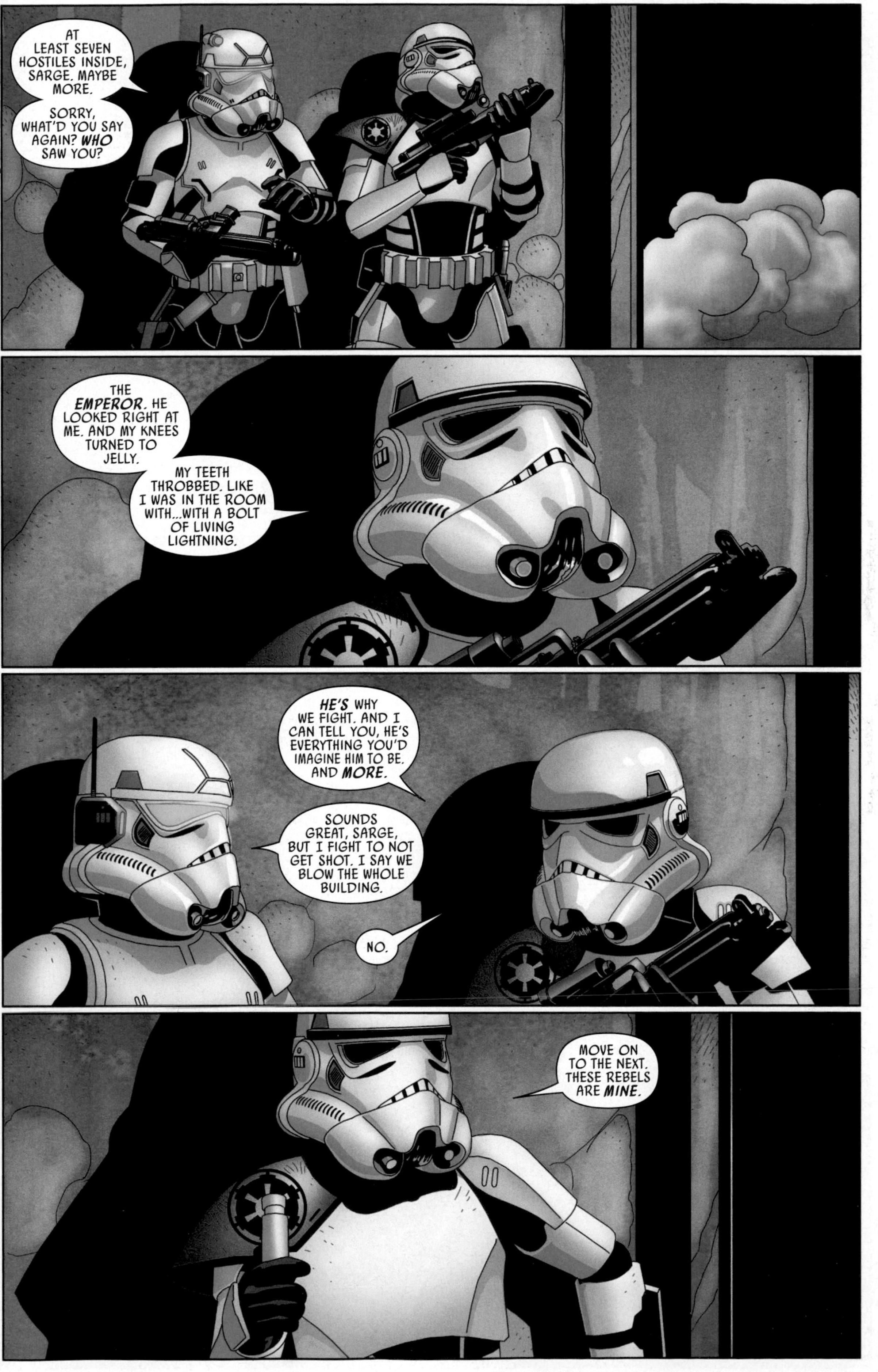
AT LEAST SEVEN HOSTILES INSIDE, SARGE. MAYBE MORE.
SORRY, WHAT'D YOU SAY AGAIN? WHO SAW YOU?
THE EMPEROR. HE LOOKED RIGHT AT ME. AND MY KNEES TURNED TO JELLY.
MY TEETH THROBBED. LIKE I WAS IN THE ROOM WITH...WITH A BOLT OF LIVING LIGHTNING.
HE'S WHY WE FIGHT. AND I CAN TELL YOU, HE'S EVERYTHING YOU'D IMAGINE HIM TO BE. AND MORE.
SOUNDS GREAT, SARGE, BUT I FIGHT TO NOT GET SHOT. I SAY WE BLOW THE WHOLE BUILDING.
NO.
MOVE ON TO THE NEXT. THESE REBELS ARE MINE.

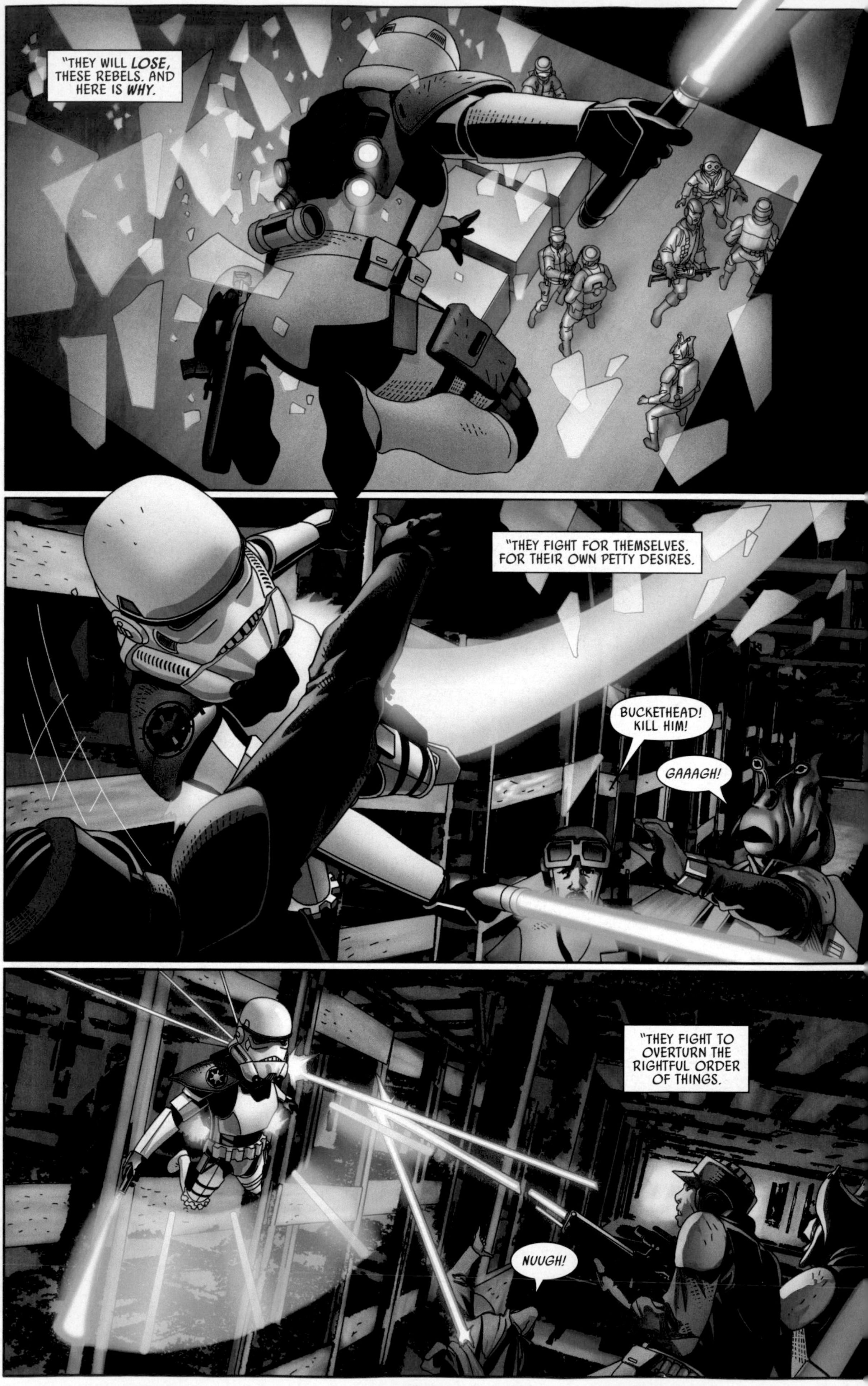
"THEY WILL *LOSE*, THESE REBELS. AND HERE IS *WHY*.
"THEY FIGHT FOR THEMSELVES. FOR THEIR OWN PETTY DESIRES.
BUCKETHEAD! KILL HIM!
GAAAGH!
"THEY FIGHT TO OVERTURN THE RIGHTFUL ORDER OF THINGS.
NUUGH!

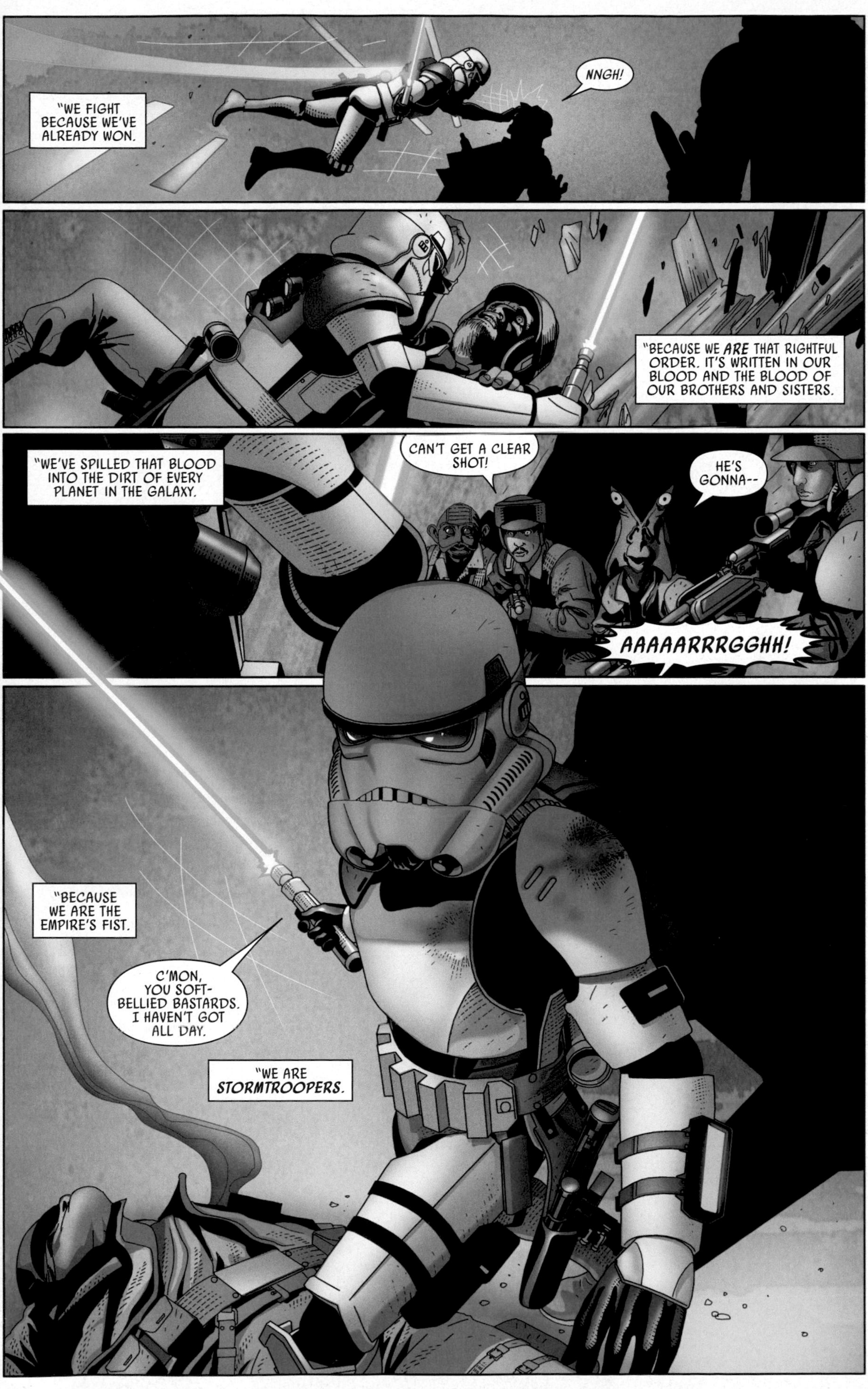
"WE FIGHT BECAUSE WE'VE ALREADY WON.
NNGH!
"BECAUSE WE ARE THAT RIGHTFUL ORDER. IT'S WRITTEN IN OUR BLOOD AND THE BLOOD OF OUR BROTHERS AND SISTERS.
"WE'VE SPILLED THAT BLOOD INTO THE DIRT OF EVERY PLANET IN THE GALAXY.
CAN'T GET A CLEAR SHOT!
HE'S GONNA--
AAAAARRRGGHH!
"BECAUSE WE ARE THE EMPIRE'S FIST.
C'MON, YOU SOFT-BELLIED BASTARDS. I HAVEN'T GOT ALL DAY.
"WE ARE STORMTROOPERS.

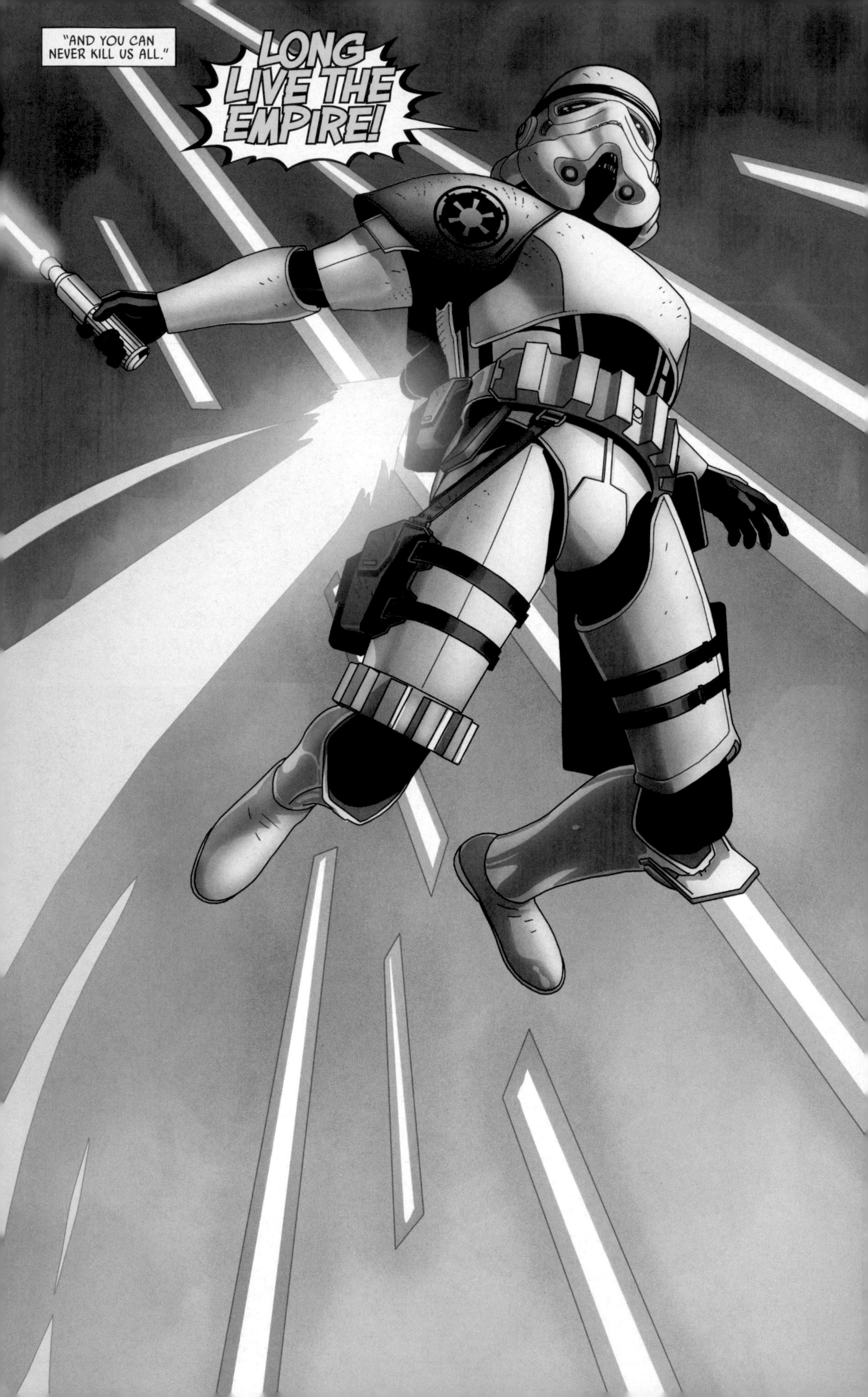
"AND YOU CAN NEVER KILL US ALL."
LONG LIVE THE EMPIRE!

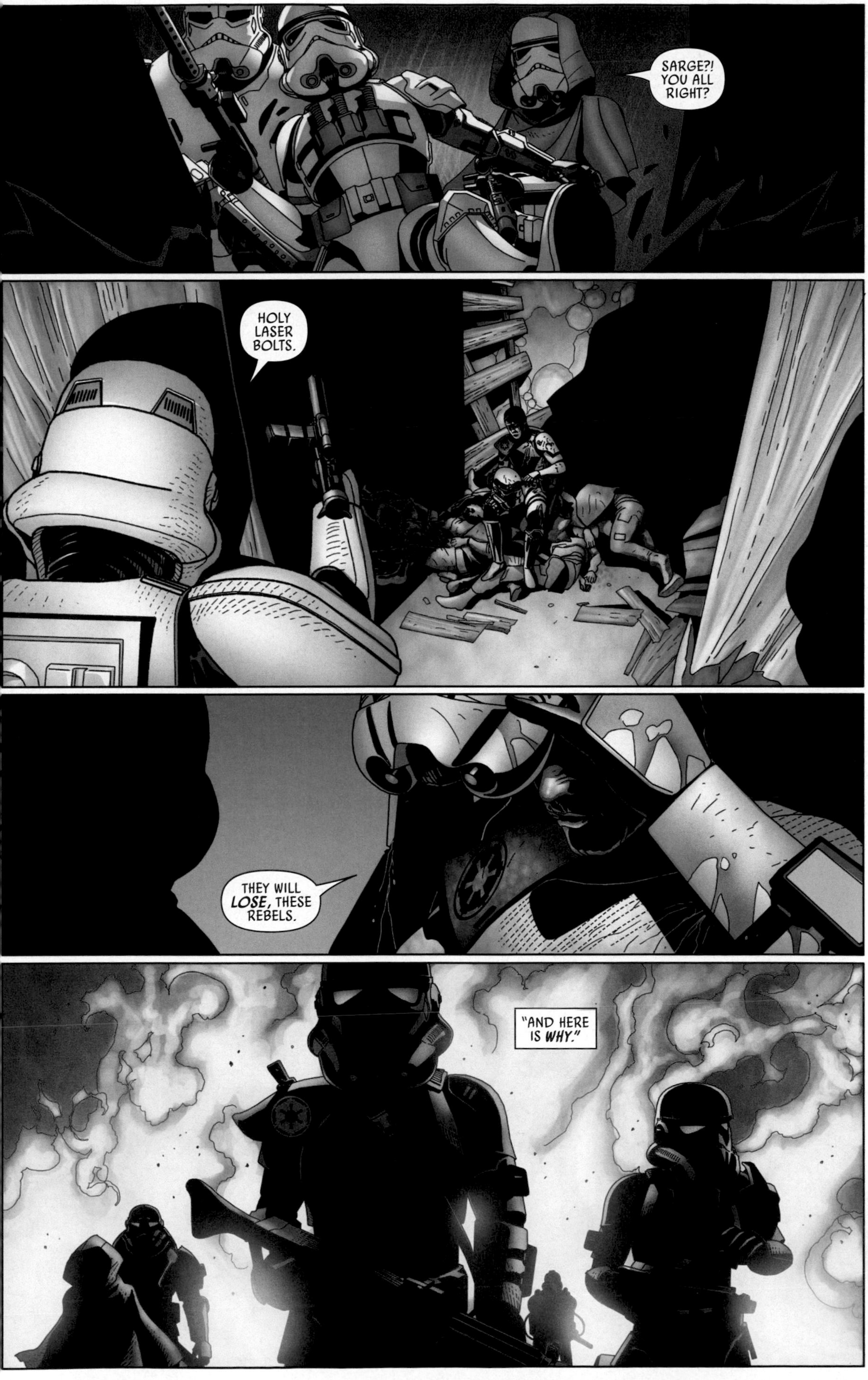
SARGE?! YOU ALL RIGHT?
HOLY LASER BOLTS.
THEY WILL LOSE, THESE REBELS.
"AND HERE IS WHY."

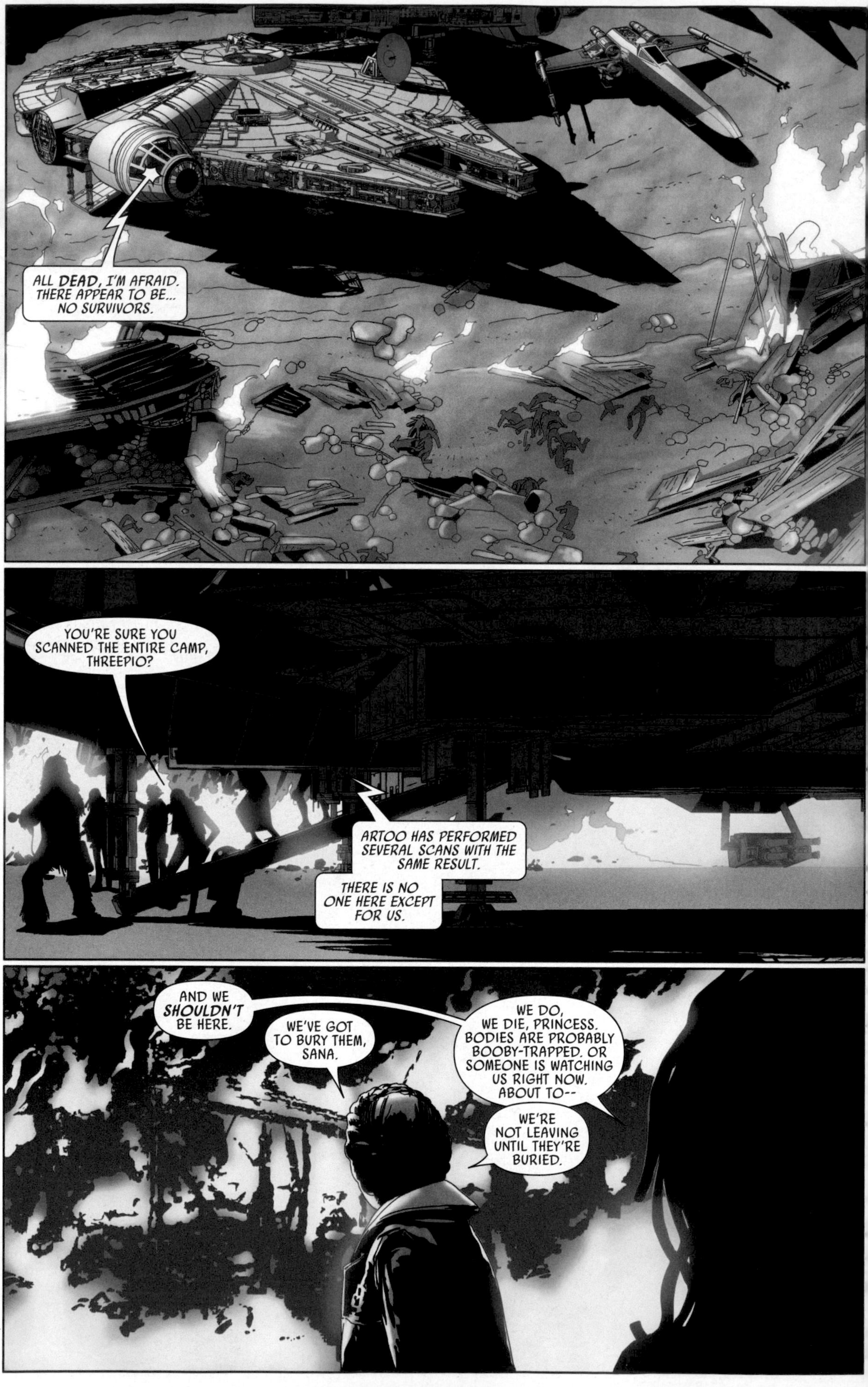
ALL DEAD, I'M AFRAID. THERE APPEAR TO BE... NO SURVIVORS.
YOU'RE SURE YOU SCANNED THE ENTIRE CAMP, THREEPIO?
ARTOO HAS PERFORMED SEVERAL SCANS WITH THE SAME RESULT.
THERE IS NO ONE HERE EXCEPT FOR US.
WE'VE GOT TO BURY THEM, SANA.
WE DO, WE DIE, PRINCESS. BODIES ARE PROBABLY BOOBY-TRAPPED. OR SOMEONE IS WATCHING US RIGHT NOW. ABOUT TO--
AND WE SHOULDN'T BE HERE.
WE'RE NOT LEAVING UNTIL THEY'RE BURIED.

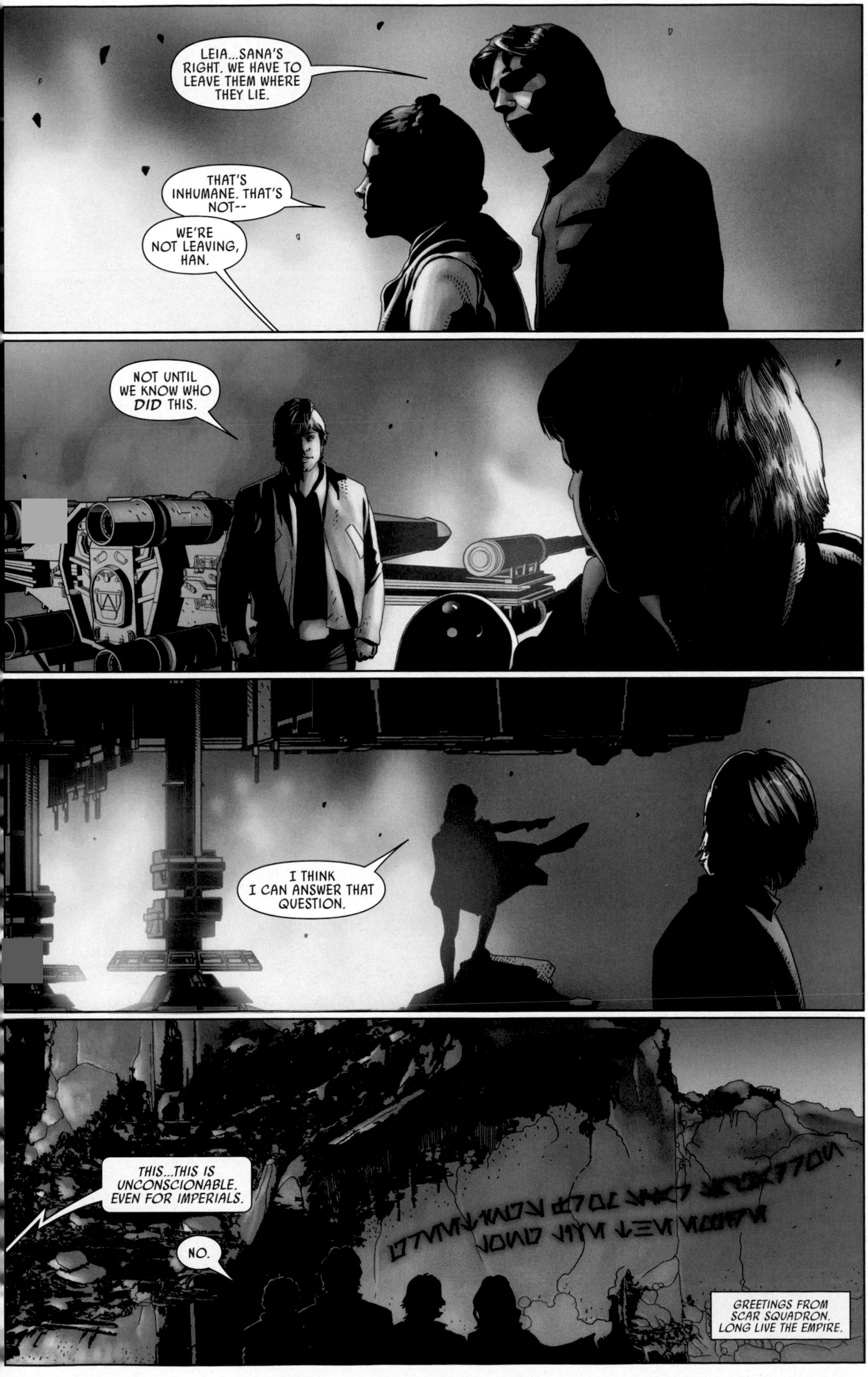

LEIA...SANA'S RIGHT. WE HAVE TO LEAVE THEM WHERE THEY LIE.
THAT'S INHUMANE. THAT'S NOT--
WE'RE NOT LEAVING, HAN.
NOT UNTIL WE KNOW WHO *DID* THIS.
I THINK I CAN ANSWER THAT QUESTION.
THIS...THIS IS UNCONSCIONABLE. EVEN FOR IMPERIALS.
NO.
GREETINGS FROM SCAR SQUADRON. LONG LIVE THE EMPIRE.

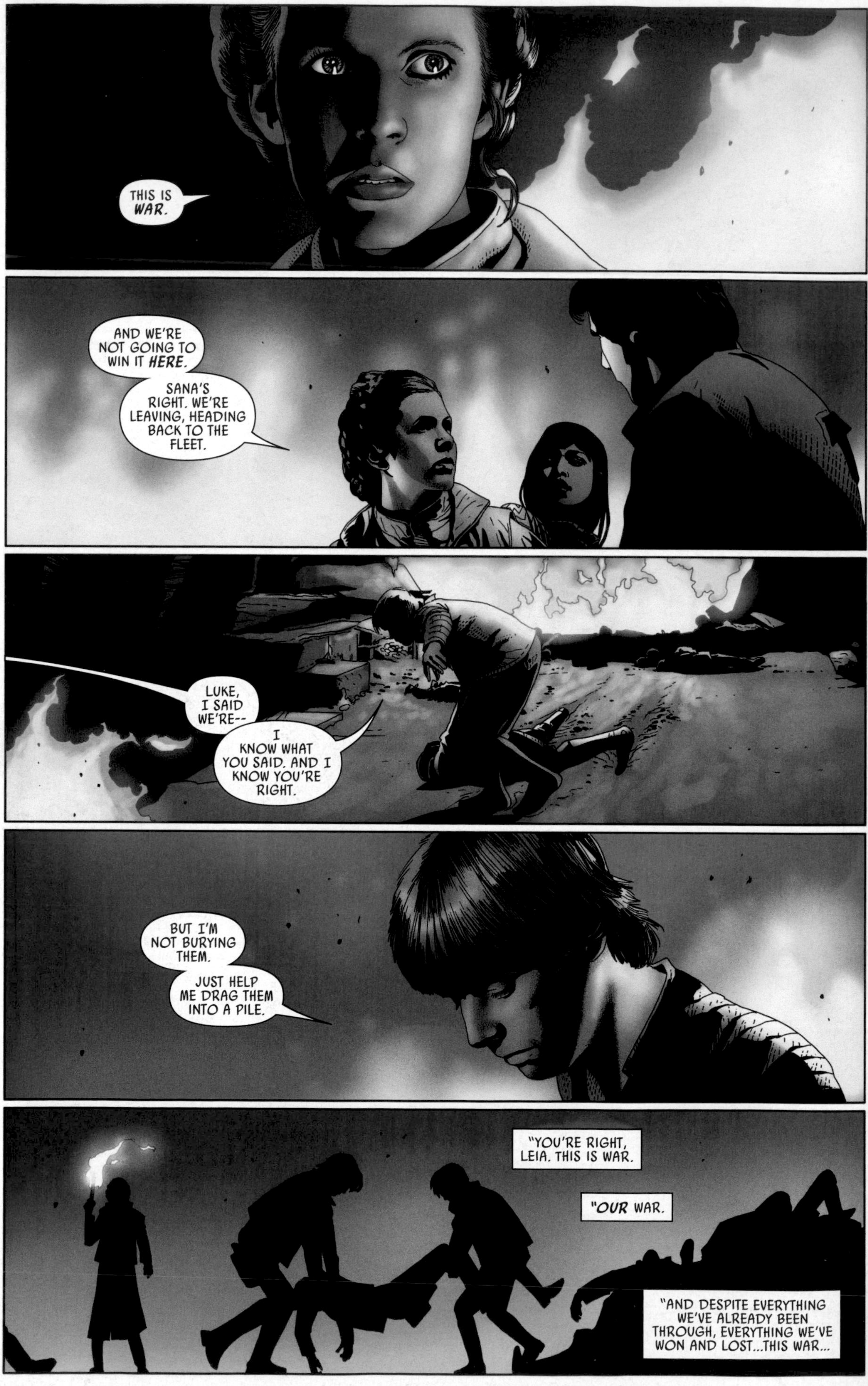
THIS IS WAR.
AND WE'RE NOT GOING TO WIN IT HERE.
SANA'S RIGHT. WE'RE LEAVING, HEADING BACK TO THE FLEET.
LUKE, I SAID WE'RE--
I KNOW WHAT YOU SAID. AND I KNOW YOU'RE RIGHT.
BUT I'M NOT BURYING THEM.
JUST HELP ME DRAG THEM INTO A PILE.
"YOU'RE RIGHT, LEIA. THIS IS WAR.
"OUR WAR.
"AND DESPITE EVERYTHING WE'VE ALREADY BEEN THROUGH, EVERYTHING WE'VE WON AND LOST...THIS WAR...

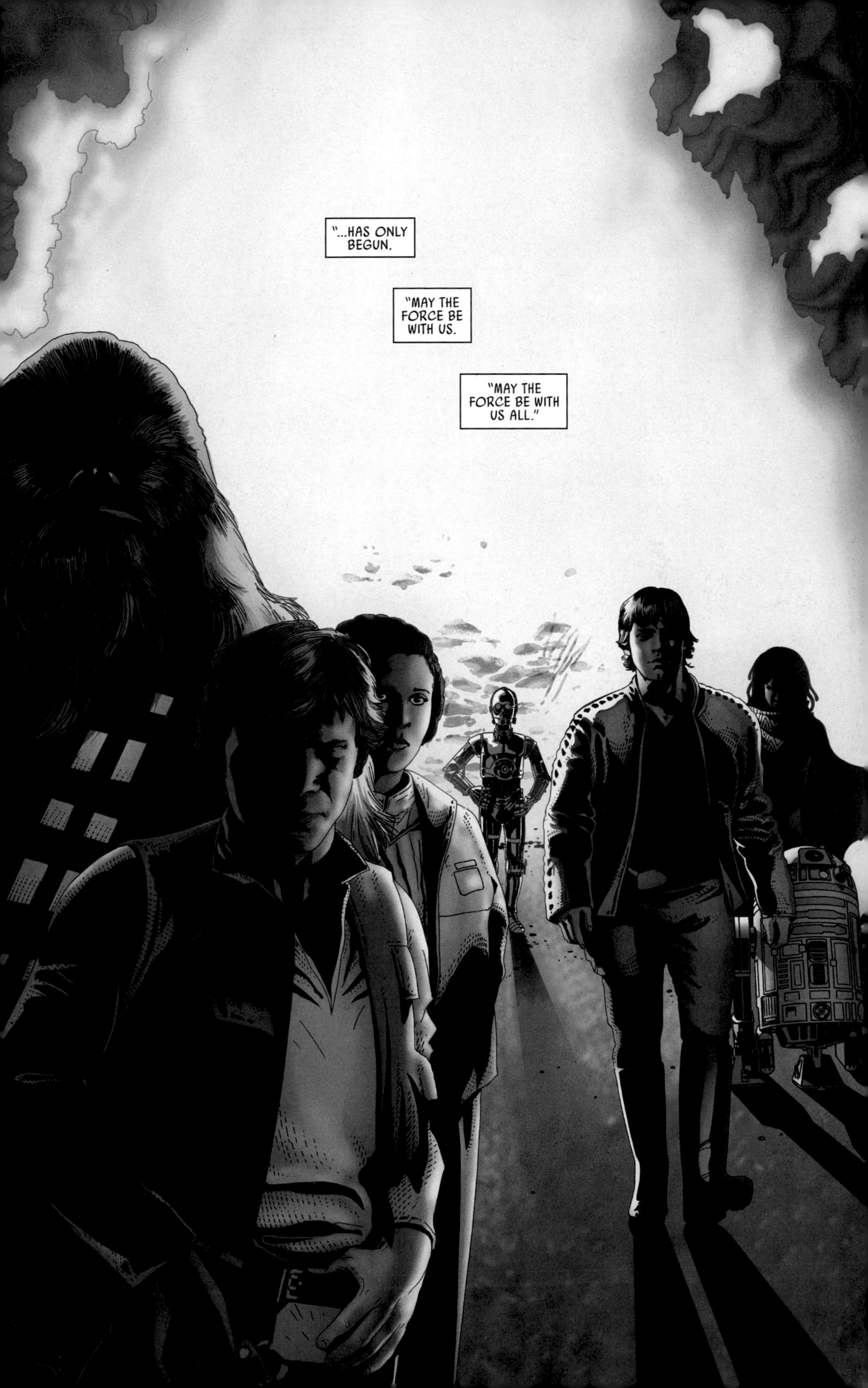
"...HAS ONLY BEGUN.
"MAY THE FORCE BE WITH US.
"MAY THE FORCE BE WITH US ALL."

THE SAND WILL PROVIDE

It is a period of survival in the galaxy. As war rages on between the Galactic Empire and the Rebellion, the battle of everyday survival continues for those trying to live a normal life.

Between the scorching heat of the twin suns on Tatooine and the vast deserts of the Jundland Wastes, the life of a Tusken Raider is not an easy one. But when the world has turned its back on the Tusken Raiders, they always have the sand to call their home....

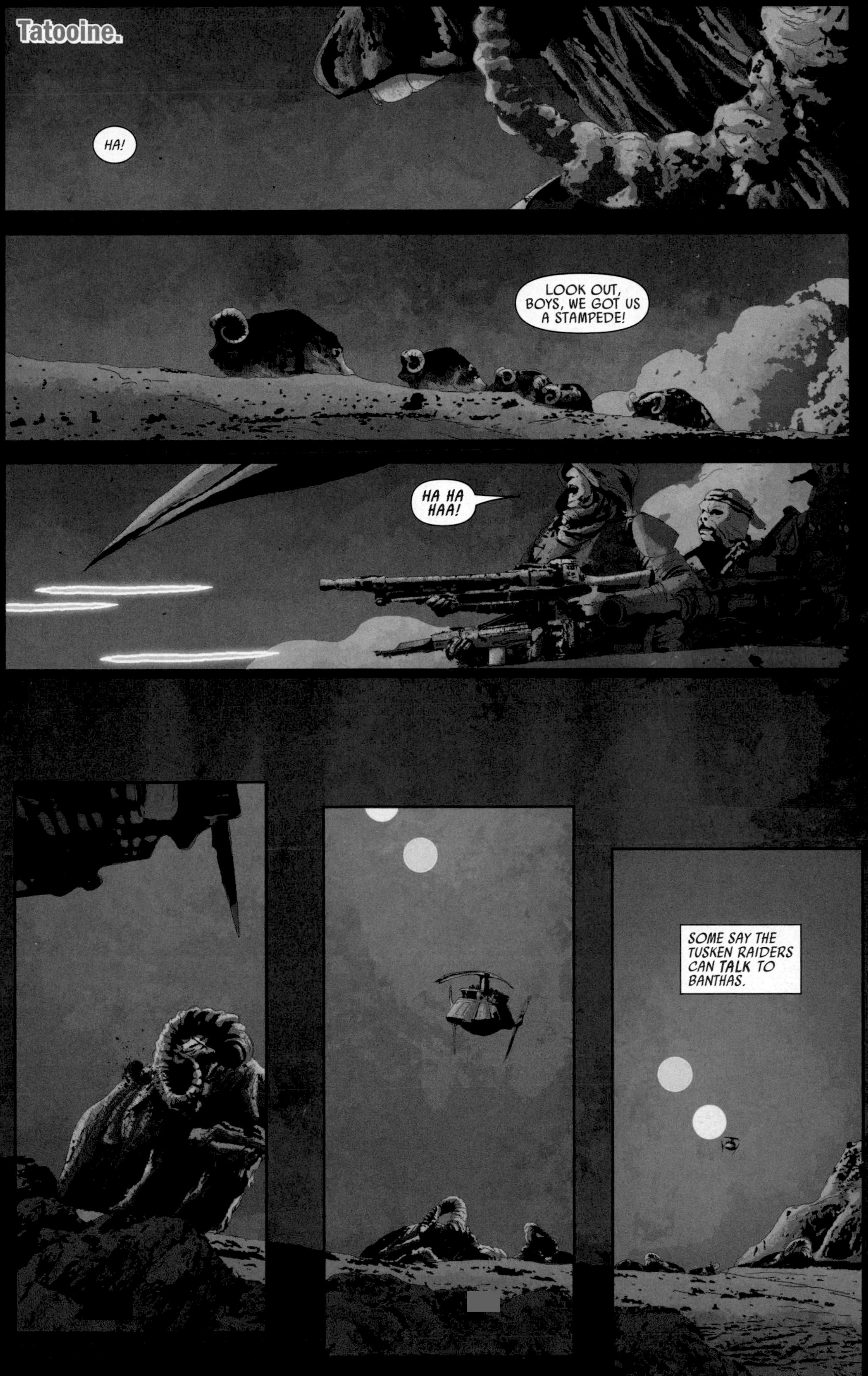
Tatooine.
HA!
LOOK OUT, BOYS, WE GOT US A STAMPEDE!
HA HA HAA!
SOME SAY THE TUSKEN RAIDERS CAN TALK TO BANTHAS.

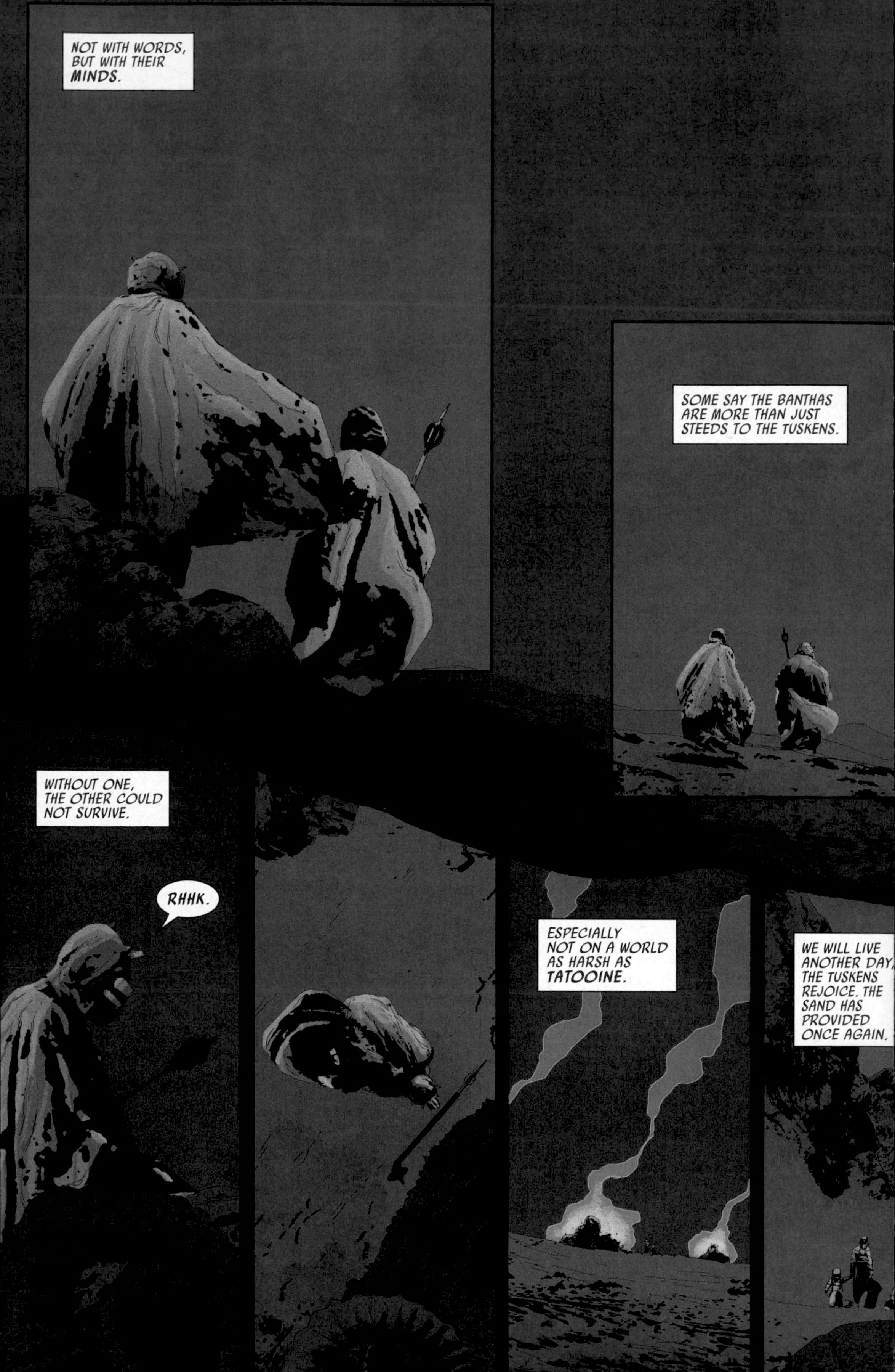
NOT WITH WORDS, BUT WITH THEIR MINDS.
SOME SAY THE BANTHAS ARE MORE THAN JUST STEEDS TO THE TUSKENS.
WITHOUT ONE, THE OTHER COULD NOT SURVIVE.
RHHK.
ESPECIALLY NOT ON A WORLD AS HARSH AS TATOOINE.
WE WILL LIVE ANOTHER DAY, THE TUSKENS REJOICE. THE SAND HAS PROVIDED ONCE AGAIN.

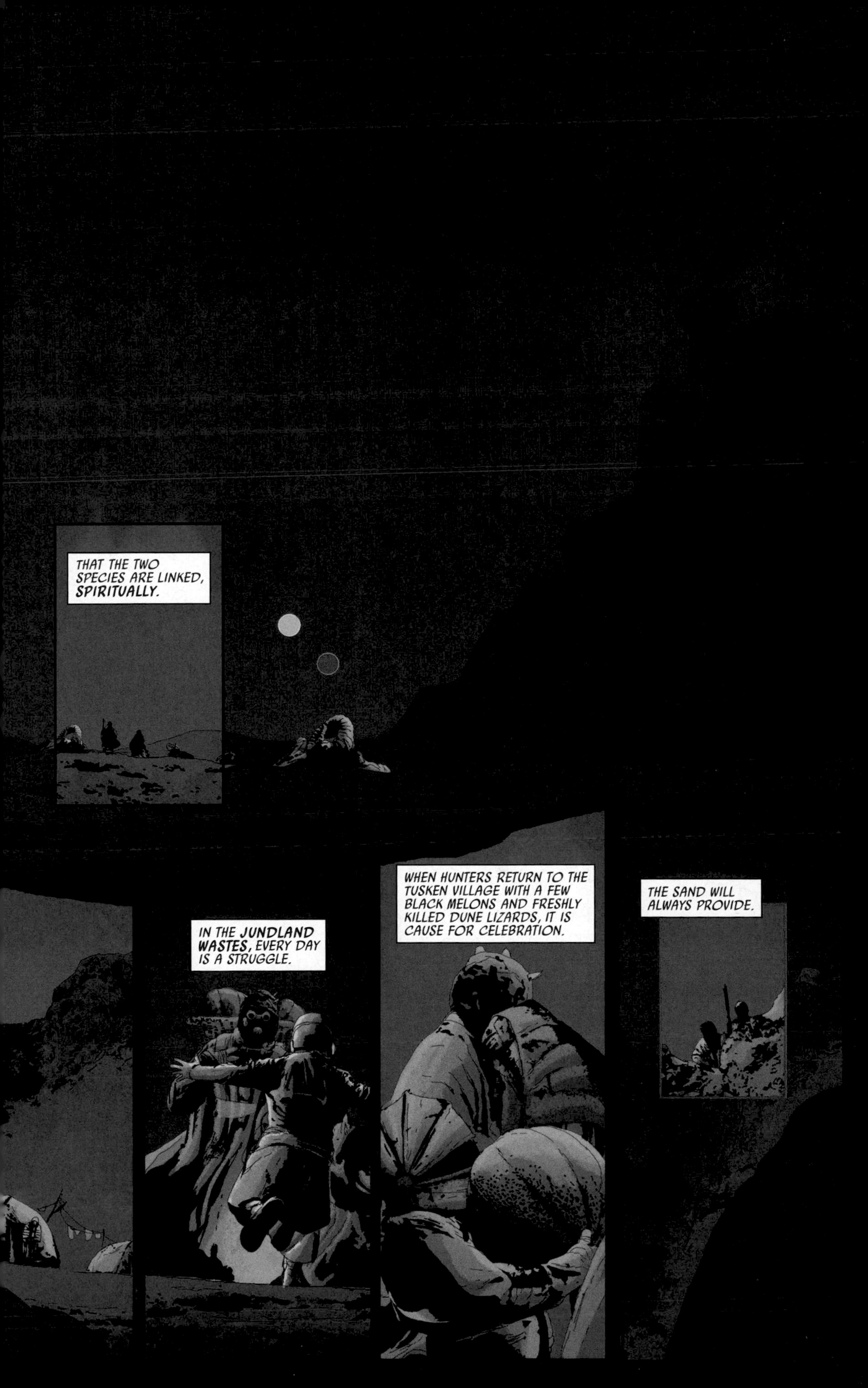
THAT THE TWO SPECIES ARE LINKED, SPIRITUALLY.
IN THE JUNDLAND WASTES, EVERY DAY IS A STRUGGLE.
WHEN HUNTERS RETURN TO THE TUSKEN VILLAGE WITH A FEW BLACK MELONS AND FRESHLY KILLED DUNE LIZARDS, IT IS CAUSE FOR CELEBRATION.
THE SAND WILL ALWAYS PROVIDE.

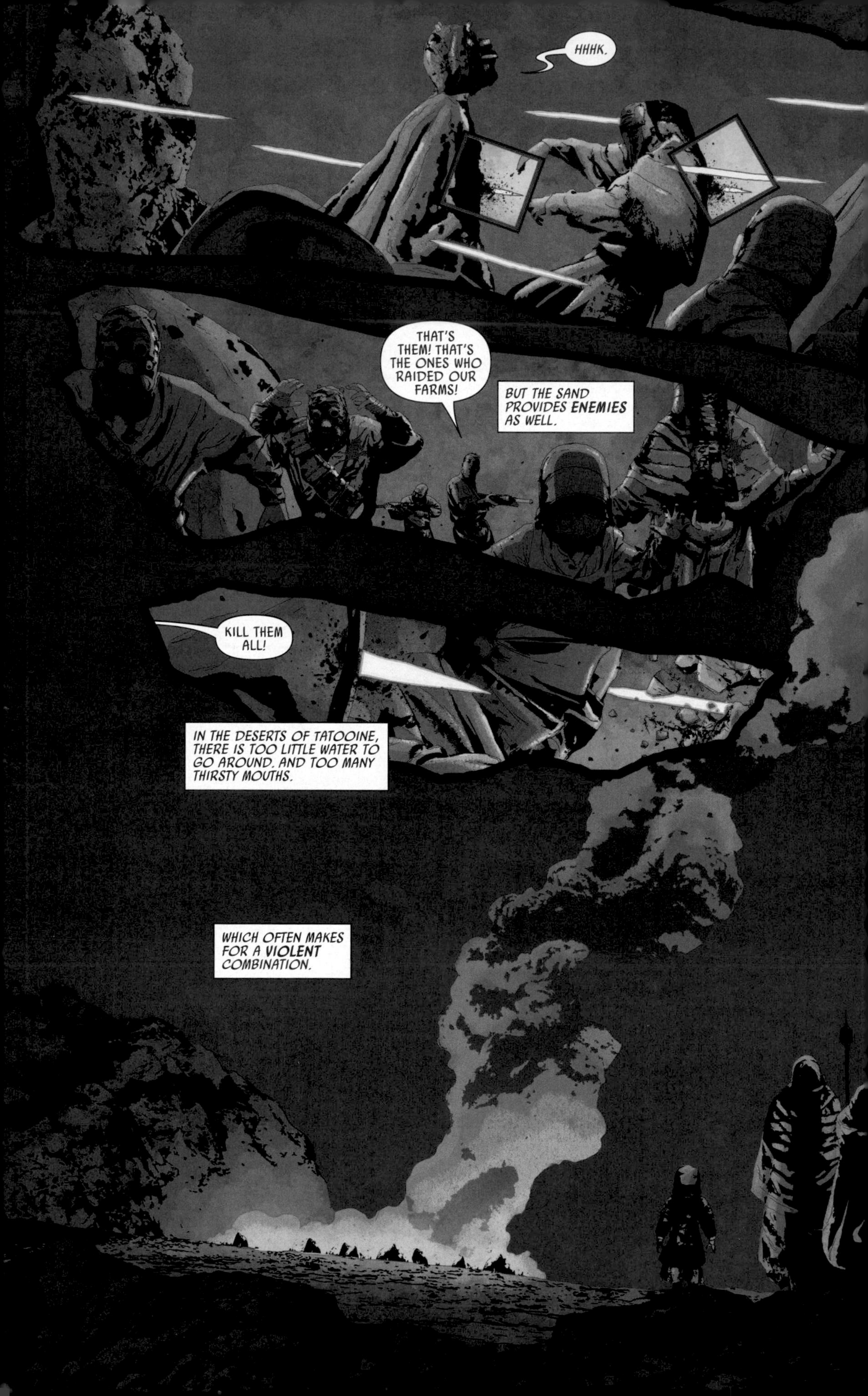
HHHK.
THAT'S THEM! THAT'S THE ONES WHO RAIDED OUR FARMS!
BUT THE SAND PROVIDES ENEMIES AS WELL.
KILL THEM ALL!
IN THE DESERTS OF TATOOINE, THERE IS TOO LITTLE WATER TO GO AROUND. AND TOO MANY THIRSTY MOUTHS.
WHICH OFTEN MAKES FOR A VIOLENT COMBINATION.

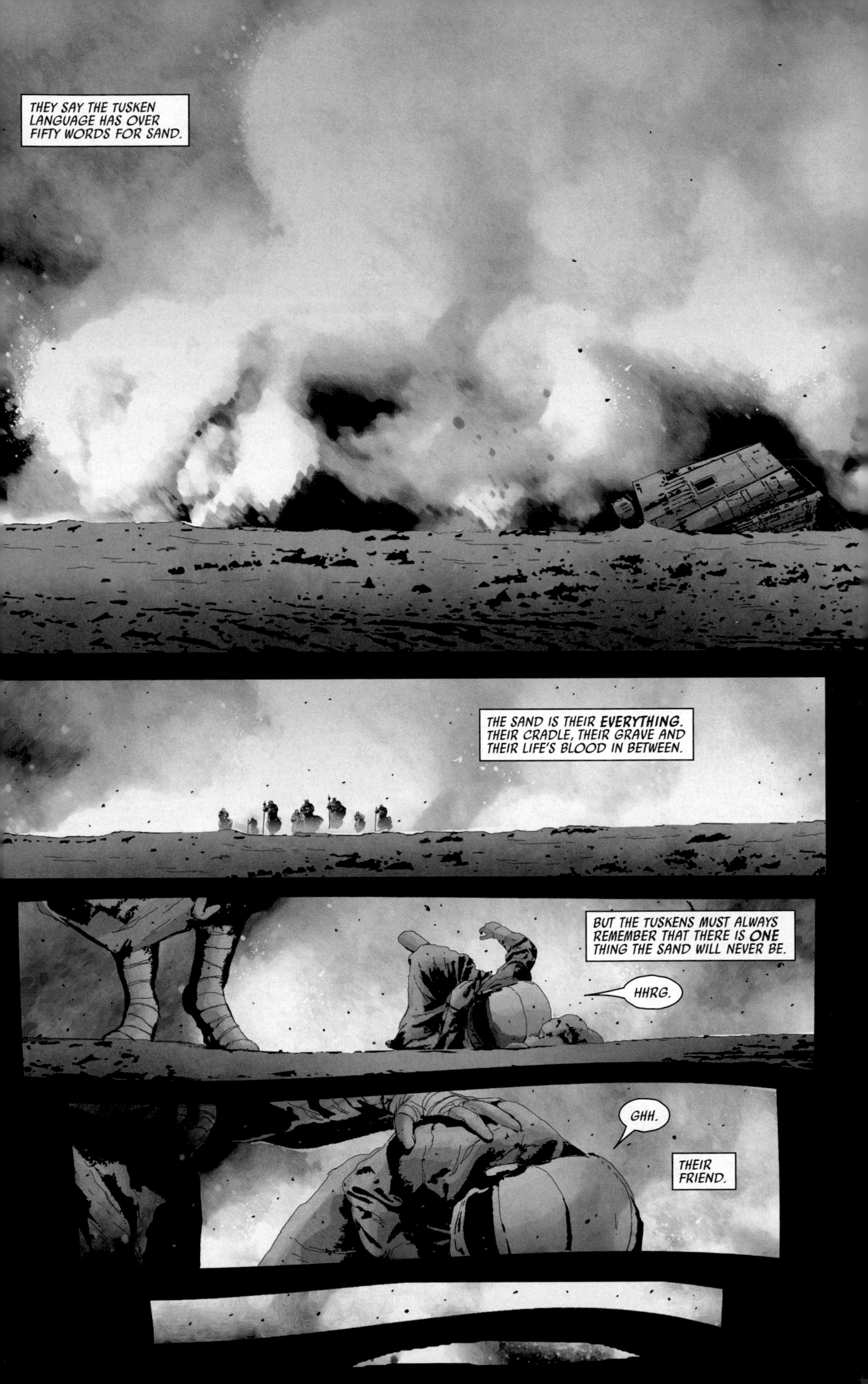
THEY SAY THE TUSKEN LANGUAGE HAS OVER FIFTY WORDS FOR SAND.
THE SAND IS THEIR EVERYTHING. THEIR CRADLE, THEIR GRAVE AND THEIR LIFE'S BLOOD IN BETWEEN.
BUT THE TUSKENS MUST ALWAYS REMEMBER THAT THERE IS ONE THING THE SAND WILL NEVER BE.
HHRG.
GHH.
THEIR FRIEND.

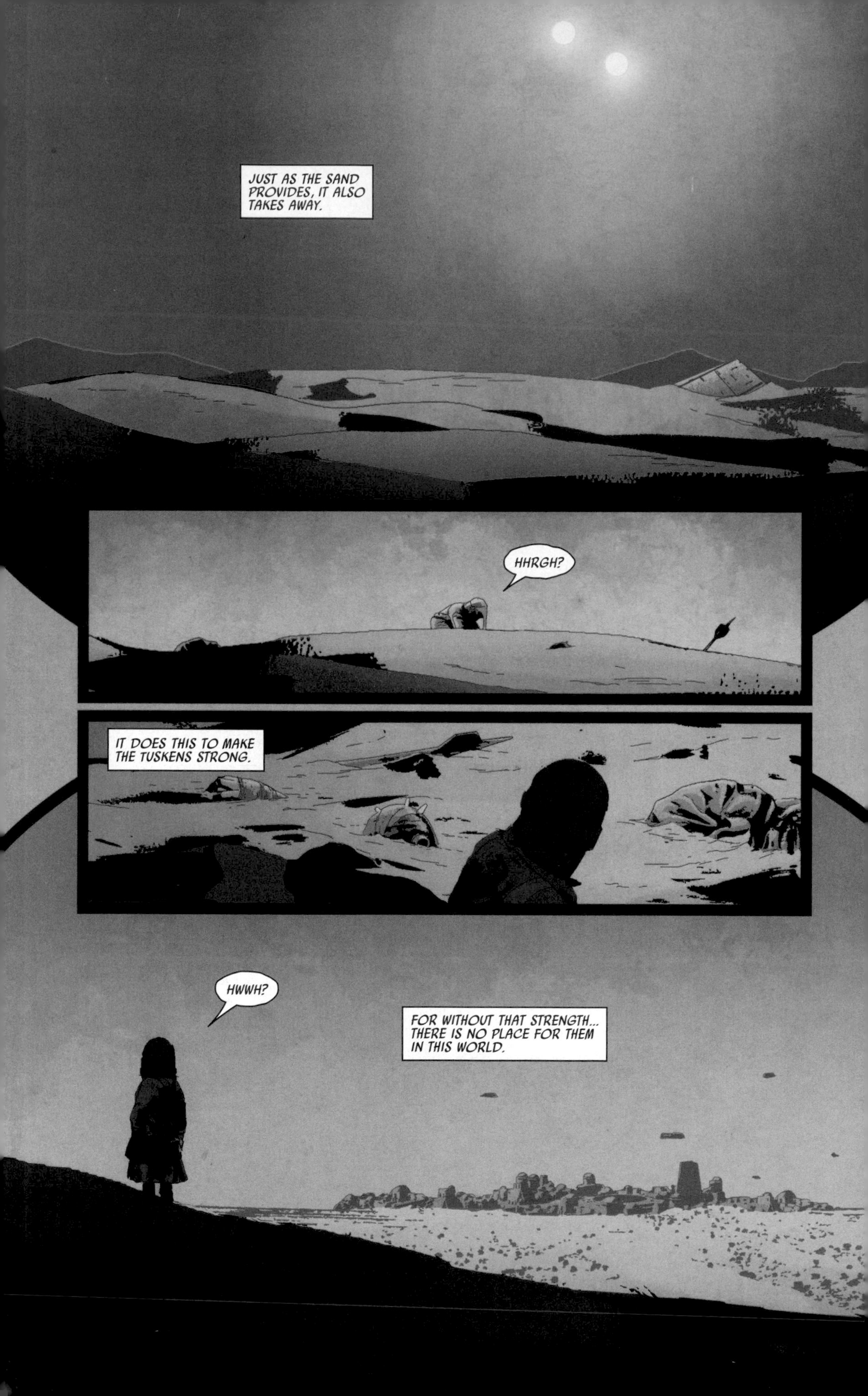
JUST AS THE SAND PROVIDES, IT ALSO TAKES AWAY.
HHRGH?
IT DOES THIS TO MAKE THE TUSKENS STRONG.
HWWH?
FOR WITHOUT THAT STRENGTH... THERE IS NO PLACE FOR THEM IN THIS WORLD.

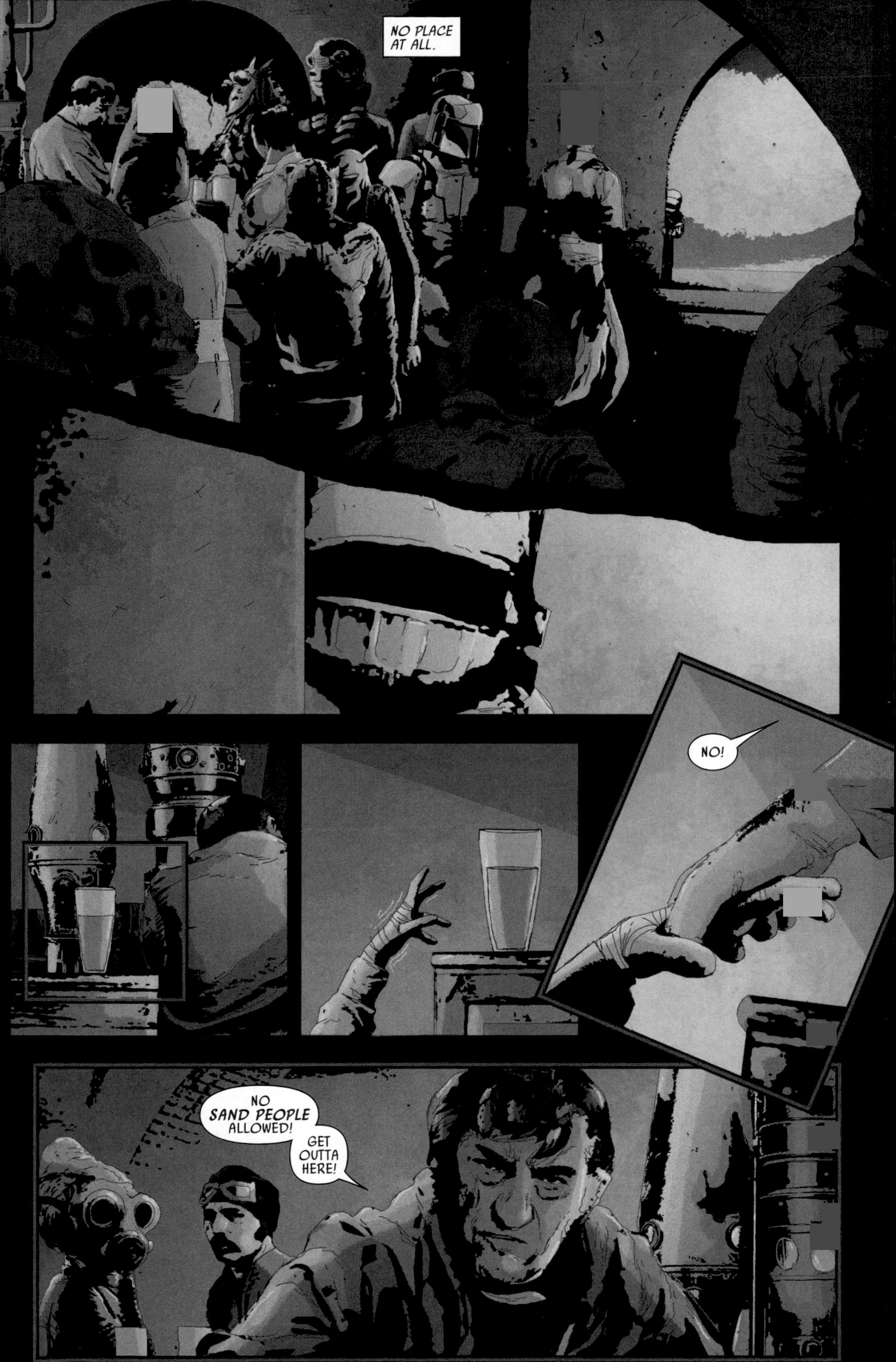
NO PLACE AT ALL.
NO!
NO SAND PEOPLE ALLOWED!
GET OUTTA HERE!

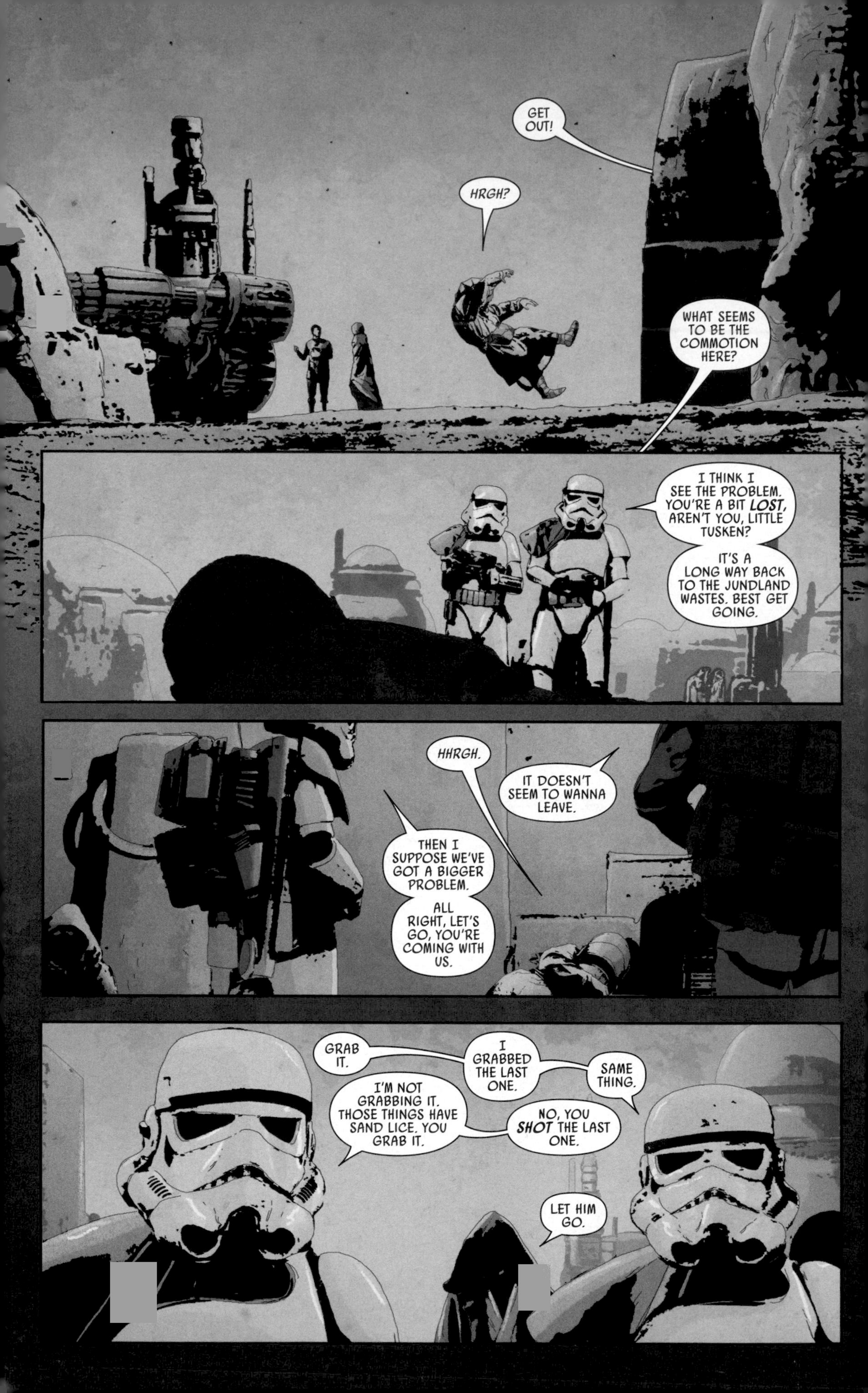
GET OUT!
HRGH?
WHAT SEEMS TO BE THE COMMOTION HERE?
I THINK I SEE THE PROBLEM. YOU'RE A BIT LOST, AREN'T YOU, LITTLE TUSKEN?
IT'S A LONG WAY BACK TO THE JUNDLAND WASTES. BEST GET GOING.
HHRGH.
IT DOESN'T SEEM TO WANNA LEAVE.
THEN I SUPPOSE WE'VE GOT A BIGGER PROBLEM.
ALL RIGHT, LET'S GO, YOU'RE COMING WITH US.
GRAB IT.
I GRABBED THE LAST ONE.
SAME THING.
I'M NOT GRABBING IT. THOSE THINGS HAVE SAND LICE. YOU GRAB IT.
NO, YOU SHOT THE LAST ONE.
LET HIM GO.

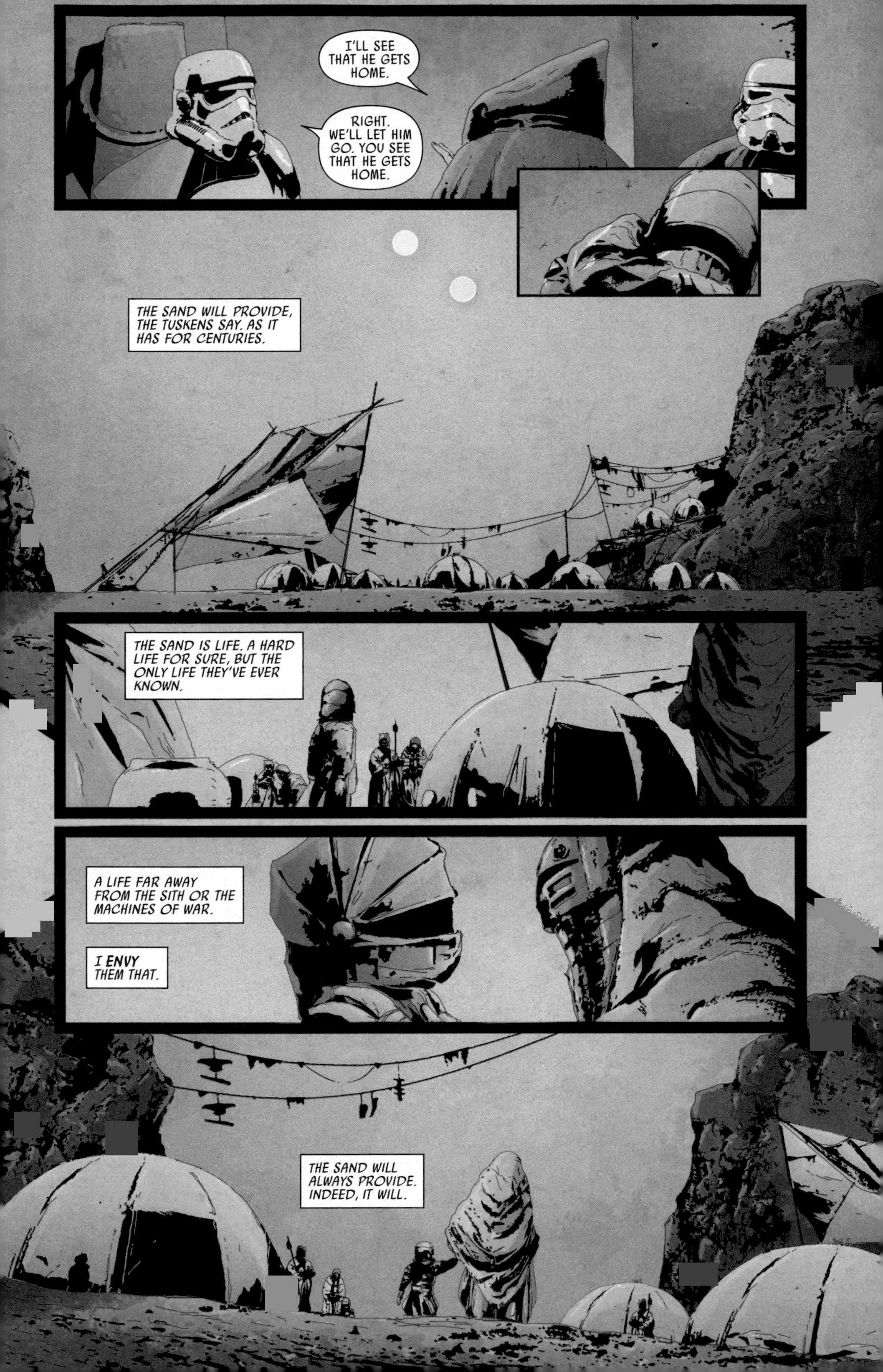

I'LL SEE THAT HE GETS HOME.
RIGHT. WE'LL LET HIM GO. YOU SEE THAT HE GETS HOME.
THE SAND WILL PROVIDE, THE TUSKENS SAY. AS IT HAS FOR CENTURIES.
THE SAND IS LIFE. A HARD LIFE FOR SURE, BUT THE ONLY LIFE THEY'VE EVER KNOWN.
A LIFE FAR AWAY FROM THE SITH OR THE MACHINES OF WAR.
I ENVY THEM THAT.
THE SAND WILL ALWAYS PROVIDE. INDEED, IT WILL.

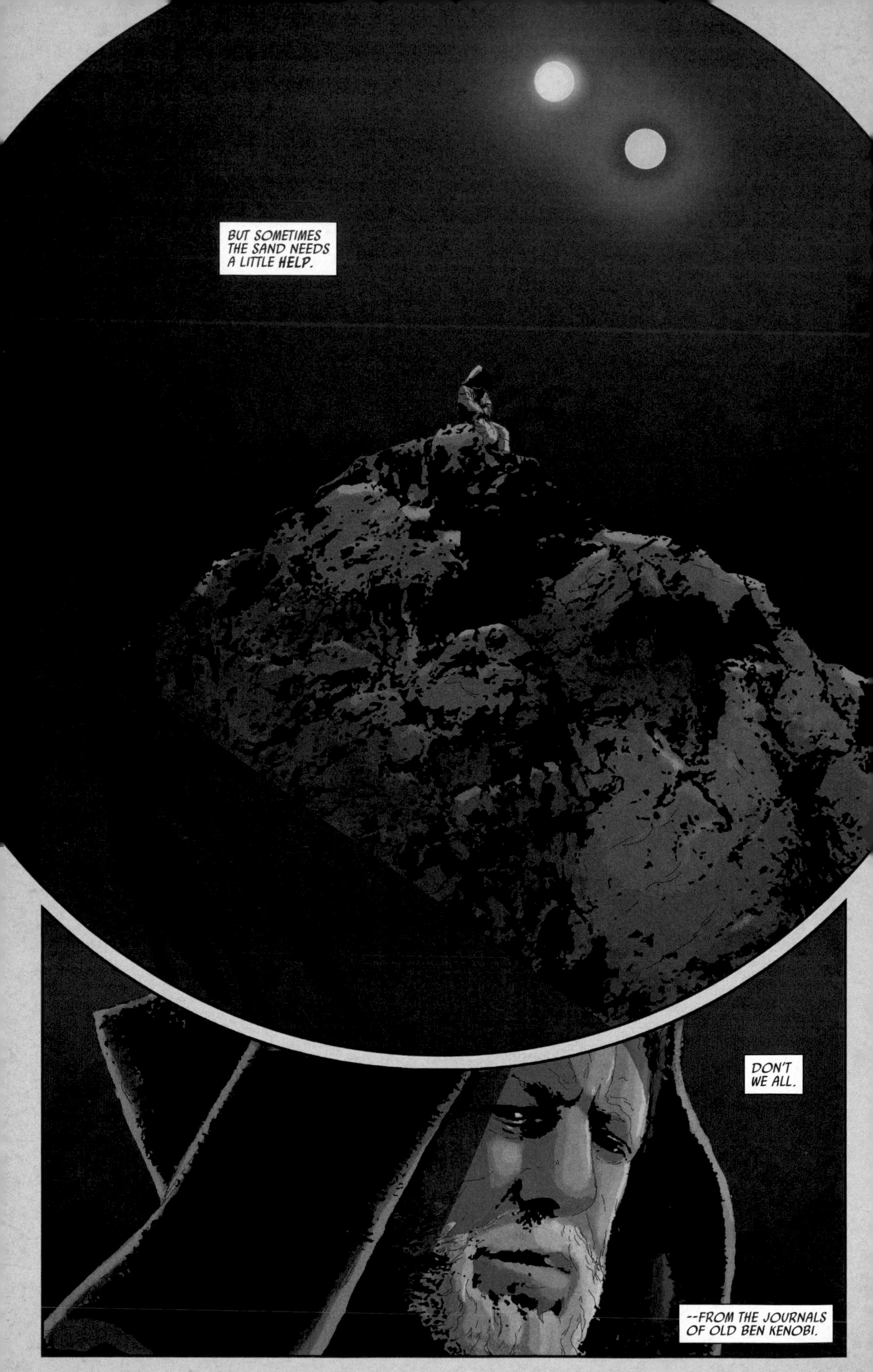
BUT SOMETIMES THE SAND NEEDS A LITTLE HELP.
DON'T WE ALL.
--FROM THE JOURNALS OF OLD BEN KENOBI.

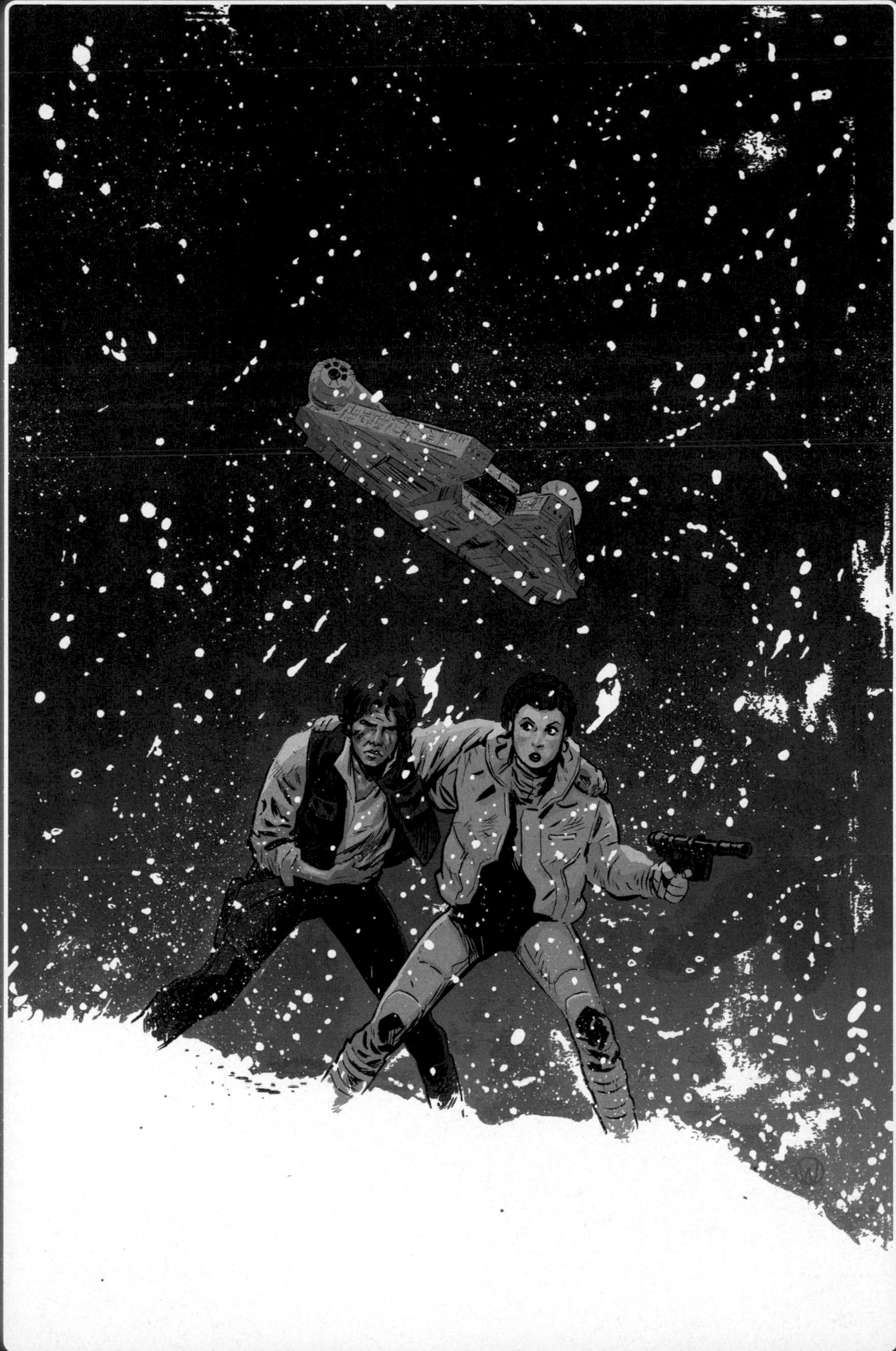

ANNUAL 3

STAR WARS
Annual III

In an effort to find a new staging ground for a hidden rebel base, Han Solo has led rebel leader Princess Leia to the planet of Odona, a remote world of harsh extremes and secret alcoves long used by pirates and smugglers to avoid the Empire.

But as their mission stretches on, Han and Leia find themselves cut off from their allies, and lost in the caves of Odona as a massive ice storm approaches....

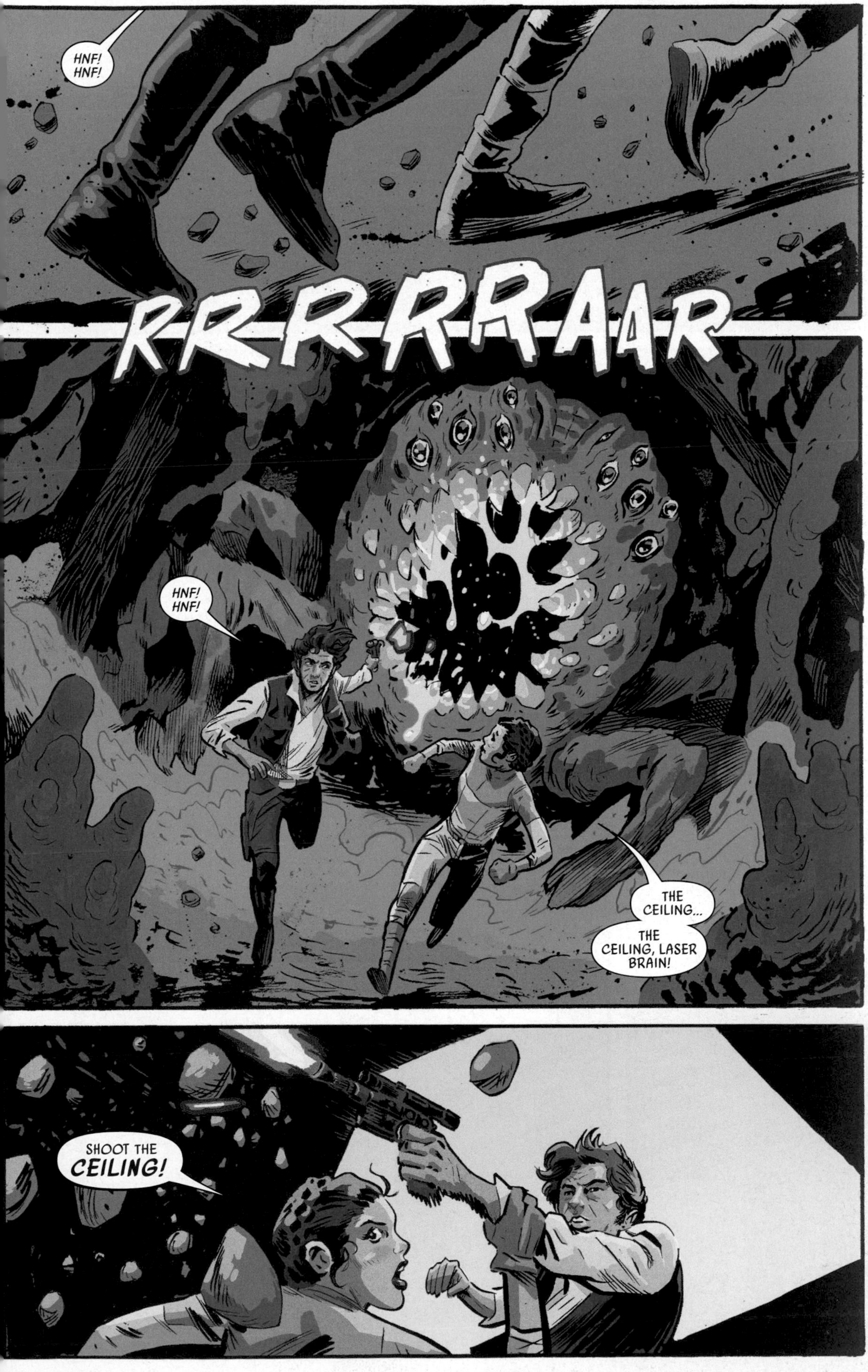
HNF! HNF!
RRRRRRAAR
HNF! HNF!
THE CEILING...
THE CEILING, LASER BRAIN!
SHOOT THE CEILING!

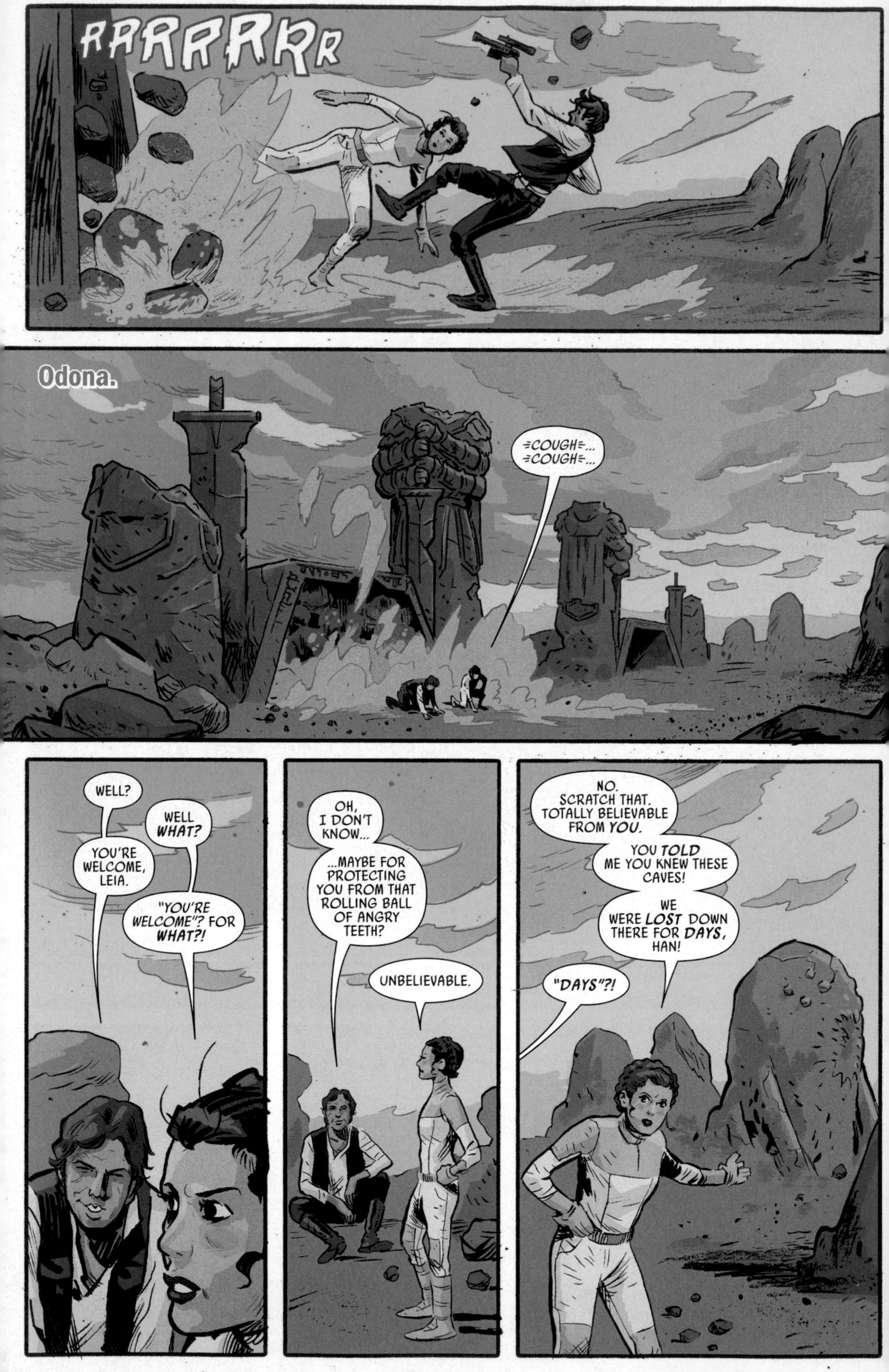
RRRRRRR
Odona.
≡COUGH≡...
≡COUGH≡...
WELL?
WELL WHAT?
YOU'RE WELCOME, LEIA.
"YOU'RE WELCOME"? FOR WHAT?!
OH, I DON'T KNOW...
...MAYBE FOR PROTECTING YOU FROM THAT ROLLING BALL OF ANGRY TEETH?
UNBELIEVABLE.
NO. SCRATCH THAT. TOTALLY BELIEVABLE FROM YOU.
YOU TOLD ME YOU KNEW THESE CAVES!
WE WERE LOST DOWN THERE FOR DAYS, HAN!
"DAYS"?!

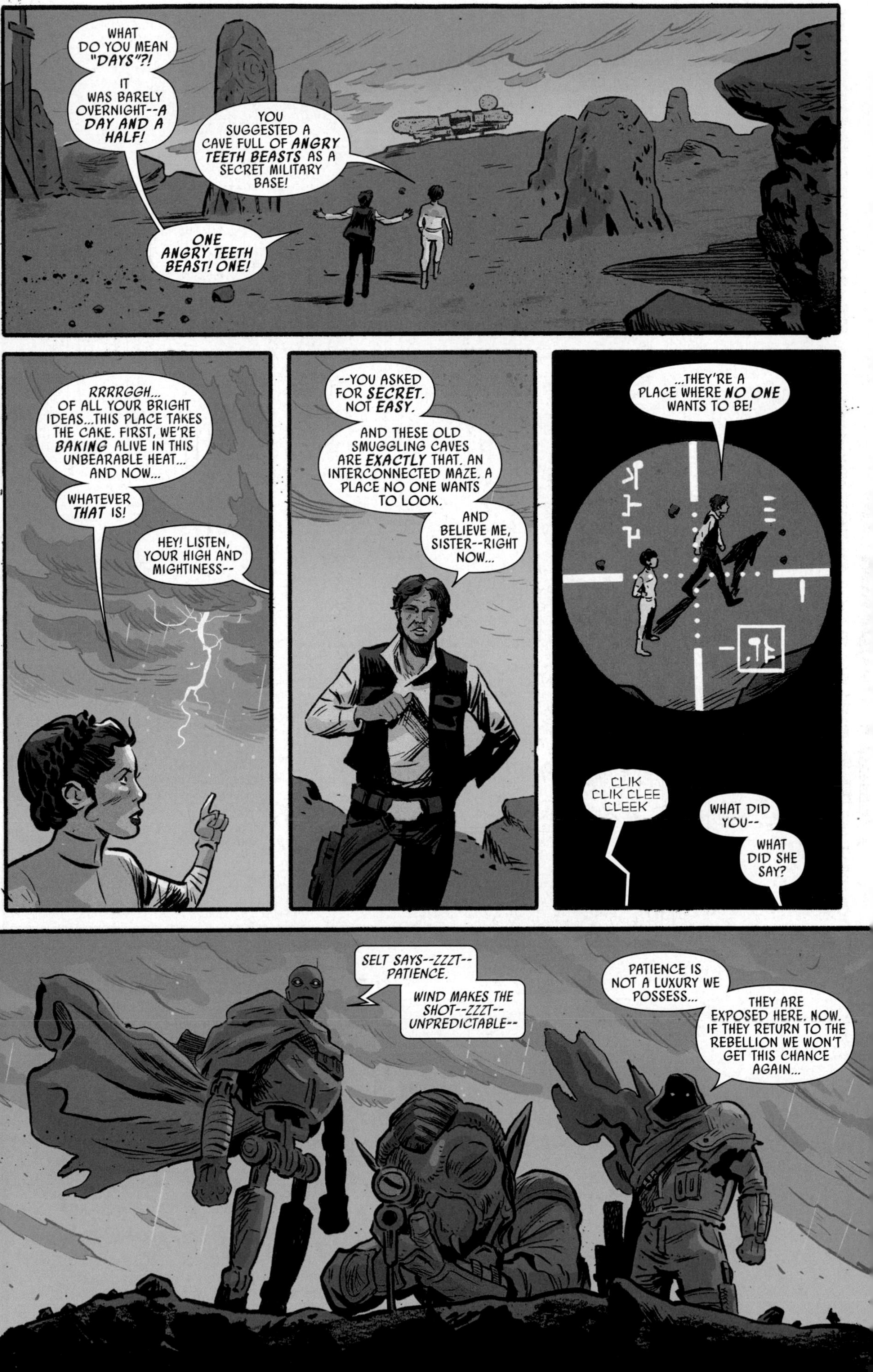

WHAT DO YOU MEAN "DAYS"?!
IT WAS BARELY OVERNIGHT--A DAY AND A HALF!
YOU SUGGESTED A CAVE FULL OF ANGRY TEETH BEASTS AS A SECRET MILITARY BASE!
ONE ANGRY TEETH BEAST! ONE!
RRRRGGH... OF ALL YOUR BRIGHT IDEAS...THIS PLACE TAKES THE CAKE. FIRST, WE'RE BAKING ALIVE IN THIS UNBEARABLE HEAT... AND NOW...
WHATEVER THAT IS!
HEY! LISTEN, YOUR HIGH AND MIGHTINESS--
--YOU ASKED FOR SECRET. NOT EASY.
AND THESE OLD SMUGGLING CAVES ARE EXACTLY THAT. AN INTERCONNECTED MAZE. A PLACE NO ONE WANTS TO LOOK.
AND BELIEVE ME, SISTER--RIGHT NOW...
...THEY'RE A PLACE WHERE NO ONE WANTS TO BE!
CLIK CLIK CLEE CLEEK
WHAT DID YOU--
WHAT DID SHE SAY?
SELT SAYS--ZZZT-- PATIENCE.
WIND MAKES THE SHOT--ZZZT-- UNPREDICTABLE--
PATIENCE IS NOT A LUXURY WE POSSESS...
THEY ARE EXPOSED HERE. NOW. IF THEY RETURN TO THE REBELLION WE WON'T GET THIS CHANCE AGAIN...

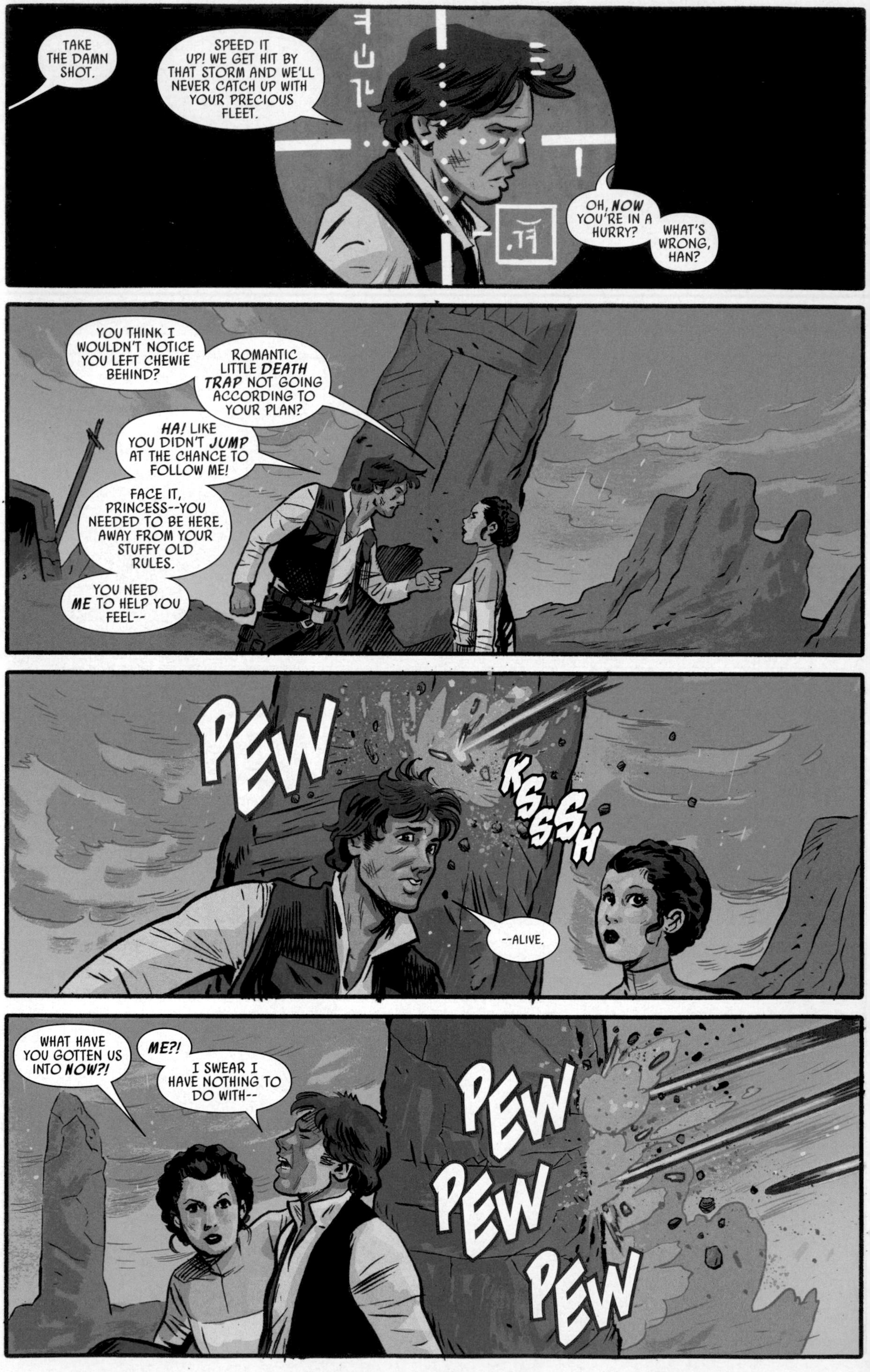
TAKE THE DAMN SHOT.
SPEED IT UP! WE GET HIT BY THAT STORM AND WE'LL NEVER CATCH UP WITH YOUR PRECIOUS FLEET.
OH, NOW YOU'RE IN A HURRY?
WHAT'S WRONG, HAN?
YOU THINK I WOULDN'T NOTICE YOU LEFT CHEWIE BEHIND?
ROMANTIC LITTLE DEATH TRAP NOT GOING ACCORDING TO YOUR PLAN?
HA! LIKE YOU DIDN'T JUMP AT THE CHANCE TO FOLLOW ME!
FACE IT, PRINCESS--YOU NEEDED TO BE HERE. AWAY FROM YOUR STUFFY OLD RULES.
YOU NEED ME TO HELP YOU FEEL--
PEW
KSSSH
--ALIVE.
WHAT HAVE YOU GOTTEN US INTO NOW?!
ME?!
I SWEAR I HAVE NOTHING TO DO WITH--
PEW
PEW
PEW

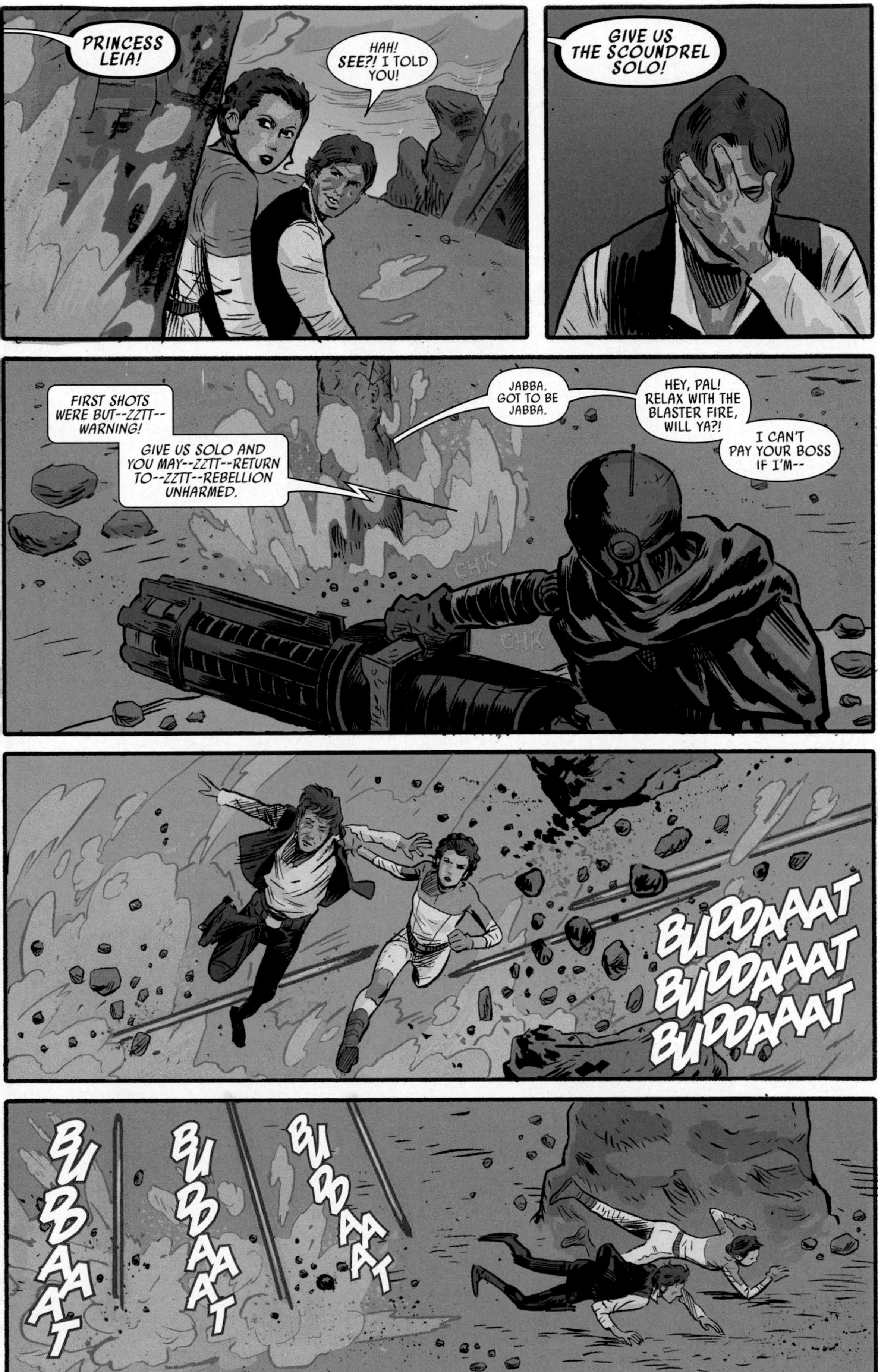
PRINCESS LEIA!
HAH! SEE?! I TOLD YOU!
GIVE US THE SCOUNDREL SOLO!
FIRST SHOTS WERE BUT--ZZTT--WARNING!
GIVE US SOLO AND YOU MAY--ZZTT--RETURN TO--ZZTT--REBELLION UNHARMED.
JABBA. GOT TO BE JABBA.
HEY, PAL! RELAX WITH THE BLASTER FIRE, WILL YA?!
I CAN'T PAY YOUR BOSS IF I'M--
CHK
CHK
BUDDAAAT
BUDDAAAT
BUDDAAAT
BUDDAAAT
BUDDAAAT
BUDDAAAT

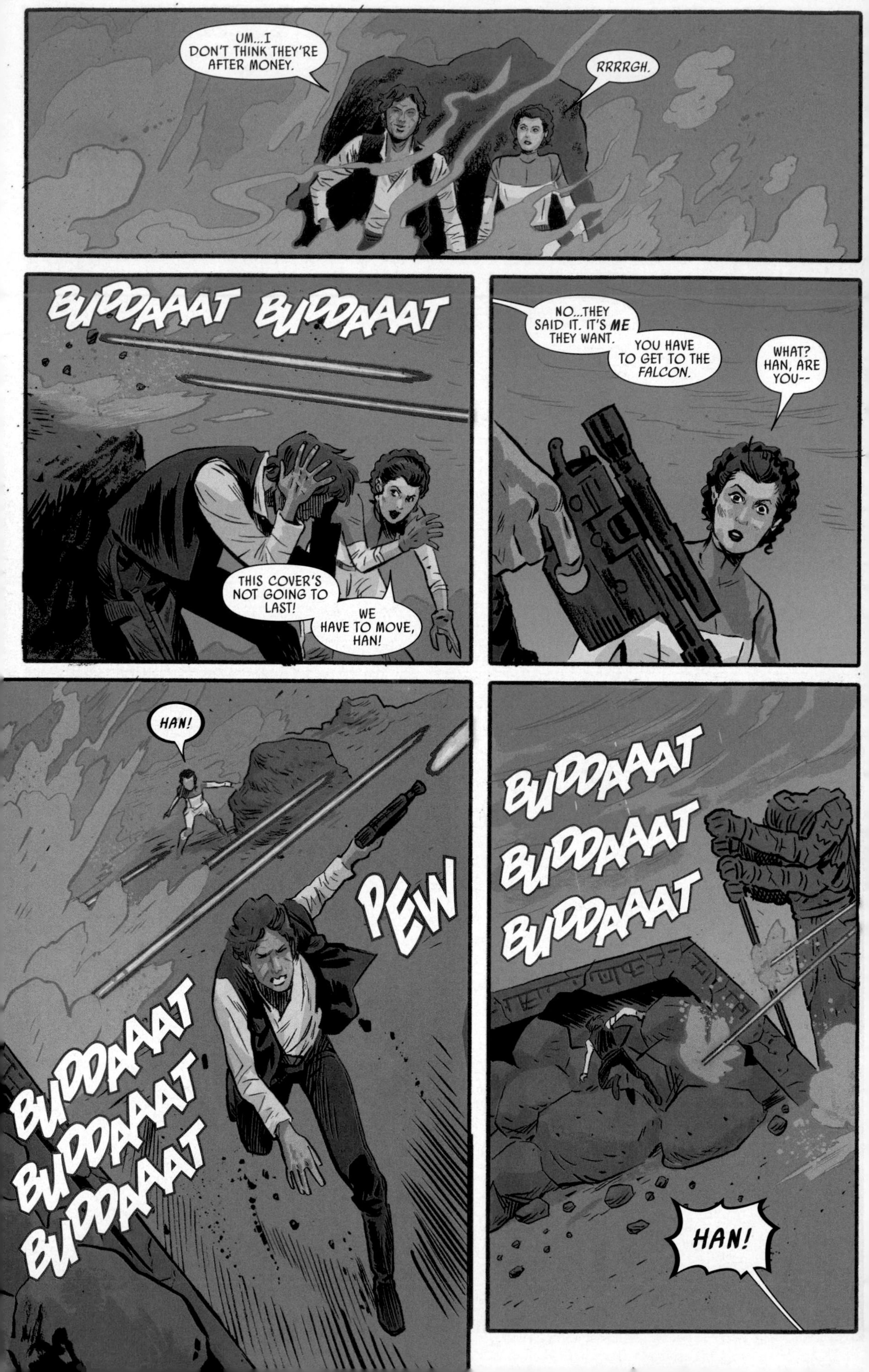
UM...I DON'T THINK THEY'RE AFTER MONEY.
RRRRGH.
BUDDAAAT BUDDAAAT
THIS COVER'S NOT GOING TO LAST!
WE HAVE TO MOVE, HAN!
NO...THEY SAID IT. IT'S ME THEY WANT.
YOU HAVE TO GET TO THE FALCON.
WHAT? HAN, ARE YOU--
HAN!
PEW
BUDDAAAT BUDDAAAT BUDDAAAT
BUDDAAAT BUDDAAAT BUDDAAAT
HAN!

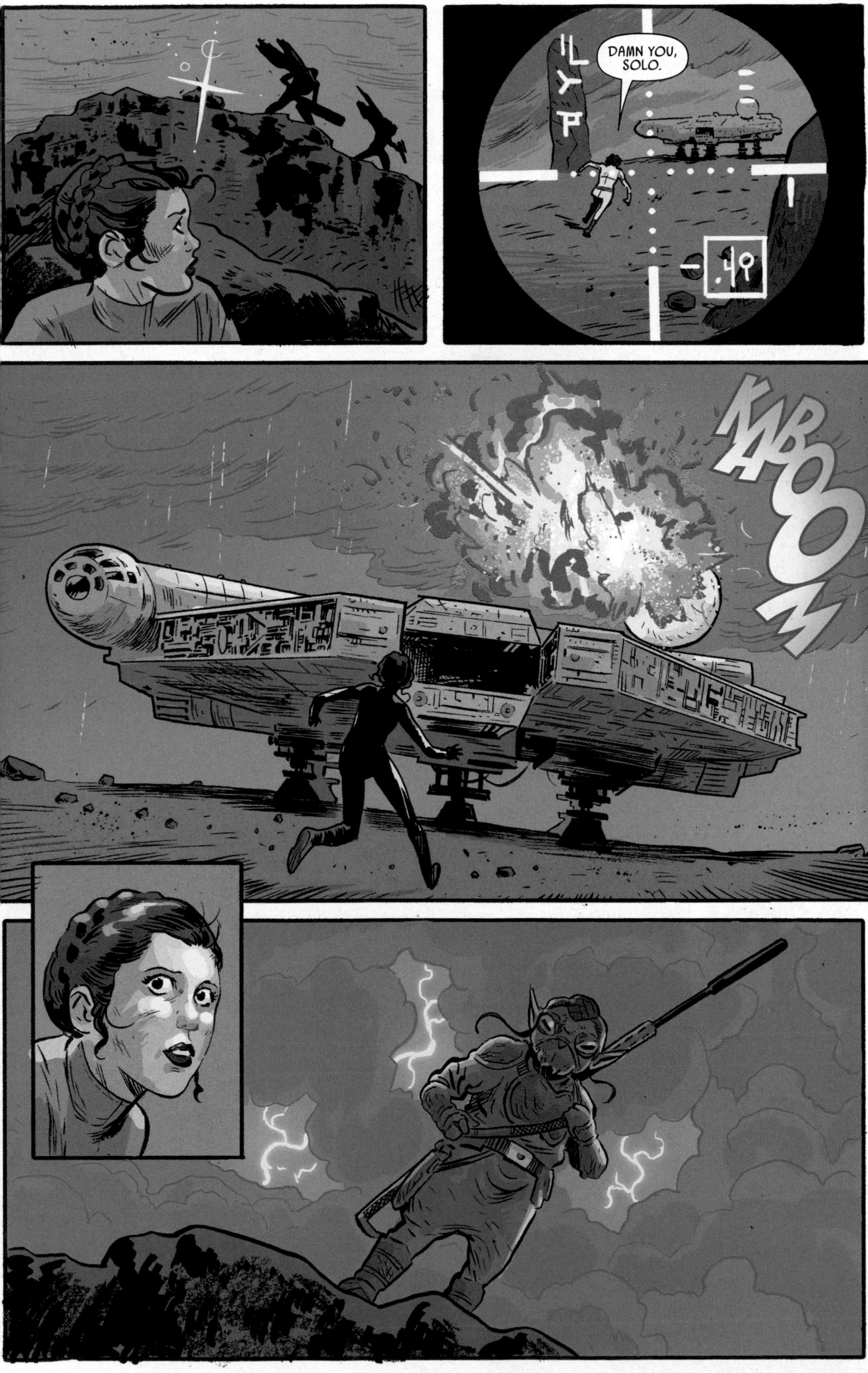
DAMN YOU, SOLO.
KABOOM

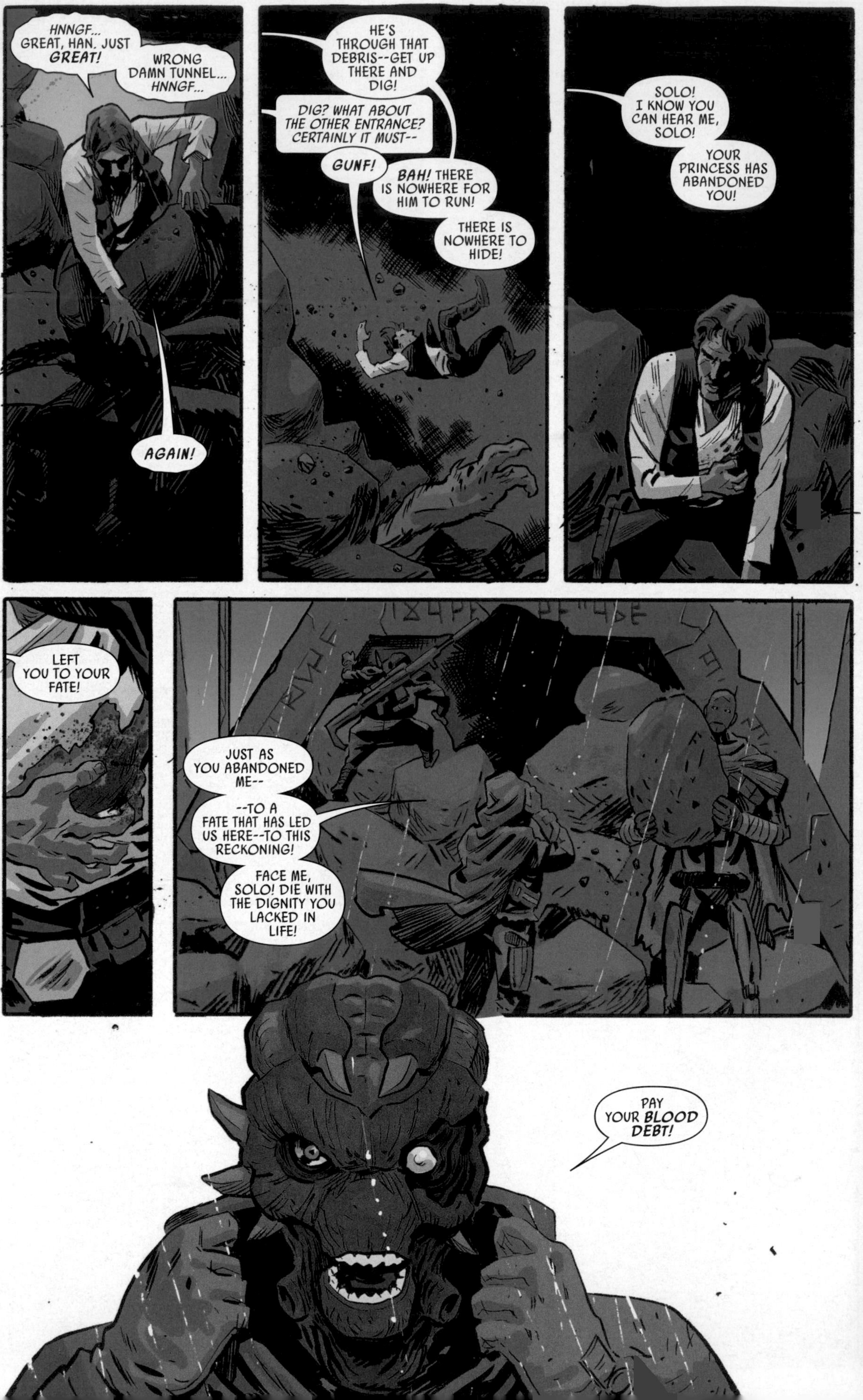
HNNGF... GREAT, HAN. JUST GREAT!
WRONG DAMN TUNNEL... HNNGF...
AGAIN!
HE'S THROUGH THAT DEBRIS--GET UP THERE AND DIG!
DIG? WHAT ABOUT THE OTHER ENTRANCE? CERTAINLY IT MUST--
GUNF!
BAH! THERE IS NOWHERE FOR HIM TO RUN!
THERE IS NOWHERE TO HIDE!
SOLO! I KNOW YOU CAN HEAR ME, SOLO!
YOUR PRINCESS HAS ABANDONED YOU!
LEFT YOU TO YOUR FATE!
JUST AS YOU ABANDONED ME--
--TO A FATE THAT HAS LED US HERE--TO THIS RECKONING!
FACE ME, SOLO! DIE WITH THE DIGNITY YOU LACKED IN LIFE!
PAY YOUR BLOOD DEBT!

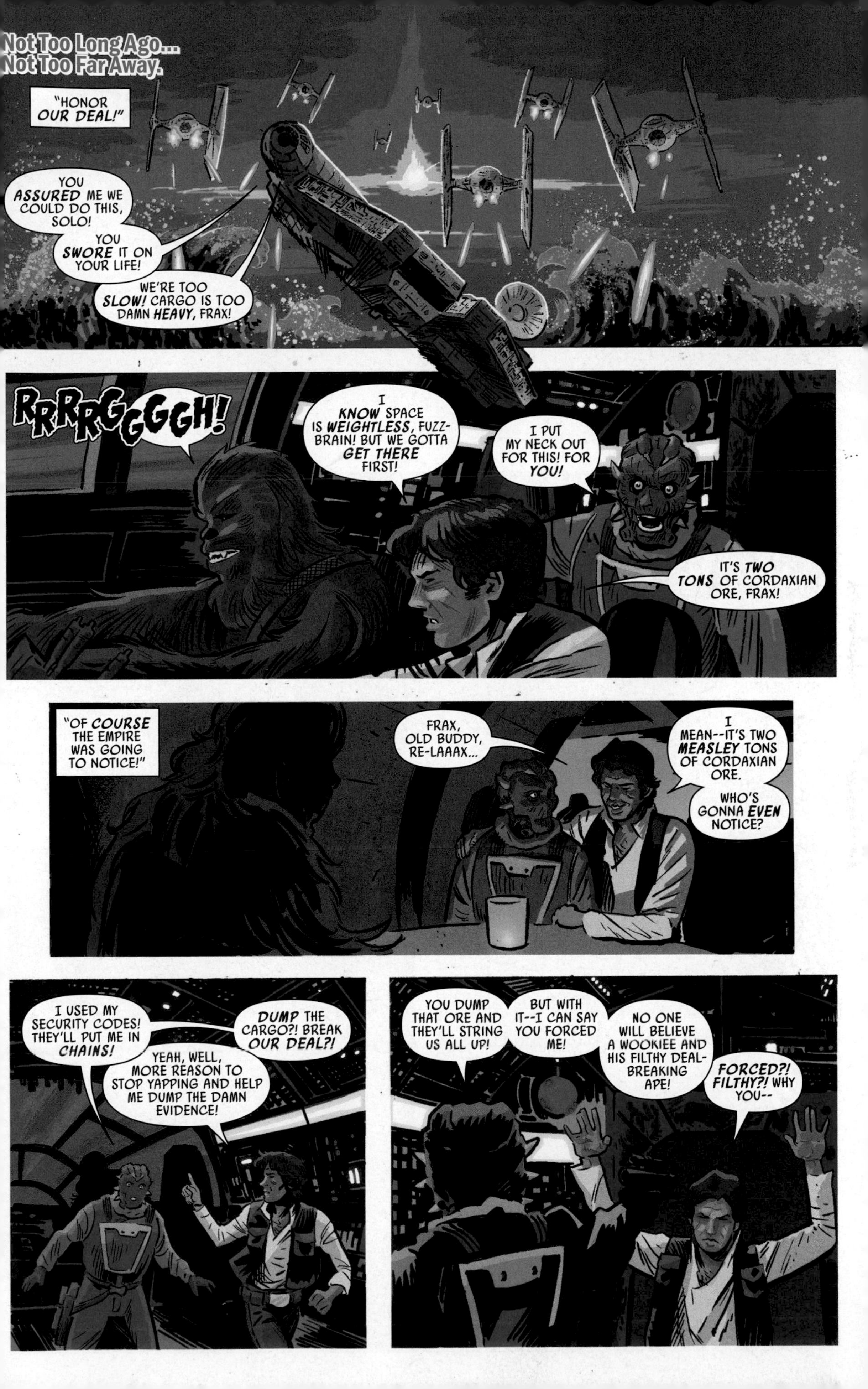

Not Too Long Ago...
Not Too Far Away.
"HONOR OUR DEAL!"
YOU ASSURED ME WE COULD DO THIS, SOLO!
YOU SWORE IT ON YOUR LIFE!
WE'RE TOO SLOW! CARGO IS TOO DAMN HEAVY, FRAX!
RRRRGGGGH!
I KNOW SPACE IS WEIGHTLESS, FUZZ-BRAIN! BUT WE GOTTA GET THERE FIRST!
I PUT MY NECK OUT FOR THIS! FOR YOU!
IT'S TWO TONS OF CORDAXIAN ORE, FRAX!
"OF COURSE THE EMPIRE WAS GOING TO NOTICE!"
FRAX, OLD BUDDY, RE-LAAAX...
I MEAN--IT'S TWO MEASLEY TONS OF CORDAXIAN ORE.
WHO'S GONNA EVEN NOTICE?
I USED MY SECURITY CODES! THEY'LL PUT ME IN CHAINS!
DUMP THE CARGO?! BREAK OUR DEAL?!
YEAH, WELL, MORE REASON TO STOP YAPPING AND HELP ME DUMP THE DAMN EVIDENCE!
YOU DUMP THAT ORE AND THEY'LL STRING US ALL UP!
BUT WITH IT--I CAN SAY YOU FORCED ME!
NO ONE WILL BELIEVE A WOOKIEE AND HIS FILTHY DEAL-BREAKING APE!
FORCED?! FILTHY?! WHY YOU--

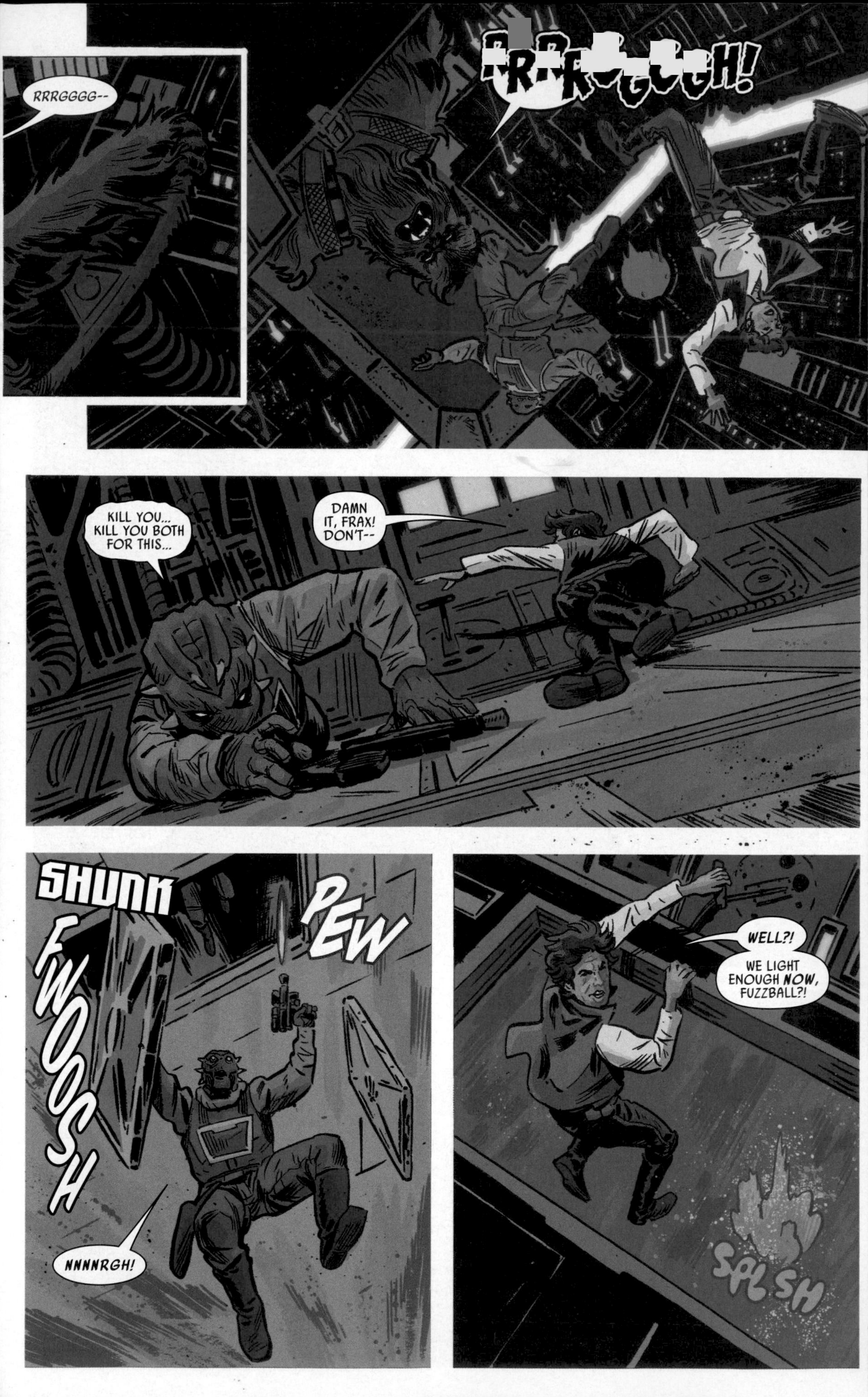
RRRGGGG--
KILL YOU... KILL YOU BOTH FOR THIS...
DAMN IT, FRAX! DON'T--
SHUNK
FWOOSH
PEW
NNNNRGH!
WELL?!
WE LIGHT ENOUGH NOW, FUZZBALL?!
SPLSH

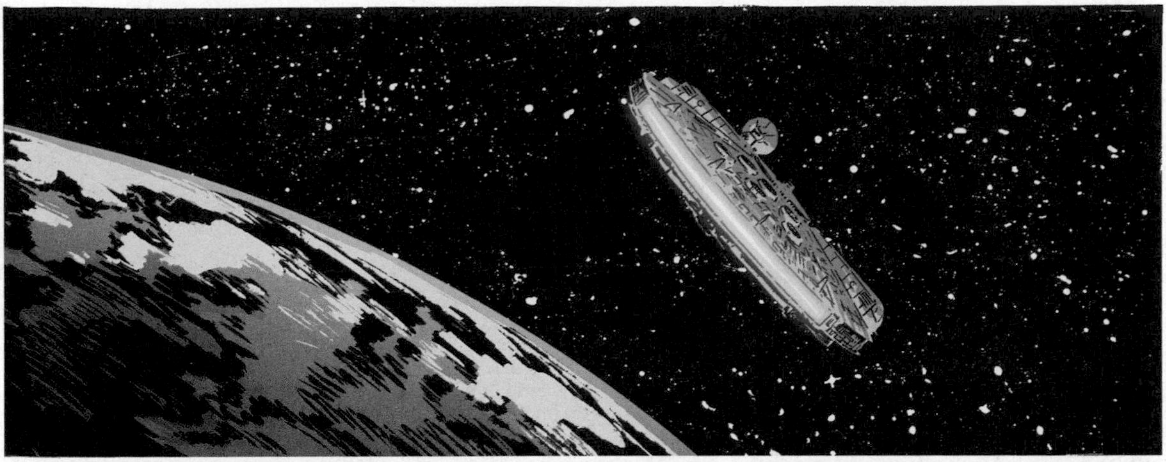

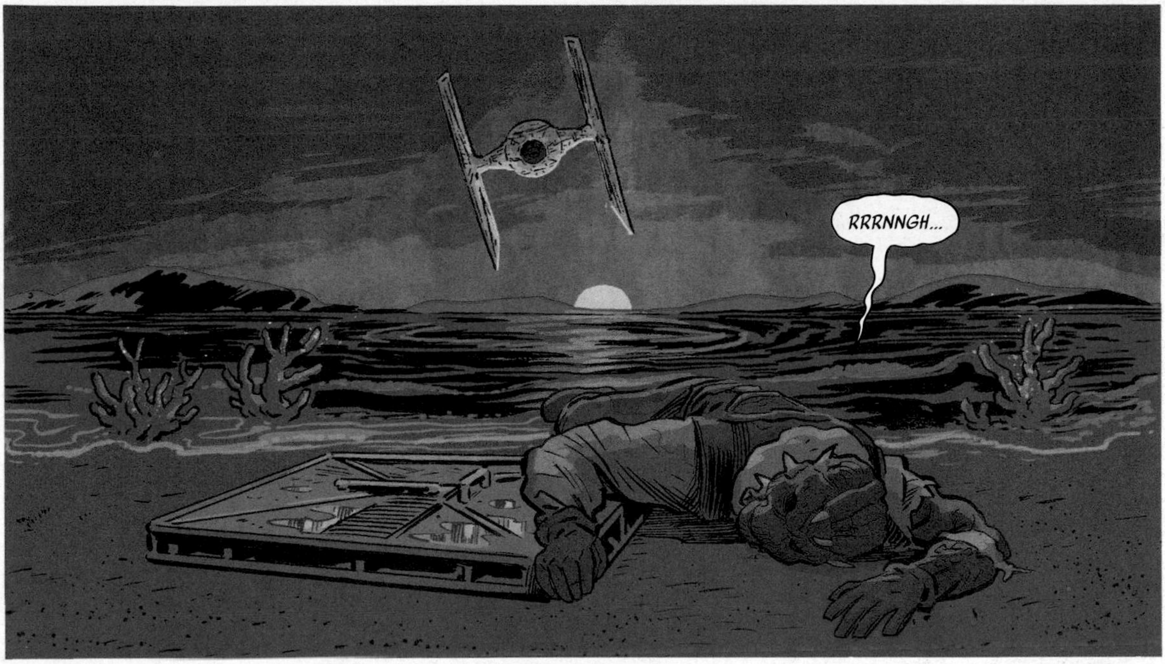
RRRNNGH...

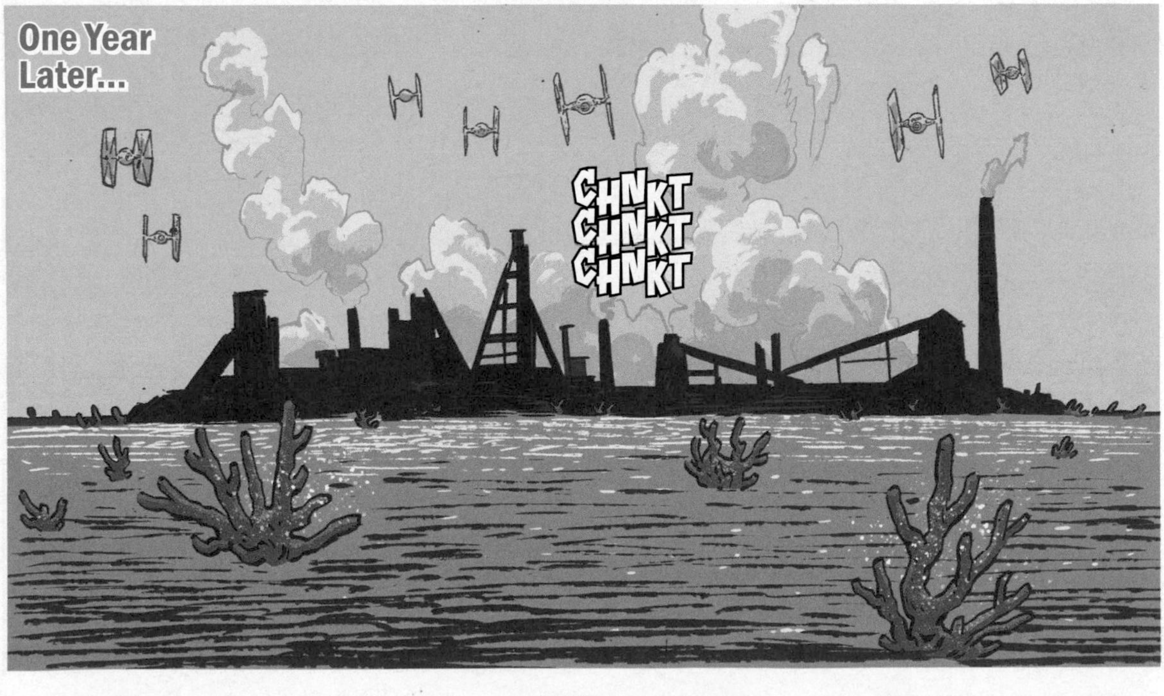
One Year Later...
CHNKT CHNKT CHNKT

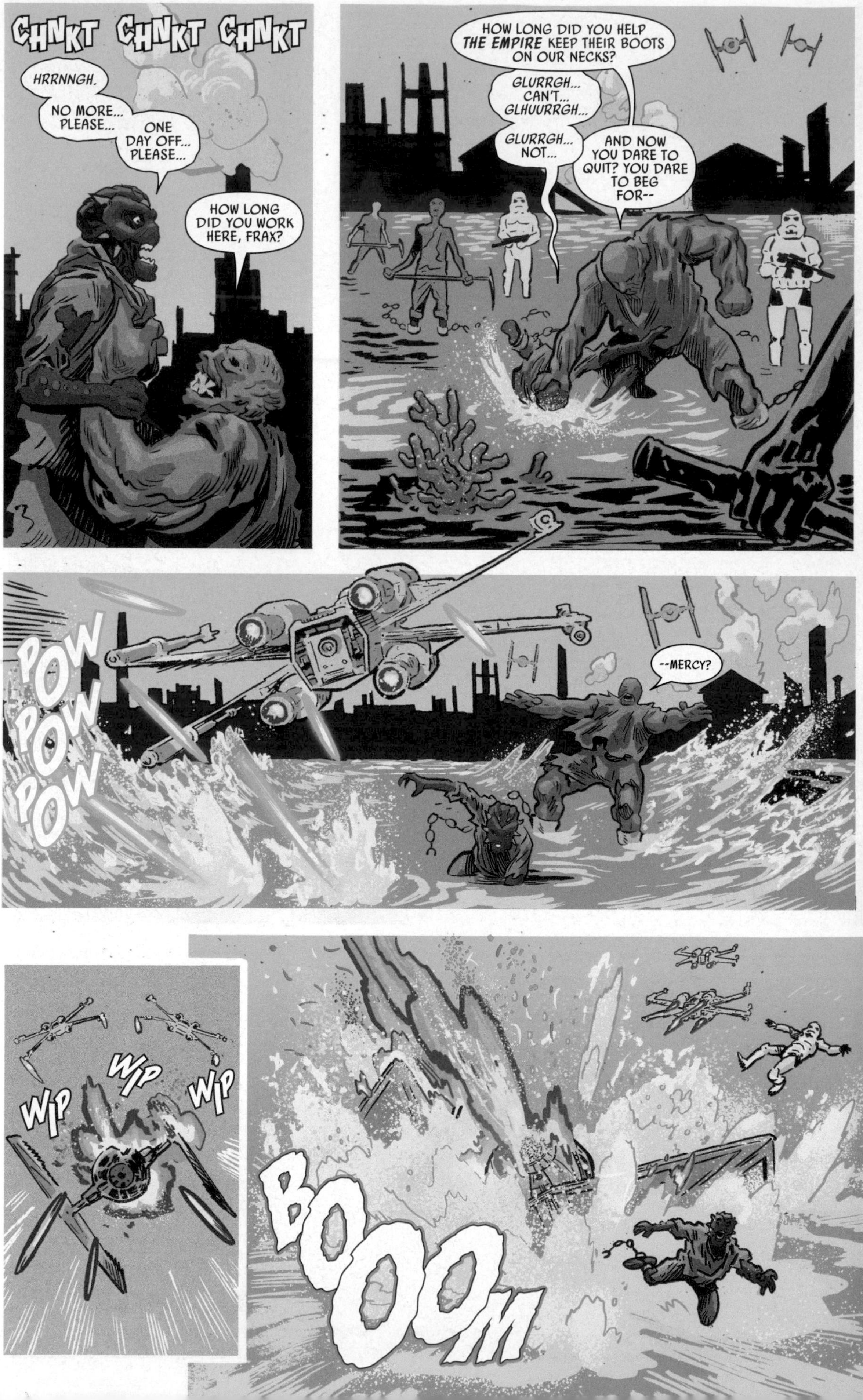
CHNKT CHNKT CHNKT
HRRNNGH.
NO MORE... PLEASE...
ONE DAY OFF... PLEASE...
HOW LONG DID YOU WORK HERE, FRAX?
HOW LONG DID YOU HELP THE EMPIRE KEEP THEIR BOOTS ON OUR NECKS?
GLURRGH... CAN'T... GLHUURRGH...
GLURRGH... NOT...
AND NOW YOU DARE TO QUIT? YOU DARE TO BEG FOR--
POW POW POW POW
--MERCY?
WIP WIP WIP
BOOOOM

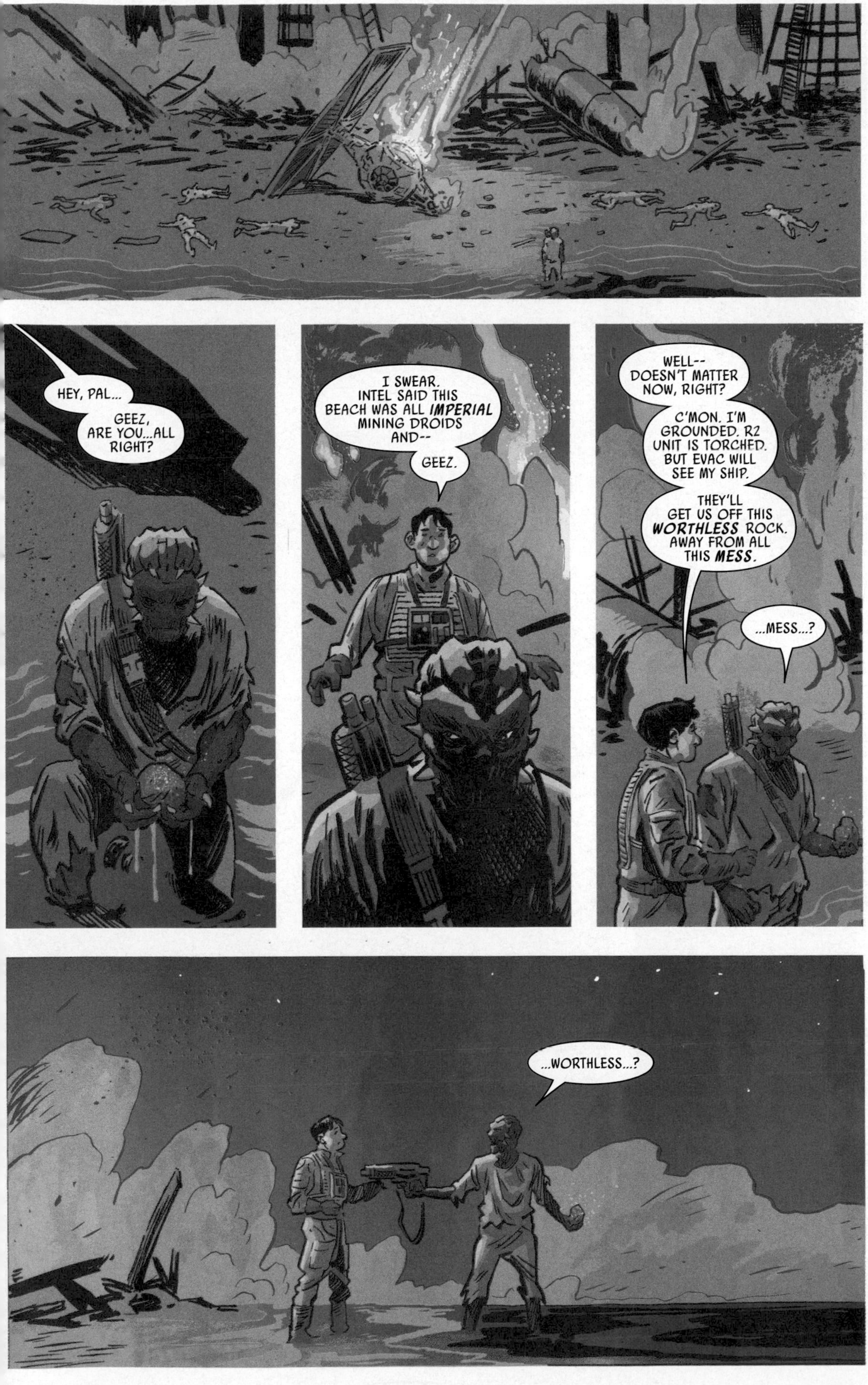
HEY, PAL...
GEEZ, ARE YOU...ALL RIGHT?
I SWEAR. INTEL SAID THIS BEACH WAS ALL IMPERIAL MINING DROIDS AND--
GEEZ.
WELL-- DOESN'T MATTER NOW, RIGHT?
C'MON. I'M GROUNDED. R2 UNIT IS TORCHED. BUT EVAC WILL SEE MY SHIP.
THEY'LL GET US OFF THIS WORTHLESS ROCK. AWAY FROM ALL THIS MESS.
...MESS...?
...WORTHLESS...?

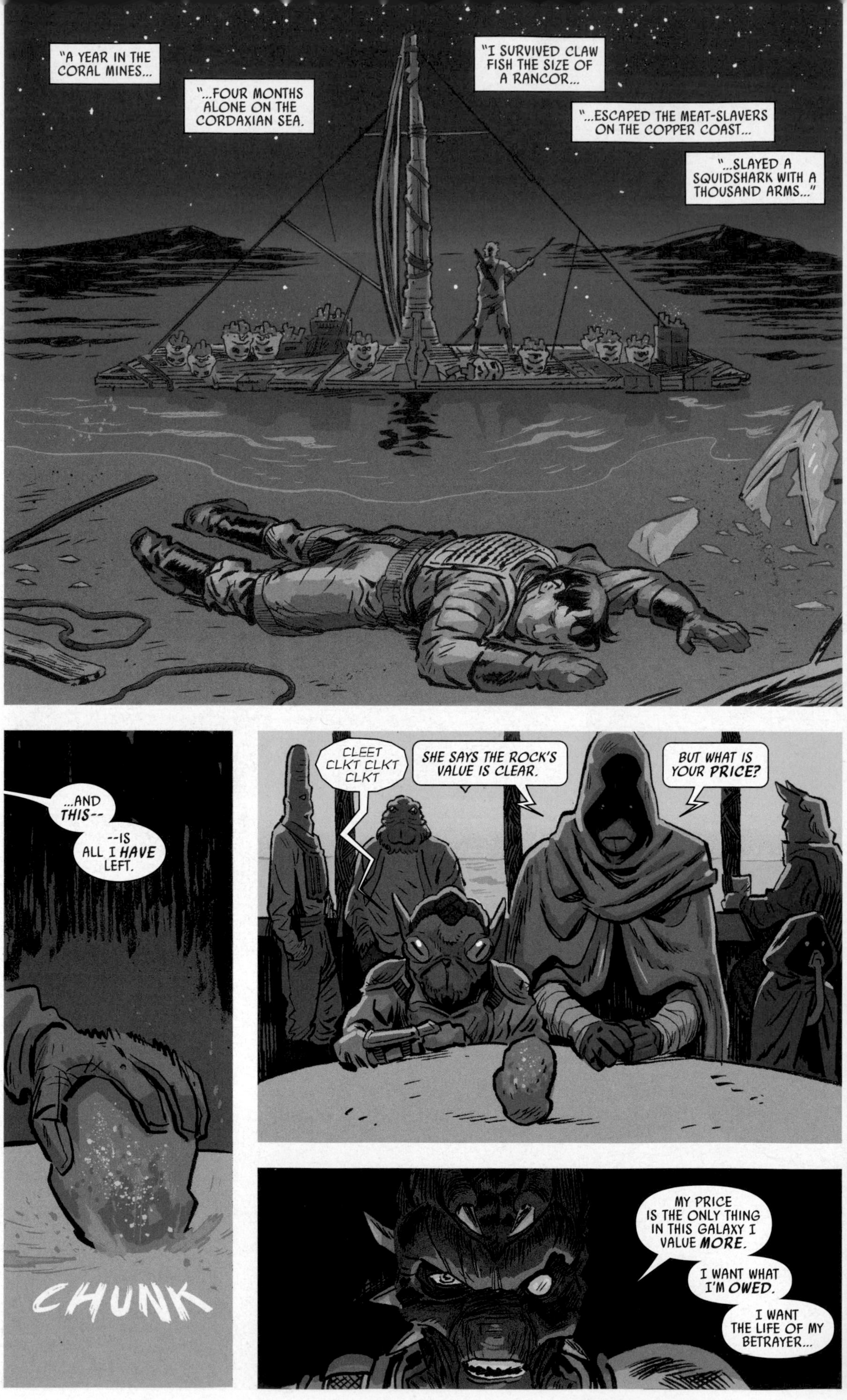
"A YEAR IN THE CORAL MINES...
"...FOUR MONTHS ALONE ON THE CORDAXIAN SEA.
"I SURVIVED CLAW FISH THE SIZE OF A RANCOR...
"...ESCAPED THE MEAT-SLAVERS ON THE COPPER COAST...
"...SLAYED A SQUIDSHARK WITH A THOUSAND ARMS..."
...AND THIS--
--IS ALL I HAVE LEFT.
CHUNK
CLEET CLKT CLKT CLKT
SHE SAYS THE ROCK'S VALUE IS CLEAR.
BUT WHAT IS YOUR PRICE?
MY PRICE IS THE ONLY THING IN THIS GALAXY I VALUE MORE.
I WANT WHAT I'M OWED.
I WANT THE LIFE OF MY BETRAYER...

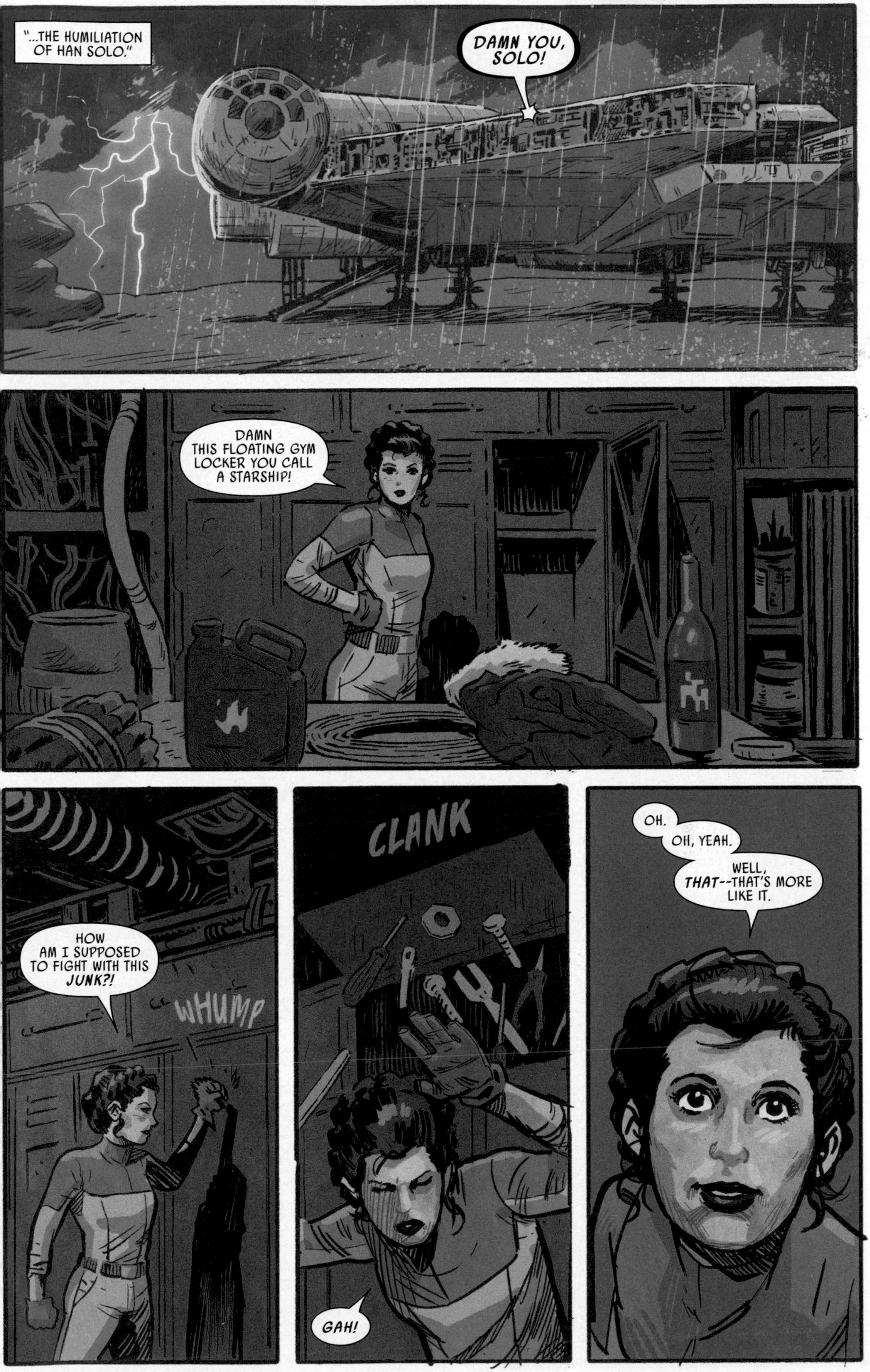
"...THE HUMILIATION OF HAN SOLO."
DAMN YOU, SOLO!
DAMN THIS FLOATING GYM LOCKER YOU CALL A STARSHIP!
HOW AM I SUPPOSED TO FIGHT WITH THIS *JUNK?!*
WHUMP
CLANK
GAH!
OH.
OH, YEAH.
WELL, *THAT*--THAT'S MORE LIKE IT.

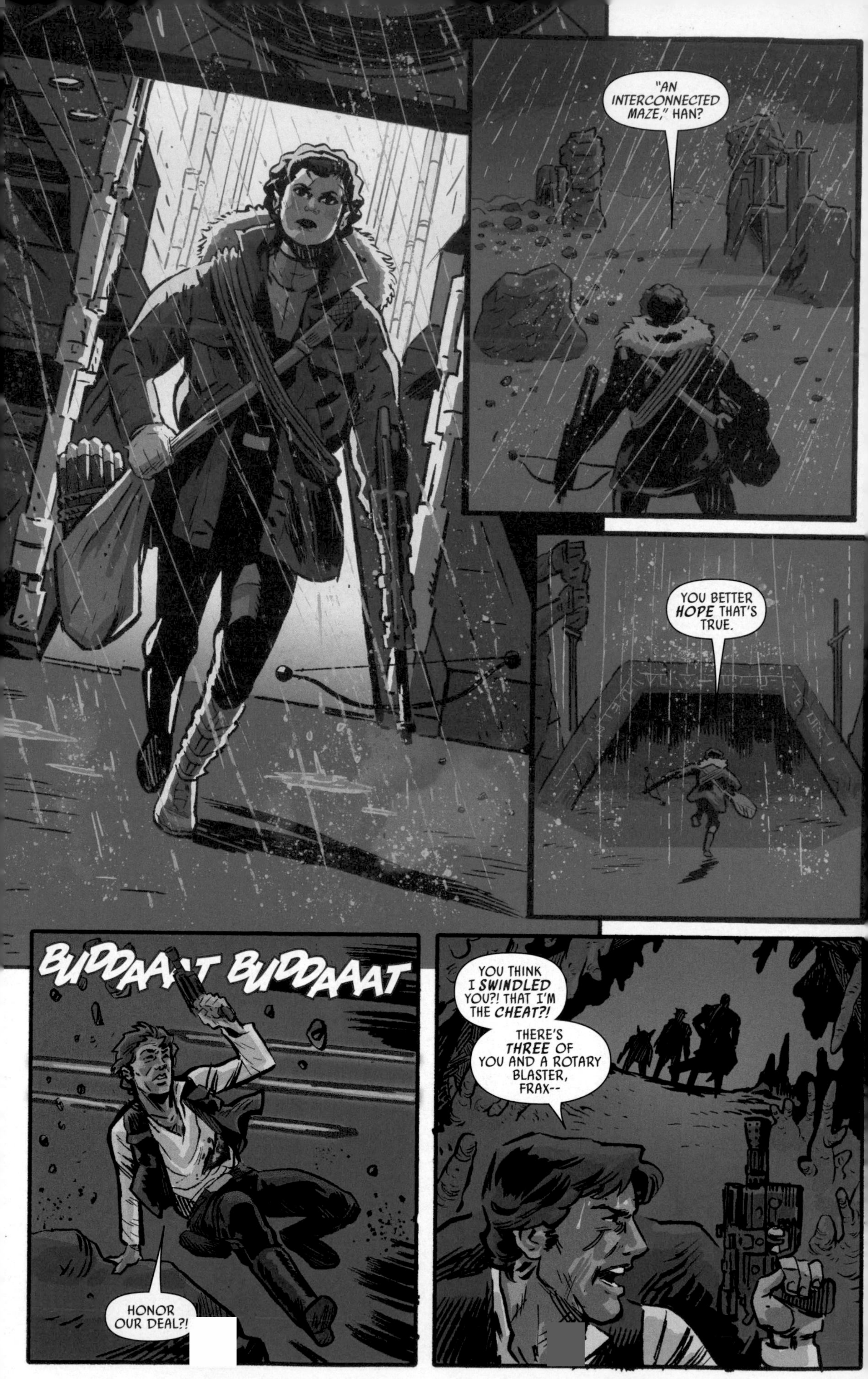
"AN INTERCONNECTED MAZE," HAN?
YOU BETTER HOPE THAT'S TRUE.
BUDDAAAT
HONOR OUR DEAL?!
YOU THINK I SWINDLED YOU?! THAT I'M THE CHEAT?!
THERE'S THREE OF YOU AND A ROTARY BLASTER, FRAX--

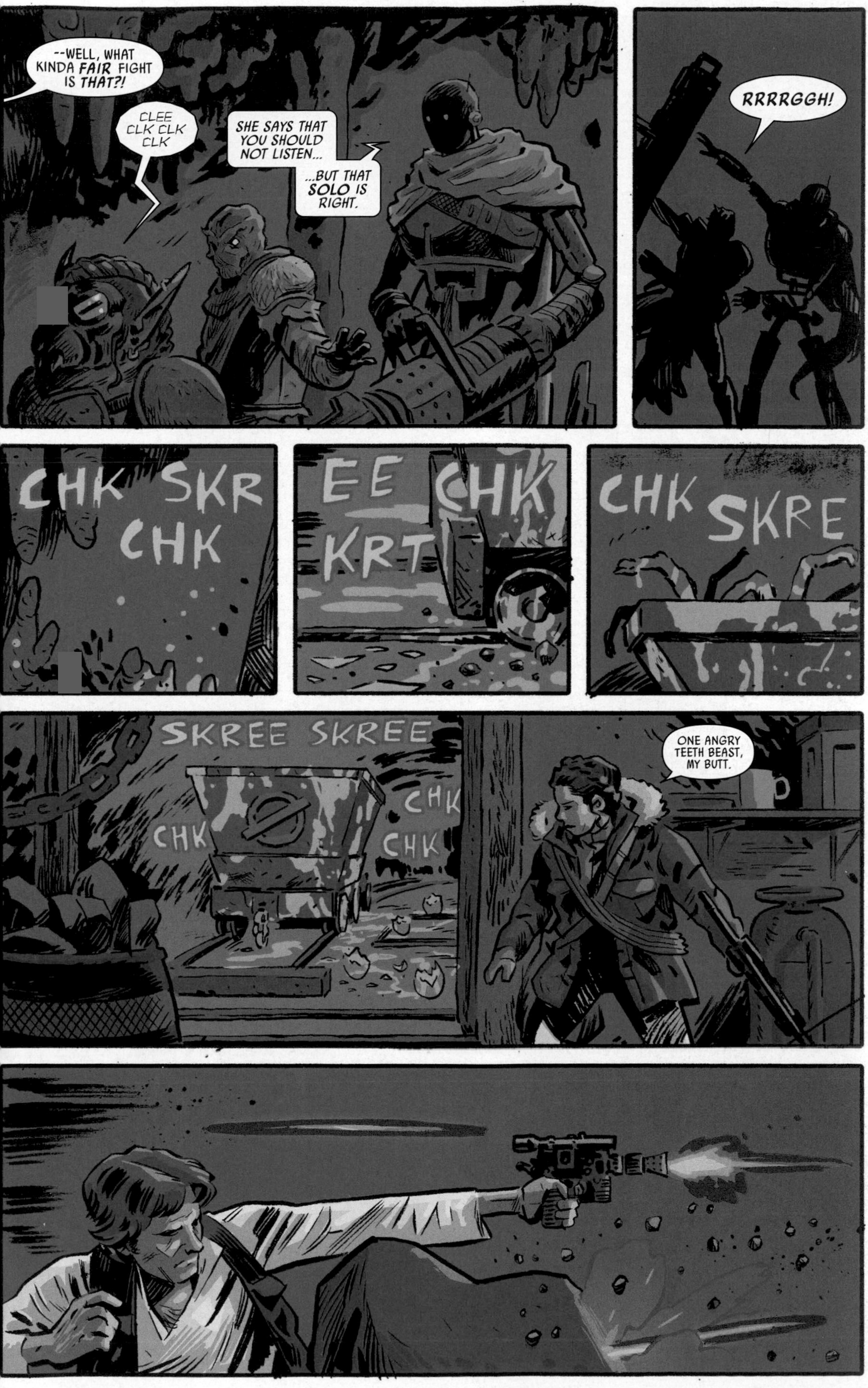
--WELL, WHAT KINDA FAIR FIGHT IS THAT?!
CLEE CLK CLK CLK
SHE SAYS THAT YOU SHOULD NOT LISTEN...
...BUT THAT SOLO IS RIGHT.
RRRRGGH!
CHK SKR CHK
EE CHK KRT
CHK SKRE
SKREE SKREE
CHK
CHK
CHK
ONE ANGRY TEETH BEAST, MY BUTT.

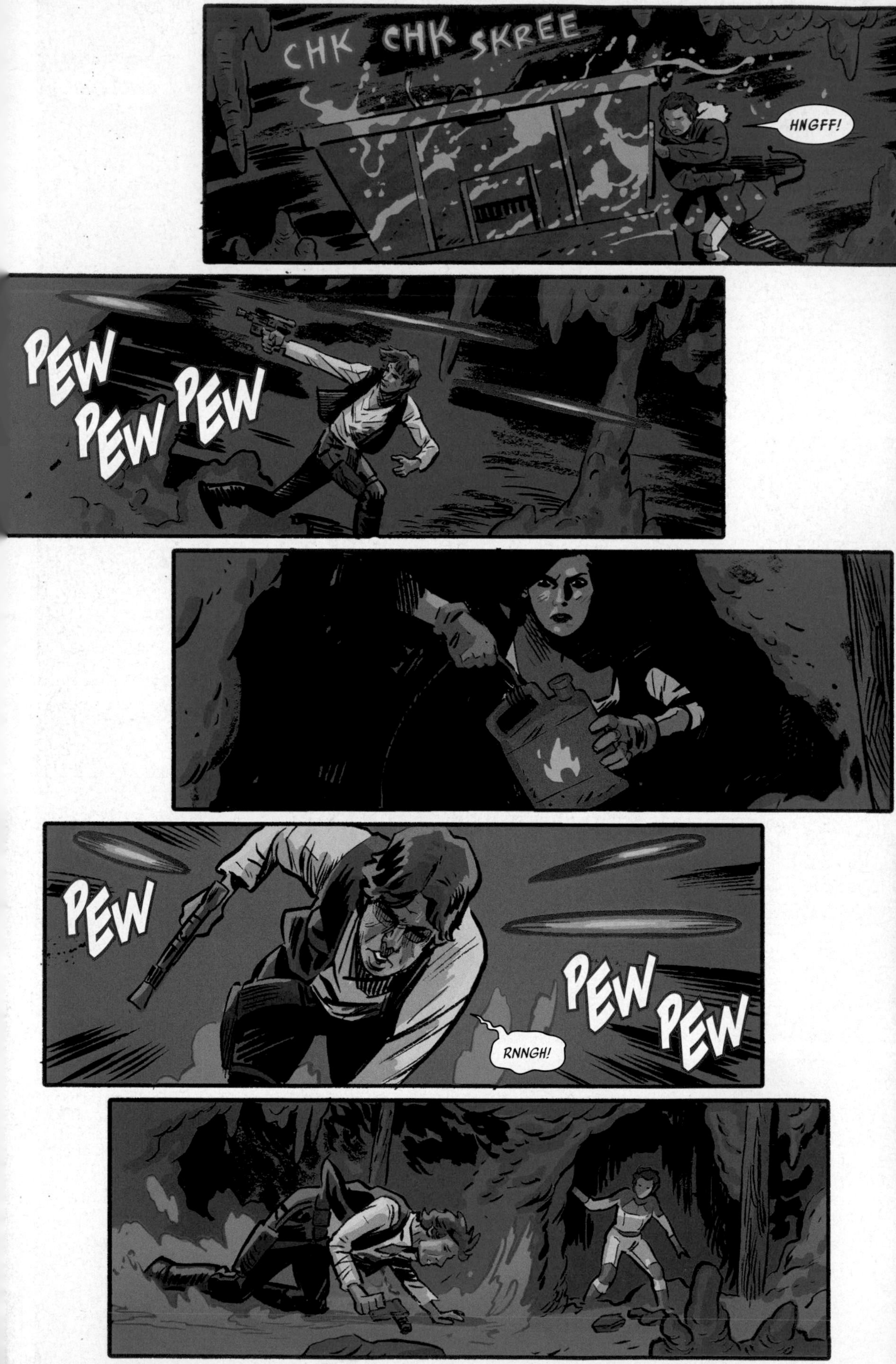
CHK CHK SKREE
HNGFF!
PEW PEW PEW
PEW
PEW PEW
RNNGH!

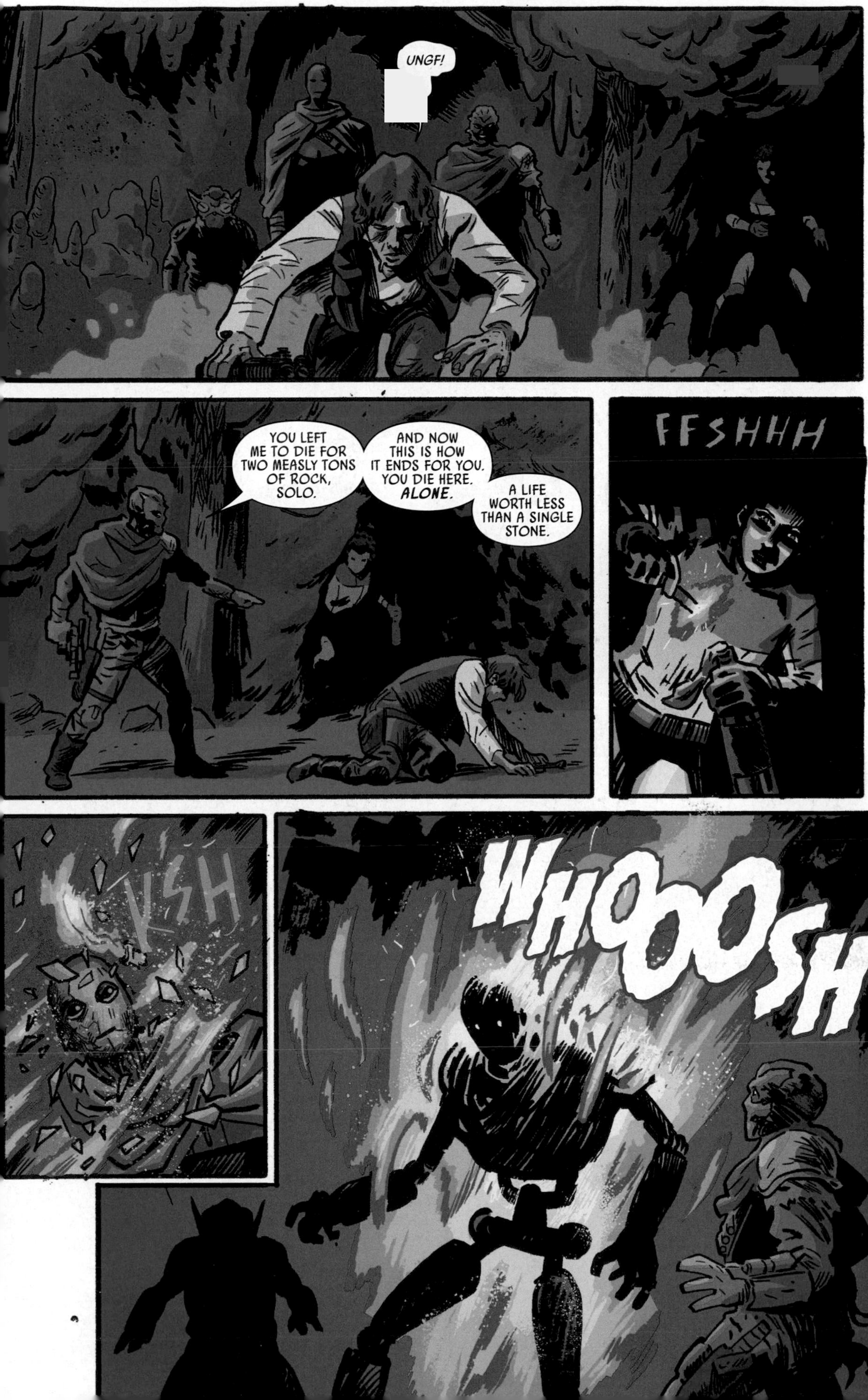
UNGF!
YOU LEFT ME TO DIE FOR TWO MEASLY TONS OF ROCK, SOLO.
AND NOW THIS IS HOW IT ENDS FOR YOU. YOU DIE HERE. *ALONE*.
A LIFE WORTH LESS THAN A SINGLE STONE.
FFSHHH
VSH
WHOOOSH

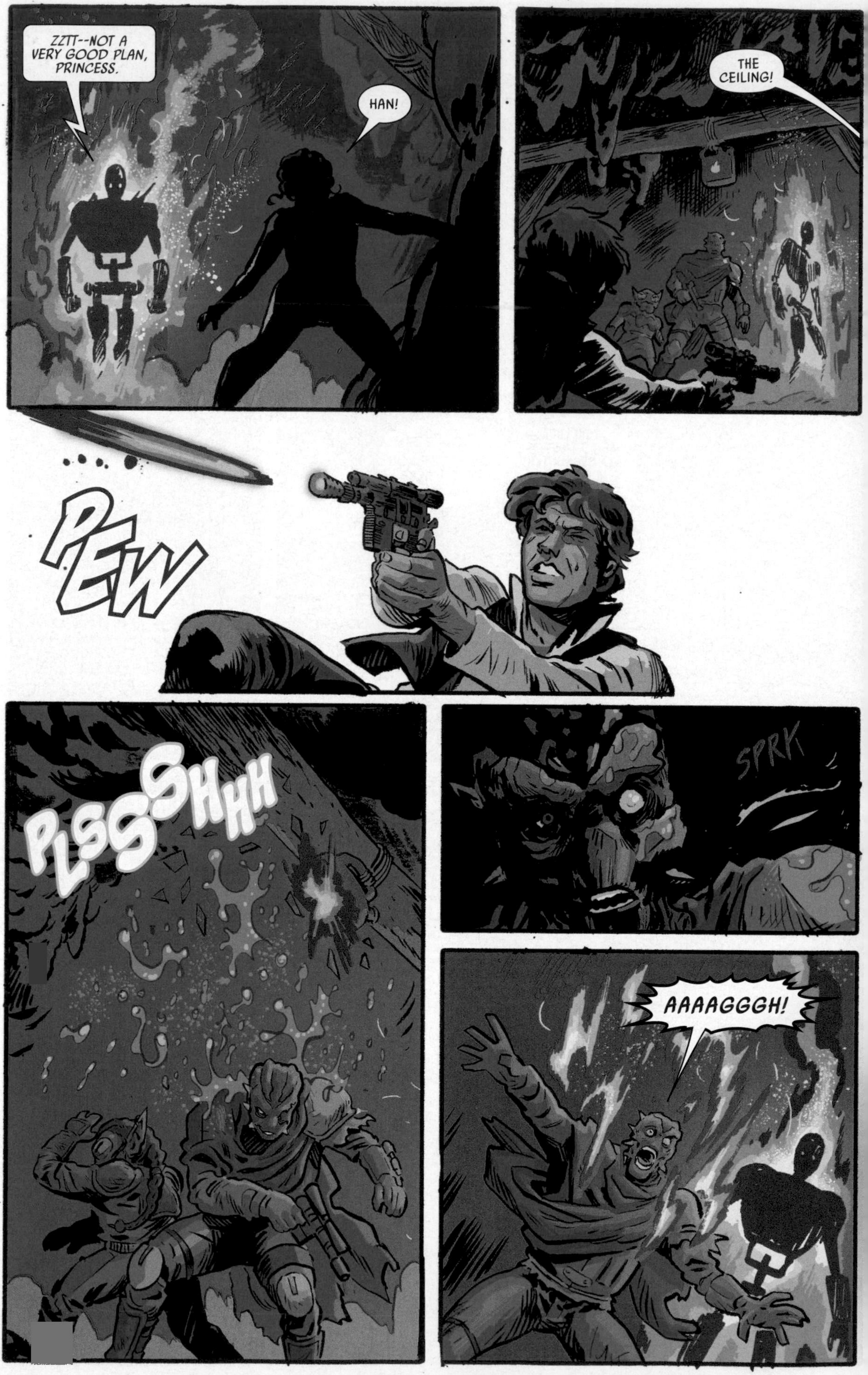
ZZTT--NOT A VERY GOOD PLAN, PRINCESS.
HAN!
THE CEILING!
PEW
PLSSSHHH
SPRK
AAAAGGGH!

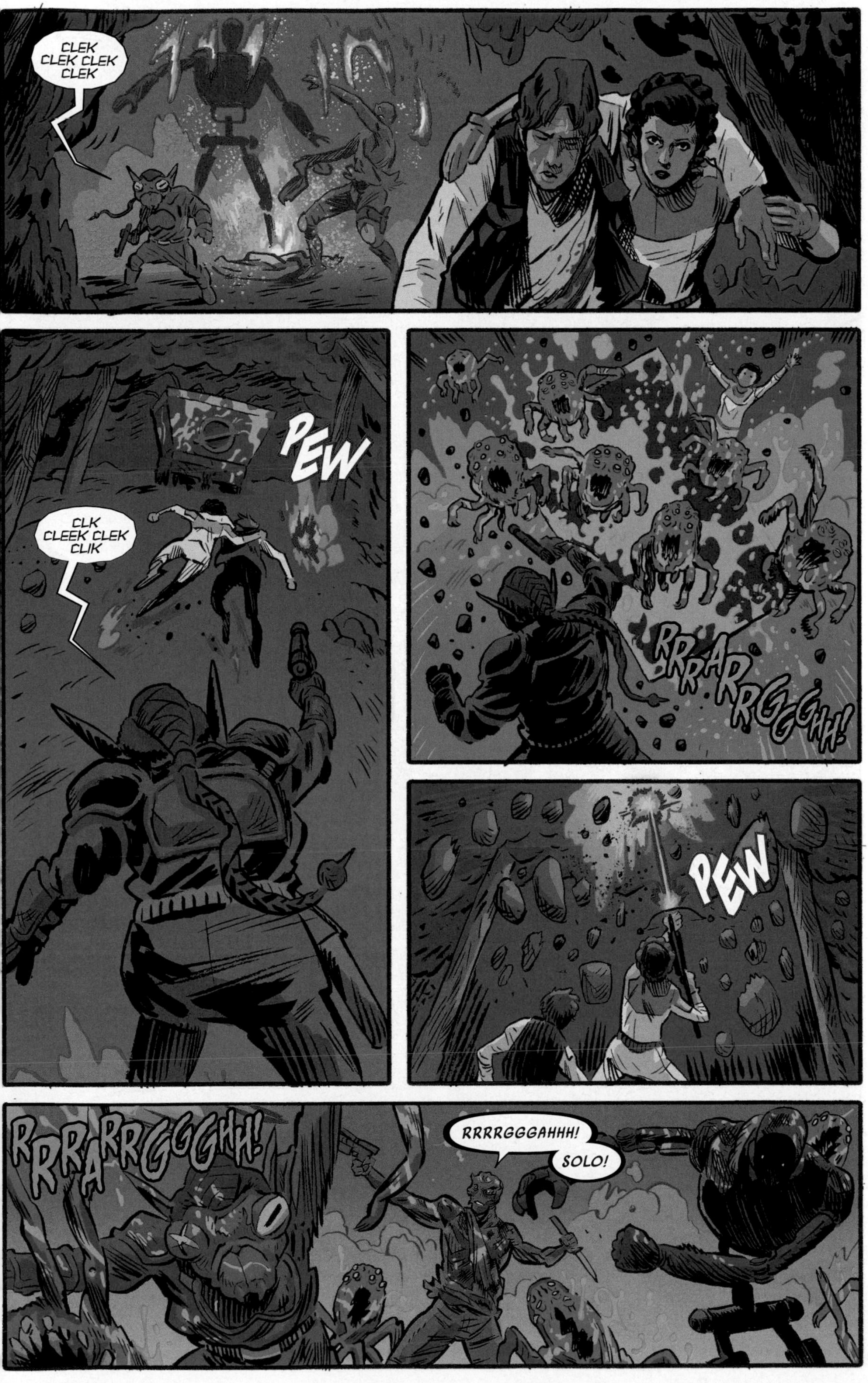
CLEK CLEK CLEK CLEK
PEW
CLK CLEEK CLEK CLIK
RRRARRRGGGHH!
PEW
RRRARRGGGHH!
RRRRGGGAHHH!
SOLO!

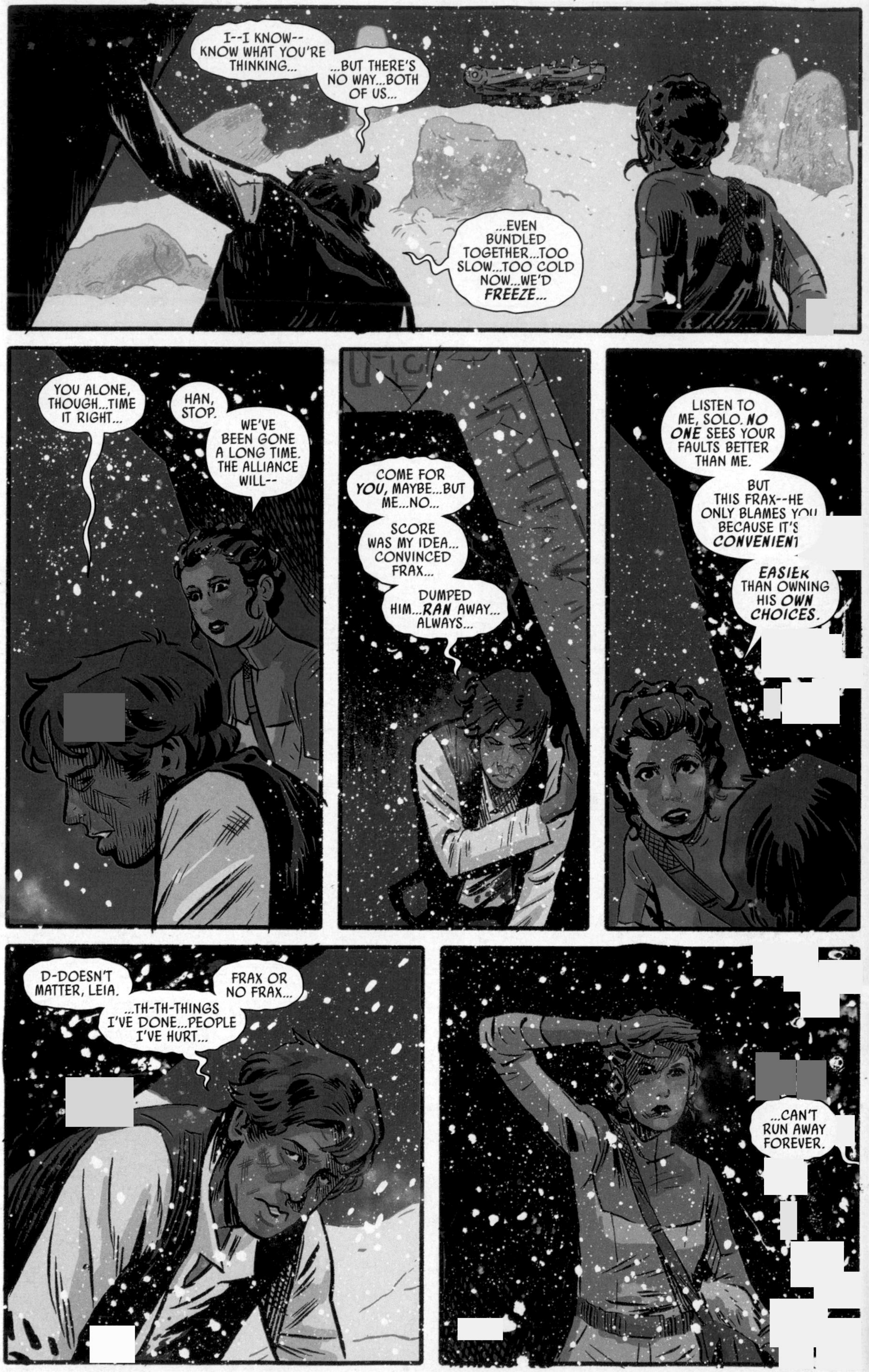
I--I KNOW--
KNOW WHAT YOU'RE THINKING...
...BUT THERE'S NO WAY...BOTH OF US...
...EVEN BUNDLED TOGETHER...TOO SLOW...TOO COLD NOW...WE'D FREEZE...
YOU ALONE, THOUGH...TIME IT RIGHT...
HAN, STOP.
WE'VE BEEN GONE A LONG TIME. THE ALLIANCE WILL--
COME FOR YOU, MAYBE...BUT ME...NO...
SCORE WAS MY IDEA... CONVINCED FRAX...
DUMPED HIM...RAN AWAY... ALWAYS...
LISTEN TO ME, SOLO. NO ONE SEES YOUR FAULTS BETTER THAN ME.
BUT THIS FRAX--HE ONLY BLAMES YOU BECAUSE IT'S CONVENIENT.
EASIER THAN OWNING HIS OWN CHOICES.
D-DOESN'T MATTER, LEIA.
FRAX OR NO FRAX...
...TH-TH-THINGS I'VE DONE...PEOPLE I'VE HURT...
...CAN'T RUN AWAY FOREVER.

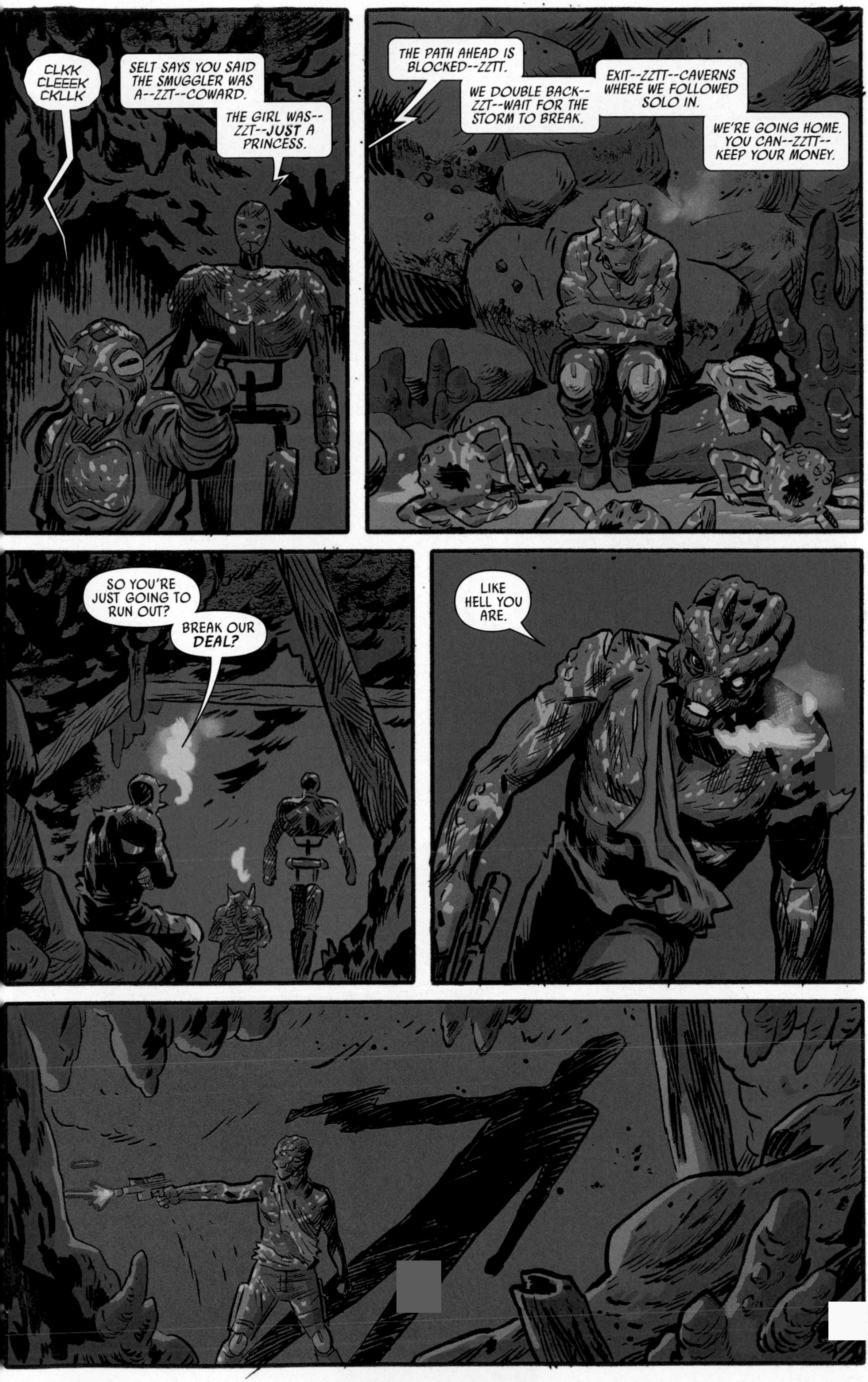
CLKK CLEEEK CKLLK
SELT SAYS YOU SAID THE SMUGGLER WAS A--ZZT--COWARD.
THE GIRL WAS--ZZT--JUST A PRINCESS.
THE PATH AHEAD IS BLOCKED--ZZTT.
WE DOUBLE BACK--ZZT--WAIT FOR THE STORM TO BREAK.
EXIT--ZZTT--CAVERNS WHERE WE FOLLOWED SOLO IN.
WE'RE GOING HOME. YOU CAN--ZZTT--KEEP YOUR MONEY.
SO YOU'RE JUST GOING TO RUN OUT?
BREAK OUR DEAL?
LIKE HELL YOU ARE.

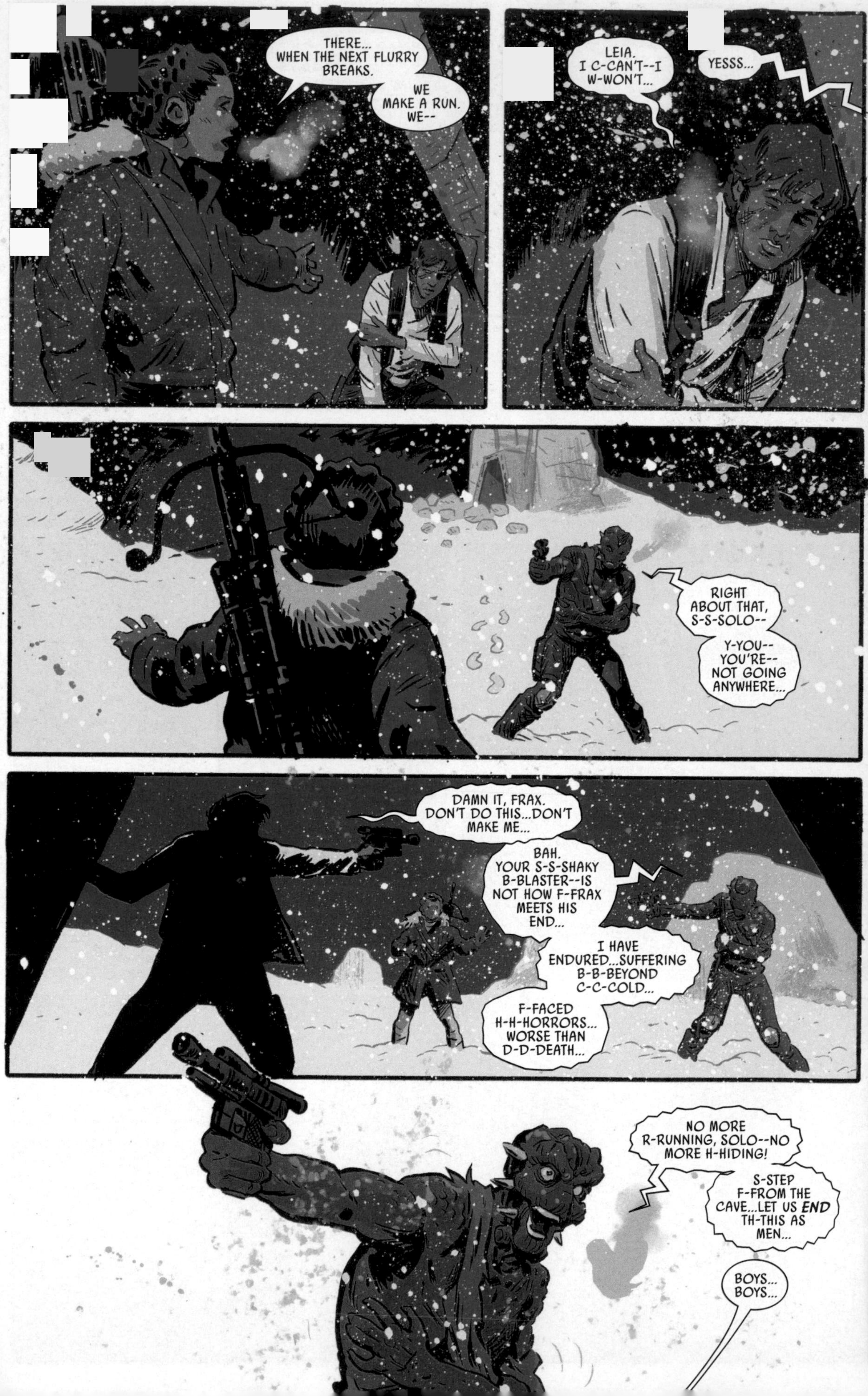
THERE... WHEN THE NEXT FLURRY BREAKS.
WE MAKE A RUN. WE--
LEIA. I C-CAN'T--I W-WON'T...
YESSS...
RIGHT ABOUT THAT, S-S-SOLO--
Y-YOU-- YOU'RE-- NOT GOING ANYWHERE...
DAMN IT, FRAX. DON'T DO THIS...DON'T MAKE ME...
BAH. YOUR S-S-SHAKY B-BLASTER--IS NOT HOW F-FRAX MEETS HIS END...
I HAVE ENDURED...SUFFERING B-B-BEYOND C-C-COLD...
F-FACED H-H-HORRORS... WORSE THAN D-D-DEATH...
NO MORE R-RUNNING, SOLO--NO MORE H-HIDING!
S-STEP F-FROM THE CAVE...LET US **END** TH-THIS AS MEN...
BOYS... BOYS...

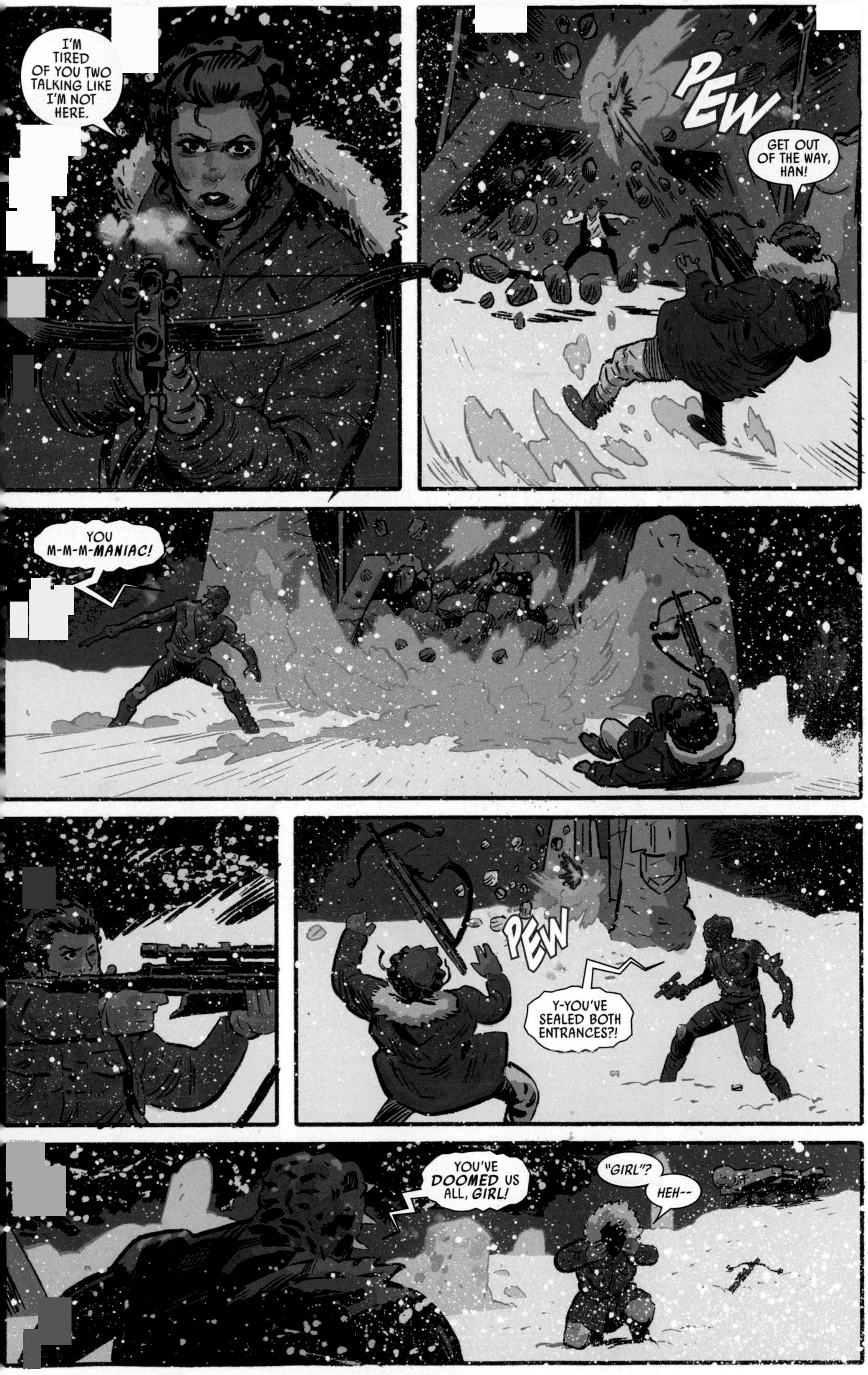
I'M TIRED OF YOU TWO TALKING LIKE I'M NOT HERE.
PEW
GET OUT OF THE WAY, HAN!
YOU M-M-M-MANIAC!
PEW
Y-YOU'VE SEALED BOTH ENTRANCES?!
YOU'VE DOOMED US ALL, GIRL!
"GIRL"?
HEH--

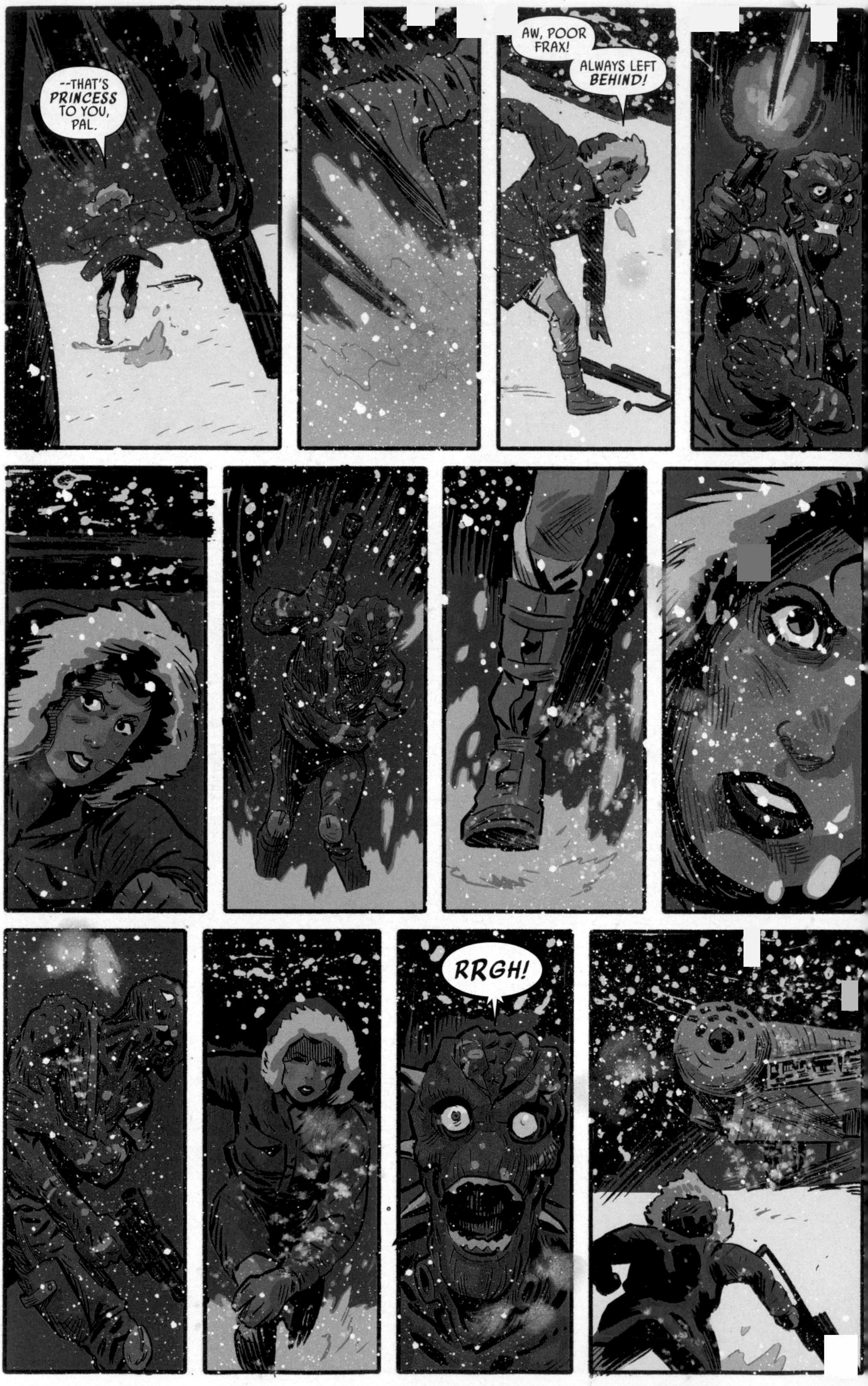
--THAT'S PRINCESS TO YOU, PAL.
AW, POOR FRAX!
ALWAYS LEFT BEHIND!
RRGH!

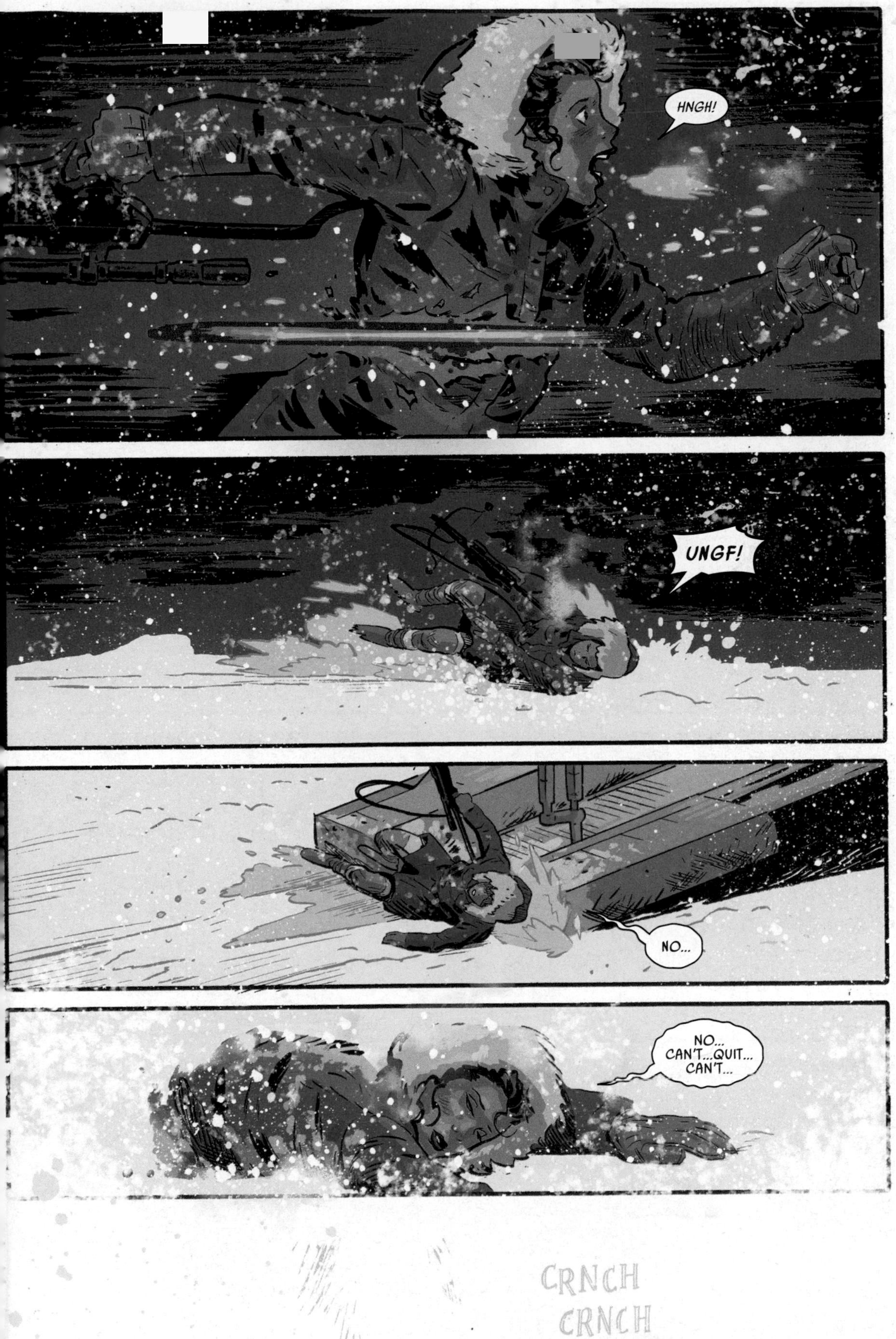
HNGH!
UNGF!
NO...
NO... CAN'T...QUIT... CAN'T...
CRNCH
CRNCH

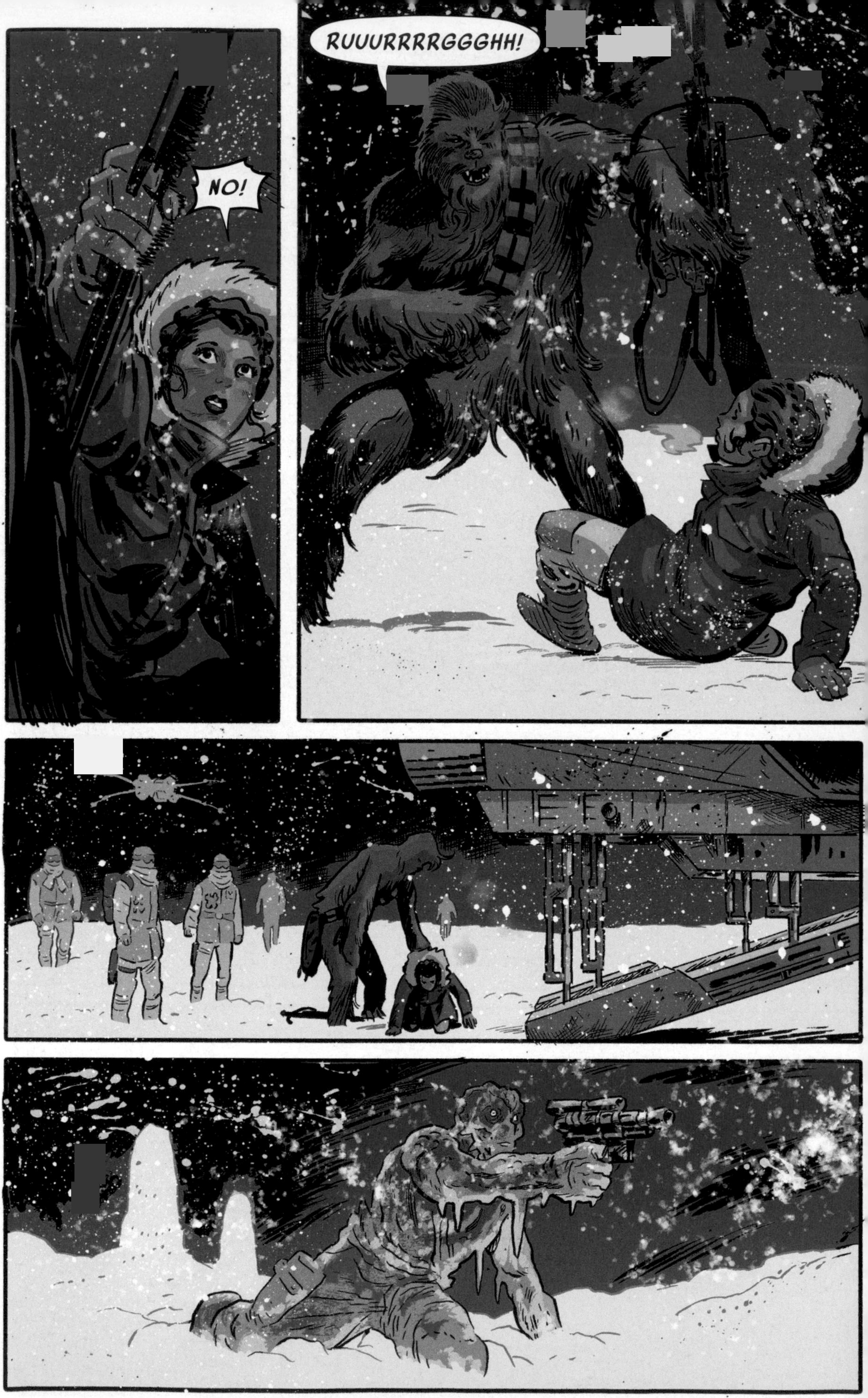
NO!
RUUURRRRGGGHH!

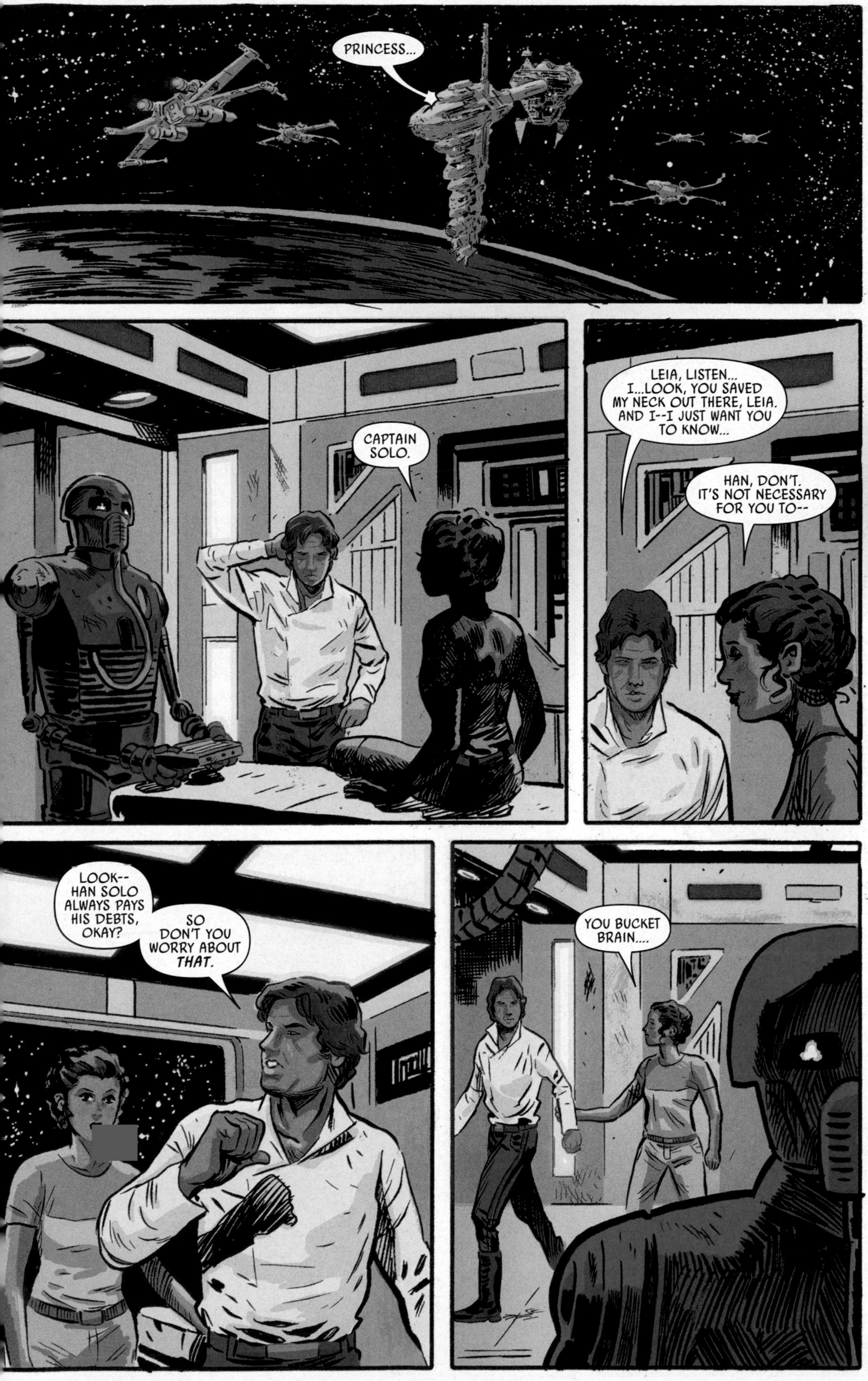
PRINCESS...
CAPTAIN SOLO.
LEIA, LISTEN... I...LOOK, YOU SAVED MY NECK OUT THERE, LEIA. AND I--I JUST WANT YOU TO KNOW...
HAN, DON'T. IT'S NOT NECESSARY FOR YOU TO--
LOOK-- HAN SOLO ALWAYS PAYS HIS DEBTS, OKAY?
SO DON'T YOU WORRY ABOUT *THAT.*
YOU BUCKET BRAIN....

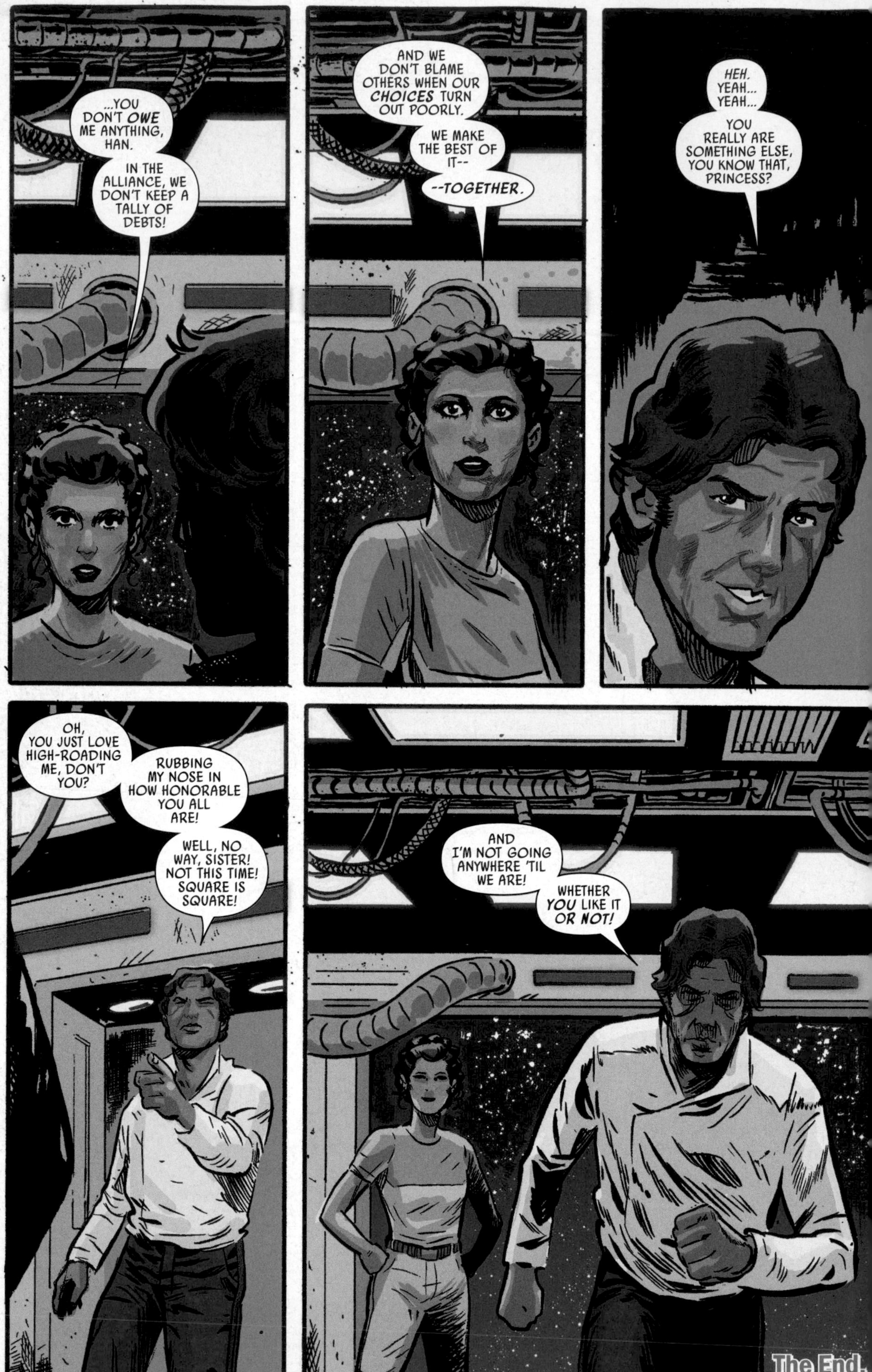
...YOU DON'T OWE ME ANYTHING, HAN.
IN THE ALLIANCE, WE DON'T KEEP A TALLY OF DEBTS!
AND WE DON'T BLAME OTHERS WHEN OUR CHOICES TURN OUT POORLY.
WE MAKE THE BEST OF IT--
--TOGETHER.
HEH. YEAH... YEAH...
YOU REALLY ARE SOMETHING ELSE, YOU KNOW THAT, PRINCESS?
OH, YOU JUST LOVE HIGH-ROADING ME, DON'T YOU?
RUBBING MY NOSE IN HOW HONORABLE YOU ALL ARE!
WELL, NO WAY, SISTER! NOT THIS TIME! SQUARE IS SQUARE!
AND I'M NOT GOING ANYWHERE 'TIL WE ARE!
WHETHER YOU LIKE IT OR NOT!
The End.

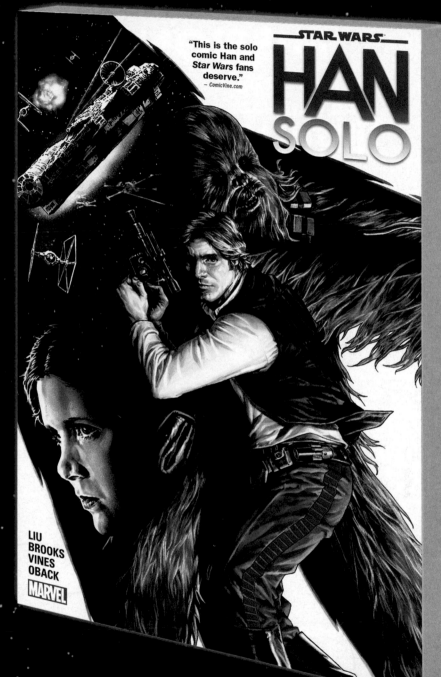

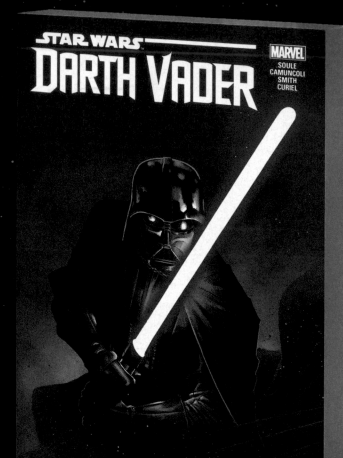

REBELLIONS ARE BUILT ON HOPE

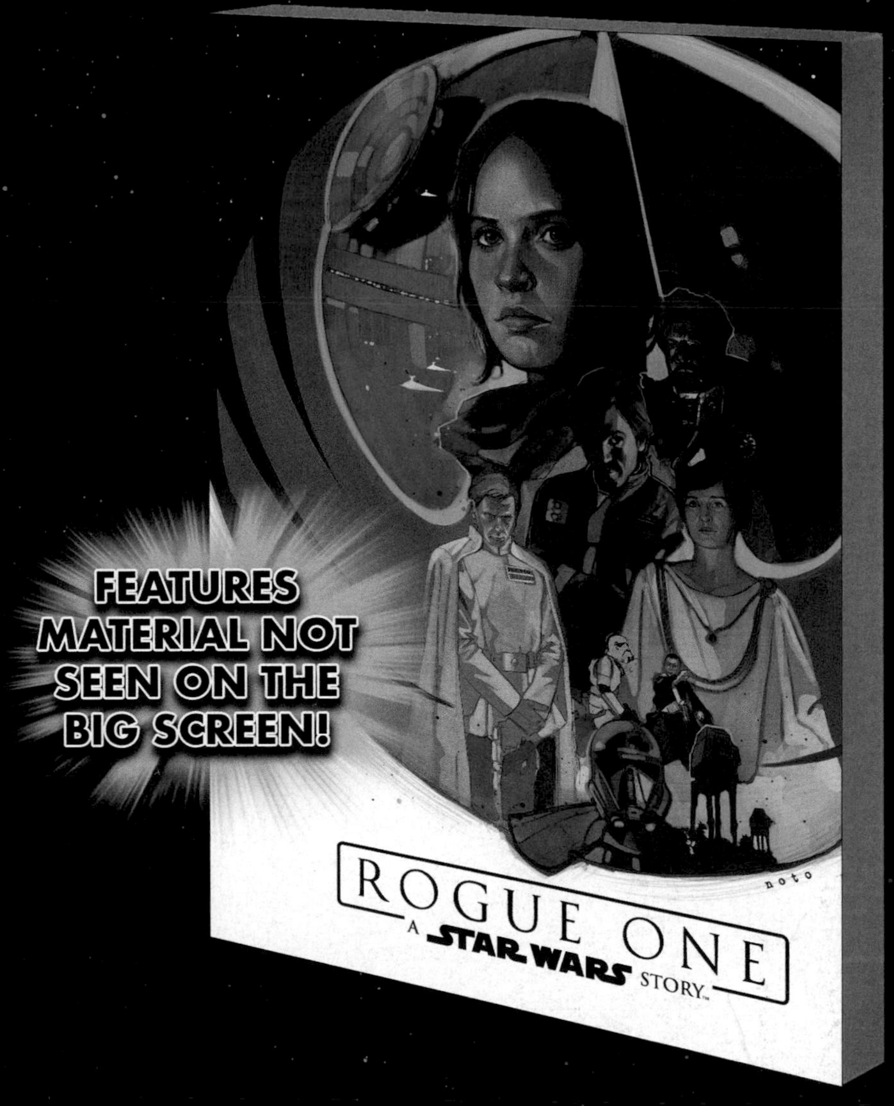

FEATURES MATERIAL NOT SEEN ON THE BIG SCREEN!

ROGUE ONE
A *STAR.WARS* STORY.

STAR WARS: ROGUE ONE ADAPTATION TPB
978-0785194576

ON SALE NOVEMBER 2017
WHEREVER BOOKS ARE SOLD

TO FIND A COMIC SHOP NEAR YOU, VISIT COMICSHOPLOCATOR.COM

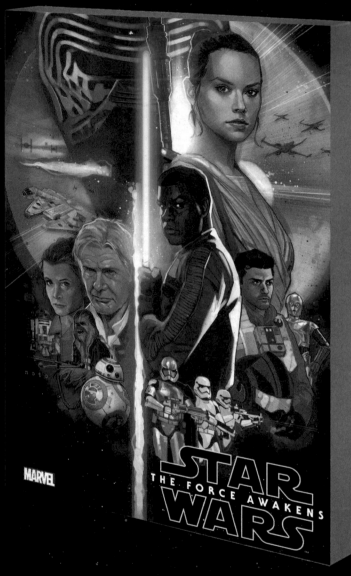